The
Imperfect
Spies

The
Imperfect
Spies

The History of
Israeli Intelligence

Yossi Melman and Dan Raviv

SIDGWICK & JACKSON
LONDON

To Dori, Jonathan and Emma
To Billie and Yotam

First published in Great Britain in 1989 by
Sidgwick & Jackson Limited

Copyright © 1989 by Yossi Melman and Dan Raviv

Also published in 1990 in the USA

ISBN 0-283-99710-9

Typeset by Rowland Phototypesetting Limited
Bury St Edmunds, Suffolk

Printed by Billing and Sons Limited, Worcester
for Sidgwick & Jackson Limited
1 Tavistock Chambers, Bloomsbury Way
London WC1A 2SG

Contents

Key Figures

The Heads of the Mossad

1951–1952	Reuven Shiloah
1952–1963	Isser Harel
1963–1968	Meir Amit
1968–1974	Zvi Zamir
1974–1982	Yitzhak Hofi
1982–1989	Nahum Admoni
1989–	[*disclosure forbidden by Israeli law*]

The Heads of Military Intelligence (Aman)

1948–1949	Isser Beeri
1949–1950	Chaim Herzog
1950–1955	Binyamin Gibli
1955–1959	Yehoshafat Harkabi
1959–1962	Chaim Herzog
1962–1963	Meir Amit
1964–1972	Aharon Yariv
1972–1974	Eli Zeira
1974–1978	Shlomo Gazit
1979–1983	Yehoshua Saguy
1983–1985	Ehud Barak
1986–	Amnon Shahak

THE IMPERFECT SPIES

The Heads of Shin Bet
1948–1963   Isser Harel
1963   Amos Manor
1964–1974   Yosef Harmelin
1974–1981   Avraham Ahituv
1981–1986   Avraham Shalom
1986–1988   Yosef Harmelin
1988–   [*disclosure forbidden by Israeli law*]

The Heads of Lakam
1957–1981   Binyamin Blumberg
1981–1986*   Rafi Eitan

The Prime Minister's Adviser on Counter-Terrorism
1972–1973   Aharon Yariv
1974–1977   Rehavam Ze'evi
1977–1978   Amichai Paglin
1978–1984   Rafi Eitan
1985–1988   Amiram Nir
1988–   Yigal Carmon

The Political Department of the Foreign Ministry
1948–1951*   Boris Guriel

* Agency disbanded

The structure of the Israeli intelligence community

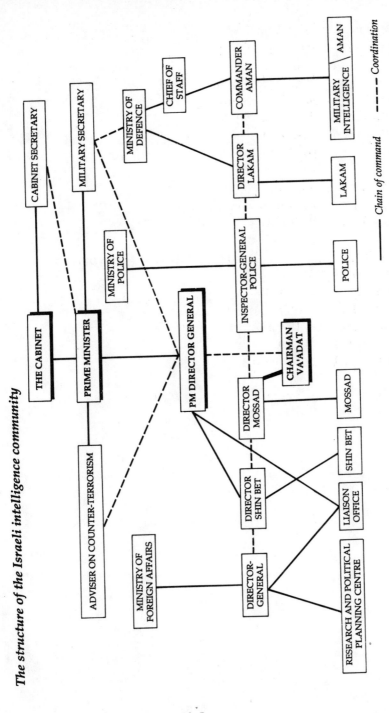

Preface

The world has always been fascinated by spy stories, and Israeli intelligence has always held a special place in the public imagination. This was easily understood in the Jewish state's first twenty years, when Israel itself was admired for its pioneer spirit and astounding achievements. Israel's intelligence community showed the same qualities: succeeding by sophistication rather than sheer size, by brains rather than brute force, and by finesse rather than financial muscle.

After the Six-Day War of 1967, the intelligence agencies continued to enjoy the praise and admiration of the world – even when Israel itself became accursed with the negative image of an occupying power. Beneath the surface, the seeds of a bitter harvest of failure in the intelligence field were sown then. The rotten fruit did not appear until the 1970s, and the stench was unavoidable in the scandals of the 1980s.

This book is an attempt to examine the roots of the disease

which began eating away at what is still a vital element of Israel's security.

No history of the Israeli intelligence community can be written without digging deeply into the early days of the secret services. Our intention is to portray the structure, politics, and people of Israeli intelligence since 1948, when the state was born and its espionage community was formed by guerilla fighters of the Jewish underground.

We cannot pretend to know everything. In a business priding itself on compartmentalization, even those who work within the secret society do not know all that is happening outside the walls of their own unit.

The obstacles before us were many and formidable. Israel's military censor insisted on brief deletions in the Introduction and in Chapters 3, 5, 6, 7, 9, 11 and 14, written by Israeli citizen Yossi Melman. In addition, Israel's intelligence agencies do not share their documents with the public, and they are not even published along with other government papers after the statutory thirty-year secrecy period. The agencies do not have any official spokesmen to be asked such trivial details as places, dates, names, or even spellings and pronunciations.

Members of the intelligence community, trained to be silent in the belief that knowledge is power, jealously guard that knowledge and selectively release only their own, biased versions.

The only intelligence operations to have caught the public eye, over the years, were successes and failures so spectacular that they could not be kept under wraps. In both the 'positive' and the 'negative' cases, however, there are heretofore hidden details which link these exploits with other operations – forming a pattern of behaviour, not previously recognized. We believe that a balanced portrait of the secret agencies and their history will help them to be better understood and more fairly judged.

While aiming to produce a comprehensive history, presented in chronological sequence, we highlight some issues in their own chapters: the use of intelligence to pursue

Jewish goals, for instance, and the advancement of Israel's secret nuclear programme.

The full story reflects the development of Israeli society, and also human factors common to all nations: good intentions and twisted aims, high-minded concepts and flawed vision, patriotism and xenophobia, love and jealousy, sex and prurience.

Our aim is to provide a balanced account – as accurate as is possible, and as complete as we can piece together. Our research has taken us to Israel and a host of other countries where Israeli intelligence has made an impact. We interviewed dozens of intelligence people, some still active and others discovering there can be life after an undercover career.

We met former chiefs of the various branches of Israeli intelligence, but also – to gain a sense of the psychology out in the field – with junior members of the community. We spoke with former directors of the CIA and other old hands of the clandestine game, to see how Israel's spies are really perceived – not by the newspaper columns, but by the professionals in capitals abroad.

A list of interviewees would be long, but they insisted that our encounters be 'off the record' for the sake of their anonymity. Still, we insisted on having a story or fact confirmed by at least two sources before including it in our book. We do not, however, publish every detail we learned. When we felt that a revelation would endanger lives, we decided that even authors and journalists have their limits.

Our thanks go to the many unnamed individuals who shared their time and knowledge with us. At Sidgwick & Jackson, director Susan Hill and her team have been most helpful in ensuring that our work not wither with age so that this book remains timely. Appreciation also goes to Professor Walter Laqueur in Washington for his good advice and abundance of ideas, to colleagues at CBS News in London and New York who contributed understanding and encouragement, to Paul Bruin for his patience with computer snafus, to Raaya Carmel and Hanna Hon for their help in the *Ha'aretz* newspaper library, and above all to our friends and families for their support. All errors and omissions, however, are ours alone.

YOSSI MELMAN and DAN RAVIV

London, April 1989

Introduction

This book illuminates the darkness which envelops the fascinating history of Israel's intelligence community, from its origins to the troubles and triumphs of today, with a projection into the future and its inevitable challenges.

Intelligence is generally defined as the collection, arrangement, interpretation and distribution of information needed in the defence against enemies and rivals, and in the pursuit of what are perceived to be vital interests. This has been true in all periods of history for all nations seeking to execute properly their foreign, domestic, and defence policies.

In addition to these raw requirements of intelligence, most modern nations have extended the actual exercise of the craft beyond those functional borders towards new horizons. In that, Israel is not exceptional.

Since its creation as a modern state in 1948, Israel has been subject to a hostile environment of wars, terrorism, international isolation and domestic subversion. Naturally, the Jewish state feels compelled to assign more tasks to its secret agencies – more, perhaps, than any other nation on earth.

Being a small country with limited resources, Israel has to use its intelligence community to the utmost. The responsibility of Israeli intelligence is, above all, to collect data on the military capabilities of the Arab countries and their intentions, to counter international and Palestinian terrorism directed against Jews and Israelis, to track the activities of the superpowers regarding the Middle East, to conduct secret diplomacy in pursuit of Israel's national goals and to prevent the enemy from discovering what is occurring in Israel itself.

Those are the traditional duties of almost any intelligence community, but Israel's agencies stand out in the choice of new horizons they pursue. As Israel perceives itself as a state of and for all the Jewish people, its intelligence is also Jewish intelligence. Clandestine emissaries keep in touch with Jewish communities, helping them to protect themselves, particularly in Arab and Communist countries. One of the agencies' central missions was to organize the illegal immigration of Jews from around the world. Israel's secret agents also launched an international manhunt for Nazi war criminals.

Israel, seeing self-defence as its prime interest, has built itself a technological infrastructure aimed at preparing, if necessary, for chemical, biological, or even nuclear war, with research into countermeasures against those types of unconventional conflict. Israeli intelligence has, on the one hand, helped the nation obtain what it needs – for both conventional and unconventional defence – while, on the other hand, preventing leaks of information about that effort.

This book will also describe in detail the intelligence community's multi-branched structure, its modes of operations, the people of the community and the ethos and values which motivate them.

There is a need, at the same time, to evaluate the connections between ends and means – the chosen methods to achieve the objectives – and to what extent the Israeli intelligence community is accountable to the political masters whose directives it is supposed to follow.

The aim, here, is not to debate basic moral questions such as: Is it right and just to have an intelligence community? It should be taken for granted that intelligence agencies do exist, like wars. Judgmental discussions of whether they should exist are irrelevant.

There are moral aspects, however, in the practice of the intelligence craft. Even in the uncomfortable frontier between just and unjust, when considering moral dilemmas such as assassinating a Palestinian terrorist, blowing up a German scientist who works for the Arab enemy, or kidnapping a Nazi war criminal, there should still be controls in the form of a coherent set of instructions.

As one Mossad veteran says, 'We are taught to lie, to steal, and sometimes even to kill, but when we return to the family – to Israel – we have to be pure and honest with our superiors.'

It is also not the intention of this book to be dragged onto the official line that friendly nations do not spy on each other. It is sheer hypocrisy, because it is simply not true. The history of Israeli intelligence is full of occasions when clandestine operations were mounted in friendly countries to obtain technological know-how and information on political intentions. Other nations' spies do the same, and the number one rule of the intelligence game is: Don't get caught.

Most other books in the field have extensively, sometimes exaggeratedly, described the great successes of Israeli intelligence – victories which fuel the human imagination to fanciful heights: the acquisition of Nikita Khrushchev's secret speech in 1956, the capture of Adolf Eichmann in 1960, the smuggling of missile boats from Cherbourg in 1969 and the daring rescue of hijacked airline passengers from Entebbe in 1976.

The other accounts stopped short, however, of failures, preferring to ignore them. It would be a disservice to

Israeli history and certainly to readers to exclude the hidden confusion of the early days – faulty recruitment of criminals and adventurers into the community, while Soviet agents penetrated the heart of the Israeli defence apparatus – and the better known scandals of the 1980s: Shin Bet's killings and cover-ups, Jonathan Pollard's espionage in the United States, the defective plotting of Irangate, the embarrassment caused by nuclear spy Mordecai Vanunu, secret trials in Israel and excessive censorship of the press.

An egregious error has lingered for decades, condensing the entire Israeli intelligence community into a single word: Mossad. The truth is much more complicated and so much more interesting.

Israeli intelligence has at least six branches, and the Mossad is only one. Glamorous and important as its missions might be, it is not considered the most essential agency to Israel's defence: Military Intelligence is bigger, has more versatile duties, and wields greater influence in the state's life or death decisions.

There are other units, each with untold stories to be told: Shin Bet, Lakam, the Liaison Office, the Counter-Terrorism Adviser, and others working silently for the Jewish state. They have all contributed both to the nation's defence and to the mishaps and errors of the intelligence community.

As is so often the case in re-telling secret operations, truth and fiction have been woven together into a patchwork which is difficult to unravel, with the facts and the distortions blurring into legends and myth.

This is not a tale of perfection. Intelligence agencies like to consider themselves as pure and good fraternities, but – as in monasteries – internal rivalries, love-hate relationships and all human traits may be found.

To say that Israel's spies are imperfect is not to imply that they have no value at all. It is not this book's intention to shatter the myth of Israeli intelligence and throw away all the pieces. The true history contains remarkable feats of skill and courage, by highly motivated operatives working for talented, professional agencies.

They are still human beings, however, not superhuman Israelis who make no mistakes. Sometimes they are right; sometimes they err. They are dedicated, prepared to work hard and even risk their lives in the defence of their nation. Their labours contribute greatly to the continued existence of the state, but it would be wrong to believe that they are irreplaceable. Individual agents have come and gone; even entire agencies have come and gone. Furthermore, the intelligence community has not been immune to the damage inflicted on Israeli morale and morals by the continuing occupation of the Arab lands captured in 1967.

After all, the intelligence brotherhood is a reflection of the total sum of its society.

I

The Death of the Informers

It was Muhammad al-Ayad's last stand, and he was making a desperate show of it. Running from window to window of his old stone house, spraying bullets from his Uzi sub-machine gun at his fellow Palestinians outside. Ayad did not care whom he might hit. He just wanted a way out.

'Ayad! Ayad!' His wife shouted the family name down the telephone to one of the Arabic-speaking Israelis who were supposed to protect them. The Ayads had been cooper-ating with the Israelis since the West Bank of the Jordan fell into their hands nearly twenty-one years earlier.

It was February 24, 1988, the seventy-eighth day of the popular revolt which had taught much of the world an Arabic word: the *intifada*, or 'uprising', was already the longest and most damaging challenge the Israeli occupation had had to face. Inspired but not distracted by the jubilation of a six-day victory in 1967, the Israelis had quickly spread their tentacles through the West Bank, the Gaza Strip, the Golan Heights and the Sinai Peninsula. The octopus, with its brain at the centre in Tel Aviv, was *Shabak* – the Hebrew acronym for *Sherut ha-Bitachon ha-Klali*, or General Security Service. Foreign analysts sometimes call it GSS, but more commonly Shin Bet, the first two Hebrew letters of the name.

Shin Bet is Israel's FBI, dedicated to fighting the state's enemies, whether foreign or domestic, within the borders of Israel and occasionally abroad. Since the Six-Day War, Shin Bet's borders included the occupied territories. Muhammad al-Ayad worked for Shin Bet.

His neighbours in Qabatiya, one of the northernmost towns in that part of the West Bank which biblically-minded Israelis call Samaria, said Ayad had been coerced – recruited did not seem quite the right word – to serve as an informer when Shin Bet had him under arrest in the first months of the occupation, when he was 20. He had been accused of causing some trouble, although no one can remember what. What matters is that to gain his freedom and later to grease the administrative wheels which ensured the prosperity of his café, Ayad agreed to give Shin Bet tips.

'It is nothing major,' a Shin Bet agent typically says to a potential collaborator. 'It is not even against the interests of your people. You all simply want to live in peace, right? So if you see some troublemakers, you just tell us and we'll do the rest. No one will have to know.'

But in the small villages, where secrets are hard to mask, Shin Bet's informers are often known. There are said to be thousands of them, among the over one million Palestinians of the West Bank and Gaza. Ayad's fate, however, was enough to make future recruitment almost impossible.

The *intifada* had taken on new vigour that week in February, as the latest clandestine leaflets from the National Unified Command of the Uprising called for a general strike and protest marches to coincide with the start of an American diplomatic initiative. The Palestinians felt they had been ignored too long. Even as the rebellion prompted Secretary of State George Shultz to fly in with a United States plan for Middle East peace negotiations, the protesters wanted to be sure that the American would pay some attention to them.

Similar scenes were played out throughout the West Bank and Gaza, but in Qabatiya, law and order gave way to lawlessness and disorder. Nationalist protesters marched through the town, shouting slogans as they passed Ayad's house, for a few days.[1] He should have grown accustomed to hearing chants such as 'With our bodies and our blood, we will destroy the traitors and liberate our land!' On Wednesday the 24th, however, Ayad panicked.

He was 40 years old, and he had cracked under pressure only twice: when he gave in to the Israelis and agreed to work for them; and, in an episode more courageous than uncontrolled, when he fired his Uzi at young Arabs whom he suspected of trying to sabotage his car. That was a few months before the *intifada* began. That was when Ayad could feel confident that shooting at other Arabs would not mean that he, himself, would be in mortal danger. The Israelis would protect him. After all, they had given him the Uzi, which perhaps more than any other weapon symbolizes the defence of Israel.

Ayad used the gun, first waving it threateningly, then firing bursts of bullets, after the protesters hurled rocks at his house. All the tensions built up since the uprising against the Israelis began were released in this unexpected, fatal confrontation. He probably did not even notice that among the thirteen Qabatiyans he hit was a small boy, a four-year-old who died instantly.

The demonstrators knew immediately. The blood was all the evidence they needed of Ayad's treason, which they had always suspected. Where cooler heads might have retreated in the face of gunfire and a dead toddler, the crowd continued to throw rocks and bottles in a relentless assault on the traitor's home.

He, however, was defending his ground. Shooting from the windows, running like a trapped rat, Ayad told his wife to telephone the Israeli military authorities in Jenin, an Arab town four miles away, to summon a rescue force.

The army was busy that day, controlling unrest elsewhere, and did not get to Qabatiya in time. Who was this Palestinian calling for help, anyway?

He was an informer, one of many lending their eyes and ears to Shin Bet in the mini-society which the Israelis could occupy but could not fully penetrate without assistance.

Admittedly, it was a difficult time for the domestic intelligence agency. Shin Bet was scrambling to identify the organizers of the rebellion, but even after hundreds and then thousands of Palestinians were arrested in the West Bank and Gaza, the underground leaflets continued to be distributed and the crowds of protesters continued to throw stones and chant angry slogans.

In the meantime, Shin Bet's director Yosef Harmelin was preparing to leave his post at the end of March. He had only served a year and a half, but he had directed the agency in the past and was only brought out of retirement as a temporary caretaker when a scandal tore Shin Bet apart. The agency was found to have habitually used torture and perjury to win convictions in court and the good names of the normally nameless security agents were dragged through the mud.

Ironically, it was also revealed in that scandal, which burst into the public eye because Shin Bet interrogators beat to death two Palestinians who had just hijacked an Israeli passenger bus, that the agents had tried to sidestep responsibility by blaming the army for killing the Arab prisoners. The army, afterwards, did not owe Shin Bet any favours, and when the *intifada* began, senior military officers engaged in private but potent criticism of Shin Bet.

Internal Israeli rivalries certainly did not help Ayad, and before any Israelis could come to save him, the informer ran out of bullets. The mob poured into his house and pinned him to the floor, and several of the angry young men used a wire to strangle him. Ayad's wife was allowed to escape, even as the frenzied crowd set fire to her home.

By the time the army did arrive, with several Shin Bet agents in an unmarked car, they found Ayad on public display: a brutally beaten body, hanging from an electricity pylon near Qabatiya's bus station. Up there, on the wire, covering the corpse, was the green, black, red and white flag of Palestine, a country which existed only in the nationalistic longings of a people who had lost all the Middle East wars.

Ayad's body was a gory symbol of rebellion, and a message to Shin Bet that its twenty-year control of the territories had broken down. Ayad was the sixty-fifth Palestinian who died in the *intifada*. The boy he killed was the sixty-fourth. By the middle of 1989, another thirty Arabs who had collaborated with Shin Bet were killed by fellow Palestinians.

The *intifada* was aimed not only at protesting the continued occupation of the West Bank and Gaza, but at shaking off Israeli military rule. And that is literally what *intifada* means in Arabic: 'shaking off'. The protesters wished to create an alternative system of government which would be dominated by the Arab inhabitants and would lead to the infrastructure of a future, Palestinian state. The organizers of the uprising, to achieve their goal, reached the conclusion that the best weapon to consolidate their own rise to power was to expose the Palestinians who had worked for the Israelis.

Leaflets and loudspeaker announcements in West Bank villages urged collaborators to come to the local mosques, where they should hand in the weapons given to them by Shin Bet and repent. If they gave up their Israeli arms and pledged allegiance to the Palestinian national cause, they were told, their sins of collaboration would be absolved.

The Palestinian uprising was precisely what Shin Bet was meant to prevent. The network of informers should have told the Israelis of any significant attempts to organize dissent. The informers ranged across Palestinian society, from factory workers to intellectuals. With their incomes supplemented by Shin Bet stipends, between $50 and $200 a month, they were supposed to keep the Israelis informed about activists who tried to turn social and professional organizations into political power centres.

Shin Bet concentrated, however, on the area in which it excelled: preventing Arab terrorism. Informers were paid handsome bonuses for tips pertaining to violent groups. Isolated terrorist crimes, such as a stabbing of a Jewish settler in the West Bank, were solved with impressive speed – thanks to information from agents planted inside guerilla cells, or purchased from informers on 'the street', or obtained by physical or psychological coercion from the dozens of 'suspects' who were usually arrested in sweeps of the area around the scene of an attack.

There was no truly dangerous terrorist threat within the occupied territories. The intelligence system accomplished that, and then it grew fat and complacent. Shin Bet agents, spreading the word that they should be addressed – when addressed – by invented, Arabic names such as Abu Ibrahim, seemed arrogant. And they were.

In the field, they knew they were hated. They knew the worst thing they could do to a political activist in a West Bank town was to pretend to be his friends. They might visit his house frequently and grin as they left, or they might shout familiar greetings from their car while driving past. Arresting a young hothead could make him a local hero. Making him appear to be a collaborator would surely ruin him.

At its headquarters in a northern suburb of Tel Aviv, Shin Bet concentrated on gathering information rather than producing informed analysis. Reports of trouble brewing here or there would lead to detentions, interrogations, and more reports being filed, suggesting names of people, villages, and refugee camps to be investigated. But the overall picture was missed.

Hardly anyone, in the intelligence community or elsewhere in Israel, wanted to believe that the Palestinians would rise up in mass rebellion. That had been the fear in the first months of the occupation in 1967, but for two decades the territories had been governed peacefully. The majority of Palestinians had cooperated, most of the time, with the Israeli authorities so as to continue their normal lives with a minimum of disruption.

A few months before the *intifada* began, the Israeli official responsible for monitoring West Bank and Gaza affairs was overheard denying the possibility of such unrest. The 'Coordinator' of government activities in the occupied territories, Shmuel Goren, was asked: 'Well, when will the rebellion in the territories begin?'

It was a somewhat aggressive conversational opening, but Israelis are not known for standing on polite formality, and in any event it was a military man who was asking. Goren seemed to be taken aback, however, and he snapped: 'No rebellion! Not ever!'

The officer persisted: 'Are you sure about what you're saying?'

Goren ended the exchange with: 'You want to bet?'

Goren was, until 1984, a senior operative with the Mossad, Israel's foreign espionage apparatus. Even in the defence ministry, he was considered a candidate for Mossad chief. He should have known whatever the intelligence community knew, and his heated conversation ironically took place at a party attended by a large number of Israeli intelligence officers. It was a wedding reception in honour of Mossad veteran Yaakov Nimrodi's daughter, Smadar. It was the party of the year in Israel, but it was not to be *the* Middle East event of the year 1987. That was to be the uprising which Goren claimed would never occur.

The *intifada* began as a loose collection of events, co-ordinated only later by the shadowy National Unified Command in its leaflets, underground radio broadcasts from Syria, and word-of-mouth instructions. It began on December 9, after the Arab leaders at their summit conference in Jordan, the previous week, had focused only on the dangers of the Iran-Iraq war, and after President Ronald Reagan and Soviet leader Mikhail Gorbachev had also not bothered to discuss the Palestinian problem at their summit, that same week, in Washington.

The immediate spark flashed in Gaza, where an Israeli truck driver on the main road through town lost control of his vehicle on Tuesday, December 8. The heavy truck struck a crowd of Palestinians, killing four and injuring seven others in what police later called an accident. To Gazans, however, it seemed to be murder, the last straw, the breaking point, the signal for an explosion of anger which had been building for over twenty years. They took to the streets the next morning, the protest movement spread to the West Bank, and it went on and on.

Shin Bet and the military governors of the occupied territories had failed to see the Palestinians as a political people. Their primary aim was to control the territories by a combination of incentives and threats, known in traditional colonial terms as a carrot and stick policy. The security forces were always so confident of keeping order, while tens of thousands of Arabs peacefully earned their crusts of bread by travelling daily to work in pre-1967 Israel, that the Israelis had not learned the lines of influence in Gaza and the West Bank.

Among the most difficult groups to penetrate were the religious zealots. Although they were Sunni Moslems, rather than the fanatical Shi'ites who rule Iran, the Gaza faithful took some inspiration from Ayatollah Ruhollah Khomeini and his revolutionaries in far-off Teheran. Ironically, Shin Bet had at times encouraged fundamentalist groups, thinking they would be a useful alternative to the mainstream support of the Palestine Liberation Organization, the PLO. It was yet another classical method of colonialism, divide and rule, which proved futile. Those same fundamentalist mosques turned against Shin Bet by encouraging the collaborators to turn themselves in.

Clashes between the Israeli army and Palestinian protesters, armed mainly with stones and bottles, led rapidly in 1988, the year of the *intifada*, to over 300 Arab deaths and a new page in the history of the Arab-Israeli conflict was turned. But equally quickly, the rebel movement became uncrushable. In the first year of the uprising, the Israelis arrested over 20,000 Arabs and held as many as 6,000 in detention at any one time. There were, however, many more taking part in the daily, even hourly, protest marches.

When the uprising began in December 1987, top Israeli defence and intelligence officials did not attach particular significance to the events. Defence Minister Yitzhak Rabin did not rush back from a visit to Washington. Prime Minister Shamir and the army Chief of Staff General Dan Shomron, in the weekly cabinet meetings, dismissed the trouble in the occupied territories as unimportant and repeatedly promised the twenty-five ministers that the unrest could easily be crushed.

It took two months for Israel's intelligence chiefs, who meet every week as *Va'adat Rashei ha-Sherutim*, the Committee of Heads of the Services, to reach the conclusion that Shin Bet and the army had failed to stop the uprising.

As well as the heads of the Mossad, Shin Bet, and Military Intelligence – Aman – the *Va'adat* meetings included the commissioner of the national police and the director-general of the foreign ministry. The presence of these two non-intelligence officials usually deterred the three agency chiefs from being entirely open and they were especially reluctant to discuss operational details of their missions. This time, however, they were so disturbed by the dissolution of the informers' network that they opened their hearts.

Harmelin, also concerned by the killing of Ayad and others, argued that Shin Bet's role was not a prophetic one. It did not have the tools to anticipate large-scale rebellion. The agency, he pointed out, had been assigned to preventing threats to the State of Israel and had done very well at that. Shin Bet would refuse to be the scapegoat for the failure of Israeli politicians to find a long-range solution in the region. Nevertheless, he did set up a new department in Shin Bet, with the mission of monitoring and analysing political trends in the Palestinian community.

The *Va'adat* members knew that the worst short-term failure had been the inability to foresee that the Palestinians would change their tactics. They had shifted from isolated terrorist attacks, involving very few individuals, to less violent but much more widespread action which could outmanoeuvre the massive military strength of Israel. The armed behemoth, even with its sophisticated weapons systems, was too clumsy to react appropriately. Israel's leaders knew that as a democratic society, the option of bringing in tanks and artillery to suppress demonstrators who were throwing stones and burning tyres was unthinkable – unlike some dictatorships in the Middle East and elsewhere.

Shin Bet's chief could report that his agents were intensifying their efforts to cut off the trouble spots from each other and from outside incitement. Israeli intelligence knew that the *intifada* was locally initiated by people in the occupied territories, but there were indications that PLO leaders outside the territories were moving quickly to jump on the bandwagon. Mossad chief Nahum Admoni revealed that one of the first acts of solidarity, for incitement and propaganda purposes, would be a voyage at sea.

The PLO, which had been formed in 1964 as an umbrella to include the various Palestinian Liberation organizations, spent around $750,000 in February 1988 to buy an old Greek car ferry, the *Sol Phryne*. It was re-named *al-Awda*, 'The Return', and was to bring 131 Palestinian exiles to the shores of Israel to dramatize their demand for a homeland. This would be an Arab version of the *Exodus*, the freighter which brought over 4,000 Jewish survivors of the Nazi concentration camps to British-ruled Palestine in 1947, only to be repulsed and forced back to Europe – to the eternal embarrassment of Britain.

Coincidentally, the *Sol Phryne* itself had been built in 1947, had sailed among the Greek islands and later specialized in transporting Christian pilgrims from Greece to Israel. In 1982, it was one of many ships which carried Palestinian guerilla fighters out of Beirut, after Israel's invasion of Lebanon.[2]

Now the PLO was planning to use the ferry to embarrass Israel. Britain's mandate over Palestine had survived only one more year after the suffering Jews aboard the *Exodus* had been turned away. Forty-one years later, the PLO could only hope, unrealistically, that Israel's rule over the West Bank and Gaza would suffer a similar fate. The imminent confrontation at sea could only be bad for Israel's international image, which was already badly tarnished by the army's brutality in attempting to suppress the *intifada*.

The threat of a PLO propaganda coup was a major subject of a *Va'adat* meeting in Tel Aviv in mid-February. Nahum Admoni was the chairman. As director of the Mossad, Admoni's job was to gather intelligence overseas and to carry out 'special tasks' beyond the state's borders.

His agents in Greece were watching the PLO as it organized the publicity-seeking 'Voyage of Return'. The passengers were being assembled in Athens, and it was openly suggested that a ship in the nearby port of Piraeus would be chartered for the voyage. The Israeli agents passed the word around local shipping circles that anyone providing a vessel to the PLO could expect to lose that ship. The Israelis also asked around and found out that the *Sol Phryne* had just been sold to Palestinians. It was not in Piraeus. It was anchored in the harbour of Limassol, Cyprus.

The men and women of Mossad compiled lists of the Palestinians who were planning to sail to Israel and these certainly included PLO men with a violent past. The ship was also due to carry dozens of journalists, television crews and even a leftist member of Israel's parliament, the Knesset. They were the PLO's insurance policy, the guarantee that the Israeli navy – which would try somehow to prevent *al-Awda* from landing – would not sink the ship.

Admoni had a brilliant idea. He told the joint intelligence committee that his men could sabotage the ship before it took any people aboard. They would have to act quickly, the Mossad chief added, because the Palestinian spokesman, Bassam Abu Sherif, was telling daily news conferences in Athens that the voyage would begin 'at any hour, any time now.' The spokesman was a heavily scarred, half-blind man. He had managed to survive the explosion of a Mossad parcel bomb in July 1972, at his Beirut home, when he was an information officer for the more radical Popular Front for the Liberation of Palestine. Sherif had lost one eye and had himself become a scarred symbol. A proposal to attack Abu Sherif was briefly considered in the Mossad, but the man had not recently been linked with terrorist violence, and it was felt that his death would not stop the PLO propaganda machine.

The Mossad chief brought his plan to sink the PLO ship, while it was still empty, to Prime Minister Yitzhak Shamir. As a former European operations chief for the agency, Shamir could see the elegant logic in stopping the voyage before it began. He did not ask for the precise details of how his ex-colleagues in the Mossad would do it, but he knew that explosives would be used. The Prime Minister was told that the aim would be to avoid loss of life, and given such an intention the mission would have been considered a failure – at least partially – if innocent passengers were killed.

Admoni also asked Shamir, however, to approve a killing. He wanted the go-ahead to assassinate a senior PLO figure who was described by Israeli intelligence analysts as a 'clear, potent, and persistent danger'. Mohammed Bassem Sultan Tamimi had the rank of lieutenant colonel in the PLO's semi-official army and he had been closely watched by Mossad agents in Jordan, Lebanon and Tunisia. They found that Tamimi was an activist in Arafat's mainstream *Fatah* faction, more a man of action than a political planner. He was 35 years old, was better known by the nickname Hamdi and worked with the Occupied Homelands Directorate of the PLO.

Hamdi signed his own death warrant by planning dozens of attacks by Palestinian guerillas inside the occupied territories, while organizing a PLO branch, *Jihad Islami*, or 'Islamic Holy War', which was meant to attract religious Moslems.

One example of Hamdi's handiwork had particularly enraged the Israelis: by the ancient Wailing Wall in Jerusalem, during an army swearing-in ceremony on October 15, 1986, hand grenades exploded among the recruits and their proud families. One Israeli was killed and seventy wounded. Whoever threw the grenades – apparently one of Hamdi's agents – got away. The Palestinian *Jihad Islami* claimed responsibility.

The Israelis were determined that Hamdi would not escape punishment.

Prime Minister Shamir approved both plans, the assassination and the sabotaging of the PLO ferry, in a simple oral statement to the Mossad director. No American-style 'intelligence finding' had to be typed out, signed and placed in the files. No parliamentary committee had to be informed of the covert action. This was war, after all. Even in public, Shamir had branded the PLO plan to sail a ship towards Israel as 'a declaration of war.'

The Mossad must have had an agent remarkably close to Hamdi, and there is no doubt that the PLO and its Occupied Homelands Directorate were thoroughly infiltrated by Israeli informers. The Israelis knew that the Palestinian colonel would be flying from Athens to Cyprus on February 13, and they also knew that Cyprus was a relatively easy venue for murder. The police on the island, divided into Greek and Turkish sectors and barely 150 miles from Israel and Lebanon, were hopeless at solving political crimes. There were simply too many incidents and the Cypriot authorities had enough problems without making enemies among Israelis and Arabs.

The only potential trouble was that Cyprus was where the *Sol Phryne*, the PLO propaganda ship, was waiting for its passengers. Whether the voyage was stopped or not, the glare of worldwide media coverage would soon come to the island. Admoni checked with Shamir, to be sure that the Prime Minister did not see a problem in the proximity of the two cases which the Mossad had been told to handle. The approval was reaffirmed.

On Sunday, February 14, the Israelis struck. They had received an excellent tip: that Lieutenant Colonel Tamimi, a.k.a. Hamdi, would be driving around Cyprus that day with Marwan Kayyali, a PLO colonel who was based in Limassol. Kayyali's job was to ship supplies to the Palestinians remaining in Lebanon, using his excellent contacts in Limassol harbour. He was also involved in arranging the voyage of the *Sol Phryne*.

From the Mossad's point of view, the two missions were coming together beautifully. Israeli agents had little trouble planting a powerful bomb in Kayyali's green Volkswagen.[3] The device could be detonated by remote control, and the men with the radio transmitter watched the automobile as it approached Kayyali's home in a small apartment complex in Limassol.

There was a third man in the car, but one of the Israeli agents – based in Cyprus – immediately identified him as Mohammed Hassan Buheis. Known as Abu Hassan, he also worked for the PLO's Occupied Homelands Directorate. Using the latitude of decision-making permitted to Israeli field operatives, they considered Abu Hassan a legitimate target, too. One of the Israelis pressed the button. The Volkswagen was destroyed by the explosion. All three Palestinians died.

Early the next morning, the port of Limassol was rocked by another explosion. This one pierced the hull of the ferryboat *Sol Phryne*, rendering it useless for the 'Voyage of Return'. The Palestinians correctly blamed Israel, but all that Defence Minister Yitzhak Rabin would say was: 'The State of Israel decided it was compelled not to let them achieve their purpose and we always do that in any way that seems suitable.'

The Monday blast injured no one. Cypriot police said a limpet mine, a simple but effective weapon commonly used by frogmen during World War II, had been attached to the *Sol Phryne*'s hull from beneath the surface of the Mediterranean. It was neat work, the explosion destroying any evidence which could trace the mine, and there was no chance of catching the attackers.

Operatives of the Mossad station in Nicosia, the capital

of Cyprus, must have had a busy time. They were certainly involved in pre-attack reconnaissance and served as look-outs. They also played host to bomb experts who came to the island for the two explosive missions.

Abu Sherif said, in Athens, that another 'Ship of Return' would be found. But the intended passengers, already tired of waiting, left Greece. The world's press lost interest. The *Sol Phryne* was repaired, but no one again suggested using it as a pale imitation of the *Exodus*. Shamir and the Mossad had got their way.

The PLO prepared a violent response, instead. It would be an act of almost personal revenge by Khalil el-Wazir, better known as Abu Jihad, the 'Father of the Holy War' who was Yasser Arafat's right-hand man and military chief. Wazir had been working closely with the Occupied Home-lands Directorate, plotting strategy for exploiting the *inti-fada*. Three of his men had just been killed by the Mossad in Cyprus and Abu Jihad was out for blood.

He sent three guerillas to Egypt at the beginning of March, where they armed themselves from a hidden PLO cache and headed across the Sinai Desert, which the Israelis had returned to Egypt in 1982 under the Camp David Accords of 1978 and the peace treaty which followed.

On March 7, the *Fatah* band had surprisingly little trouble crossing the border from Sinai into the Negev Desert on foot. They were not immediately detected, and they managed to shock the Israeli defence establishment, whether they knew it or not at the time. The guerillas hijacked a passenger bus in the desert that same day, perhaps aware that they were stopping and boarding the daily run bringing employees, with their high security clearances, from the Negev capital Beersheba to the ultra-secret nuclear reactor at Dimona. It was an indirect attack on Israel's most secure facility.

The bus was stopped at a roadblock and after pretending to negotiate, an anti-terrorist unit of Israel's police assaulted the bus. All three hijackers were killed. Three of the Israeli nuclear workers also died, however, and the PLO declared the raid a victory. Yasser Arafat said the victims were connected with Israel's clandestine atomic bomb factory, 'the most dangerous military target in the Middle East.' The PLO attack was a contribution, of sorts, by the guerilla fighters outside 'Palestine' to the uprising by their brethren living under occupation.

That was on Monday. On Thursday, March 10, Mossad chief Admoni told his fellow intelligence chiefs, Shin Bet's Harmelin and Aman's director General Amnon Lipkin-Shahak, that with around thirty days' preparation, Mossad and the army could together strike at the root cause of the upsurge in terrorist violence. The *intifada* was bad enough, Admoni said. Infiltrations were intolerable. He suggested that Abu Jihad be killed.

As chairman of the joint committee, the Mossad chief won quick approval from his colleagues and from Prime Minister Shamir. It was also explained to the inner cabinet, the ten top ministers from among the large, unwieldy twenty-five-member full cabinet. The Prime Minister told the bipartisan inner group that the PLO had to be sent a clear message that its 'military' side would not be allowed to gain any advantage from the unrest in the occupied territories. Liquidating Arafat's top aide would inject fear into the Palestinian leader's heart, just when he might think that the Israelis were running scared during the *intifada*.

Some ministers realized that behind the official explanation hid another motive for assassinating Arafat's deputy. It would be a 'show-off' operation, to boost the morale of the Israeli public, which had suffered because of the inability to suppress the *intifada*.

Meeting so soon after the shock and anger of the bus hijacking, most of the government ministers readily agreed. The Deputy Prime Minister, Shimon Peres, raised objections, however. He is leader of the Labour Party, rival to Shamir's Likud bloc, and while this was not strictly a party line issue, Peres seemed concerned that an attack on the top leadership of the PLO – for the first time in nine years – could ruin diplomatic efforts to find a solution to the

Palestinian problem, through negotiations with Egypt and Jordan.

The Labour side of Israel's coalition government, believed in surrendering most of the occupied territories in exchange for peace treaties. Shamir and his Likud did not. Also objecting to the assassination plan were two other Labour ministers, former air force chief Ezer Weizman and the former president of Israel, Education Minister Yitzhak Navon.

In terms of military experience, however, the two senior ministers on the Labour side agreed with the Likud and Shamir in this case. Defence Minister Rabin and Police Minister Chaim Bar-Lev were both former army chiefs of staff, and they both believed in sending the PLO a stern warning. Approving an air raid on a military target is, admittedly, more impersonal and easier. But Abu Jihad himself was a military target.

Rabin, Bar-Lev, and the Likud ministers were intrigued by the idea of striking again in faraway Tunisia, Arafat's headquarters since the Palestinian guerillas had been forced to flee from the Lebanon. Israel's military morale had been lifted by the air force's longest air raid ever, which destroyed many of the PLO's buildings near Tunis in October 1985. A morale booster would help again, with the army now pinned down with unpalatable policing chores in the occupied territories. And after all, Abu Jihad had gone too far.

The Mossad was the perfect instrument to end the recent escalation in the renewed 'war of spooks' between Israelis and Palestinians – similar to the killings and counter-killings across Europe and the Middle East in the 1970s.

No formal vote was taken in the inner cabinet. None was required under Israeli law. In any event, a show of hands would have produced a seven-to-three majority in favour of execution.

Shamir told his ministers that the Mossad director would need the participation of élite units of the Israel Defence Forces, the IDF. The PLO military commander would be killed in Tunis, nearly 1,500 miles from Tel Aviv, and while the raid had not yet been planned in detail it would likely resemble the assault on Beirut on April 9, 1973. At that time, in an operation coordinated by Mossad agents who entered Lebanon with false identities, IDF commandos killed fifteen senior Palestinian operatives in their homes. The chief targets were Abu Jihad's predecessor Yussuf Najjar and two other leaders of the notorious Black September terrorists who were blamed for the massacre at the 1972 Munich Olympics.

The inner cabinet told the Mossad and the army to begin their planning. In charge were Israel's top general, IDF Chief of Staff Shomron, and his deputy, General Ehud Barak. Barak had deep intelligence and commando experience and was involved in the raid on Beirut fifteen years earlier. Now he was to work with the intelligence men again and their task was to duplicate the success of 1973, even though the distance to be covered this time was fifteen times greater.

General Barak had plenty of cooperation from *Agaf ha-Modiin*, the army's 'Intelligence Branch' which is better known as Aman. Its director, General Shahak, had also been with the commando forces in Beirut. In 1973, Shahak was known as Amnon Lipkin. It is fairly common for Israelis to change their European Jewish names to Hebrew biblical names and even more common in Israel's intelligence community for a family name to be changed during a senior officer's years of service. 'Shahak' was a powerful choice, as it is the Hebrew word for pulverize. The Aman director liked the mission and he had a gut feeling that it would succeed.

The intricate planning for the raid on Tunisia would seem to any military strategist to be a tremendous amount of trouble for the sake of killing one man. But imagine what the Americans or British, in World War II, would have done to get rid of a senior German or Japanese general. And would not the Germans have felt they were crippling the morale of the Allies if they could have assassinated General Eisenhower?

Removing a senior commander from enemy ranks would not win the war, but the Israelis badly needed a victory four months into the *intifada* and the experience of the 1970s had taught the Mossad that assassinating top terrorist leaders caused severe disruption in the PLO and its splinter groups. It made them fear the Israelis; it made them hesitate in planning their violence; it forced them into making mistakes. Perhaps even more than the fact that the Israelis needed a triumph, they believed that the Palestinian resistance movement needed to suffer a blow.

The Mossad, Shin Bet and, occasionally, Aman had been keeping a close eye on Wazir for years. Agents and informers in Arab countries and inside the PLO itself reported to Tel Aviv frequently and fully on his movements. An Israeli handwriting expert, Aryeh Naftali, had been asked by the Mossad in 1983 to produce a psychological analysis based on a sample of Arabic writing. Only later did he learn that the notorious Abu Jihad was the subject of his report, a man whom he described as highly intelligent, a good organizer with a precise, analytical mind and great reserves of strength.[4]

Official Israeli files also noted that among PLO politicians, Abu Jihad was a great conciliator. He helped hold the organization together, because both Arafat and his violent rivals would listen to him.

He was a strong believer, however, in achieving victory through 'armed struggle'. At the age of 19, in 1954, he was arrested by the Egyptian Army for laying mines in the Gaza Strip. The Wazirs lived there, under Egypt's rule, after Khalil's father fled the original family home when the State of Israel was born in 1948. In 1955, the junior Wazir became a guerilla by attacking a water facility on the Israeli side of the border. A few years later, he met Yasser Arafat and other young Palestinian professionals, and in Kuwait in 1959 they formed *Fatah*, a small organization which managed eventually to take over the entire PLO. He remained at Arafat's side throughout, seeking support in the early years by touring all the Arab and Communist countries, and later wherever the PLO was making its home, directing the guerilla war while Arafat shaped his own image into that of a diplomat.

At Mossad headquarters in Tel Aviv, Admoni and his operations' planners studied their files on the raid into Beirut. Looking at how Israeli agents had been infiltrated into an Arab country, it appeared to be as easy in 1988 in Tunisia as it had been in 1973 in Lebanon. Six Mossad agents, using false British and Belgian passports to pose as tourists and businessmen, had flown to Beirut in order to acquaint themselves with the buildings to be attacked and had hired six roomy cars.

In Tunisia, there would be only one target. The Mossad would need only three agents, to hire three cars. This time, they used Lebanese passports and spoke perfect, Lebanese-accented Arabic. The two men and a woman flew in as tourists. They travelled separately, and appeared as relaxed as the other two million tourists who visit Tunisia in an average year.

As in the Beirut raid, the Israeli navy – led by *Shayetet 13*, its élite 'Fleet 13' of frogmen – later brought the army commandos to the beach near their target. Unlike the brief cruise to the Lebanese coast, the navy's missile boat had to leave Israel around the same time that the Mossad agents arrived in Tunis on Tuesday, April 12. The boat was then in position to deliver approximately thirty soldiers to the North African coast on Friday night, the 15th. The men were members of *Sayeret Matkal*, the Reconnaissance Unit of the General Staff: hand-picked commandos, under the personal command of the army chief of staff.

Copying the Beirut plan, the élite troops landed on a tourist beach near Tunis aboard rubber dinghies in the dead of night. As in 1973, the Mossad agents were waiting on the shoreline. They had rented two Volkswagen mini-buses and a Peugeot station wagon. It was a short drive from the beach at Rouad to the Sidi Boussaid suburb where Abu Jihad lived with his wife, also a PLO activist, and two children – a daughter, who was 14, and a two-year-old son.

Another two sons and one daughter were students in the United States.

The Israelis had the advantage of two technological improvements which gave the commando force more security than their counterparts had had in Beirut in 1973. The first was the use of an Israeli Boeing 707 jet, outfitted with military communications gear, flying over the Mediterranean barely thirty miles north of Tunisia. Because it stayed within a civilian air lane known as Blue 21, just south of Sicily, the Israeli pilots were in touch with Italian air controllers, and the plane could pose as an El Al charter flight. It was a bit unusual, but flight controllers do not have the time or inclination to ask about every extra flight ostensibly between Israel and Europe.

For the clandestine mission, it was like having the Israeli generals on the spot, and decisions could be made by the commanders without any delays, because Generals Barak and Shahak were aboard the converted airliner in easy contact by two-way radio with the commandos.

The other technical development was a device which enabled the Israeli team on the ground to jam the telephones of the Sidi Boussaid neighbourhood near Abu Jihad's villa. At around one o'clock in the morning of April 16, one mini-bus and the station wagon parked just one block away from the house. They plugged their device, which caused an immediate short-circuit, into a telephone junction box previously located by one of the Mossad agents. The two vehicles were packed with troops in civilian clothes, holding their Uzi submachine guns between their legs, and they simply waited. In Beirut, their counterparts had had to fight PLO units and the Lebanese Gendarmerie to protect the main mission. This time, if necessary, they would battle PLO security forces or even the Tunisian army.

Eight commandos, driven by the Mossad woman in the other Volkswagen mini-bus, pulled up in front of Wazir's home. In two task forces of four men each, they swiftly assaulted the house. They had practised on a similar villa in Israel. Such rehearsals, with models of the target, often specially built, are considered absolutely necessary before embarking on complex missions behind enemy lines.

One team, responsible for on-site security, killed Wazir's driver, who was sitting in the PLO leader's car, having brought Wazir home around ninety minutes earlier at midnight. Also, using pistols fitted with silencers, they shot dead a Palestinian guard in the basement of the house. Their task was to eliminate anyone who might stand between them and their quarry.

The other team, assigned to the target himself, broke down the front door and began the search for Abu Jihad. They immediately used their silenced pistols to kill a Tunisian guard and then they spotted Khalil el-Wazir at the top of the stairs.

Abu Jihad had a small pistol in his hand. He had grabbed it when he heard the unusual noises outside and downstairs. He had been up late that night, watching videotaped news coverage of the *intifada* which he was busily trying to coordinate from abroad. He did not have a chance to aim or fire his weapon. Four Israeli commandos pumped seventy bullets into him with startling rapidity. After travelling the huge distance from Israel, they were not going to take the chance that Wazir might survive. His right hand, which had clutched the gun, was nearly severed. At age 52, Abu Jihad was dead.

There was no need for further killing. The guerilla leader's wife, who called herself Umm Jihad, 'Mother of the Holy War', said later that she fully expected to be shot.[5] She even turned to the wall, preparing to wait for the bullets. Instead, one of the Israelis shouted to her daughter in Arabic: 'Take care of your mother!' And with that, the commando force ran to the mini-bus and drove off at high speed. Wazir's wife and daughter were not entirely certain, but they believed they saw a woman among the attackers, wielding not a gun but a video camera to record the assassination. It is possible that in this age of portable television technology, the assault was videotaped for future training and morale boosting.

Israeli intelligence had once again proved its unrivalled excellence at carrying out a delicate and complex mission. All that the Tunisian authorities could find were footprints on the beach, ten miles from Wazir's house, and the three hired cars.

The PLO, naturally, blamed Israel, but the Israelis could have kept the entire matter secret. Unfortunately, it would not then have had the desired deterrent effect, so official Israeli sources provided two American news outlets, NBC Television and the *Washington Post*, with fairly complete accounts of what the Mossad and the army had done. Ezer Weizman, the minister most strongly opposed to the assassination, publicly shook his head, telling reporters: 'It does not contribute to the fight against terrorism. It distances the peace process and will bring greater hostility. It also makes us more vulnerable around the world.'

The Military Intelligence chief, General Shahak, however, was quoted in that week's issue of the official army magazine *Ba-Machaneh*, 'In Camp'. In the extract from an interview with him before the killing of Abu Jihad he said, 'Anyone directing terrorism is a suitable target for elimination.'

Shahak was enunciating one side of what had been a long and heated debate behind the closed doors of the intelligence community: Are assassinations of Palestinian leaders worthwhile? If so, should the targets be at the very top of the guerilla groups? In the 1970s and early 1980s, that was the prevailing dogma and Israel either killed or tried to kill PLO chiefs. Several attempts were made on Yasser Arafat's life, including both aerial bombings and car bombs in Beirut, when Israel laid siege to the city in the summer of 1982.

Later, however, the counter-argument seemed to prevail – that it was better to confront the devil that Israel knew rather than the unknown PLO leaders who might take control once he was gone. A new generation of guerilla chiefs could be more radical, bloodthirsty, and unpredictable.

The compromise reached between those two conflicting views was expressed by Brigadier General Gideon Machanaymi, the Prime Minister's deputy adviser on counter-terrorism, who in 1985 devised the philosophy that only leaders of small terrorist groups were appropriate targets. A prime example would be Sabri el-Banna, alias Abu Nidal, the 'Father of Struggle', who was responsible for two hundred of the bloodiest attacks against Israeli, Jewish, British and American civilian targets in more than twenty countries. General Machanaymi advocated that in cases of such small organizations, fully controlled by one man, once the leader is eliminated the organization ceases to exist. Then, an assassination accomplishes something.

The same reasoning lay behind the attempt by Israel, the following year, to capture an entire planeload of Palestinian terrorists – seeking economies of scale – by intercepting a Libyan executive jet on its way to Damascus. Israeli intelligence had learned that several leaders of extremist groups, far more radical than Yasser Arafat, had gathered for a terrorist summit in Tripoli, Libya, on February 4, 1986. Among them were Georges Habash, Nayef Hawatmeh, Ahmed Jibril, and even Abu Nidal – a veritable who's who of notorious killers. With the support of Libya's Colonel Qaddafi, they plotted against Arafat's moderated policies and vowed 'to intensify the struggle against the conspiracies of Zionism and American imperialism.'

The Mossad and Aman located the terrorist chiefs and received a seemingly precise tip, from informers, as to what flight they would be taking back home to Syria. As the jet passed the Israeli coast, four F-16 jets forced the Gulfstream airliner to land at a military airport in the north of Israel. But as the passengers were led out of the plane with their hands up, the Israeli intelligence operatives found that there were no wanted men among them – only Syrian officials, including a senior Ba'ath Party man who was close to President Hafez el-Assad.

Two months later, the Syrians sought revenge by way of a remarkable plot to blow up an Israeli airliner. Brigadier

General Muhammad el-Khouli of Syrian air force intelligence recruited a freelance Palestinian terrorist, Nezar Hindawi, and instructed him to find a dupe who would carry a powerful bomb aboard an El Al flight. He met a naïve Irishwoman in London, promised to marry her, made her pregnant, and then sent her as a human bomb onto a Tel Aviv-bound aeroplane. It was only the superb vigilance of the El Al security staff, trained by Shin Bet experts, that led to the discovery of a sophisticated bomb inside her handbag. The British authorities captured Hindawi and sentenced him to forty-five years in jail. At least something worked right, after the failed attempt to gain a significant advantage in the war against Palestinian terrorists by capturing all the chiefs in one aerial net.[6]

Was there some lasting gain to be accrued in 1988 from killing Abu Jihad? Most Israelis were in no state of mind, distracted and frustrated by the *intifada*, to ponder such questions. In general, there was praise for the intelligence community and Israel's soldiers. It was quickly realized, however, that the army and Shin Bet were still left to grapple with the day-to-day violence of the *intifada*. Abu Jihad's death made no difference.

Ironically, the protests and the attempts by soldiers to suppress them were especially ugly when Abu Jihad was being buried in Damascus, Syria. Five more Palestinians were killed in the West Bank and Gaza that same day.

The names of the dead and wounded were listed, as martyrs and heroes, in the leaflets of the National Unified Command of the Uprising which called for general strikes and other protests. They were especially maddening to the Shin Bet men who had never heard such language used in the day-to-day life of the West Bank and Gaza. Meanwhile, identical messages were being heard on an AM radio station which popped up out of nowhere – *Radio al-Quds*, 'the Holy', the Arabic name for Jerusalem. Aman's direction-finding equipment quickly told the Israelis that the station was in southern Syria, apparently operated, with the approval of Damascus, by a radical splinter of the PLO. It was a puzzle as to how the broadcasters could see and quote from the leaflets so quickly, unless they were composed in Syria or Jordan overnight and smuggled into the West Bank by Palestinian travellers crossing the River Jordan bridges.

Shin Bet's counter-measures appeared increasingly desperate, and even ridiculous. The security agents published their own, forged leaflets signed by the National Unified Command, calling, in persuasive Arabic, for continued rebellion but changing all the details of the commercial strikes meant to shut shops and factories. The Israelis, hoping to fight harassment with harassment, were sowing confusion as to the location and times of the work stoppages.

On the streets of the Palestinian villages, there were two sets of leaflets: the genuine instructions for the *intifada*, and the deceptive instruments of disruption distributed by Shin Bet. One of these, in early July 1988, called for a continuous seven-day strike, much longer than any previous protest shutdown. It turned out to be a fake, in the hope that Arabs unwilling to give up their livelihood for an entire week would lose their faith in the uprising's organizers.

The security agents had already tried to eliminate the leaflets by watching all the print shops in the West Bank and Gaza. Two Palestinians, found to have thousands of the propaganda pamphlets in their truck during a routine search at a roadblock, were closely questioned.

Finally, amid triumphant publicity, Shin Bet sent the army to raid the al-Arz Printing Company on the Arab, eastern outskirts of Jerusalem. The owners, brothers Musa and Ali Darwish, were arrested. The security authorities triumphantly leaked the story to Israel's most respected newsmen, who in all seriousness told the public that night that a severe blow had been dealt to the *intifada*.

For some Israelis, the sickness of the occupation had taken hold. It was simply absurd to watch one of the most sophisticated armies in the world, and the highly praised intelligence community, celebrate the seizure of an ageing printing press. The leaflets continued to appear and in November 1988 they called on the Palestinians to pour into the streets to celebrate the declaration of their independent state – by the decision of the Palestine National Council in Algiers.

The Palestinian leaders hoped to duplicate the spontaneous explosion of joy, on the streets of Tel Aviv and other Jewish areas exactly forty-one years earlier, when the United Nations decided to create the State of Israel. Perhaps acting on the same memories, Israel's security chiefs decided, as a high priority, to prevent the celebrations. Perhaps uniquely in the history of military occupations, Israel resorted to such steps as switching off the electricity in the entire West Bank and Gaza Strip. This was not a measure of collective punishment to stop the local populace from having hot water, cooked food, laundered clothes, or reading lights. The objective was simply to prevent them watching television and enjoying the sight of Arafat and his PLO politicians declaring the theoretical creation of their own state in the West Bank and Gaza.

That night, as the curfew was clamped down, Israeli soldiers found themselves chasing children who were waving the green, black, white and red Palestinian flags, who were throwing firecrackers into the air, and attempting to dance and sing until soldiers came along to disperse the revellers.

The leaflets which directed all these activities were distributed, with surprisingly little trouble, around once a week. They were well written and bore the hallmarks of organized backing for the uprising. In more than two decades of occupation, Israel had tried to encourage Palestinians to create their own leadership as an alternative to the hated PLO. They tried many tactics, including the creation of quisling organizations called Village Leagues. These West Bank 'leaders' failed to lead, and Israel then argued that there was no one with whom to negotiate peace.

In the *intifada* the Palestinians did create their own leadership, the National Unified Command of the Uprising. It successfully remained underground, but appeared to have a hierarchical structure based on local committees in the various towns and villages of the West Bank and Gaza. Its aim was to consolidate the desire of the Palestinians, living under occupation, to develop alternative institutions to those imposed by the Israelis.

The committees assigned specific tasks which included cleaning streets, fighting prostitution and drug trafficking, and even the killing of collaborators. Shin Bet had the urgent task of penetrating the committees and the National Unified Command at the top, but they were unable to do so.

In a bid to repair the damage and make some headway, after banal and trivial attempts to use their might instead of their minds, Israel's intelligence community eventually devised new tactics which were in the mould of the old, but successful method of utilizing secret military units.

Using codenames such as *Shimshon* and *Duvdevan*, 'Samson' and 'Cherry', the army formed special units of soldiers in civilian dress, assigned to mingle with the local Palestinians.[7]

It was a repeat performance of the army's activities in the Gaza Strip in the early 1970s, when terrorists were imposing a reign of violence, defying the presence of Israeli soldiers. One day, in the summer of 1970, a small fishing boat flying the flag of Lebanon arrived on the Gaza shore. Six people hurried onto the beach, and the local Gazans found Lebanese newspapers, cigarettes, and groceries aboard. The Israeli army immediately sent squads of troops and helicopters to sweep the area, in what appeared to be a serious and thorough search for Arabs who had infiltrated from the sea. The chiefs of the guerilla cells in Gaza, impressed by how important these new arrivals from Lebanon must be, broke the usual underground rules of compartmentalization and secrecy to contact them.

The contacts, and the supposed Israeli search, continued for three days, but then at a clandestine night-time meeting with local guerilla leaders, the six newcomers pulled out guns and killed them.[8] These were Israeli army commandos on special assignment.

The tactics which had been used earlier in Gaza, to combat

terrorism, led foreign journalists to reach the conclusion that the new Samson and Cherry units had similar instructions. Based on claims by the Palestinians, they reported that soldiers in civilian clothing in 1988 were shooting *intifada* activists. Israeli authorities strongly denied that their troops had been instructed to adopt a 'shoot on sight' policy as allegedly carried out by British forces in Northern Ireland against the IRA.

Whatever the truth of the 'death squad' claims, there is no doubt that the special army units, coordinated by Israeli intelligence, used unorthodox tactics. America's ABC News accused Shin Bet of sending agents, masquerading as an ABC camera crew, to pick up Nezar Dadouk. Shin Bet was apparently afraid that he might flee if identifiable Israeli authorities were seen entering the West Bank town Salfit, twenty miles north of Jerusalem. Dadouk was wanted for allegedly throwing firebombs.

According to witnesses, two Israelis who said they were from ABC approached the young man and suggested they would like to interview him. He got into their car, which had apparently genuine ABC News signs and stickers, and later the family was informed that Nezar was under arrest. As punishment for his alleged crime, the army sent in bulldozers to demolish his house.

The president of the network's news division, Roone Arledge, sent a telex to Prime Minister Shamir, which said: 'I have been informed that security forces in Israel have impersonated ABC News personnel in order to arrest a Palestinian Arab. ABC News is deeply distressed by this and insists that an investigation be conducted immediately to ascertain who authorized such an action.'

Undercover Israelis were, from time to time, monitoring events while driving in cars marked 'Foreign Press'. In the West Bank and Gaza, nearly free access to Arab villages was enjoyed by foreign correspondents, and especially the American media, who were courted by both Israelis and Palestinians. Each side wanted support and sympathy from the United States.

Israel and its security services were under worldwide examination. After a full year of rebellion in the occupied territories, truths about the Israeli intelligence community which had been buried for too long were surfacing. It is true that amateurism, arrogance, brutality, complacency, mistakes and rivalries between agencies had all occurred at various times in the history of the community. Never before, however, had they come in such abundance and during such a concentrated period of time.

It was a major and painful change from the optimistic vision held by the founders of Israeli intelligence.

2

First Steps

A handful of men dressed in khaki arrived – prudently, in separate cars and taxis – at 85 Ben Yehudah Street on a typical summer day in Tel Aviv: a hot and humid June 30, 1948. They hurried, individually, into a whitewashed apartment building identical to the others in the ordinary residential neighbourhood. Up one flight of stairs, however, behind a door with a sign saying 'Consultancy Services', was the headquarters of Shai.

Shai was the acronym for *Sherut Yediot*, Hebrew for 'Information Service', the intelligence arm of the underground, pre-independence army of Palestine's Jews known as the *Haganah*, which means 'Defence'. The Haganah had been swallowed up by the nation's new army, the Israel Defence Forces, with the birth of the State of Israel on May 14. Six weeks later, this was to be the end of Shai and the beginning of the Israeli intelligence community.

Shai's 47-year-old commander, Lieutenant Colonel Isser Beeri, chaired the last meeting of his highly effective force, his small eyes darting from man to man as they took their seats around an old, wooden dining table. These half-dozen fathers of Israeli intelligence chatted as they skimmed the headlines of that day's newspapers – filled, as usual, with reports from the various fronts of Israel's War of Independence. The battle for the state's existence had begun on its day of birth.

Beeri cleared his throat for attention: 'I have just come from a meeting with *ha-Zaken*,' using the Hebrew phrase meaning 'the Old Man' to refer to David Ben-Gurion, the charismatic first Prime Minister of Israel who was also directing the war as defence minister.

The Shai officers unconsciously sat a bit more erectly, as an announcement from the white-haired oracle of Israel appeared forthcoming. A mere 62 years old, Ben-Gurion was the nation's elder statesman and guiding light, bar none.

Beeri kept his men waiting a moment longer. 'Before we turn to the agenda which brought you here,' he said, 'here is the latest information on the fighting.' He told his colleagues that while Israel's army had halted the far more numerous enemy, the Egyptians continued their build-up only twenty miles from Tel Aviv while the Syrians threatened kibbutz farms near the Sea of Galilee. The picture was far from bright in Jerusalem, besieged by the Arab Legion of Trans-Jordan.

'However,' Beeri added, 'the Prime Minister is looking beyond the present situation.' In the long run, Ben-Gurion had just finished telling the Shai chief, defence would have to include intelligence. Not good intelligence; great intelligence.

The immediate 'agenda', as Beeri put it, was how to carry out the Prime Minister's instructions: to disband Shai, using its people and structure as the basis for a newly organized community.[1]

It was not to be simply a new name for Shai. Instead, the Haganah's intelligence arm would digest itself and other pre-state Zionist underground groups to produce four agencies in a community:

• **Military Intelligence:** Beeri announced that he would henceforth head the dominant agency in the new community. Known later as Aman, what was then 'the Intelligence Department' of the army was assigned widespread functions. These ranged from collecting information on Arab armies, through censoring Israeli newspapers, to maintaining security within Israel's army, and on to a bit of counterespionage. Beeri was recognizable by his dark eyebrows, his deeply cleft chin, and white hair – not nearly as exuberantly scattered as Ben-Gurion's ghostly fringe – flanking his bald scalp. Above all, literally, he was so tall that his nickname was *Isser ha-Gadol*, 'Isser the Big'. He was Isser Birentzweig when born in 1901, but like most of Israel's pioneers he chose a Hebrew family name as a break from Jewish roots of oppression and prejudice in Europe. In the Haganah and Shai since 1938, he had proved himself a fanatic on one subject: corruption. He could not stand it. Israel, to him, could, should, and would be a perfect society.

• **A domestic secret service:** Beeri told Isser Harel, whose speciality in Shai had been surveillance on right-wing Jews who rejected the authority of Ben-Gurion and the Haganah, that he would be director of a security service later called Shin Bet. Harel was just in the process of changing his name from Isser Halperin, with which he was born in Russia in 1912. His new post suited him well, because in his view enemies within could be just as dangerous as the enemies outside Israel's borders. Harel believed in a strict code of conduct for Israel's defenders, and he also resembled Beeri except for darker hair and complexion, bigger ears, and a lack of physical stature which led to his contrasting nickname: *Isser ha-Katan*, 'the Little'.

• **A foreign intelligence service:** Beeri informed Boris Guriel that as the new chief of the foreign ministry's Political Department, he would be part of the new intelligence community with responsibility for collecting information outside Israel. Born in Latvia some fifty years earlier as Boris Gurvitch, Guriel already had plenty of experience with foreigners. As a British soldier in World War II, he was captured by the Germans, and after surviving that ordeal his job in Shai was to spy on the British mandate authorities in Palestine.

● **The Institute for Aliyah B:** Beeri added that *ha-Mossad le-Aliyah Bet*, 'the Institute for Aliyah B',* would continue to do its secret work under the direction of Shaul Avigur, although its original mission of smuggling Jews into Palestine would naturally change now that immigration into Israel was perfectly legal. When set up by the Haganah in 1937, the agency's name distinguished it from the legal *aliyah*, or 'immigration', by the lucky few Jews who received entry permits from the British.

Born in 1899 in Latvia as Saul Meyeroff, Avigur had helped set up Shai in 1934 and in 1948 was busy as Ben-Gurion's deputy defence minister, buying weapons abroad for the war of independence. He took the name *Avigur* – 'Father of Gur' – in memory of his son, Gur Meyeroff, who died in Israel's first war. Avigur did not attend the intelligence community's birth in Tel Aviv, and neither did the other founder of Shai, Reuven Shiloah. But as a special adviser to the Prime Minister, it was Shiloah who conceived the reorganization.

Shiloah's name never found its way onto the list of national heroes revered by Jewish students around the world – from Biblical warriors to the soldiers of modern Israel. The men and women who work in the secret world of espionage rarely receive the recognition they deserve. Shiloah, however, should be remembered as Israel's 'Mr Intelligence'.

A short man, with blue-grey eyes behind professorial glasses, Shiloah focused his penetrating gaze on whomever he spoke to, radiating a combination of secrecy and strength. He was as silent as the Sphinx but was insatiably curious, delving into the tiniest details of any subject which caught his attention.

---

* In spite of the similarity in name, this organization should not be confused with today's espionage agency, the Mossad.

Feeling as though under interrogation, colleagues who talked to Shiloah invariably noticed the scar on his right cheek, a lasting reminder of shrapnel which hit him when an Arab car bomb exploded in March 1947 near the Jerusalem offices of the Jewish Agency, which was the unofficial government for the Jews of Palestine before their independence.

Shiloah was good at asking questions but volunteered very little information. He was a 'lone wolf', keeping to himself and doing his best work behind the scenes. He was a methodical planner, an analytical thinker who delivered his recommendations free of emotional colouring or additives. His projects were always anchored in the firm ground of reality. But in his personal life, he loved mystery.

'Shiloah used to give different and contradictory details in interviews and questionnaires that he filled in about his life, even where the facts were of no special significance, as if in order to surround himself with total secrecy,' biographer Hagai Eshed wrote.[2]

'When Reuven Shiloah took a taxicab,' his friend Abba Eban, the extraordinary Israeli diplomat, reminisced, 'he would never tell the driver his destination. Only a short and laconic order: "Move." And when the driver lost his patience and asked, "But where to?" Shiloah would direct his penetrating and distrustful gaze at the man, as if he were facing a dangerous spy.'[3]

He was a born secret agent, although there was no indication of that in December 1909, when he entered the world with the name Reuven Zaslanski. The family lived in an Orthodox Jewish neighbourhood of Jerusalem, then ruled by Turkey's Ottoman Empire. Reuven's father, Yitzhak Zaslanski, was a rabbi who gave his four children – two sons and two daughters – a craving for general knowledge, rather than stopping with the religious education which dominated community life.

Reuven's teachers noted that he was a serious and talented student. He rarely had much to say, but occasionally he displayed a sense of humour. He excelled in drama, displaying an acting skill which he would later employ in his intelligence work. He was also an independent thinker, and by high school he had abandoned kosher food and the rest of his family's religious lifestyle.

He could be charming, when he cared to be, and while teaching Hebrew to new immigrants from America he began to court Betty Borden, a social worker from New York. They were married in 1936.

His other great love was the Haganah, where Ben-Gurion and the other commanders quickly took note of his talents. As they pushed him up the ladder of leadership, he repaid them with unswerving devotion.

As part of his enlistment in the ranks of top Zionist activists, he shortened his name from Zaslanski to Zaslani, and later he adopted his codename in the underground, 'Shiloah'. No name could have suited him better, because the word 'Shiloah' is derived from the Hebrew word *shaliah*, an 'emissary', and he was repeatedly used as a high-level envoy on various secret missions for Ben-Gurion.

This was not yet real intelligence work, but Shiloah's hush-hush travels contained the first seeds which would later sprout into his view of intelligence: clear identification of enemies, the comprehensive collection of information about them, and the perpetual search for allies. Heavily outnumbered in the Middle East, the Jews had to know, quickly and with certainty, how to distinguish between friends and foes.

Shiloah's first foreign assignment came in August 1931, before he had reached his twenty-second birthday. The Jewish Agency planted him deep in the Arab world: in Baghdad, capital of Iraq. His cover was a job as a school-teacher. He also presented himself as a part-time journalist, which made his trips around the country appear quite natural. In three years of supposed interviews for his news-paper articles, Shiloah assembled an impressive network of information sources.

The most memorable lessons Shiloah learned came while trekking in the mountains of Kurdistan in northern Iraq, where he forged contacts with the stateless, non-Arab mountain dwellers. He never forgot the Kurds, and as he developed his personal vision of the future Israeli espionage community he focused on the need for clandestine alliances with all the non-Arab minorities of the Middle East. In a sense, the Jews could have friends dotted around the periphery of the Arab world. Shiloah's 'peripheral philosophy' became a lasting tenet of Israeli intelligence.

When he returned to Jerusalem in 1934, the Haganah assigned him to the job of forming a professional intelligence department to protect the long-range interests of the Jewish community in Palestine. Shiloah worked on the project with Meyeroff/Avigur, and in a short while they created Shai. Shiloah's on-the-record job was as a liaison officer between Ben-Gurion's Jewish Agency and Palestine's British governors.[4]

When World War II broke out in Europe, Shiloah seized the opportunity to deepen the relationship. Nazi Germany was the common enemy of both the Jews and the British. Shiloah helped set up a Jewish Brigade within the British Armed Forces – a move which showed great vision, because the Brigade later was part of the foundation of the Israeli army.

The war was frustrating for the Palestinian Jews who could save only a handful of their European brethren from the Nazi extermination camps, but it was also a learning experience for Shiloah and his men. Fighting in every available way, they picked up priceless skills of infiltration, reconnaissance, and outright masquerade when sending Jewish agents behind enemy lines: those of Aryan appearance into German-held territory in Europe, and those who looked and spoke like Arabs into Syria and Lebanon, then ruled by pro-Nazi Vichy France.

Twenty-six Jewish paratroopers, recruited by Shiloah for British intelligence, were dropped behind Nazi lines in the Balkan countries. Some, such as Hannah Senesh and Enzio Sereni, were taken prisoner and executed as spies – entering a heavenly hall of fame as Jewish heroes. Others, such as

Yeshayahu (Shaike) Trachtenberg-Dan, survived to experience further exploits in Israeli intelligence.

Shiloah was not only learning during the war. He was making powerful friends, who later could help the Jews in their widening struggle against the Arabs for control of Palestine. He had the opportunity to forge strong relationships with British army intelligence officers in Jerusalem and Cairo. In a similar and more significant fashion, World War II saw the beginning of contacts between the Zionist movement and American intelligence. Shiloah shared drinks and ideas with agents of the Office of Strategic Services, which in 1947 became the nucleus of the Central Intelligence Agency.[5]

These ties were strengthened after the war and were the platform for building vital links between the CIA and Israeli intelligence. Shiloah's wartime activities are clear evidence of his wisdom and his ability to take a long-term, strategic view of the importance of intelligence in modern times.

Lecturing his fellow founders of the Jewish state, teaching themselves how to run a modern country in their people's ancient homeland, Shiloah called intelligence a 'most essential political tool'.[6] In a world with few public declarations or statements of intent, it was Shiloah who defined the secret side of Israeli diplomacy and foreign policy:

• Enemy Number One of the Jewish community was the Arab people, and Arab society had to be penetrated by professional agents.
• Israeli intelligence also had to think beyond Palestine, as a 'Jewish-Zionist' protector of Jews throughout the world.
• Clandestine work should be based on modern technology, keeping up with the latest espionage methods by maintaining ties with friendly agencies in Europe and the United States.[7]

Although he did not attend the Ben Yehudah Street meeting which disbanded Shai and introduced the new state's intelligence structure – considering it a 'purely technical' session – Shiloah watched over the fledgling community like a guardian angel. And he found much to worry about in Isser Beeri.

On the afternoon of June 30, 1948, only a few hours after assuming the mantle of military-intelligence director, Beeri carried his sense of duty to an extreme never repeated in Israel's history. He convened a kangaroo court, which hurriedly convicted an Israeli army officer of treason and immediately had him executed.

The accused man was Captain Meir Tubianski, who had served in the Haganah and after independence was in charge of setting up the first permanent Israel Defence Forces base in Jerusalem. He also held a civilian job with the Jerusalem Electricity Company, and Tubianski's Israeli colleagues were suspicious about his relationship with the company's British managers.

Early in the 1948 war, Jordanian artillery was scoring devastatingly accurate hits on Israeli bases. Shai's Jerusalem commander, Major Binyamin Gibli, had concluded that there must be a spy in the Israeli ranks, and it seemed logical that Tubianski could be feeding information to his electricity-company bosses, who in turn would advise the British officers who led Trans-Jordan's Arab Legion. Tubianski had, after all, been a major in Britain's Royal Engineers during World War II and was known to be an anglophile.

The circumstantial evidence was enough to sentence him to death. The judges, convening in a derelict house near the main Jerusalem–Tel Aviv road, were Beeri, Gibli, and two other Shai officers.

No detailed notes of the brief trial were kept. All the judges except Beeri claimed later that they were merely interrogating the suspect, that they did not know they were imposing any sentence to be enforced. But that very afternoon, Tubianski was shot by an impromptu firing squad, watched by soldiers who could hardly believe that Israelis were killing one of their own.

'A traitor! They are going to execute a traitor!' One

witness recalls hearing the shouts of fellow infantrymen: 'We sat down on the rocky hill and watched. A young man dressed in khaki was being moved along by a group of seven young soldiers. They were just kids, dressed sloppily. They sat him on a chair. They didn't even cover his face with a handkerchief. Then they moved away a bit. We heard the cocking of the Czech rifles. It was all quiet. The sun set. Only a short volley disturbed the peace. The man fell from his chair.'[8]

A few hours later, Beeri informed the Prime Minister that, after 'a field court martial', an army unit had shot a traitor. An emotional letter from Tubianski's widow later that year prompted Ben-Gurion to order an official enquiry, which cleared the captain's name and ordered that compensation be paid to his family.

On that same final day of June 1948, Beeri's Shai men in Haifa, the northern port city with a mixed Jewish–Arab population, were torturing a friend of the Jewish mayor who was considered too liberal. The Shai agents were pressing for evidence that Mayor Abba Khoushy had gone beyond being 'soft' on Arabs – that he was a traitor to the Zionist cause.

Their victim was Jules (Yehuda) Amster, and Beeri had Amster arrested on May 15, 1948, the very day that Israel's independence was declared. Amster was a taxi owner and, behind the scenes, he was Mayor Khoushy's right-hand man. Amster was charged with espionage, and his nightmare lasted for two and a half months in a secret detention camp. Amster's property was confiscated, and his investigators – first, officially, Shai, and then the new military intelligence agency – tortured him mercilessly. They pointed pistols at him, as though about to blow his brains out. They beat him, dripped water on his head, pulled his teeth out, burned the soles of his feet, and injected drugs into his bloodstream. He was released, without any charges being pressed, on August 1.

The unwarranted arrest and the torture which followed it were kept secret for many years. Only in 1964 did the defence ministry agree to pay compensation to Amster. It was clear, all along, that Beeri had been trying to wring a confession out of Amster that would implicate his friend, Khoushy. Beeri even fabricated evidence that the mayor had spied on the Haganah for the British. Ben-Gurion learned of the forgery, and Beeri was on his way out.[9]

The last straw was the killing of a wealthy Arab in the summer of 1948. The victim was Ali Qassem, a double agent employed by military intelligence to penetrate Palestinian Arab militias. Suspecting, due to several mishaps, that Qassem was in fact a triple agent – working, above all, for the Arabs – Beeri's agents shot him.

Ben-Gurion, in his dual capacity as minister of defence as well as Prime Minister, ordered a comprehensive investigation of the Qassem case. Beeri was suspended from the army in November, and then a military court convicted him of manslaughter. He was demoted to private, and then put on trial again for the illegal killing of Tubianski and the torture of Amster. Beeri denied the charges, but he was again found guilty and sentenced to a symbolic one-day jail term.[10]

The man who was the first commander of military intelligence and the most active force in the new espionage community had lasted only six months in that position. Beeri was brought down by his own narrow-minded view of national security. He had no time for political gamesmanship – or even human rights, for that matter. The state had to be protected, and Beeri's world was as simple as that.

He learned bitterly that he was wrong. Behaviour which the authorities of a totalitarian state might get away with would not be tolerated for long in Israel – a nation determined, from its beginning, to be a democracy. Beeri continued to claim, until his death of a heart attack in January 1958, that he was innocent. His son, Itai Beeri, insisted, years later, that Isser the Big had only been following Ben-Gurion's orders.[11]

Beeri's downfall was the sort of shock which could have crippled the intelligence community for many years. Ben-Gurion, however, wisely chose Colonel Chaim Herzog as the new military intelligence chief, and the fact that he had been Beeri's deputy provided vital continuity. In addition, Herzog's friendship with Reuven Shiloah – who avoided all the domestic misdeeds and concentrated on strategic planning and foreign affairs – helped heal the wounds which cut deep into the community's young flesh. Herzog would go on to even bigger and better things, as Israel's president in the 1980s.

Deciding to take a more active, hands-on role in administering the community, Shiloah established a coordinating body which he himself chaired. He called it *Va'adat Rashei ha-Sherutim*, 'the Committee of Services Chiefs', and it first convened in mid-1949 with Shiloah and Herzog joined by Isser Harel for Shin Bet and Boris Guriel for the foreign ministry's Political Department.

Yehezkel Sahar, chief of the national police, was invited to take part, because, while the police were not ordinarily privy to all state secrets, they did constitute the country's largest security force.[12] Shaul Avigur of Aliyah B, mainly concerned with gathering immigrants rather than intelligence, did not take part. The other service chiefs, newly grouped and meeting frequently as the *Va'adat*, soon faced an unusual challenge remembered as 'the revolt of the spies'.

The revolt was led by Asher Ben-Natan, who was known as Arthur – his code name in the pre-state Jewish underground. His good looks brought him a nickname, 'Arthur the Handsome', and he earned a reputation for success with the opposite sex. More generally, in the small family of Israeli intelligence, Ben-Natan was seen as a man who believed in enjoying life.

Born in Austria in 1921, he escaped the Nazis by moving to Israel in 1938. To help even more Jews find a way to their historic homeland, he joined Shaul Avigur's Aliyah B and served as intelligence coordinator in postwar Vienna while posing as a journalist with the name Arthur Pier. Later, he joined the foreign ministry as operations chief in Guriel's Political Department.

The department, despite its innocuous title, was the overseas arm of Israeli intelligence. Guriel's operatives were in charge of planting agents in Arab countries and forming ties with foreign security services. A rare, written record of Ben-Natan's work in France, Italy, and other nations can be found in a report he sent to Prime Minister Ben-Gurion: 'We are gathering information on Arab property and the economic relations between Europe and the Arabs.'[13] This was in the early days of the state, when every small detail seemed new and exciting to Israel's first spies.

The Political Department's operatives had diplomatic cover in the Israeli consulates and embassies in London, Rome, Paris, Vienna, Bonn, and Geneva – potentially advantageous, because diplomats enjoyed immunity from prosecution; but less useful operationally, because the agent was openly connected with his government and many host countries act under the suspicious assumption that foreign diplomats are spies.

Until 1950, Israel's agents in Europe reported to Ben-Natan's headquarters in Paris, which had remarkable autonomy from Guriel. Later, Ben-Natan was generally in Tel Aviv, receiving reports and issuing operational orders. Each 'station', in the various European capitals, had its own network of agents – mostly non-Israelis who sold information. Some of the leads they provided helped operatives in Europe sabotage military shipments on their way to Arab countries.

There was also, however, some smuggling by the Israelis in their 'off hours'; not for personal greed, but to finance various clandestine activities after the finance ministry refused to pay all the bills and expense accounts submitted by Ben-Natan's team.

The Political Department's greatest achievement was obtaining the 'order of battle' – the war plans – of the Syrian army, from an agent planted in Damascus. Such information was considered vital to the Jewish state, still facing a strong threat from its neighbours.

In general, however, the material obtained by Ben-Natan and his men was not highly regarded by their political bosses. Perhaps it was because of Ben-Natan's style.

He and his senior operatives, including Gershon Peres – brother of a future Prime Minister – behaved as they imagined spies ought to behave. They dined at elegant restaurants in Paris and Geneva, drank at the most fashionable watering holes, and used the lobbies of Europe's finest hotels as meeting places. Their extravagance was diametrically opposed to the puritanical, socialist spirit then prevalent in Israel. This provoked much anger, especially on the part of Avigur and Shiloah – the two founders of Israeli intelligence.

Guriel was not bothered, however, and shrugged off charges that his men in Europe lined their own pockets with unauthorized, phony expenses. There were even rumours that Political Department personnel had laid their hands on secret Swiss bank accounts belonging to Jews who were gassed in the Holocaust.[14]

Beyond the complaints about style and finances, the rest of the intelligence community was upset about the work performance of the Political Department. Its rivals – in Aman, Shin Bet, and Aliyah B – cursed Guriel's men as mere amateurs masquerading as professionals and rarely contributing to Israel's vital defence.

Shiloah, as chairman of the *Va'adat*, was under great pressure from Ben-Gurion and military chiefs to produce precise information on the capabilities of the Arab armies. There was a growing fear in 1950 that with the Korean War raging and the Cold War chilling relations between the United States and the Soviet Union, the Arab states might feel inspired by international tension to launch their own second round against Israel to reverse the defeat they suffered in 1948–9.

The Jewish state's leaders were less interested in Guriel and Ben-Natan's speciality: the Arabs' political plans, their economic projects, and what was happening in their leaders' bedrooms.

Lieutenant Binyamin Gibli was the Political Department's most bitter opponent. He was a young and enthusiastic officer who served as deputy to Chaim Herzog and then replaced him as Aman director when Herzog moved to Washington as military attaché in April 1950.

A major mark against Gibli was the fact that he had been one of the judges who sentenced Meir Tubianski to death. Ben-Gurion appointed Gibli to the top post in military intelligence primarily to ensure the continuity still needed after Beeri's downfall and Herzog's departure. The Prime Minister was sending a dangerous signal, however: that he was willing to sacrifice ethical considerations upon the altar of efficiency.

In any event, unprecedented inefficiency was the result. Gibli decided to launch an all-out campaign against the Political Department, and he found an ally in Shin Bet chief Isser Harel. As ascetic as he was professional, Harel had complete disdain for the Political Department's lavish style and its low productivity.

In the disarray which followed, both Gibli and Harel sent their own operatives abroad. Guriel simply rolled up his sleeves for a fistfight, and his Political Department encroached on Shin Bet's territory by sending burglars to break into Soviet-bloc embassies in Tel Aviv. Harel was furious.[15]

Guriel's European operatives considered themselves members of an exclusive club as intelligence agents posted overseas, and they scorned the coarseness and lack of civility of 'Gibli's military men and Harel's policemen'. Ben-Natan sneered that the new arrivals could never blend into the cultured and refined society of Europe. Needless to say, the various Israeli spies were not working in concert.

The security services of France and Italy, which were especially friendly towards Israel, could not believe what was happening. They were confused by a huge number of conflicting requests from Israeli liaison officers. This was a classic case of a power struggle, and the intelligence community's foreign friends did not know how to react. They did know that Israel, surrounded by hostile nations, could not afford the luxury of infighting.

Ben-Gurion was outraged, and he ordered Reuven Shiloah to put an end to the chaos. 'Mr Intelligence' would be given the opportunity to bump some heads together and re-organize the community. Shiloah declared that the Political Department would be disbanded, forcing Boris Guriel to resign. Guriel's European network was told to expect new orders from new commanders.

Ben-Natan, however, refused to give in. A few days after Shiloah's coup, he assembled his senior operatives at Lake Geneva on March 2, 1951. 'Arthur the Handsome' and his equally comely collection of wine connoisseurs and gourmands were in a huff, and in a final burst of snobby pique they collectively submitted their resignations. They would not work for any of the other intelligence agencies. They would just pack up their toys and go home.

Ben-Natan enrolled in an international relations course in Switzerland, and his men refused to hand over their records to Shiloah. They would not give him guidance on ongoing operations. In some European stations, they even burned secret files. Israel's European spies simply declared a strike.[16]

The revolt never stood a chance. Shiloah, armed with the Prime Minister's full backing, carried out a thorough reorganization of the intelligence community, right over the heads of the men who refused to play the game. Responsibility for special assignments was transferred, lock, stock, and barrel, to the Aman military intelligence agency under Gibli. He quickly established a top-secret 'Unit 131' to plant agents in Arab countries.

Out of the ruins of the Political Department arose *ha-Mossad le-Modiin ule-Tafkidim Meyuhadim*, 'the Institute for Intelligence and Special Tasks' – better known as the Mossad. For a short while, the new agency had other names: first 'the Central Institute for Coordination', and then 'the Central Institute for Intelligence and Security'. However, the day of Shiloah's strike-breaking reorganization, April 1, 1951, is considered the Mossad's date of birth.

Ben-Gurion appointed Shiloah as the first director of the Mossad, which was directly subservient to the Prime Minister's Office. This was the first time that American influence was felt in the Israeli intelligence community. The previous model, of overseas espionage answerable to the Foreign Minister, as with Britain's MI6 Secret Intelligence Service, was abolished. In the United States, the Central Intelligence Agency is under the President, and in Israel the Mossad is under the Prime Minister.

There was one clear difference. The CIA always had an operations department. When the Mossad was founded, however, it had to get along without one. The Mossad's function was simply to collect facts, not to do anything about them.

It was difficult, in the weeks which followed, to assess the long-term damage caused by the revolt. Because of deep distrust between the intelligence chiefs in Israel and operatives abroad, however, it was also difficult for the community to function. Shiloah, now officially an agency chief as well as *Va'adat* chairman, was so preoccupied with internal matters, that he paid insufficient attention to what was happening overseas.

Some sort of big mistake was just waiting to happen. An embarrassing failure could practically be anticipated. But it was not. It happened in Iraq, just as the reorganization took effect and the Mossad was born.

Two somewhat mysterious men, dressed in nearly identical, shortsleeved, open-necked shirts walked into the Tel Aviv factory of Techno-Kfitz, a manufacturer of springs. The men from the government – for their appearance and demeanour suggested nothing else but government men – asked to see one of the company managers, Yaakov Frank.

'Reuven Shiloah would like to talk to you,' they told the solidly-built thirty-year-old.[17] It was January 1951, and Shiloah's formal role in government was hazy, certainly to an Israeli public which had never been told about the *Va'adat*. Frank had heard of Shiloah, and agreed without hesitation to meet the almost legendary spy.

Frank had been an enthusiastic member of the Haganah, and after fleeing a manhunt by the British in Palestine he worked for the Institute for Aliyah B in New York. He did his bit for the Allies in World War II as an American soldier, fighting the Japanese in the Pacific. Severely wounded in the Philippines in October 1944, he returned to Israel as it became independent in 1948, with US citizenship and a monthly pension from the Pentagon.

Recovered to near perfect health, Frank was about to be called into active service again. The two shadowy officials drove him to the *Kirya*, the 'Town Centre' – the name used for the military and defence-ministry compound so large that it comprised its own small neighbourhood on the eastern edge of Tel Aviv. They escorted Frank into one of the buildings, where there was no plaque or sign mentioning 'intelligence', and to Shiloah's private office.

The chief of Israel's intelligence community was sitting at his desk, looking down at the younger man's file. 'I see, Frank, that you helped Aliyah B bring Jews to Israel, and then you were an army major,' Shiloah said. 'You have the kind of background we're looking for.'

'What would you like me to do?' said the redheaded Frank, who had always agreed to any mission for Israel.

'I want you to go to Iraq,' Shiloah replied. 'Our man in Iraq is about to end his tour of duty, and we want you to take over our station in Baghdad.'

'I agree, under one condition,' said Frank, 'that I be given full authority there.'

'Certainly,' Shiloah agreed. 'You will be responsible for the immigration of the Jews from there, as well as for the collection of information.'

'But isn't Aliyah B responsible for getting the Jews out?' insisted Frank, a veteran of that agency but unsure who his next employer would be.

Shiloah told him: 'Don't worry. Everything is being coordinated.'

After a quick briefing by Shiloah's staff, Frank was invited for a chat with Foreign Minister Moshe Sharett, who stressed the importance of the Baghdad operation and assured Frank that the State of Israel stood behind him. Feeling fully confident, the new recruit left for Iraq a few days later.

Three weeks after he was first approached, Yaakov Frank found himself on a flight from Tel Aviv to Teheran, bearing a false Israeli passport in the name of Yitzhak Stein. In the Iranian capital, Frank/Stein was met by the station chief, Zion Cohen.

'Tell me, Zion,' Frank wondered, 'who am I working for?' Was he working for Shiloah? And what agency would that be? For Aliyah B? For Guriel's Political Department? For Gibli's Military Intelligence?

'I have no idea,' Cohen replied. 'I am completely in the dark. I have the feeling that Tel Aviv is busy with other things.'

Frank waited in Teheran for over two months, doing absolutely nothing. But when Cohen, trying to help, gave him a false passport as the basis for a new cover identity, it only inflamed Frank's anger. The passport would force him to become Ismail Tashbakash, a rug merchant from Bahrain. He had thought his cover story would be that of a Canadian businessman. He spoke English well, had visited Canada a number of times, and believed that the years he spent in the United States would enable him to get away with it.

Now he was supposed to be an Arab from the Persian Gulf. 'My facial features are European, not Arabian. It is true that I spoke a little Arabic, but with a Palestinian accent. I found it hard to believe that, in the circumstances, I would be able to operate as required,' he recalls. 'I was boiling mad. For God's sake, I said to myself, how can they do this to me? Is this the way a secret agent is to operate?'[18]

He had no one to whom to complain. He considered returning to Israel, but his patriotism prevented his quitting the mission. Even without specific orders, he decided to carry on. First, he burned every document he had which linked him with the Jewish state. Frank/Stein/Tashbakash then bribed some smugglers to transport him from Iran into Iraq, no easy task because of the many police checkpoints, on April 20, 1951. His true torment was only now to begin.

Frank had believed Tel Aviv's promise that it would send a coded message to the Baghdad station to advise of his arrival. When his long and tiring journey was over, however, and he knocked on the door of the planned contact, a Jewish family, he found that he was totally unexpected.

It was, ironically, the first night of Passover, the major Jewish springtime holiday, and the family – celebrating the traditional *Seder* banquet – refused to allow the newcomer to stay the night. Naturally, they feared he might be an agent for the Iraqi police. Frank's pathetic pleas fell on deaf ears, and even one of the *Seder* guests who should have known better, Mordecai Ben-Porat, refused to listen.

Ben-Porat was Aliyah B's principal operative in Baghdad. An Iraqi-born Jew who had emigrated to Palestine, he served in the Israeli army and was sent back to Iraq in the autumn of 1949 to organize the illegal departure of Jews. He borrowed the identities of two Jews who had already left Iraq, and he would alternate between two false names, 'Zaki Habi' and 'Moshe Nissim'. It was not a completely undercover existence, however, as far too many people knew his true identity.

In the disarray then reigning in the intelligence community, Ben-Porat was also in charge of other secret operations. A technique known in the espionage business as 'compartmentalization' would have been far safer, but instead the immigration organizer also ran a network of agents, mainly Jews, who fed him military and political tidbits. They were linked to headquarters in Tel Aviv by two-way shortwave radio, and the Baghdad station used the coded callsign 'Berman'.[19]

Just inside the Jewish family's front door, and within earshot of the *Seder* table, Frank had the uncomfortable task of telling Ben-Porat that his mission was to take over Ben-Porat's station. The incumbent chief refused to yield, claiming that his team of agents and the heads of the Jewish community, who knew of his secret activities, would not agree to the change.

Frank, by now so tired that he could barely control his anger, was further enraged when Ben-Porat drove him to the large Hotel Semiramis. Frank knew that any foreigner who checked into a hotel would have to register his passport with the police, and the risk could undermine his mission.

It was not the first time that Ben-Porat quarrelled with a colleague. Exactly a year earlier, in April 1950, 'British businessman Richard Armstrong' arrived for talks with the Iraqi government on behalf of the American Near East Air Transport Corporation. His real name was Shlomo Hillel, and he worked for the Institute for Aliyah B. The obscure American airline had covered its tracks carefully so as to disguise its close ties with the Israeli government. No one knew that in 1948 and 1949 the company had flown all the Jews of Yemen to Israel in another secret Aliyah B operation codenamed 'Operation Magic Carpet'.[20]

The Iraqi parliament had just passed a law permitting every Jew who wished to do so to leave the country, provided they gave up their Iraqi citizenship. This was surprising from a regime which had declared war on Israel and arrested hundreds of Jews for Zionist activities. The explanation lay in the attitude of the Prime Minister who opened the emigration gates, Toufik al-Sawidi. He was also the chairman of Iraq Tours, which – by no coincidence – was appointed agent for Near East Air Transport of the US. In other words, and by a roundabout method, the head of Iraq's government received bribes and kickbacks from Israeli intelligence.

The Prime Minister was not unique. Hillel/Armstrong and his Aliyah B agents made sure that Sawidi's opponent and predecessor, veteran politician Nuri as-Said – who would later be Prime Minister again – would also benefit. The airline awarded a maintenance concession to Iraqi Airways, which was run by Colonel Sabah as-Said, Nuri's son.

Ben-Porat insisted on being closely involved in the clandestine contacts. Headquarters in Tel Aviv had to tell him to butt out, and from May 1950 to January 1952 the operation managed to bring around 150,000 Iraqi Jews to Israel by air. The direct flights supplanted Ben-Porat's much smaller operation, which smuggled Jews overland from Iraq to Iran and then flew them to Israel. They refused to help, perhaps acting without consulting the Israeli controller.

Frank was not aware of all the details or of the unpleasantness between Hillel and Ben-Porat. He was trying to sort out his own conflict with Ben-Porat. Based more on emotion than rational logic, Frank decided to remain in Baghdad until his life was clearly in danger. Not surprisingly, he found that he was being followed by Iraqi security men. He changed taxis a few times to shake off the tails, and then he approached Ben-Porat's operatives to ask for their aid in fleeing. They refused to help.

Frank remained calm and went into a travel agency, bribed one of the employees, and arranged a flight and an exit visa for himself. He had enough sense to fly to Beirut rather than to a European capital, as the Iraqi secret police kept a much tighter watch on flights to Europe than to Arab destinations.

Frank/Stein/Tashbakash had been in Baghdad for only a week, but even after leaving his troubles were not over. He transferred at Beirut and flew on to Turkey, intending to catch a flight to Tel Aviv. The Israeli consulate in Istanbul, however, refused to believe his story and to grant a visa to a 'rug merchant from Bahrain'. That, after all, was the only identity Frank could prove with documents. It took the consulate three days before it finally gave 'Tashbakash' a visa for Israel. Even then, Frank was thinking as a patriotic agent and urged the consul not to stamp the visa into the Bahraini passport, which would render it useless in the future. No Israeli secret agent could use a travel document that had an obvious link to Israel. But the consul, a supreme bureaucrat, stamped in the visa anyway.

The flight to Tel Aviv was uneventful, but no one came to Lod airport to receive him. Adding to Frank's puzzlement, when he went to Shiloah's office the next day – now part of the new Mossad – the intelligence chief simply refused to meet him.

Nearly forty years later, Frank is as angry as ever at his

intelligence handlers, charging them with 'amateurism and dilletantism which almost cost me my life. The right hand knew nothing of what the left hand was doing. Disorganization ran rampant. We were fortunate that they, the Iraqis, are even worse than we.'

Frank was not surprised, therefore, when he heard a month after returning to Israel that the Israeli undercover ring in Baghdad had collapsed.

Ben-Porat was arrested several times, in fact, and repeatedly withstood brutal interrogation by the Iraqis. He finally escaped to Israel, on one of Hillel's Jewish emigration flights which he had so resented. A second Israeli arrested with him, however, could not possibly maintain his cover story of being a Persian merchant. He could not even speak Farsi. His real name, he confessed to the Iraqis, was Yehudah Tajar. He was a veteran of the *Palmach*, the élite 'Storming Forces' of the Haganah, sent to Baghdad by the Political Department – before it was disbanded – as case officer for a group of young Iraqi Jews and Arab hirelings who collected strategic information for Israel.

Ben-Porat and Tajar were supposed to have been working in parallel, but definitely not together. Ignoring all rules of compartmentalization, they met often, spoke to each other in Hebrew, and even sang Israeli songs when driving by car. Such elementary errors caused the network of Jewish spies to fall like dominoes.

The Iraqis arrested some one hundred Jews, one after another, and seized a huge cache of arms. A show trial convicted twenty Iraqi Jews in November 1951, and two were hanged. Tajar was sentenced to life imprisonment. He was deported nine years later, however, after Mossad agents established contact with the new Iraqi ruler, Colonel Abdel Karim Qassem, and secured Tajar's freedom in exchange for information on plots by Iraqi dissidents against Qassem.

Among other crimes, the defendants were convicted of four acts of sabotage. One was a bombing which caused minor damage to the United States Embassy's public information centre. The biggest and most surprising attack, though, was a grenade explosion in the Masouda Shemtov Synagogue in Baghdad. At the time, hundreds of Jews were at prayer. Four of them, including a twelve-year-old boy, were killed, and around twenty were injured.

The astounding accusation, that an Israeli spy network bombed a synagogue, shocked Iraqi Jews. The charge formed the basis of rumours circulating among Iraqi immigrants to Israel who suddenly suspected that their departures may have been hastened by Israeli agents waging terrorism. The Iraq Jews were already disgruntled, blaming the European-born leadership of the Jewish state for thrusting them into primitive camps with little or no sanitation. Ben-Gurion was so annoyed by the rumours that in 1960 he ordered Harel to set up an internal enquiry. A three-man committee submitted a top-secret report which said: 'We could not find any factual evidence that Israelis or Jews were involved in throwing explosives.'

By then, however, Israeli intelligence lost all benefit of the doubt because a similar string of bombings was revealed in Egypt when a Jewish espionage and sabotage network was uncovered.

At least Yaakov Frank had the good sense not to become involved in the Egyptian affair. Similar to the springs which he went back to making at his factory, Israeli intelligence kept bouncing back at Frank. About two weeks after his return from near-capture in Baghdad in 1951, nondescript Mossad agents with limitless *chutzpah* once more visited the Tel Aviv workshop and suggested that he might want to volunteer again – this time on a secret mission to Cairo. Frank refused to listen and threw them out.

Egypt, as the largest of the neighbouring Arab states, had always been of primary interest to Israeli intelligence – much more than Iraq. An extremely unfortunate Aman operation began when military intelligence Unit 131 decided to send Avraham Dar to Cairo, despite his obvious weaknesses. He had been a *Palmach* officer in the 1948 war, but he had no great reputation for either leadership or analytical abilities. As the grandson of a Jew who had been born in Aden, his dark skin made it difficult for Dar to appear British, as his cover story demanded.

On the other hand, his English was excellent, and he had worked for the Institute for Aliyah B. He arrived in Egypt in May 1951 as John Darling, representative of a British electronics company. 'The name Darling was not chosen by chance,' Dar recalled years later. 'The name of one of the British army officers in Egypt was Darling, and the family ties that I ostensibly had with him might be useful to me.'[21]

After Dar had settled in under his cover – even the authentic Darling believing that they were related – he began working on the true goal for which he had been sent: to establish a network of 'sleeper' agents who, when the time came, would be called upon to carry out secret assignments. Dar/Darling set up two cells of young, dedicated Jews who were supporters of the State of Israel. They were even brought secretly to Israel in 1952 for training.

Almost all of these Egyptian Zionists were rank amateurs. Unit 131 instructors had trouble making their lessons in tradecraft stick: invisible ink, coded radio broadcasts, and surveillance techniques were as strange to these second-rate agents as nuclear physics might be. No one in Israel's intelligence community seemed to protest, however. There were, after all, a few exceptions. Among the more talented espionage students was Eli Cohen, who a decade later would be considered 'the best spy' of the Jewish state.

One of the female operatives, Marcelle Ninio, set up a travel agency in Egypt with secret Israeli funding. Popular for her vivacious personality and memorable beauty, Ninio was the link between the two Egyptian cells.

The recruits 'slept' for three years, until the agreed code-word was transmitted from Tel Aviv to Cairo in June 1954, activating Operation Suzannah. A group of young army officers led by Colonel Gamal Abdel Nasser had seized power in Cairo in 1952, overthrowing King Farouk and declaring a republic. Aman reached the conclusion that the time had come to stir up some unrest. The agency's secret cells were finally going to do something, although Dar/

Darling was no longer their case officer. He had been replaced by Avraham Seidenwerg.

Seidenwerg was the son of a Jewish politician in Austria who had died in a Nazi concentration camp. The younger Seidenwerg moved to Palestine, changed his name to Avri El-Ad, and excelled in the *Palmach*'s battle for Jerusalem in 1948. He was a major at the age of twenty-two, but his army career ended when he looted a refrigerator in a captured Arab village and was court-martialled.

By the end of 1951, scorned, unemployed, and divorced, Seidenwerg/El-Ad met Avraham Dar and Mordecai Ben-Zur of Unit 131. They saw him as excellent material for a dangerous mission in enemy territory, because he had nothing to lose and would be grateful for the opportunity to rehabilitate himself.

Unit 131 borrowed the identity of a kibbutz member of German origin named Paul Frank and assigned it to its new recruit. Seidenwerg/El-Ad/Frank went to West Germany for nine months to close any gaps in his cover story, and he even underwent a unique and painful operation to reverse his circumcision – so that he would not be identified, if naked, as a Jew. He told the German surgeon that he was a non-Jew who could not stand his sexual partners thinking he was Jewish. The doctor sympathized fully.[22]

The Israeli spy sailed to Cairo as wealthy businessman Paul Frank in December 1953. He was quickly accepted into the growing community of Germans in Egypt, many of whom had a Nazi past they wished to escape.

As case officer of the intelligence network in Egypt, Seidenwerg/El-Ad/Frank committed every mistake in the book. He knew all of his agents – not just a top few – and even visited them in their homes. They and their families could identify him, if the worst should happen, even though they called him 'Robert'.

On June 30, 1954, he went to Alexandria with the long-awaited codeword. Operation Suzannah meant sabotage. The bombing targets were not Egyptian military facilities. They were cinemas, post offices, and American and British institutions. The aim was to provoke the anger of Washington and London against the Egyptians, and to portray the new government in Cairo as unstable and unreliable.

The somewhat bizarre mission began with the bombing of a post office in Alexandria. Philip Nathanson, at nineteen the youngest of the Zionist operatives, and Victor Levi carried the primitive incendiary devices in eyeglasses cases. There was only minor damage, and Egyptian military censorship forbade any publication of the event. As a result, Egypt's image did not suffer at all.

A week later, more ambitious instructions were given by codewords during an Israel Radio programme. Seidenwerg/ Frank ordered his team to place bombs in the Cairo and Alexandria libraries of the United States Information Centre. This time, both the local and international press reported the explosions. Unit 131, in Tel Aviv, was pleased.

On July 22, two bombs went off in Cairo. One of them, however, was still in the pocket of Philip Nathanson. A police officer helped extinguish the burning trousers and then arrested Nathanson. It was the end of Operation Suzannah, which would haunt Israel's intelligence community like a ghost.

For many years, Israel denied any connection with the bombings in Egypt. Censors prevented the Israeli press from mentioning the topic. Well over three decades later, the question persists: who gave the orders? Ben-Gurion had just retired to his kibbutz in the Negev. The new Prime Minister, Moshe Sharett, knew nothing of the affair. Defence Minister Pinhas Lavon took most of the blame, in part because he already had a reputation for keeping secrets to himself.

Lavon admitted that he was aware of a sleeper cell in Egypt, but he denied ordering that it be activated. He suggested that the army Chief of Staff, General Moshe Dayan, might have been responsible. Dayan denied it, but Aman chief Gibli stated that he had received orders from his military superiors.

In the following years, a number of investigations found

that intelligence operatives had lied. Documents had been forged or destroyed. Almost everyone concerned had covered-up something. The schism in the government could not be bridged. Ben-Gurion returned to serve as Prime Minister and obsessively demanded that his party, Mapai, investigate the case over and over.

The 'Lavon Affair', as it became known, had a huge political impact in hastening the decline of the Mapai Party. In time, the entire Socialist bloc began to lose its grip on the Israeli electorate, culminating in the 1977 victory of Menachem Begin's right-wing Likud bloc.

The ones who suffered the most, two of them paying for it with their lives, were the young Jews of Egypt who had spied for Israel. The Jewish state had let them down. Nathanson was the first to break under interrogation. As in Iraq, the Egyptian security police found it easy to roll up an unprofessional espionage network. Ninio, the travel agent and liaison, was arrested. So was Max Bennett.

Meir (Max) Bennett was born in Hungary in 1917 to a family of Orthodox Jews from Germany. In 1935, his family arrived as illegal immigrants to Palestine. Out of gratitude, he was a secret agent for Aliyah B, and there he acquired the dual identity he retained until his dying day. Avraham Dar recruited him into Aman, where his command of six languages brought him to many nations on varied missions – rising to the rank of major by the time he was sent to Egypt in 1951.

As in the case of Seidenwerg/El-Ad, Bennett was given a German cover identity. It was something of a favourite choice for the simple reasons that Israel had many German-speakers and that few people would expect a German to be working for the Jewish state. There was also a deeper reason: West Germany's intelligence service was helping the Israelis set up their cover stories, complete with passports and other documentation, because of German feelings of guilt after World War II and the Holocaust.

According to Bennett's cover story, he was a former Nazi representing a German company which manufactured prosthetic devices. Later, he became the chief engineer in Egypt for Ford Motors. Beneath the surface, Bennett was an exceptional intelligence man. Ford's most important client was the Egyptian army, and this gave the Israeli spy a great deal of access to military men and bases.

His wife was not supposed to know where he was, and he would first send his letters home to an address in London. Once, one of his operators erred and forgot to remove the Egyptian stamps. Jean Bennett suddenly knew where Max was. She believes such amateurism characterized the entire affair.[23]

Bennett himself, however, dutifully carried out his assignments. One was fatal. 'It was a stupid error by his operators,' Avraham Dar said years later. 'There had been a break in their contacts with the Seidenwerg/Frank network, and they chose the easiest way to transfer money to them. The rules of compartmentalization in intelligence forbid any connection between two different networks, especially when their assignments are totally different. But the operators acted stupidly. Thus Bennett met with Marcelle Ninio and with Frank, and gave them the money.'[24]

Under interrogation, Ninio told what she knew about Bennett. The Egyptians broke into his home, stripped him, and, when they saw that he had been circumcised, beat him cruelly. On December 21, 1954, Max Bennett slashed his wrists in a prison cell in Cairo and died the day before he was to stand trial. It appears that he realized that, as the highest-ranking Israeli spy, he was doomed. Bennett preferred not to be humiliated.[25]

Still, Israel stubbornly denied involvement. Bennett's body was sent to West Germany for burial, but in 1959 it was secretly disinterred and flown to Israel for reburial. His grave was unmarked. The authorities told his widow about the reburial only a day before it took place. All of the family's requests for an explanation as to the circumstances of his death were turned down by the intelligence community. Only in 1988 did Israel admit officially that Bennett had been an agent, and, at a ceremony in the Defence Minister's office in Tel Aviv, he was posthumously awarded the rank of Lieutenant-Colonel.

The Israeli authorities were similarly unhelpful to the other captured agents in the 'Lavon Affair'. Two were hanged in 1955, and four others were sentenced to long prison terms. Israel rejected an Egyptian offer to exchange them for Egyptian prisoners of war captured during the 1956 Suez campaign. Chief of Staff Dayan was firmly opposed to a deal, fearing it would embarrass Israel.[26] Only in 1968, after the Six-Day War, were Marcelle Ninio, Philip Nathanson, Robert Dassa, and Victor Levi exchanged for thousands of Egyptian POWs.

The only member of the network who escaped capture was the Israeli operator. Under the name of Paul Frank, he even dared to remain in Egypt for two more weeks. Upon returning to Tel Aviv, Seidenwerg/Frank became Avri El-Ad again, and Aman sent him on another military intelligence mission to Europe. Only Shin Bet chief Isser Harel was opposed to this, as he suspected that El-Ad could have been a double agent. His easy escape from Egypt seemed sinister.

It was not the first time that a senior Israeli intelligence operative was accused of working for the Egyptians. The shadow over El-Ad was reminiscent of the case of David Magen, who spied for Israel in Italy and Egypt before falling foul of his superiors. His original name was Theodore Gross, and he was born in the early 1920s to a Hungarian Jewish family. The Gross family moved to South Africa, and Theodore later went to Italy to study music. An accomplished singer, he appeared in operas in Italy and Mexico. World War II brought him to the British army, where he changed his name to Ted Cross and became an intelligence officer on dangerous assignments in Italy and Germany.

When war broke out in Palestine in 1948, Gross/Cross felt obliged to move to Israel and join its army. Because of his experience and his knowledge of English, German, Italian, Spanish, and French, he was recruited into the foreign ministry's Political Department by Arthur Ben-Natan. In

Israel, the volunteer spy was known by the Hebrew name David Magen, but he was sent to Italy as Ted Cross to run a network of Arab agents who were gathering military and political information for Israel.

In 1950, Magen/Cross was sent to Egypt, where he operated a string of local informers. Shiloah and his new Mossad inherited their man in Cairo from the Political Department but did not keep him for long. In 1952, he was ordered to leave Egypt, and from a transit stop in Rome he flew to Tel Aviv.

Magen was immediately arrested, tried, convicted, and sentenced to fifteen years imprisonment for spying for Egypt. Without authorization or reporting his actions, Magen/Cross had made contact with Egyptian intelligence personnel. In his defence, he claimed that he had done so in order to deceive Egyptian intelligence – to propose that he become a double agent while remaining loyal to Israel.

Magen's alibis were not accepted by the prosecution or the court, in part because of evidence that in Italy he had been involved in drug deals, and had even been imprisoned for doing so.

Many members of the disbanded Political Department continued to believe that Magen/Cross did not betray Israel. Boris Guriel testified on his behalf during the trial, claiming that Shiloah and his Mossad had rigged a false case against Magen to ruin the reputation of the Political Department. The campaign for parole led to his release in 1959, after seven years in prison. Gross/Magen/Cross changed identities one more time. He married, raised a family, and lived in Israel with a deep sense of injustice until his death in 1973 – an anonymous man without his true identity or his life story known to the people of his adopted country.[27]

There were similar disagreements, within the intelligence community, about Avri El-Ad in 1955. Aman, now led by Major General Yehoshafat Harkabi since Gibli was forced to quit over the 'Lavon Affair', continued to believe in El-Ad. Isser Harel, however, doggedly followed his own instincts. Without telling Harkabi, Harel sent Shin Bet operatives to Europe to trail the suspect.

Shin Bet reported that El-Ad contacted an officer at the Egyptian military attaché's office in Bonn and gave him secret documents about Israeli intelligence. The Aman agent was immediately flown back to Israel, interrogated for nine continuous months by Shin Bet, and put on trial in July 1959. He was accused of spying for Egypt.

Hoping to save his skin, El-Ad confessed his part in concealing the truth about the 'Lavon Affair', saying that officers in Aman's Unit 131 had conspired to blame Defence Minister Lavon for the failure of Operation Suzannah in Egypt. Still, El-Ad was sentenced to ten years in prison after one of the most secret trials in Israeli history. Military censors forbade the press from printing details. The newspapers referred to the entire affair only as *Esek Bish*, the 'Rotten Business'. Gibli was identified as 'the senior officer', Ben-Zur as 'the reserves officer', and Avri El-Ad as 'the third man', as a bizarre homage to Graham Greene's cinematic thriller.

All the same, Shin Bet interrogators were unable to break El-Ad and force him to confess that he had helped Egyptian intelligence, or to admit that he had betrayed his comrades in Cairo and Alexandria. After his release from prison, El-Ad moved to California and wrote a book charging that Isser Harel had framed him.[28]

The Israeli people were not told exactly what was rotten in their nation's intelligence community, but it was clear that not all had gone well in the 1950s. The operations in Iraq and Egypt contained almost every error in the espionage textbook. They could be excellent case studies as to how an intelligence service should not behave. Israel used inexperienced operatives who were not qualified for their missions and were not fully briefed before going abroad. The chain of command back home, at headquarters, was left vague and defied definition.

Even though intelligence chiefs had decided after the fiasco in Iraq not to employ local Jews in future missions,

Egyptian Jews were used in Operation Suzannah. Their employment not only brought about the downfall of the espionage networks, but it also placed the entire Jewish community in danger of reprisals.

There were, however, some important silver linings in the clouds of Iraq and Egypt. Many of the Israeli agents exhibited dedication to their mission, an impressive ability to improvise when necessary, level-headedness under pressure, and an ability to make do with very little. These qualities would continue to be among the most striking characteristics of the Israeli intelligence community. But true, consistent professionalism had yet to be developed.

Some changes were made, as early as just after the Iraqi spy ring collapsed. The Institute for Aliyah B was disbanded in March 1952, although, similarly to the Political Department people the previous year, the Aliyah B staff objected. They charged that Reuven Shiloah's Mossad was trying to grab their impressive assets.

Aliyah B was indeed something of an economic empire, and certainly a massive travel agency. It owned ships and planes. Furthermore, after the conclusion of immigration operations from Romania, Hungary, Poland, and Yemen after the 1948 war, the only justification for Aliyah B's existence was the immigration of the Jews from Iraq. Once that was completed, there was no need for the specialized secret agency.

To apply bureaucratic cement to the change in authority, Shiloah and his assistant, Akiva Levinsky, went to the trouble of signing a memorandum with the Jewish Agency which put the Mossad in charge of immigration from the Arab countries – specifically, 'underground activities in order to make contact with Jews and to bring them to Israel.' The Jewish Agency promised to pay the bills. This became the pattern of operations in the future.[29]

Shiloah, meantime, was in bad health after a head injury suffered in a car accident. He also felt that he was under pressure from an ambitious Isser Harel. Indeed, Prime Minister Ben-Gurion noted in his diary on May 24, 1952:

'Isser came to me. In his opinion, Reuven has failed in his task.'[30] A consensus built up that while Shiloah was brilliant, he was not much good at running an agency.

On September 20, 1952, after only eighteen months as first director of the Mossad, Shiloah submitted his resignation to Ben-Gurion. Asked to recommend possible successors, Shiloah named the obvious candidates: Levinsky, Gibli, and Harel.

Ben-Gurion chose Harel. His perseverance and rectitude had impressed the Prime Minister. Harel would become, in the following decade, the supreme chief of Israeli intelligence.

Until his death in 1959, Shiloah continued to carry out some special assignments for Israeli foreign policy – with an eye towards his old stomping grounds in espionage. He had come to the conclusion that Israeli intelligence suffered from poor political and strategic analysis, and he hoped to eliminate naiveté, narrow-mindedness, and ignorance in the community. Gaining powerful foreign allies would help.

Equipped with his old wartime contacts, Shiloah embarked on a one-man mission to establish and expand links with the espionage services of the West, especially those of Britain and the United States. A growing network of contacts abroad would turn the Mossad into an alternative foreign ministry for Israel.

3

Strategic Alliances

'We are very interested in having a cooperation agreement with you,' Prime Minister David Ben-Gurion said to the surprised head of the CIA. This was in May 1951, in the old offices of the CIA, opposite the Lincoln Memorial in Washington, DC. The Israeli leader happened to be in the United States on a private visit, the first of its kind after the war in the Middle East. His declared purpose was to participate in the launch of fundraising by the sale of Israel Bonds in the US. Ben-Gurion used the visit for diplomatic purposes, too.

'The Old Man' met President Harry S. Truman and a secret luncheon was arranged for him with the director of the CIA, General Walter Bedell Smith, and his assistant, Allen Dulles. Even before Ben-Gurion left Israel, Reuven Shiloah, then still head of the Mossad, suggested that the Prime Minister propose intelligence cooperation between the two countries.

It was a far-reaching notion. Israel, which was ruled by

left-wing parties, was considered to be a socialist state. The kibbutz, the unique Israeli farm cooperative which enshrined the principle of sharing assets among members according to their needs, was regarded as the embodiment of the Communist dream. Israel's economy, too, was based on the principles of collectivism and public ownership of most of the means of production. 'Capitalism' and 'free market' were considered dirty words in the national lexicon of Israel. But especially disturbing, from an American point of view, was the fact that Israeli-Jewish sentiment was believed to favour the Soviets, largely due to the aid which the Eastern bloc had tendered in the first days of the new state.

Had it not been for a speech supporting a Jewish state by Andrei Gromyko, the Soviet ambassador to the United Nations, Resolution 181 – which decided on the partition of Palestine into two states, Jewish and Arab – would not have been adopted. At Moscow's behest, Czechoslovakia and Yugoslavia supplied weapons and ammunition to the newborn state and they played host to Israeli pilots for training. Furthermore, the readiness of Romania, Hungary and Poland to permit their Jews to emigrate added to Israel's sparse manpower.

Shiloah bucked the beliefs of the establishment by urging that Israeli foreign policy should abandon its pro-Soviet orientation, and strengthen its ties with America. His ultimate aim was to arrange a defence treaty with Washington, and to have Israel join the American-led North Atlantic Treaty Organization (NATO). As a first step towards this, he suggested secret contacts between the CIA and the Mossad.

Ben-Gurion and senior government officials did not believe there was much chance that Shiloah's proposal would be accepted, but they felt, at the very least, that the effort should be made. One can therefore understand how surprised Ben-Gurion was when Bedell Smith and Dulles gladly endorsed the idea.

This was not the first meeting of the American general and 'the Old Man'. They had met immediately after World

War II, when Ben-Gurion visited Holocaust survivors in the displaced persons camps of Germany, and Bedell Smith, who was then chief of staff to General Dwight D. Eisenhower, Commander of the Allied forces in Europe, had accompanied the Zionist leader on his tour of inspection.

The extermination of six million Jews in Auschwitz, Treblinka, Dachau and other Nazi death camps, and the sight of the hundreds of thousands of refugees who survived, left an indelible impression on many American soldiers who served in Europe during the war. Israel, for its part, was well aware of how to maximize the memory of the Holocaust, when emotional manipulation appeared necessary. The sympathy and guilt felt by some Western leaders could be useful when the Jewish state requested political and military aid.

Israeli diplomats stressed, time and again, the necessity of their country being strong, so that there would never be another Holocaust. This was possibly a cynical exploitation of the unspeakable horrors of the war era, horrors which remain unique in human history, but it worked. Among the persuaded were Bedell Smith and Dulles. In Washington, Ben-Gurion reached an understanding with the CIA chiefs to have talks begin immediately on pressing ahead with cooperation.

A month later, Shiloah was sent to Washington, to agree the final details of a formal but secret agreement. He held long meetings with Bedell Smith, Dulles and especially James Jesus Angleton.[1]

Angleton had also been influenced profoundly by the Holocaust. He was a man of contradictions. He intensely disliked his childhood home, Arizona, where the climate was supposed to help counter his tuberculosis. In 1933, when he was 16 years old, his father moved to Milan, Italy, to find employment. After a few years abroad, Angleton returned to the US to study at Yale, where he started a literary magazine with a remarkable set of contributors including Ezra Pound, Archibald Macleish, William Carlos and William Cummings.

In 1943, Norman Holmes Pearson, one of his teachers at Yale, recruited Angleton to the counterespionage department of the Office of Strategic Services. This was a unit composed of intellectuals, Ivy Leaguers and eccentrics. Angleton was a little bit of all three.

After he joined the American secret agency, it became clear that he had a quality which was singularly appropriate for someone working in intelligence: he had a suspicious mind, which always sought to search for hidden meanings beyond those which met the naked eye.[2]

Angleton served the OSS in Britain and Italy, where he recruited informers and uncovered Nazi and Fascist spy rings. Among his best sources of information were the Aliyah B agents in Italy, who were involved in smuggling Jews to Palestine.[3]

Angleton was especially impressed by the ability of the Jewish underground and its representatives in Europe. He was aware of several efforts to strengthen the ties between the Zionist underground and America's spies, thwarted by the opposition of the British who were ruling Palestine. When Shiloah and the CIA did reach their cooperation agreement in 1951, Angleton was pleased.

The agreement laid the foundation for the exchange of strategic information between the CIA and the Mossad and committed them to report to each other on matters of mutual interest. Israel and the US pledged not to spy on each other and to exchange liaison officers attached to their embassies in Washington and Tel Aviv.

To add flesh to the skeleton agreement, however, they had to overcome one major obstacle. Angleton, promoted to be head of counterespionage of the CIA, was an obsessive opponent of Communism. Israel, with its socialist values and its links with the Soviet bloc, was considered by him to be a high security risk.

Angleton was concerned that the immigration of Jews from Eastern Europe would provide a pipeline for Soviet spies to penetrate Israel, as a launching pad into the West. The Communist authorities could easily blackmail Jews who were leaving for Israel, by threatening to harm their relatives who remained behind. The acting US Secretary of State, Robert Lovett, noted: 'The admixture of European races in Palestine offers a unique opportunity for Soviet penetration into a highly strategic area,' and the new US military attachés in Israel were instructed to observe 'Soviet activities and should be thoroughly familiar with Soviet tactics.' The Americans also believed that the Russians were infiltrating Israel's army.[4]

Shiloah was aware of Washington's fears and did not merely make promises in response. He persuaded them that Israel's intelligence community was already on the same wavelength. Shiloah told the CIA that Aliyah B and Isser Harel's Shin Bet were already giving close scrutiny to the new Jewish arrivals from behind the Iron Curtain.

Harel did not like being pushed around by the Americans. They seemed to prefer a one-sided relationship, he felt, getting as much information from Israel without giving much. Harel stood against Shiloah's apparent desire to be liked by the Americans at all costs, but Shiloah convinced Ben-Gurion that the price of vetting the immigrants was worth paying until the CIA's trust was won.

What finally persuaded Angleton and the CIA was Israel's contention that 'from the bitter could come the sweet', in the words of the Bible – that the new immigrants should not be feared; they should be used. After all, the Jews had come from all walks of life and had intimate knowledge of the Soviet military establishment, science, economics and politics. Israel began feeding such data to the US and even agreed to put some of its agents at risk in the Soviet bloc, by allowing the CIA to use them.[5]

In return, Israel was permitted to purchase special technology for its intelligence needs, including eavesdropping devices and electronic code-breaking equipment. Israeli officers were sent to the US to learn how to use the equipment.[6] To oversee all of this, two excellent intelligence men were dispatched to Washington: Colonel Chaim Herzog, the new military attaché, and Shiloah's close friend

Teddy Kollek, as counsellor in the Israeli embassy. Kollek already had experience, before 1948, in buying weapons for the Zionists and running networks of American sympathizers.

Israel's true breakthrough into the ranks of US strategic allies was the intelligence coup of 1956. Rumours had been flying for weeks about historic decisions declared in a secret speech by Soviet leader Nikita Khrushchev to the Twentieth Congress of the Communist Party in February. Dulles, by then the CIA director, had a few excerpts of the speech but hankered for the complete text. Neither the Americans nor British secret agents in Europe or Russia could satisfy the CIA's hunger.

In the middle of May, Israeli intelligence came through. The Israelis surprised Angleton with a copy of the full Khrushchev text. The feat proved that even a tiny intelligence organization, which lacked the financial and human resources of the superpowers, could achieve great things. What Dulles and Angleton did not know was that, on this occasion, it had been a matter of pure luck for the Israelis. Senior members of Poland's Communist Party received the text, and one handed it to a journalist who in turn shared it with Israeli intelligence. A leak to the press was rare in Eastern Europe and Israel made an indelible impression on Angleton and the CIA brass by sharing the text immediately.[7]

Angleton became Israel's great advocate in American intelligence and defence circles. Given the pro-Arab bias of most of the State Department and Pentagon, and some CIA personnel, Angleton's views were like an oasis in the desert for the Israelis. He was even able to counter or distort information obtained from other sources which was liable to harm Israel. When the US military attaché in Tel Aviv sent a report in October 1956 that Israel was planning to attack Egypt, Angleton claimed that the information was not accurate. That helped to maintain the smoke screen which cloaked the preparations for war.[8]

Admiration for the Jewish state became an obsession

with Angleton, who fell captive to the magic of Israeli intelligence. He zealously insisted on being the sole handler of the Israeli 'account', as the CIA called it, even after becoming counterespionage chief. 'Angleton had one major responsibility other than counter-intelligence – Israel – which he had traditionally handled in the same totally compartmented fashion as counter-intelligence,' then-CIA director William Colby wrote.[9]

He was furious when others tried to make contacts with the Israelis, without his knowledge. His jealousy reached its peak in 1971 and possibly indicated the paranoia, which led to his removal from his position three years later. When Peter Wright, his counter-intelligence counterpart in Britain's domestic MI5 security service, visited Washington, Angleton filed an official complaint to Sir Martin Furnival Jones, the British agency chief. Angleton suspected that Wright had conducted secret negotiations behind his back, regarding Israel and the Middle East, with other CIA officials. The British did not bother responding to the letter.

On other occasions, Angleton did not conceal his suspicions of Lord Victor Rothschild, a scion of the famous banking family. Rothschild was a former British intelligence operative, dating back to World War II. As always in intelligence, 'once an agent, always an agent', and he maintained close ties with his former employers in London while nurturing personal friendships with the leaders of Israeli intelligence. Angleton resented Rothschild's contacts.[10]

Angleton opened a wedge in the American wall of suspicion about Israel, and in his dozens of visits to Jerusalem – where he loved to stay at the King David Hotel, overlooking the walls of the Old City – he paved the way for the special strategic ties between the US and Israel. Within sight of the hotel, Israel dedicated a 'memorial corner' to its valued American friend. On a rock quarried in the Jerusalem hills, the inscription, 'In memory of a dear friend, James (Jim) Angleton', appears in Hebrew, English, and Arabic. It was unveiled at a gathering attended by present and former heads of the Israeli intelligence community. This was in November 1987, the year after he died.

Sharing reminiscences at the ceremony, Teddy Kollek, now mayor of Jerusalem, told how he met Angleton for the first time when touring CIA headquarters in September 1950. The Israeli happened to bump into Kim Philby in the corridor. This was very surprising to Kollek, for he knew Philby from Vienna. Kollek hurried over to Angleton's room and asked him: 'What is Philby doing here?'

Angleton replied, 'Kim is a good friend of ours and is the MI6 representative here in Washington, as the liaison officer with the CIA.'

Kollek pulled no punches. He had never liked Philby, possibly because Philby's father, an eccentric Orientalist, had converted to Islam and settled in Saudi Arabia in order to serve as a special adviser to the Saudi royal family. Kollek felt that the father's views must have rubbed off on the son, and the Israeli did not hesitate to tell Angleton what was bothering him.

Kollek had first met Philby in Austria in the 1930s and had even attended the Briton's wedding to a Communist Jew. This was a part of his past which Philby concealed when he joined British intelligence.[11]

Around the time that Angleton heard about Philby's past from Kollek, senior British diplomats Guy Burgess and Donald Maclean defected to Moscow. They exposed the tremendous extent to which the Soviets had infiltrated British intelligence, and Angleton launched a search for other traitors in the Western secret services.

It was clear that a senior official had alerted Burgess and Maclean to take flight, and Philby was suspected of being the 'third man'. It was difficult to believe, however, because he was so high up in MI6 and held an exemplary record in World War II intelligence. Angleton ignored Kollek's information, but the American later admitted he regretted his error, which further fuelled his obsessive hunt for Soviet moles.

Part of the hunt involved a British woman visiting Israel.

Flora Solomon was the daughter of a wealthy Jewish banker in Czarist Russia who had moved to England. She worked for the Marks and Spencer chain of stores, and like her employers she was an ardent Zionist. On one of her frequent trips to Israel, she attended a cocktail party where she met an old friend, Lord Victor Rothschild. Solomon, who hated the anti-Israel and pro-Arab newspaper articles written by Kim Philby, then a journalist in Beirut, made a disparaging remark to Rothschild: 'As usual, Kim is acting as his operators in Russia tell him to.'

Rothschild responded with surprise: 'What do you know about Philby's Russian operators?'

Solomon told him how Philby had tried to recruit her in 1940 to work for Soviet intelligence. Philby described his work to Solomon as 'secret and dangerous', and when she did not consent, he asked her not to tell anyone about it. In 1961, after telling Rothschild, she told the Mossad – confirming Kollek's suspicions.[12]

Rothschild told his friends in British intelligence. But in typical British manner, to avoid embarrassment at all costs, MI6 allowed Philby to flee to Moscow.

The British, in the end, were impressed that the Israelis knew so much. Just as with Angleton in the US, a number of senior officials in British intelligence, including Peter Wright and Maurice Oldfield, came to appreciate the Mossad's abilities. Under their influence, MI6 and the Mossad signed a cooperation agreement, similar to the pact between the Mossad and the CIA.[13]

Oldfield was of medium height, with a round face, and bespectacled. A sharp eye could even pick out certain similarities between Reuven Shiloah and Maurice Oldfield. It is true that Shiloah respected British intelligence and the elegant manner of its agents, but the link would not have been forged without Kollek. He had met Oldfield at the end of World War II, when the Briton was in Military Intelligence, collecting information on Arab and Jewish nationalist movements in the Middle East.

Over the years, the two became fast friends. Oldfield told

Kollek that he had always admired Zionism. Kollek was very taken with Oldfield's personality, and their friendship would yield significant dividends in the 1960s, when Oldfield became director of MI6. Novelists Ian Fleming and John LeCarré were also impressed by Oldfield, and Fleming's M in the James Bond books and LeCarré's George Smiley were modelled on the MI6 chief.[14]

Oldfield, like Angleton, always made sure to protect Israel's interests in the hostile British establishment. In London, Oldfield and his successor were better able to press their case because of the benefits reaped from the hidden ties with the Jewish state.

Roy Guindon was an officer with the Royal Canadian Mounted Police, the Mounties, who are responsible for Canada's security. In 1959, he was sent to his country's embassy in Moscow as a security officer and codes operator. Guindon soon earned a reputation as a womanizer, and when the embassy's ladies spurned his advances, word of his frustration reached the KGB, the Kremlin's *Komitet Gosudarstvennoy Bezopasnosti*, the Committee for State Security. The KGB, famed for its efficiency, set a classic trap for the Canadian. As bait, they used Larissa Fedorovna Dubanova, who was young, attractive and sensual.

By arranged coincidence, Guindon found himself seated next to Dubanova at the Bolshoi Ballet. By another coincidence, she spoke excellent English. Roy and Larissa carried on an affair for a number of months, until she informed him that she was pregnant. The KGB hurriedly arranged a secret and illegal wedding and now had Guindon exactly where it wanted him. Under the threat of never seeing Larissa again, Guindon supplied the Soviet secret service with Canada's diplomatic codes. For quite a while after Larissa said that she had had an abortion, Guindon continued to supply his operators with valuable services, which even included planting electronic bugs in the Canadian embassy. Later, he was transferred from the Moscow to the Washington embassy and continued to work for the KGB.

His 'wife' was permitted to visit him from time to time.

His treason only came to light when he was transferred to Israel. Shin Bet learned of his actions after Guindon was careless and spoke about his 'work' on the phone. Israeli intelligence informed MI6 of Guindon's treachery. The British, in turn, told the Canadian Mounties, who quickly used a pretext to lure Guindon to London. Security officers then took him to Ottawa. Guindon confessed his guilt and, in return for his full cooperation, was not tried.[15]

About twenty years later, the heterosexual factor again proved its worth in Israeli–British cooperation. In August 1979, a young, attractive Scotswoman named Rhona Ritchie joined the British Foreign Office, where she was able to practise the many languages she knew. After leaving school in her birthplace, Dundee, she had studied law in Glasgow and Paris. She dreamed of a diplomatic career, and in July 1981 her dream seemed to be fulfilled. She was sent to serve Great Britain in Tel Aviv as a press attaché. Three weeks later, Ritchie was invited to a diplomatic cocktail party given by Egypt's new embassy – established after the peace treaty with Israel – to celebrate Egyptian Revolution Day.

A simple handshake with a dark, handsome, young man put Ritchie's career on the slippery slope to disgrace. She fell in love, at first sight, with Rifaat al-Ansari, second secretary of the Egyptian consulate. Israeli intelligence did not have to exert any great effort to uncover the ties between them. The two lovers did not even attempt to hide their relationship. They were seen at dozens of diplomatic receptions, or stealing kisses by candlelight in the small restaurants on Yirmiyahu Street in northern Tel Aviv.

Perhaps the hot and humid summer of Tel Aviv and the heady feel of liberation, so far from the dreary climate of Scotland, thawed the senses of the British diplomat. She soon not only acceded to her Egyptian lover's advances, but also to his requests for information on secret cables which were sent to her embassy from London.

At the end of November, she handed Rifaat a top secret document which gave details of the forthcoming visit of the British Foreign Secretary, Lord Carrington, to the Middle East. If this information had reached the wrong hands, such as a terrorist group, it could have endangered Carrington's life.

Shin Bet decided to put an end to the dangerous romance before it was too late. The Israelis gave a detailed report to the British. Ritchie was summoned to London on some supposed business and arrested.

She admitted her guilt, expressed contrition, and co-operated with her interrogators. After a trial at the Old Bailey criminal court, she was given only a suspended sentence on November 29, 1982. The prosecutor, Sir Michael Havers, said: 'I must admit that the behaviour of the accused was more foolish than evil. She permitted herself to be so carried away by her involvement that she laid open to him secret telegrams.'

Ritchie's world collapsed completely when she found out that her lover had a wife and children who had remained behind in Cairo. In truth, as the Israelis informed their British counterparts, Ansari was a professional intelligence officer using his good looks for espionage purposes. Britain's sensationalist press had a field day, with headlines such as 'Virgin Diplomat Cheated by Romeo of Cairo' and 'Don Juan of the Nile'.[16]

Completely out of the headlines, the secret ties, based on the compatible personalities of the veterans Angleton, Oldfield, Kollek, and Shiloah, gave Israel a clout it would not have otherwise enjoyed. On top of the benefits of good bilateral relations, Israel's intelligence community was able to play a central role in the strategic planning of the United States and Britain in the Middle East – and not only in intelligence affairs. Washington and London were highly concerned, in the mid-1950s, about the deep inroads made by the Soviet Union in the region.

Moscow's influence was especially visible in Egypt, where the Soviets equipped Colonel Nasser's army. Iraq and Syria followed into the same camp. The Americans and the British decided to get rid of the 'Red Pharaoh', as Nasser was dubbed by them. CIA and MI6 agents began plotting his death and the downfall of other radical regimes.

Washington and London were fond of forming pacts in regions considered strategic but uncertain. Their aim was to surround pro-Soviet regimes in the area with a ring of solid, pro-Western allies. It was clear to Oldfield and Angleton that the Arab nations in these pacts would never allow Israel to become a formal member. The Western intelligence chiefs suggested a neat alternative to Shiloah: that Israel should clandestinely participate in the strategic envelopment.

The developing views of Washington and London fitted in neatly with Israel's earlier discovery that it could profitably maintain secret contacts with its supposedly hostile neighbours. Shiloah himself took part in clandestine meetings with Trans-Jordan's King Abdullah and his prime minister, senior officials and military men over a three-year period. Only Abdullah's assassination in July 1951 prevented the signing of a peace treaty with Israel.[17] There were other contacts, often built on bribery, within the Egyptian and Iraqi leadership.

Shiloah realized, however, that the ability of Israeli agents to gain access to Arab leaders could not change the basic political and strategic facts of the Middle East: that the inner circle of Arab states would continue to hate the State of Israel and to object to its very existence.

Shiloah also knew that there were other geographic and ethnic factors in the Middle East. The inner circle was surrounded by an outer circle, the periphery, of non-Arab states; and the Arab states themselves had religious and ethnic minorities. The peripheral nations and the minorities suffered, as did Israel and the West, from the rise of Arab nationalism and radicalism. The idea which developed out of this assessment can be summarized in the dictum: the enemies of my enemy are my friends.

Any force which opposed or fought Arab nationalism

THE IMPERFECT SPIES

was considered to be a potential ally of Israel: the Maronite minority in Lebanon, the Druze in Syria, the Kurds in Iraq and the Christians in southern Sudan, who all suffered under the yoke of the Moslem majorities in their countries. The concept was known as 'the peripheral alliance', and Israel put its intelligence community in charge of this covert side of the nation's foreign policy. The Mossad usually had some assistance from, or coordination with, the CIA and MI6.

Together with the British and the Saudis, Israeli intelligence supplied finance and arms to the royalist forces in North Yemen between 1963 and 1965, to aid their fight against the republican regime and Egyptian military units. The Israelis wanted the Yemeni war to continue, because it kept the Egyptian Army far away and busy.[18]

For similar reasons, Israeli intelligence also began to foster ties with the Kurdish minority in southern Iraq. The Kurds were fighting against the central government in Baghdad to obtain autonomy. Shiloah had formed the first links with them in the 1930s, but the apex of the secret relationship came in the 1960s, when Israeli military experts advised and trained the fighters of Mustapha Barazani, the Kurdish leader of the rebellion. In 1966, Prime Minister Eshkol sent junior cabinet member Aryeh (Lova) Eliav – a legendary agent for special assignments – to the Kurds as his personal courier. The Israeli envoy and his team found themselves riding mules in the Western mountains of Iraq, carrying a field hospital for his Kurdish friends.[19]

American and British efforts to establish a clandestine pro-Western treaty with Israeli participation were particularly strenuous in 1958, when anti-Western, pro-Nasser nationalism was scoring impressive gains. Nasserists came close to gaining control of Lebanon. In Iraq, Colonel Qassem seized power after murdering Nuri Sa'id and the Hashemite royal family. Similar perils faced the Hashemite royal rulers of Jordan.

Washington and London advised Israel to participate in two cooperative groupings: the 'northern tier' of the peripheral alliance, tying Israel to Turkey and Iran; and the 'southern tier' linking Israel with Ethiopia. All these states bordered Arab countries, were involved in border disputes with them, and feared Soviet subversion as well as Arab nationalism. Turkey was high on the list.

In December 1957, the Turkish Prime Minister Adnan Menderes met a special emissary from Israel, Eliyahu Sasson, and arranged a follow-up session in June 1958 for intelligence officials of the two nations. The Israeli team was headed by Shiloah, even though he had not held any official Mossad position for years. Both Prime Minister Ben-Gurion and Foreign Minister Meir believed that Shiloah was the most appropriate person for these secret missions. Ben-Gurion himself flew to Ankara to see Menderes in August and Meir saw officials in Istanbul.[20]

Shiloah reached an agreement for comprehensive co-operation between the Mossad and the Turkish National Security Service, the TNSS. Around the same time, a similar pact was agreed with SAVAK, the Farsi acronym for *Sazmani-Amniyat Va Kisvar*, the State Intelligence and Security Organization.

At the end of 1958, the three secret agencies established a formal cooperation group called Trident, which held half-yearly meetings of all three service chiefs. The co-operation agreement with Turkey allowed the Mossad to gather intelligence on the activities of Soviet spies in Turkey, and the Israelis told the Turks about Soviet operations against Turkey from elsewhere in the Middle East. Turkey helped by passing on information which its agents had collected, primarily on Syria's intentions towards Israel. The Israelis also trained Turkish secret agents in counterespionage techniques and the use of technological devices.

In the case of Iran, the clandestine cooperation can be traced back to Zion Cohen, the Aliyah B agent who was recognized in 1949 by the authorities in Teheran as *de facto* representative of the Israeli Government. Iran's national airline agreed to fly Jewish refugees, who had crossed the border illegally from Iraq, directly from Teheran to Tel Aviv. After British and American agents arranged the overthrow of Prime Minister Mohamed Mossadegh in 1953 and restored the Shah to his throne, all the parties involved reached the conclusion that their interests required further cooperation among the intelligence services. Senior Mossad officials, led by Isser Harel and his deputy Yaakov Karoz, met in Paris and Rome in September and October of 1957 with SAVAK's first chief, General Taimour Bakhtiar.

Israel's main goal in its ties with Iran was to encourage pro-Israeli and anti-Arab views among Iranian government officials. The relationship was deep and all-embracing. The Mossad helped train SAVAK agents and then worked with the Iranians to aid the Kurdish rebellion against Iraq.[21]

Whether the joint projects were military or civilian in character, Israel put its intelligence community in charge of them. On the Iranian side, the Shah, his own family, or trusted aides personally supervised the cooperation and often reaped financial gain.

Visiting Tel Aviv on July 18, 1977, Iran's deputy defence minister Hassan Tufanian, according to a top secret Israeli memorandum, told Defence Minister Ezer Weizman: 'You and we in Iran can be two defence fortresses, and we can cooperate together. We are the only two countries in the region that can depend on each other.'

Weizman, pressing for joint military projects, urged Tufanian to finance the development of various missiles. 'You must have a ground-to-ground missile, a country like yours. You will see the firing tomorrow,' Weizman said of one new weapon. 'You will enjoy it. It is a very impressive piece of machinery. We started working on it in 1962.'

The Iranian general, in reply, pressed for intelligence: 'There is something started in India. What is your information about that?'

Weizman, turning to an aide, said: 'The Indians are very careful with us, aren't they?'

The Israeli assistant replied: 'They are, but we can find out.'

Weizman assured his Iranian friend: 'Any intelligence you want, let me know.'[22]

Iran decided to participate in joint ventures and purchased huge quantities of Israeli weapons, amounting to $225 million in 1978 and including Uzi submachine guns for the Shah's imperial guards. Iran's fighter aircraft were maintained by Israel Aircraft Industries and Iran became the largest supplier of oil to Israel.

Several corporations, owned jointly by the Israeli Government and the Shah's relatives, were established, including a shipping line named Trans-Aseatic, with tankers carrying oil directly from Abadan to Israel's southern port, Eilat. There was also the company which ran the Eilat-Ashkelon oil pipeline, where Iran's part-ownership was such a secret that even the US was amazed when it found out. An American analyst noted with surprise: 'His Imperial Majesty said it was open to Iran to use the Israeli pipeline, particularly since they had an interest in the line.'[23]

Iran was one of Israel's most important allies, until the Ayatollah Khomeini toppled the Shah and turned Iran into an Islamic republic in 1979. Then, the Israelis fled.

The ups and downs of the northern tier of their peripheral alliances were mirrored in the southern tier, in Africa.

Sudan provided a further playground for Israel to manipulate events for its own purposes and adapt them when necessary. In 1954, when Sudan was in transition to independence, under joint British and Egyptian administration, Egypt's President Nasser tried to intervene in the general election. In Cairo, slogans called for 'the unity of the Nile valley', and in Sudan's capital, Khartoum, the officers in the ruling clique feared that Nasser might attempt to occupy their country.

Members of the populist Umma Party and nationalist Mahdia movement rushed to London, hoping for guarantees of British support against Egypt. Nasser's plan to nationalize the Suez Canal and expel British troops from the canal zone seemed likely to help the Sudanese gain sympathy. They were also banking on Prime Minister Anthony Eden's hatred for Nasser.

The Sudanese delegation was not satisfied, however, with London's response. The Foreign Office, as opposed to MI6, believed in appeasing Nasser. The Sudanese happened to mention to MI6 contacts that they were even willing 'to join with the Devil' to halt Egypt's expansionism. This led the British intelligence men to suggest that they should indeed deal with the Arab world's Satan – namely, Israel. The Israelis – with British help – would teach Sudan to develop its cotton fields, based on Israel's own success in making the desert bloom.

The populist parties ended up losing the election, but secret contacts between Sudan and Israel continued until 1958. Their highpoint was reached at a clandestine meeting in August 1957, at the Plaza Athenée Hotel in Paris, between the Israeli Foreign Minister, Golda Meir, and Abdallah Khalil, the Sudanese Prime Minister. The contacts ended abruptly the following year, when Khalil was overthrown by his army.

New leaders came and went in Khartoum until 1969, when Colonel Gaafar Numeiri took over in yet another military coup. He established a Free Officers' Movement, emulating Nasser – a move which only intensified the civil war which had been tearing Sudan apart for some years. The rebels were the tribes in the South, mostly black African Christians, who felt they were discriminated against by the Arab central government. They established the Nile Liberation Movement and a military wing known as Anya-nya, complete with European mercenaries who were veterans of the Belgian Congo's civil war.

From the moment that Numeiri seized power, the Mossad decided – in coordination with the CIA and MI6 – to help the Sudanese rebels. The Israeli concept was divide and rule, to foment disagreements within the Arab world. The logic was simple. Anya-nya was fighting Numeiri. Numeiri was Nasser's friend. Nasser was the enemy of Israel, so Israel would side with Anya-nya.

Mossad agents arrived from their stations in Nairobi and Addis Ababa to coordinate military aid for the guerilla fighters. For a number of months, Israeli cargo planes flew over the Red Sea and dropped firearms, ammunition and medical equipment into southern Sudan for the rebels. Military advisers trained Anya-nya fighters in guerilla warfare.[24]

With almost clockwork precision, the Israeli pendulum swung back precisely ten years later. The Mossad's aid to the rebels ended and Israel was again working with the central government in Khartoum. The Israelis found that their interests lay in cooperating with President Numeiri once it became clear that he was pro-Western.

Further east, the Israelis, Americans, and British found Ethiopia to be a more stable, pro-Western country, and obviously of prime strategic importance, overlooking as it does the sea lanes leading into the Red Sea and on towards Suez and Eilat. Trade relations were used to advance clandestine diplomatic relations with Ethiopia's Emperor Haile Selassie, who considered himself a descendant of the ancient Hebrew tribe of Judah and used its symbol, a lion, as his emblem.

After an Israeli consulate was opened in Addis Ababa, the diplomats were followed by agricultural advisers, professors who founded the University of Addis Ababa and, of course, military advisers and intelligence personnel. The Israelis helped the Ethiopian emperor train his security forces and Israel was permitted to build a powerful listening post which monitored Arab radio traffic.

A company named Red Sea Incoda served as the springboard for the penetration of the southern tier. It was owned by the government of Israel and based in the French colony of Djibouti, also vitally important because just a short and easy voyage across the Bab el-Mandeb strait lay Yemen, with Saudi Arabia beyond.

The company bought meat in Asmara, in the Eritrean province of Ethiopia, and employed ritual slaughterers and rabbis to make sure it was kosher. The beef and lamb were warehoused in Djibouti, and then transferred by ship to Israel. As for what meat has to do with intelligence and strategic interests, Israel, in its political isolation and economic fragility, has always sought reliable sources for its essential commodities – such as the Iranian oil. Most of Incoda's business was genuine business, but it was also used for other purposes.

From time to time, the company found itself engaged in the good works called intelligence. Incoda could be trusted to carry out its assignments, especially after Asher Ben-Natan was appointed company manager in 1953. After resigning two years earlier from the Political Department, he had been forgiven by Ben-Gurion for the revolt of the spies. 'The Old Man' gave Ben-Natan the directorship in Djibouti.

Incoda's radio transmitter was used to send intelligence messages, especially information obtained about Arab activity in Ethiopia. The French authorities in Djibouti turned a blind eye to the espionage side of the meat company.

In the coming years, the link with France would be of tremendous value – and of far more strategic importance than oil, meat or listening posts.

4

Lakam and the Nuclear Bomb

'Pack your bags at once,' was the message received in September 1956 on the radio at the Red Sea Incoda company in Djibouti. A few days later, Asher Ben-Natan flew back to Tel Aviv and went straight to the Ministry of Defence.

He was greeted by the young director-general of the ministry, Shimon Peres who said, 'The Old Man wants you to leave for Paris immediately to renew your contacts from your Political Department days. You'll be a special represen-tative of the defence ministry for all of Europe. But it is better that you don't ask too many questions. Everything will be clarified soon.'

About a month later, on October 23, Ben-Natan believed that the smoke was finally clearing. He was at a heavy wooden table in a private villa in a suburb of Paris and pinched himself to believe what he was seeing.

Around the table sat more than a dozen men, including two famous Israelis: the Prime Minister and Minister of Defence, David Ben-Gurion, and the Chief of Staff of the army, Moshe Dayan, with his black eye patch, a constant reminder of a wound he had suffered in action, in 1942, on behalf of British intelligence against the French Vichy forces in Syria.

Ben-Natan focused primarily, however, on several characters who were less well known to him. Settling into their chairs were the French Prime Minister Guy Mollet, Defence Minister Maurice Bourges-Maunoury, Foreign Minister Christian Pineau and various assistants and advisers, some of them wearing army uniforms and others in civilian clothes. Facing them was Selwyn Lloyd, Great Britain's Foreign Secretary, surrounded by his advisers.[1]

History books refer to this meeting as the 'Sèvres Conference', that being the name of the Parisian suburb where the secret talks took place. At the end of exhaustive discussions, the final details were hammered out for the war that would be known in Israel as the Sinai campaign and worldwide simply as Suez.

On October 29, Israeli paratroops and ground forces began moving into Egypt – across the Sinai and towards the Suez canal. In accordance with the Sèvres plan, France and Britain then issued an ultimatum to the armies of Israel and Egypt, instructing them to freeze their forces several miles from the canal. As agreed, Israel accepted; but Egypt refused. The French and British had got their excuse to drop paratroops into the canal zone on November 5 and to take over the strategic waterway.

The Israeli army, meanwhile, had completed the rapid conquest of the Sinai. It appeared that the goal of the Sèvres Conference had been achieved and the many months of planning by military men and intelligence services had borne fruit.

Israel's aims in the war were to destroy the Egyptian Army, which was benefiting from Soviet-bloc aid, and to break the Egyptian blockade of the sea lane to Eilat. Publicly, Israel said that it was trying to stop Palestinian terrorist attacks from Egypt.

British Prime Minister Anthony Eden, motivated by his

pathological hatred for President Nasser of Egypt, hoped to restore British control over the canal which Nasser had nationalized. Eden expected – with the French – to get rid of Nasser, who was riding a wave of radicalism in the Middle East against Western interests.

The French were primarily concerned in stopping Nasserism, the great inspiration to the FLN, the National Liberation Front, which was fighting the French occupying forces in Algeria.

Even before the Sèvres Conference, France had begun to arm Israel for the war to come. Since April 1956, French cargo planes and ships had arrived in the darkness of night and unloaded an abundance of weaponry: tanks, fighter planes, cannon and ammunition.

The project required close intelligence cooperation. The head of Military Intelligence, General Yehoshafat Harkabi, was sent to Paris for talks with his counterparts in French military and civilian intelligence. They decided to institutionalize the contacts, so a permanent Military Intelligence representative was stationed in France. Isser Harel, by now directing both the Mossad and Shin Bet, protested this independence, which he found excessive. He demanded a monopoly for himself of the contacts with French civilian intelligence, but Harel was forced to back down – not the only time he would be forced to do so.[2]

Israel and its partners also dabbled in some disinformation. Israeli intelligence operatives, just a few days before the Sinai attack, made a point of spreading false rumours that Israel was planning to attack Jordan. After all, Palestinian guerillas, frustrated by the lack of progress towards solving their problem, were infiltrating into Israel with frightening regularity. The deception was successful, and the CIA's James Angleton assisted by keeping the truth under his hat. If President Eisenhower did know, he certainly acted as if he were totally surprised and hurt.

Both Israel and Britain had thought that the US would take their side, as part of the strategic alliance built up by their intelligence agencies, but they were sorely disappointed. The Americans and the Soviets, for different reasons, forced the Suez invaders to withdraw. The humiliation dealt the final blow to the British and French claim to be superpowers.

Despite its military victory, Israel suffered a severe political defeat: its image as a progressive, socialist state seeking peace was cast in the shadow of involvement in an imperialist plot. Beneath the surface, however, lay the larger truth: Israel was now an ally of France. This alliance, which was dubbed 'the bridge over the Mediterranean',[3] enabled Israel to establish a nuclear conspiracy.

The notion that Israel, a small state in the Middle East, would be capable of developing nuclear weapons was considered by some to be presumptuous, rash and financially insane. Only the four victors of World War II had nuclear arsenals. And yet, far before the Sinai campaign, Ben-Gurion set his sights extremely high. He had even begun examining the possibility of building a nuclear reactor in Israel in the midst of the 1948 war.

The Prime Minister had summoned an expert from Paris, Maurice Surdin, who was described in Ben-Gurion's diary notation of December 20, 1948, as 'the builder of the French atomic oven'. A Jew born in the Crimea in 1913, he moved to Palestine as Moshe Surdin but later settled in France where he studied physics. He was involved, after World War II, in a project of CEA, the French Commission for Atomic Energy which developed the French atom bomb.

'Ben-Gurion was very interested in the topic, the atom,' Surdin recalls. 'He was very interested in the details.'[4] Nothing came of the meeting, but Ben-Gurion and his cluster of young advisers refused to abandon the idea. They envisioned the acquisition of nuclear power as compensation for Israel's tiny size and meagre human resources.

Ben-Gurion and his aides sought to develop a nuclear option in the belief that it would serve as a final guarantee for the continued existence of the Jewish state.

General Dayan, an enthusiastic supporter of the idea, spelled out his philosophy in more precise terms: 'If the arms race continues in the Middle East – and it will continue and get worse – we will reach the stage when there will be a tank in every Israeli courtyard; at the entrance to each home there will be an armoured personnel carrier; and on the roof will be a helicopter. The state will simply go bankrupt. Israel is like the body of a mammoth – that is, the army – supported upon the two financial limbs of a stork. We need to have a small army, which is efficient, cheap, even professional, for ongoing security and for limited engagements – with nuclear weapons for a general confrontation. Otherwise, we will regress to economic strangulation.'[5]

Israel's cabinet formed the Israeli Atomic Energy Commission, the IAEC, in 1952. Its chairman was Professor Ernst David Bergman, a brilliant chemist born in Germany in 1903, who moved to Palestine in the early 1930s and founded the science corps of Israel's army. While researching cancer, Bergman was also director of the defence ministry's science department and a leading supporter of the nuclear option.

Almost at every opportunity, Ben-Gurion and his team, including scientists, considered the possibilities of purchasing a nuclear reactor. The chance presented itself in 1955, when President Eisenhower's 'Atoms for Peace' programme provided a small, five-megawatt research reactor at Nahal Sorek, ten miles south of Tel Aviv. The facility, however, was limited by American inspections and the reactor was too small to produce anything of potential military use.[6]

Shimon Peres saw a one-time opportunity to obtain something bigger – from France. This came after January 1955, when Guy Mollet's socialist government took power in Paris. Mollet took a tough line on Algeria and thus had much in common with Israel's anti-Nasserist views. The fact that Israel had a socialist administration also helped.

Whenever Peres was in France, which was often, he raised the possibility of purchasing a reactor. He acted in the capacity of diplomat, intelligence officer and arms buyer. Foreign Minister Golda Meir did not care for such hyperactivity and her complaint against Peres was that he was turning the defence ministry into a second, independent foreign ministry. But there was more than that to the protest: Meir and the 'old guard' of the ruling Mapai Party did not want Israel to go nuclear.

Peres, however, had the total backing of Ben-Gurion and he was therefore able to continue his efforts. In the months before the Sinai Campaign, Peres's request for a reactor became an integral part of the secret collusion between the two countries.

The French had no moral qualms about sharing nuclear knowledge. After all, they had developed their own nuclear programme secretly in two stages. First, they built reactors for civil needs, and only in 1954 for military needs. France ignored the strong opposition expressed by the US to its nuclear independence.

The turning point came on September 21, 1956, in a country villa about a hundred miles south of Paris. There, Peres met Bourges Maunoury, the Defence Minister who was busily planning the attack on Egypt. The French were beguiled by the notion that Israel would take part, hoping that Israel's troops would do the dirty work for them.

On that autumn day, Bourges Maunoury sought to ensure Israeli participation by acceding, finally, to Peres's repeated requests on the nuclear front. On behalf of the French government, the defence minister offered the Israeli a sweetener in the form of a reactor.[7] For the first time in human history, one state had agreed to supply nuclear know-how to another, without requirements for safeguards and inspections.

Only now did Ben-Natan understand the true reason why he had been appointed as the ministry of defence's representative in Europe. He had not been sent to Paris to aid in the preparations for the Suez invasion, but to help acquire a second Israeli reactor. Reinforcing Peres's arguments, Ben-Natan lobbied in various French ministries for the idea of a large reactor, not just the small installation the French may have had in mind.

The Israelis knew that time was running out. The French

Fourth Republic was on the verge of collapse. The public had had enough of political instability and governments collapsing every few months. Many were calling for the return to power of the hero of the Second World War, General Charles de Gaulle. Peres and Ben-Natan knew that whoever would succeed the socialist government in Paris would undoubtedly refuse Israel's nuclear request.

Bourges Maunoury, now Prime Minister, knew this full well. On his last day in office, literally a few hours before his government fell in a no-confidence vote in the National Assembly, he granted Israel's request. On October 2 and 3 1957, Bourges Maunoury and Foreign Minister Christien Pineau signed two top secret documents with Peres and Ben-Natan: a political pact outlining the scientific co-operation between the two nations; and a technical agreement to supply a large, 24-megawatt reactor, with the necessary technicians and know-how.[8]

Even as Israel finally obtained its large nuclear reactor, there was growing concern among scientists and some senior politicians that a dangerous nuclear arms race could follow. Seven of the eight members of the IAEC resigned in protest and formed the Committee for the Denuclearization of the Middle East Conflict. There were heated debates, but the subject was shrouded in such deep secrecy that the arguments were never made public.

This did not seem to disturb Ben-Gurion and his 'young Turks', who still had Professor Bergman as a one-man IAEC and put him in charge. If anything, they were pleased that fewer people would now have the privilege of knowing about the project.[9]

It was considered the ultimate secret of the Jewish state and the nuclear programme was subject to more security measures than anything else in the history of a country, already prone to secrecy.

Peres, knowing that knowledge is power, insisted on keeping it out of the hands of others. This was the defence ministry's darling project. Therefore, he did not ask the existing intelligence community – as might be expected –

to take care of the security and secrecy aspects of the project. He believed that now Israel was deciding to become a nuclear power, it needed a nuclear intelligence agency. Until then, the responsibility for obtaining technical and scientific information lay with Aman and the Mossad. Peres, however, established a new secret agency and put Binyamin Blumberg in charge of it.

Blumberg was an experienced security officer, with many years in pre-State defence and intelligence affairs. After 1948, he joined the ranks of Shin Bet, where he was responsible for the maintenance of security inside the ministry of defence. He never needed any lectures or guidelines on how to maintain silence. He himself was the high priest of secrecy.

When he left Shin Bet, on Peres's invitation, he moved to a modest office in the defence ministry. To conceal his work, he named his new unit the Office of Special Assignments.

A few years later, the name was changed to *Lishka le-Kishrei Mada*, the Science Liaison Bureau or SLB, which the few insiders who knew about the agency called Lakam, its Hebrew acronym. The unit then moved from the defence ministry compound to an office building on Carlebach Street, in central Tel Aviv.

Backed fully by Peres, Blumberg tried to conceal the existence of the agency even from the other branches of the intelligence community – even from Isser Harel. 'Lakam was established behind my back and without my knowledge,' Harel, head of the Mossad and Shin Bet in those days, recalls angrily. 'I had my suspicions. I knew that someone was running around the ministry of defence dealing with various matters and that when he saw anyone from the Mossad, he would make a point of crossing to the other side of the street. It was a mysterious body, formed in a conspiratorial manner. Deceptively. Even Ben-Gurion did not know of the establishment of the experimental unit from which Lakam grew.'[10]

Blumberg was not bothered by the complaints and envy.

His concern, in this regard, was to seal the reactor project from any leaks, and this he successfully did.

Israel constructed its nuclear facility, under strict secrecy and with active support from France, in the Negev desert – in the middle of nowhere, midway between the Dead Sea and Beersheba, the Negev's 'capital'. Hundreds of French technicians and advisers were involved under the bilateral agreement and all requisite equipment was shipped in from France.

To conceal the three years of heavy construction – near the immigrants' town of Dimona – Israel used the cover story suggested by Blumberg: that a 'textiles factory' was being built. The security chief was able to protect the secret on the ground, but a gathering storm came in by air. On a high-flying reconnaissance mission, an American U-2 jet photographed the facility and US intelligence analysts had no trouble identifying its true purpose.

Foreign newspapers began to speculate about the Dimona project and domestic political pressure forced Ben-Gurion to admit, in the Knesset in December 1960, that Israel was building a second nuclear reactor – for peaceful purposes, he assured Israel's parliament. The Prime Minister made his partial disclosure for another reason, not known at the time: pressure from Paris.

As early as 1958, when de Gaulle became President, the French attitude towards Israel began to change. De Gaulle aimed at reconciliation with the Arab world and even offered independence to Algeria – a policy which would be at the expense of Israel. He also suspected that the Israelis planned military uses for their Dimona reactor. Israel should have anticipated trouble, but Peres was such a francophile that he reassured his colleagues that the 'bridge over the Mediterranean' would never collapse.

The Israelis eventually understood the new realities, and Ben-Gurion flew to Paris to see de Gaulle on June 13, 1960. Meeting in the Elysée Palace, they reached a compromise. The French President asked bluntly: 'Why does Israel need a nuclear reactor at all?'

Ben-Gurion promised it would only be for peaceful uses. He flew home, repeated his reassurances in the Knesset, but did not mean what he said. It was business as usual on the nuclear front – or almost as usual because it would become even more clandestine.

The 24-megawatt heavy-water reactor at Dimona could produce enough plutonium for at least one Hiroshima-sized, 20-kiloton bomb each year, but the crucial question was whether the French would also supply Israel with a reprocessing plant capable of extracting the plutonium from the reactor's spent fuel rods. François Perrin, son of a Nobel laureate and the scientific head of the French *Commissariat à l'Energie Atomique* from 1951 to 1970, indicated that reprocessing was an indirect part of the original 1957 agreement. While his commission, under de Gaulle's new policy, had refused to supply a reprocessing plant, it had also turned a blind eye to Israel's attempts to obtain one. Furthermore, it had even permitted a private company named St Gobain, which supplied these plants for France's military reactors, to sell its technology and plans to the Dimona project.[11]

As Israel faced a more difficult task in obtaining what it needed for nuclear development, Blumberg's Lakam recognized the need to expand its activities and, at times, to depend on cooperation from the other secret agencies. The old wounds began to be healed. Blumberg also introduced the work habits of a professional secret service: compartmentalization and the ability to work undercover in the field.

The cover was hardly a fiction. Lakam personnel were sent abroad as science attachés to the large Israeli embassies in Europe and the United States. Blumberg's people were required to report directly to his headquarters in Tel Aviv. The scientific advisers were required to purchase every publication in the field and to make social and professional connections with scientists in countries where they were posted.

Israeli scientists who travelled abroad on sabbaticals or research projects were asked to do favours for Lakam, although they usually did not know who precisely was asking. For their government, they would keep their eyes open for the latest developments in their fields and would obtain manuals, plans, and publications. There was no need to apply pressure to persuade most of the scientists. Their institutes belonged to the Israeli Government and the universities are closely linked to the establishment, as well as benefiting from government finance. Like most Israelis, scientists are brought up on patriotism.

In a few cases, Israeli scientists were even asked to steal scientific material. This was often done in an amateurish fashion, which was liable to endanger both the scientists and those who served as the equivalent of their 'case officers' – generally the science attachés – who enjoyed diplomatic immunity.

One senior Israeli scientist, who was studying in an important scientific institute in a West European country, tells of secretly photocopying various documents on a regular basis. He brought the copies home and once a week the scientific attaché of the Israeli embassy would come to pick them up. But the attaché displayed an unconscionable lack of responsibility, sometimes arriving late for meetings or not showing up at all. The two were lucky that the host country suspected nothing.

It is doubtful whether these dangerous and borderline cases came to the attention of Blumberg. Even if reports did reach him, they were insignificant when compared with the tremendous success of his venture overall. In the early 1960s, when diplomatic troubles were brewing with France, Blumberg began to seek alternative sources of supply for the Dimona reactor. The first success was with Norway. The Oslo government agreed to a secret sale of 21 tons of heavy water to Israel.[12] As soon as this supply was guaranteed, Lakam began to look for uranium. An important source was found in the person of Zalman Shapiro.

Shapiro was born in 1921 in Canton, Ohio – an American with a keenly felt Jewish background. His father was an Orthodox rabbi of Lithuanian origins and the younger Shapiro had suffered anti-Semitic abuse. Also, many members of his family had perished in the Holocaust. He earned a PhD in chemistry in 1948. It was the year that the State of Israel was proclaimed and that provided great inspiration to Shapiro. He joined the Zionist Federation and the Friends of the Technion, Israel's top technological university.

At the Westinghouse Corporation, he worked on constructing the *Nautilus*, the first nuclear submarine of the US Navy. In the mid-1950s he started his own company, Numec, the Nuclear Materials and Equipment Corporation, in Apollo, Pennsylvania.

Shapiro's company supplied uranium for nuclear reactors in the US, but the company seemed to have an inordinate number of foreign visitors, mainly from France and Israel. This did not escape the notice of the US Atomic Energy Commission, which in 1962 rebuked the company for its lax security precautions and its slipshod record-keeping. It was only in 1965, however, that a routine AEC inspection made a significant discovery: Numec's warehouse records showed more than 110 pounds of enriched uranium to be inexplicably missing. Enriched uranium is used in the manufacturing of nuclear weapons.

The AEC investigators were unable to obtain clear proof that the material had been transferred elsewhere or that Numec had committed any crime. The FBI, too, which had been invited to investigate the case and had concentrated on Shapiro's relations with Israel, could not arrive at any clear conclusion. Federal authorities also ruled that Shapiro's limited ties with Israel did not require him to register as a foreign agent. By 1968, however, the suspicions had grown that the missing uranium had been sold or somehow shipped to Israel.[13]

The American intelligence community, believing that Israel had obtained a large quantity of enriched uranium, went into action. The CIA and the FBI began a thorough investigation. Shapiro was placed under surveillance, and his telephones were tapped. He was brought in for questioning and he told of a meeting he had had at Pittsburgh airport with Avraham Hermoni, the Lakam attaché in Washington.[14]

Israel was concerned about the new-found American attitude on the nuclear question. In previous years, largely due to the influence of James Angleton in the CIA, the US authorities had been content to let the Israelis do as they wished. In effect, Angleton was protecting Israel's nuclear secrets.[15] Now, Angleton's influence had diminished and the new CIA director Richard Helms was far more suspicious about Israel.

To ascertain the situation in Washington, four Israelis – including Hermoni, Raphael (Rafi) Eitan, and Avraham Bendor – dropped in on Shapiro's Numec plant. In an application for US government clearance, Eitan listed himself as a chemist with the Israeli defence ministry. He was, in fact, a Mossad agent, and Bendor was with Shin Bet. They were on special assignment for Lakam – now that Blumberg had repaired relations with the other secret agencies. Their objective was a form of damage assessment, to find out what the American authorities knew about the Israeli nuclear project.[16]

Eitan and Bendor would later occupy senior positions in Israel's intelligence community, and would be linked to a number of sensational cases – the most admired and the most condemned in the history of the secret services of the Jewish state.

In November 1968, in a joint operation with the Mossad, Blumberg's agents stole 200 tons of natural uranium – in 560 drums merely marked Plumbat – from the deck of a cargo ship. A German chemical corporation named Asmara, through subsidiaries, had bought the uranium from a Belgian company, *Société Général de Minaro*. The uranium was loaded at Antwerp harbour onto a ship named the *Scheersberg A*, which flew a Liberian flag of convenience. Its captain declared that the ship's destination was Genoa.

It never arrived in Italy and instead the *Scheersberg A* simply 'disappeared' from the registry. After entering the

Mediterranean, it had sailed east rather than south, where it should have headed according to its declared destination. Somewhere between Cyprus and Turkey, it had rendez-voused with an Israeli cargo ship. At the beginning of December, a few days after its brief disappearance, the *Scheersberg A* anchored in the port of Iskenderun in Turkey. There was no longer any uranium on board. The ship was owned by the Mossad and from amidst this confusion of countries and companies, Israel had managed to snatch fuel for the Dimona reactor.

The atomic energy agencies of the European Economic Community were so astounded and puzzled by the incident that they decided not to publicize it.[17]

Another coup enabled Israel to get its hands on 40 tons of uranium waste which had been bought in Luxembourg, transported to Britain and then transferred to the Jewish state. Israel's acquisition of all of these materials, plus the fact that the country bought uranium directly from South Africa,[18] made it clear that Israel was constructing something extremely secret at Dimona: an arsenal of weapons.

There is, by now, no doubt that Israel has become the sixth nation to have joined the nuclear club, together with the United States, the Soviet Union, France, Britain, and China.

Blumberg's appetite for action kept growing. He offered his services – and his offer was accepted – to act as a 'theft contractor', not only for the nuclear project, but also for the entire Israeli defence industry. Lakam's budget was paid by interested parties, either owned or controlled by the government.[19]

At the same time that Israel was in the process of con-structing its nuclear reactor, it decided on the need to acquire ground-to-ground missiles. This was certainly no coincidence, for there was little sense in developing nuclear weapons if there were no reliable means to deliver them to their targets. As Ezer Weizman once said, in a secret meeting when he was defence minister: 'All missiles can carry an atomic head. All missiles can carry a conventional head. They carry all sorts of peculiar heads.'[20]

Blumberg's men managed to obtain know-how from various sources and they kept up-to-date on the latest scientific and technological developments in the world. Lakam's efforts helped Israel know which weapons to seek from potential foreign suppliers. A large step forward came when France agreed to sell ground-to-ground missiles to Israel. Israel's speciality was adapting – not quite copying – the inventions of others. In Weizman's words, referring to the French: 'We improved their equipment.' Thus, the MD 660 missile provided by France begat a family of Israeli missiles: first the Luz, and then the Jericho.[21]

The 1967 war marked a turning point for Lakam, as for almost everything and everybody else in Israel. Thanks to its success in acquiring the needed nuclear materials, Lakam's assignments were extended to other fields of science and technology. A new challenge was the fact that President de Gaulle imposed an embargo, after the war, and even refused to deliver armaments, boats and aircraft previously paid for by Israel.

There were five missile boats, anchored in the harbour of Cherbourg, which the Israelis believed they owned but the French refused to deliver. Israel's secret agents resolved the stand-off by entering the shipyards, by a series of ruses well timed to succeed on Christmas Eve in 1969, and simply sailed off into the Mediterranean with the ships which the Mossad and Israeli navy believed to be rightfully theirs. The three-thousand-mile voyage ended with a jubilant public reception in Haifa.

Lakam's business flourished. Anything unobtainable by legal means was obtained by theft or bribery. An outstandingly valuable coup took place in Switzerland, where the Israelis penetrated a company manufacturing engines for the French Mirage warplane. It was a joint operation of Lakam, the Israeli army and the air force. They exploited certain weaknesses of a Swiss engineer, Alfred Frauenknecht: his resentment of his company, his need for money so as to afford having a mistress and his sympathy with Israel after the Six-Day War.

Colonel Dov Sion, Israel's military attaché in Paris who happened to be Dayan's son-in-law, took the first step. He met Frauenknecht a few times, took him out to dinner and sized him up. Before long, Lakam's agents found that the Swiss engineer agreed to supply blueprints for the Mirage – not only for the money, but also for ideological reasons. At first, he met Israeli operatives in hotels or restaurants, where he would hand over photocopies of the blueprints. To speed up the operation, Frauenknecht got his nephew to help him photograph documents, place them into boxes and deliver them to Israeli agents who took them to Germany. Eventually, these activities were noticed by the Swiss authorities, who arrested the engineer and quickly elicited a confession.

Frauenknecht said he had been promised a million dollars for the Mirage plans and had so far received $200,000 from the Israelis. On April 23, 1971, a Swiss court found him guilty of espionage, but he spent only a year in prison.

Within half a year, Israel was flying a new warplane, the Nesher, which had the benefit of some of the Mirage technology. On April 29, 1975, Israel proudly unveiled its latest jet fighter: the Kfir. It bore an uncanny resemblance to the French Mirage and the man responsible for that – Frauenknecht – was there. But the government did not even pay his airfare and refused to have anything to do with him. Overall, he felt forgotten and abandoned by his operators.[22]

While Frauenknecht became bitter, Binyamin Blumberg's reputation within the intelligence community grew to mythic proportions. Lakam's achievements led his colleagues to conclude that they were dealing with a real genius.

Lakam was a private fiefdom. Not only did Moshe Dayan continue to give Blumberg and his men full support, the Defence Minister was simply not interested in what Lakam was up to. He made his assistant, General Zvi Zur, responsible for Lakam's activities.

The general, who had been army chief of staff in the early

1960s, gave Blumberg a free hand, which extended even further when Shimon Peres, after an absence of eleven years, returned in 1974 to the defence ministry – this time as minister of defence.

Although Peres seemed to have no touble working with Blumberg, there were others who lodged various complaints against the Lakam chief. They questioned his financial judgments and his alleged favouritism toward his personal friends. Defence ministry authorities felt compelled to look into these charges, but they were never proved. On the contrary, the few people who claim to have known the inscrutable Blumberg describe him as modest and ascetic.

After Menachem Begin and his right-wing Likud bloc took office in May 1977, the efforts to dismiss Blumberg intensified. In the eyes of the new administration, he was linked to the old Labour Party establishment. The deputy minister of defence, Brigadier General Mordecai Zippori, suspected that some of Lakam's operations involved laundering money. In 1979, Zippori tried to persuade his boss, Weizman, to fire Blumberg on the grounds that there were no controls over him. Weizman, in response, convened a meeting and secured Blumberg's agreement to report to the minister in the future. At that meeting, the Lakam chief's critics claimed that he had a definite preference for sidestepping official channels in favour of certain Israeli businessmen. ...

In May 1985, the United States uncovered ties between a corporation named Milco of California and the Israeli ministry of defence. The connection had been made by a Hollywood-based Israeli who helped the ministry when he could. Milco's owner, Richard Smyth, was charged by a federal grand jury with smuggling 810 krytrons, electronic devices which can be used as detonators of nuclear bombs, to Israel. Smyth required a special licence to export krytrons, but had he applied for one the US Government would have refused on the grounds that Israel had not signed the nuclear non-proliferation treaty.

FBI investigators found that eighty per cent of Milco's business dealings were with Israel, and that these had begun as early as 1973. Smyth was freed on $100,000 bail, but three months later did not appear for his trial. He disappeared, though sightings of him were reported in Britain and in Israel.

Israel apologized to the US after the case hit the headlines, stating that the detonators were meant for medical purposes and had not been used in its nuclear programme. As the Americans demanded, all 'unused' detonators were returned.[23]

That year, a number of other incidents were reported in the US in which Israeli government corporations, such as Israel Military Industries, were involved in shady deals with American corporations. Some of the Americans were even put on trial. Government officials, especially in the US Customs Service and the FBI, did not hide their outrage at Israel's conduct.

For many years, the US Government refused to accede to Israel's request that Israeli defence ministry representatives, who were in America to purchase arms and equipment, be given diplomatic immunity – a status finally granted in 1988.

The American authorities were suspicious of the Israeli arms buyers, as they were of nearly every scientist who visited from Israel. Professor Yuval Ne'eman received just such a reception.

'Professor, I am from the department,' an unfamiliar voice on the telephone announced. 'Can we meet?'

Ne'eman, a famous Israeli physicist, was temporarily at a research institute in Pasadena and he thought that the person on the other end of the line was a member of one of the academic departments. To his consternation, the man who arrived for the appointment introduced himself as an investigator for the US Justice Department.

'Are you Colonel Ne'eman?' the investigator, who turned out to be an FBI agent, asked.

'Yes,' answered the Israeli, who explained that until the early 1960s he had indeed been a colonel in his country's military intelligence service, but had left the army years earlier and now worked at Tel Aviv University.

'But we know that you are still involved in spying,' said the American. 'I'd advise you to stop immediately.' Ne'eman vehemently denied the allegation, and the conversation ended on the spot.

A short time earlier, Ne'eman had visited the federal laboratories in Livermore, near San Francisco and one of its employees had evidently reported this to the FBI. Considering what the Americans had recently seen of Israeli activities, a tour of Livermore – where nuclear research was conducted – was enough to cause suspicion to fall on an Israeli professor. A little later, after Ne'eman moved to the University of Austin, in Texas, yet another justice department official paid a visit – demanding that Ne'eman register as a 'foreign agent' of the Israeli Government.

Doing so would have harmed Ne'eman's reputation as a physicist and would have seriously affected his ability to meet with colleagues. In addition, his movements within the US would have been restricted by law. Ne'eman tried to use his American contacts to prevent having to register. He turned to his friend, Professor Edward Teller, father of the US hydrogen bomb; he spoke to Senator John Tower of Texas; but it was all in vain.

This humiliating incident was only taken care of through the intervention of the Mossad. Its liaison officer in Washington approached the CIA about Ne'eman. According to American practice, only if one of the intelligence agencies asks that a person's status as a 'foreign agent' be revoked, can this be done. The CIA, as in so many cases in the past, intervened on behalf of its Israeli counterpart. The threat against the Israeli professor was removed.

The astonishing fact in Lakam's history is that, despite all of its espionage activities, foreign intelligence agencies were not aware of its existence. A secret report written by the CIA in 1976 and purporting to survey the entire intelligence community of Israel, mentioned its high interest in science and technology but never referred to a Lakam or a Science Liaison Bureau.[24]

The Americans, the West Europeans, the Soviet bloc and even Israel's Arab enemies all showed a great deal of ignorance about Israeli intelligence. They identified the entire community totally with the Mossad. For almost all foreign analysts and so-called experts, the Mossad was a synonym for Israeli spies. The man who did the most to propagate that myth was Isser Harel.

5

Harel's Crusades

'Isser, I need five thousand dollars.' Dan Pines, an editor of the newspaper *Davar* had come to see Isser Harel on his first day as head of the Mossad, September 20, 1952.

'Why do you need the money?' asked Harel.

'What, you don't know?' Pines said with obvious surprise, as he launched into a long, complicated story about an espionage network he was running in the Soviet Union.

Harel listened patiently, but his instincts made him suspicious. He could hardly help it. 'Dan, give me a few days to acclimatize and I'll give you an answer.'

The Mossad chief smelled embezzlement; it was a sixth sense he had developed as head of Shin Bet. A commission of enquiry was appointed. As was the custom in the early days of the Jewish state, members of a commission of enquiry were selected only from the ruling Mapai Party and not from a mixed parliamentary committee. This guaranteed that anything embarrassing remained within the 'family' – especially intelligence affairs.

Pines was a respected journalist who used his close contacts with Ben-Gurion and cabinet ministers for personal gain. In December 1951, Pines persuaded Foreign Minister Moshe Sharett and Mossad chief Reuven Shiloah that he had established secret links with a senior Soviet government official.

With the activities of the Institute of Aliyah B being wound down, Shiloah was concerned that Israel was losing touch with the Jews of the Soviet Union. He believed Pines's claim that a Zionist underground could be formed in Russia and sent the journalist to Europe on this secret mission.

For nine months, exploiting Shiloah's lack of control over the intelligence community, Pines continued to deceive both the Mossad and Foreign Minister Sharett. The amateur spy claimed to have had secret meetings in Paris, New York and Copenhagen with emissaries of the Russian underground. Each time he returned to Tel Aviv, Pines received full reimbursement for his expenses – until Harel arrived on the scene.

The commission of enquiry found in March 1953 that Harel's suspicions were well founded. Pines had invented the Soviet Zionist cell, assisted by friends abroad who sent him telegrams and invitations without knowing what he was doing. Pines had cooked up the scheme because his daughter was very ill and he needed a great deal of money to buy her medication which was only available in Europe.[1]

The ease with which Pines deceived Shiloah could only be explained by the fact that this was a time of disarray in the intelligence community. The spy ring in Iraq had collapsed and rivalries had forced a reorganization of the secret agencies.

It was a definite pointer to the future that it was Harel who exposed the deceitful journalist. Ben-Gurion had chosen him to be Mossad chief, largely because of his suspicious mind.

Harel's dynamic rise was a logical result of new political circumstances. Four years after the State of Israel's birth, Ben-Gurion turned his attention to domestic issues: the absorption of hundreds of thousands of new immigrants, severe austerity measures and bitter political struggles. These concerned him more than foreign policy.

It was thus only natural that Ben-Gurion was more interested in Shin Bet than in the Mossad or Aman. Harel found the Prime Minister's door open to him, much more than it had been to Shiloah and his assistants.

When Shiloah resigned in September 1952, Harel became the 'emperor' of the Israeli intelligence community. Ben-Gurion created a special title for him: the *Memuneh*, 'the one in charge' of the intelligence community. He was also chairman of the *Va'adat*, the 'Committee' of the heads of the secret services. Shin Bet received a new nominal chief, first Yitzhak (Dizzy) Dorot and then Amos Manor – often referred to as Yoel Morag to protect his true identity. But Harel pulled all the strings in both Shin Bet and the Mossad.

Harel concentrated tremendous power within his grasp, more than any intelligence chief of any western power had ever been able to obtain. One man had powers equivalent to those of the FBI and CIA combined. Isser 'the Little', who had the qualities of both J. Edgar Hoover and Allen Dulles, enjoyed this unprecedented position and the unlimited trust and appreciation of Ben-Gurion.

In return, Harel displayed unlimited loyalty and agreed to undertake almost anything for the government. He happily transformed the intelligence community into a political tool of Ben-Gurion and his Mapai Party. The Prime Minister and his colleagues were democrats, but they could not resist occasionally identifying their political interests with those of the state. Harel sent agents, who were often reluctant, on what should have been police duties: to fight black marketeers and, together with Military Intelligence, to open thousands of letters sent abroad in a search for currency smugglers and subversives.[2]

Mapai's approach was simple. In a sense, part of the party's Bolshevik heritage led to an attitude of those who are not with us are against us. Accordingly, Shin Bet men were infiltrated into Israel's other political parties.

First, it was eyes to the Right. As a reflection of the gut hatred that Ben-Gurion felt for Menachem Begin, the former commander of the Irgun underground who now led the Herut political party, Harel kept Begin and his people under surveillance. Harel reported to the Prime Minister that Herut intended to establish 'a mini-underground' in the army.[3] The suspicions were groundless, because Begin had transformed himself into a true parliamentary democrat, but in the words of a Hebrew expression, Harel 'saw even the shadows of mountains as mountains.'

In the following months, Shin Bet broke several small and insignificant dissident rings which were linked to religious zealots and the political Right. One of them, calling itself *Brit ha-Kana'im*, the 'Covenant of the Zealots', fought to renew the ancient kingdoms of Israel in the old religious tradition. Bearded and garbed in the dark clothing of the Orthodox, these Jews set fire to cars, a restaurant and a butcher's shop that sold non-kosher meat.[4]

Shin Bet penetrated the zealots and then arrested them. It was clear that they were naïve amateurs, but Harel did his best to portray them as mortal dangers to democracy. Shin Bet was thus able to be depicted as an efficient and sophisticated organization – one to be feared.

Using similar public relations techniques, Harel took credit for foiling the attempted assassination of Transport Minister Ben-Zion Pincus. Shaaltiel Ben-Yair and two other young veterans of Lehi the notorious Stern Gang, were arrested on charges of plotting an anti-religious campaign. They allegedly intended to plant a bomb near the minister's home, as a protest against his introduction of public transport restrictions on the Sabbath. Buses were forbidden to travel on the Jewish day of rest, as part of a political deal between Mapai and the religious parties. Ben-Yair, who would later work in the intelligence community, was tried but acquitted for lack of evidence.[5]

After Harel finished building his reputation by liquidating the 'plots' on the Right, he turned his attention to the Left. He put political parties and publications under his microscopic scrutiny. The magazine *Ha-Olam ha-Zeh*, 'This World', was one of Shin Bet's prime targets. The weekly, a mixture of juicy gossip, sex scandals, and investigative journalism, advocated reconciliation with the Palestinian Arabs. Its editor, Uri Avneri, called on Ben-Gurion to show magnanimity by allowing the creation of a Palestinian state, despite Israel's victory in the War of Independence. In the early 1950s, that was sheer heresy. Ben-Gurion and his centrally controlled method of government were natural targets for the poisoned darts of the weekly. The ruling party hated Avneri and declared war on his magazine.

The political establishment organized a boycott against *Ha-Olam ha-Zeh*, but the publication had its loyal readers and circulation rose even further when it accused the Tel Aviv police chief of corruption. That charge was too much for Isser Harel. The police chief just happened to be Amos Ben-Gurion, the Prime Minister's son.

In an attempt to silence Avneri, Shin Bet began publishing its own weekly called *Rimon*, 'Pomegranate', on August 1, 1956. Harel tried to disguise the ownership of the new magazine, but its true proprietor was quickly discovered. *Rimon* launched a war of words against *Ha-Olam ha-Zeh*. It was really the mirror-image of Avneri's publication – but, unfortunately for Harel, clearly worse. After three years, even Shin Bet could not afford to finance *Rimon* any more and it folded.

The precedent that had been set was dangerous for a democratic state: the secret services had published their own magazine with a clearly political line, using taxpayers' money, in order to fight another publication.[6]

It was quite natural for Avneri to coin the phrase 'apparatus of darkness' to refer to Shin Bet. His magazine depicted the agency as a monster, which did not hesitate to use cruel methods to infringe civil rights. This may have been an exaggeration, but if there was a kernel of truth in *Ha-Olam ha-Zeh*'s depiction, it especially applied to Harel's treatment of the Israeli Left. The seeds of his firm anti-Communism and black-and-white outlook could be found in his personal background.

Born in 1912 as Isser Halperin in Vitebsk, in the Volozhin region of Czarist Russia, he was the youngest of four children of a Talmudic scholar and wealthy businessman. He would grow up much as he was as a child: short and hyperactive. These were exciting times and Harel recalls the visit of Soviet revolutionary Leon Trotsky to Vitebsk. Little Isser might well have been swept along with the revolutionary current, but for his thorough Jewish education. His father would read to his sons from Hebrew books and told them about Zionism.

Ironically, and this would not be the only irony in his life, Isser the teenager joined *Ha-Shomer ha-Tza'ir*, the leftist Young Guards, which later developed into the Mapam political party – hated by Harel in Israel.

In January 1930, one of the lucky few chosen by his Zionist movement, Isser Halperin was sent to Palestine and joined a kibbutz. After five years, Isser and his new wife Rivka left the kibbutz and opened an orange-packing business. When World War II broke out, he joined the Haganah and in 1944 its intelligence branch, Shai.[7]

His eight years in the underground were an excellent training ground for Harel, who had chosen a more Hebrew-sounding name, and prepared him for his post-war career. In the midst of the 1948 war, Ben-Gurion noted Harel's talents, and at age 36 he became the first director of Shin Bet – appointed at the Ben Yehudah Street meeting in June which reorganized Israeli intelligence.

Four years later, when Shiloah fell from grace in September 1952, Harel was also appointed head of the Mossad. At age 40, it was generally agreed that he looked at least 50. But Harel's tired, elderly appearance could be deceptive, for he had the limitless energy of a young boy. It was not the only paradox in his character.

In his personal work habits, Harel reflected the Soviet-Bolshevik style of the Israeli intelligence community. He probably could have risen quite high in the KGB establishment in Moscow – had he not hated the Russians so much.

The great majority of Israelis would have had no quarrel with his obsessive hatred of Communists, because Israel's Communist Party was certainly considered subversive by most citizens. As with other Communist parties in Europe, the Israeli party's loyalty was primarily to the Soviet church, its bible of revolution and its high priest Josef Stalin. In a Zionist state, they were not Zionists. The exposure of several Israeli Communists as spies was more than sufficient to justify the means taken by Shin Bet against the Communist Party – surveillance and wiretapping – but when Harel turned such methods against Mapam, he was going too far.

Mapam, a leftist party, was socialist but believed in the Jews' rights to have a state of their own. The party was more active than any other in building new Jewish settlements and kibbutzim. Its members served wholeheartedly in the army and several rose to very senior military ranks. On the other hand, when its leaders realized that Ben-Gurion wanted to turn Israel away from socialism, they angrily ceased all political cooperation with him. And when they worshipped Stalin as 'the sun of the nations', Harel did not need any substantial evidence to pounce on them.

On January 29, 1953, Natan Peled, the Mapam party secretary, opened his hands in a dramatic gesture at a Tel Aviv press conference and revealed a tiny radio transmitter. He told the journalists that the bugging device had been found under the table of the Mapam leader, Meir Ya'ari.

Peled said the party had long suspected that its private discussions were being leaked, somehow, to Ben-Gurion. The microphone and transmitter were found, he said, and then two burglars were discovered attempting to break into Mapam headquarters with skeleton keys. They were caught by party members and turned over to the police. The judge, Peled noted, had been extremely lenient – imposing a minimal fine and two-week prison terms – and did not care to investigate the circumstances. Peled wondered why.[8]

Peled offered his own answer. He said the two men were Shin Bet operatives dispatched by Harel, on orders from

Ben-Gurion and the Mapai Party. They denied the allegations, but Mapam had inside knowledge. The party had its own spies working in Shin Bet – part of a security department which spied on other parties and planted agents inside the intelligence community. Harel had fired a senior Shin Bet operative, Gershon Rabinovitz, as early as January 1951 for his pro-Mapam leanings. Other moles continued at work.

Harel made the Israeli Left, especially Mapam, his personal obsession. In his eyes, Mapam was an 'agent party' of the Soviet bloc. He even suspected that the party planned a military putsch, in which it would take over the country.

These suspicions against Mapam soon assumed new dimensions, when Harel discovered that two senior party members were Soviet spies. The *Memuneh* was positively angry when they tried to excuse their deeds with identical explanations to those given by the leaders of Mapam. They claimed they were Israeli patriots, who had been in contact with the Soviets to urge that Israel change its pro-Western orientation to a more balanced one.

In the first case, a Tel Aviv court sentenced Aharon Cohen to five years in prison for espionage. As a Middle East expert, he was arrested in 1958 by Shin Bet's counterespionage department after regular meetings with a Soviet diplomat stationed in Tel Aviv who was a KGB officer. Mapam leaders rushed to Cohen's support and accused Harel of using the case to attack the party. Cohen himself admitted, in his appeal to the supreme court, that he had met Russians but had not given them any secrets. The judges halved his prison term.[9]

The second Soviet agent linked to Mapam also claimed, until his dying day in prison in 1966, that he was innocent. Lieutenant Colonel Israel Beer argued that his motives were pure and patriotic. The evidence against him was incontrovertible, however, and the court had ample reason to sentence him to fifteen years in prison for espionage.

Beer was born in Vienna in 1912 and was a socialist from an early age. In his autobiography, he related how he joined Austria's Social Democratic Party and took part in street fighting against fascists before Hitler marched into Vienna in 1938. He volunteered for the international brigade fighting Generalissimo Franco in Spain and studied at the military academy in Austria. In 1938, Beer moved to Palestine, made known his military experience and was welcomed into the Haganah. His socialist views, his liberal education and his expertise in military matters helped him befriend the military leaders of the Jewish community.

After the 1948 war, when his hopes of becoming deputy chief of staff of the army were not fulfilled, he resigned and took up work as the military correspondent for an Israeli newspaper. Around that time, he swapped his political allegiance from Mapam, where he was in the party security department, to the more centrist Mapai. He befriended security chiefs including Shaul Avigur, Shimon Peres and even the Prime Minister. Ben-Gurion gave Beer access to his private diary and asked him to write the official history of the War of Independence. It was an excellent observation post, allowing Beer to see the most sensitive and secret documents on the defence of Israel.

When the nominal head of Shin Bet, Amos Manor, hesitated before taking action against Beer, Harel moved in. On March 31, 1961, he ordered Beer's arrest. He was caught red-handed by Shin Bet agents, while handing over a file of documents to Victor Sokolow, a KGB officer under diplomatic cover in Tel Aviv. The file contained extracts from Ben-Gurion's diary and a secret report on an Israeli defence corporation.[10]

Suspicions had begun to fall on Beer five years earlier. It was General Moshe Dayan who half-jokingly asked: 'What is that spy doing here?' This was just before Ben-Gurion, Dayan and their entourage went to France for their secret negotiations at Sèvres which sent Israeli, British and French troops to Suez. Dayan suddenly realized that Beer was at the clandestine assembly point, even though he was not going to fly to Paris.[11]

The driving force behind the suspicions against Beer was definitely Harel. Beer's troubles began with his unauthorized contacts with West German intelligence chief General Reinhard Gehlen of BND, the *Bundesnachrichtendienst* or Federal Intelligence Service.

Beer's autobiography reveals remarkable similarities to the British traitor Kim Philby. Both were Communist sympathizers, recruited by Soviet intelligence in the Spanish civil war as sleeper agents to be activated later. Beer, like Philby, penetrated the very heart of the security establishment of his own country, becoming a highly valuable asset of the Soviets and ending his career as a successful journalist.

In court, however, Beer admitted that he had invented his past. It was understood that he was simply a pathological liar who 'polished' his past. He had never received a doctorate in history, as he boasted, nor had he ever set foot in Spain. Confusion over who he really was became even greater when he went to the trouble, from prison, to deny totally his courtroom confession and to claim his original life story was true.

Despite the confusion surrounding Beer's personal past, Harel was able to discover the truth about his espionage activities. Beer had been 'awakened' in 1956 by a TASS journalist in Tel Aviv, who instructed the Israeli to penetrate West German intelligence.

Gehlen and his BND enjoyed a special place in NATO's plans for the defence of Europe in the 1950s. Gehlen had worked in World War II for Hitler's military intelligence, *Abwehr*, running spies in the Soviet Union. Now that he was working in coordination with the CIA and MI6, Gehlen had revived his sleeper agents in Russia and the Soviets were aware of the threat posed by BND. Moscow wanted someone to find out what Gehlen was doing, and Beer – a senior Israeli who would be trusted in Bonn – could probably find out.

The West Germans, anxious as always to please the Israelis, gave Beer a surprising amount of access to the German Army, NATO installations and American and other bases. Beer even obtained, for his Soviet handlers, the name of a contractor who had built US nuclear missile sites in

Europe. As a by-product of his espionage ventures, he gave the Soviets information on Israel's purchase of arms, visits by Israeli officers to Europe and the morale of Israel's army. The Russians paid him cash and it seems so banal that Beer simply spent all the money on women, bars and good restaurants.[12]

The truth is that even if Beer had never existed, the Americans would still have had good reasons to suspect the ability of the Israelis to prevent moles from penetrating their security establishment. Since its birth in 1948, little Israel was a big target for Soviet intelligence and a massive sieve when it came to leaking secrets. The Russians were interested in both its geographical location and its wide-spread contacts with the West. Soviet agents included Eastern European diplomats, journalists and scientific and commercial delegations.

A vast network of agents was needed to support this intensive activity and the Soviets had some sixty employees in their Tel Aviv embassy. Around half were agents of the KGB or GRU, the *Glavnoe Razvedyvatelnoe Upravlenie*, the military's Chief Intelligence Directorate of the General Staff. They recruited Israeli agents, often local Communists, but as they knew that these people were under suspicion and Shin Bet surveillance, the Soviets tended to prefer others in the Israeli establishment. From time to time, they were very successful.

In the summer of 1955, one of the wives of a senior Israeli diplomat in one of the Soviet bloc countries, returned to Israel for a visit. She met a Soviet diplomat and they became lovers. Shin Bet, watching the Russian, immediately found out, invited the woman to the agency's headquarters and asked her to break off all contacts with her lover.

At the same time, to protect the husband from being blackmailed, he was summoned, without explanation, to Austria. To his great astonishment, Harel was waiting for him in his hotel room in Vienna. Without mincing words, the *Memuneh* told the cuckolded diplomat the facts of life: his wife was sleeping with a Soviet and therefore he would

be transferred out of the Eastern bloc. The diplomat understood the necessity of the step, but he was, of course, very
shaken by both the adultery and his sudden career change.[13]

It is not surprising, then, that Israel's diplomats were
warned, before leaving for Eastern Europe, not to become
entangled in any love affairs. In fact, the foreign ministry
refused to send single men or women beyond the Iron
Curtain and security officers were posted in every embassy
to watch for potential blackmail. Such precautions, however, can never be foolproof, when human lust, passion and
weakness are at play.

In February 1959, a senior Israeli diplomat in Eastern
Europe received a letter which said:

Dear Sir,
Some time ago, a number of sensitive pictures came into
my possession, which testify to your intimate relationship
with Miss Dagmar Novotna. If I use these pictures for
blackmail against you or against the woman involved in
these pictures with you, it will no doubt be unpleasant
for you and for Miss Dagmar Novotna. I have thought
about it and have reached the following conclusion. The
matter can still be covered up – provided you come to
Vienna in the near future to speak to my assistant. He is
completely trustworthy. You must arrive in Vienna by
the end of February. I suggest that you stay at the Hotel
Sacher. I would request your reply within 14 days from
the receipt of this letter.[14]

The diplomat, in spite of the great unpleasantness to himself
and his family, informed the foreign ministry of the attempted blackmail. His superiors hurriedly removed him
from the Eastern bloc. On the other hand, they mistakenly
sent Ze'ev Avni there.

Avni's true name was Wolff Goldstein. He was born in
Switzerland to Jewish parents who were Communists.
When Vladimir Ilyich Lenin sought refuge before the
October Revolution of 1917, he stayed with Goldstein's

parents. As a youth, Wolff became enchanted with Marxism–Leninism. Soviet spies recruited him and he went to Moscow for an intelligence course with the intention of being planted in Israel's government. He arrived during the battles of 1948 and managed to join the foreign ministry with unbelievable ease. He joined the economics department which was so small that it urgently needed staff. As was the custom in those early days, Wolff Goldstein changed his name to its Hebrew equivalent, Ze'ev Avni.

While Avni was a minor Israeli functionary, he was sent on some important missions. At the beginning of the 1950s, he was stationed in the Israeli embassy in Brussels as an economics counsellor. At the time, secret negotiations were being held with West German officials on the payment of reparations to Israeli Jews who had suffered in the Holocaust. Avni reported regularly to the KGB on all aspects of the negotiations.

He was later posted to Belgrade, Yugoslavia, where he caused the greatest damage to Israel's secrets. His responsibilities involved commercial relations between the two countries, but because of a chronic shortage of manpower he was also allowed access to the embassy's top secret section: the communications and codes room. Avni learned to operate the code machines which were used for all communications between the foreign ministry in Israel and its embassy in Yugoslavia.

His willingness to work overtime at deciphering communications was accepted gratefully. Soon the Soviet spy had obtained the secret code of the Israeli foreign ministry and he passed it on to the KGB. The Soviets were thus able to record and decode all messages, including the most secret, from Israel's diplomats and intelligence agents operating at embassies in Eastern Europe.

Harel, constantly surveying the diplomatic lists with his good counterespionage instincts, found cause to doubt Avni and his enthusiasm. A trumped-up reason was used to summon him to Tel Aviv in April 1956. Unaware that he was in trouble, Avni flew home and was arrested by Harel's

Shin Bet. Under interrogation, Goldstein/Avni broke and confessed everything – a 'debriefing' which the Israelis found most useful. He was so cooperative that after being sentenced to fifteen years in prison, he was planted in the cell of another traitor, El-Ad/Frank of the spy ring in Egypt, as an informer for Shin Bet.

Goldstein/Avni was released after ten years. He went back to his childhood home in Switzerland, but returned to Israel a few years later. With the agreement of the intelligence chiefs, he assumed a new identity and took up residence in a farming community north of Tel Aviv where he works as a psychologist.[15]

It would be superficial to believe that Harel was only motivated, in his pursuit of Israeli traitors, by his personal hatred of Communism. As Shiloah before, Harel wanted to prove to the CIA that Israel was a reliable partner who could be trusted. As he was uncompromising by nature, a crusader in search of perfection, Harel tried to prove that he could be even holier than the Pope. If Allen Dulles of the CIA and John Foster Dulles, his brother in the State Department, saw a Red under every bed, Harel was out to demonstrate that even pink had to be eliminated from Israel's sheets.

The *Memuneh*'s disappointment was therefore great, when he discovered that Professor Kurt Sitta had penetrated Israel's scientific community. Sitta was born in 1910 in the Sudetenland in Czechoslovakia, to a German family – not a Jewish one. Sitta studied in Prague, where he was considered to be a genius in mathematics and physics. The Gestapo arrested him and he was imprisoned in the Buchenwald concentration camp because his wife was Jewish. He met senior Communist prisoners there, who, after the war, assumed high offices in Czech intelligence. After the war, they arranged a job for him in a special branch of Soviet bloc espionage.

After studying in Britain, Sitta became a physics professor at the University of Syracuse in New York, but the FBI concluded that he was a Communist spy. He was interrogated and offered the opportunity to be a double agent. It was under such circumstances that Sitta left the US in 1953 for Brazil. Two years later he was invited to lecture at the Technion in Haifa, Israel's foremost technological institute, where he quickly became chairman of the physics department.

Sitta's success, as a non-Jewish foreigner in Israel, provided a golden opportunity for the Czechs. An intelligence officer at their embassy in Tel Aviv met the professor frequently between 1955 and 1960.

On the clear and somewhat cool night of June 16, 1960, two men knocked on the door of Sitta's villa on Horeb Street, in an exclusive suburb of Haifa which faces the Mediterranean much as San Francisco overlooks its bay. The men were sent by Harel and they arrested Sitta on suspicion of spying for Czech intelligence.

Given Harel's reputation as an over-zealous spycatcher, Sitta's arrest sent shock waves through his friends in the Technion and the political leadership of Israel. They could scarcely believe the charges, but when some of them attended his trial they were shocked again by the extent of their colleague Sitta's espionage.

He had taken a special interest in the Israel Atomic Energy Commission run by Professor Bergman. It may have been coincidence but Sitta was arrested just two days before Israel's experimental nuclear reactor in Nahal Sorek was operational. The damage, however, that Sitta caused to Israel's scientific interests was much greater and it is not surprising that his name is mentioned in the same breath as the Rosenbergs in the US and Klaus Fuchs in Britain, who betrayed their countries' atomic secrets to the Soviet bloc.

Sitta was sentenced to five years in prison, but Israel – to end the embarrassment – hastened to commute his sentence and set him free to take up a new academic life in West Germany.

Harel and the Israeli secret services, on the other hand, launched efforts to repair the damage done to their record as molehunters, quite impeccable up until Sitta. They claimed he was but a small fish, recruited under blackmail – that Czechoslovakia would harm his elderly father still living there. Harel's version held that Sitta had only handed over insignificant information, not touching on nuclear matters. He also tried to blame the FBI for not giving Shin Bet information on Sitta's background.[16]

In defence of Harel, Shin Bet faced many limitations and difficulties in its first twenty years. It was a very small organization with only a few hundred employees and financial restraints, but a great many tasks were entrusted to it.

Shin Bet was divided into two divisions: support and operations. The support division had departments of administration, interrogation and legal counsel, technology, coordination and planning, and logistical supplies for operations.

The operational branch of Shin Bet had three departments.

Protective Security was responsible for guarding Israel's embassies and other representatives abroad, protecting the prime minister and other officials, and securing Israel's defence industry.

Arab Affairs had the primary task of monitoring subversion among the Arab minority within Israel's borders who lived under military administration until 1965.

Non-Arab Affairs, which was the largest and most important of the departments, with the mission of counter-espionage, surveillance of foreign diplomats and delegations, and fighting subversion by Communists and other political extremists.[17]

Israel learned, long ago, to make do with little. Most security services in the world assume that to keep a person under surveillance around the clock, thirty operatives are required to work in shifts. In the Israeli intelligence community, on the other hand, because of a serious and chronic shortage of manpower, this job is usually assigned to no more than ten agents, who have to work overtime and are stretched to the limit. They are often helped by cadets, for whom this is training for the future, when they will become full agents in the secret services.

If a suspect is an agent of a secret service, it is obvious that he has been given special training in how to shake off those who are trailing him. In the Communist countries, all members of any delegation are also given this training, including those who are legitimate visitors and not spies, so that they, too, will appear suspicious and throw the scent off the trail of the true espionage agents. Shin Bet has found its operatives trailing foreigners to supermarkets, department stores and other public places where surveillance is difficult, so that their time was wasted watching innocent people.

Shin Bet, therefore, has had to set its priorities with utmost care. Based on tips, suspicion, or purely by chance, the Israelis keep a close eye on some people and ignore others. The lack of human resources was the reason why Sitta was not deemed 'worthy', for many years, of being on a watch list. It was a fatal error.

The agency was also pressed by its duty to monitor the activities, not only of Communist nationals, but of the embassies of friendly countries including the United States.

In the first months of Israel's existence, the US Army attaché in Tel Aviv, Colonel E. P. Archibald, discovered that his telephone was bugged.

A year later, an Israeli agent attempted to blackmail an official of the American consulate in Jerusalem, hoping to force him to work for Israel. The consular clerk had an Israeli lover, who was being pressured to extract information from the diplomat. The authorities even concocted a story that the young woman needed an abortion.

In 1954, security officers at the US embassy in Tel Aviv found microphones which had been concealed in the ambassador's office. In 1956, bugs were found attached to two telephones in the home of the military attaché. Shin Bet also made crude attempts to seduce the American marines who guarded their embassy in Tel Aviv, using women and money.[18]

Most of these efforts produced nothing of value, but Harel continued to use his imagination and refused to be bound by etiquette or tradition. Above all, he believed in recruiting the best. He ordered all members of the community to keep their eyes peeled for those with potential and talent.

Harel himself persuaded Ben-Gurion in 1955 to recruit the most talented members of the former Lehi underground – despite the Prime Minister's distaste and dislike for them. In the strained and highly politicized atmosphere prevailing in Israel at that time, this was a move of unparalleled boldness. Right-wing former terrorists had been blocked from civil service jobs, even from teaching, on the grounds of being security risks. Harel, who had watched them closely, felt they had been neutralized, that they posed no real danger and that their experience in conspiratorial and underground techniques should be exploited.

The new Shin Bet and Mossad men included Yitzhak Yezernitzki, who changed his name to Shamir. He had served as head of the Lehi or Stern Gang, and would later become prime minister. Yaakov Eliav was sent to Spain. Yehoshua Cohen, who had been involved in the murder, in 1948, of United Nations mediator Count Folke Bernadotte of Sweden, was assigned to be Ben-Gurion's bodyguard. Shaaltiel Ben-Yair, who only four years earlier had been suspected of attempting to assassinate a cabinet minister, was sent under another identity to Egypt and became one of Israel's most successful agents.[19] David Shomron was posted to the Mossad station in Paris, and Eliyahu Ben-Elissar became a case officer in Europe. These right-wingers were eternally grateful to Harel for rescuing them from quarantine and giving them the opportunity to prove their value to Israel.

Harel instilled in his agents pride in belonging to an exclusive fraternity. 'You are rare creatures in a game reserve,' he would often tell his subordinates. The salaries paid to employees of Shin Bet and the Mossad were in line with those paid to ordinary civil servants, averaging around

$18,000 a year in Israel, around twice that amount on foreign assignment. But with all the demanding and dangerous work, day and night, meetings in railway stations, hotels or small restaurants, Harel demanded that his agents feel a sense of pride that they were in a community which was the cream of the crop.

His agents also knew that trips abroad, a rare luxury in those days and almost unavailable to the common Israeli, were one of the fringe benefits of their work. Those who toiled in the support division, not normally in the field, were also eligible for this fringe benefit. From time to time, technicians, mechanics, or secretaries were sent abroad on missions which did not require any specific skill, such as acting as couriers or for guard duty.

In return, Harel demanded from his men total loyalty and utter commitment to their assignments. Harel himself set the example: work, not waste. Rather than lodging himself in expensive hotels or eating at elegant restaurants, he would choose cheaper and more ascetic alternatives – even though he travelled frequently to Europe, the United States and South America.

When, in the 1950s and 1960s, there were severe restrictions in Israel on foreign currency and the amount permitted an ordinary Israeli leaving the country was $100, members of the intelligence community were given special authorization to take out large sums of money. After all, this money was meant to finance special operations, to pay informers, for the agents' expenses and for bribery. Harel would return whatever money he had left at the first bank he saw upon arriving at Lod airport.

Operatives did not have to supply receipts for their expenses. Their word of honour and a written report, when they returned, were sufficient. Lurking beneath the honour system, however, was a strong hand with regard to financial matters.

If an agent was caught lying or misappropriating funds, even a few measly dollars, or if he did not have a satisfactory explanation for his expenses, he was subject to a disciplinary hearing before a special internal court of the intelligence community, headed by a judge selected from the judicial service. Anyone found exploiting the intelligence profession by smuggling home appliances, televisions, or later, video cassette recorders into Israel was fined and warned. In severe cases, the person was dismissed immediately.

Such was the case with an Israeli agent who was sent to Europe to meet two informers who worked for him in one of the Arab countries. He wined and dined them for a number of days and gave them a good time, including visits to brothels. When the case officer returned to Tel Aviv, he gave a detailed report of his expenses. Among others, he included the cost of the prostitutes. His superior at Mossad headquarters was not pleased: 'I certainly understand the need to spend money on your agents,' he said, 'but why the hell does the State of Israel have to pay for your whoring?'

The officer was formally rebuked and the Mossad accountants also took a closer look at his previous expense reports. These, too, showed dubious entries and the man was fired without the customary termination grant.[20]

A complaint was once received about a Shin Bet man who was having an affair and using his agency-provided car to drive his girlfriend around. While there certainly was a standing order not to use official cars on personal business, the man's Shin Bet bosses instead asked him to end the love affair – which was attracting attention. Had this come to the notice of the puritannical and family-oriented Harel, his reaction would have been even sterner.

The greatest deviation from the high personal standards set by Harel was the conduct of Mordecai (Motke) Kedar. Israel put its trust in him at the end of the summer of 1956, in the *Ta'am Tov*, or Good Taste, café. It was then an 'in' place in northern Tel Aviv.

Colonel Yuval Ne'eman, of Military Intelligence, was at the café with Kedar, giving him a final briefing before his departure for Argentina on a secret mission for Unit 131, the operations department of Aman. He was to settle down there for a long time, so as to build his cover story before being sent to Egypt as a spy.

Kedar was born in Poland in the early 1930s, and at the time was named Mordecai Kravitzki. He was abandoned by his mother, brought to Palestine by his grandfather, and lived in Hadera, an agricultural town north of Tel Aviv on the road to Haifa. In his youth, he showed signs of high intelligence, leadership qualities, a strong physique and a tendency towards crime.

In the 1948 war, Kravitzki/Kedar served in the tiny Israeli navy, but went AWOL due to disciplinary problems. In the early 1950s, he was a leader of Hadera's small but violent underworld. His gang of criminals stole cars and handled stolen property, and the police linked his name to armed robbery and murder cases. Kedar was arrested, but the authorities did not have enough evidence to press a case against him. Residents of Hadera's gangland feared Kedar more than they did the police and they refused to cooperate.

Kedar moved to Tel Aviv, became a regular at various Bohemian cafés, beguiled women and lived a life of leisure and extravagance without anyone knowing where he got his money. At the recommendation of one of his friends, he went to a psychiatrist named Dr Rudi for treatment.

The good doctor happened to work for the intelligence community. He was known for rather bizarre preliminary interviews with potential recruits, where he would clench his pipe between his teeth and ask a first question such as: 'How often a month do you engage in sexual intercourse?' or 'How often did you masturbate before you lost your virginity?' The would-be agent's reaction was noted, as Dr Rudi posed a more serious follow-up question such as: 'Would you please tell me why you're willing to take a mission you might not return from?'[21]

Dr Rudi performed the miracle of declaring Kedar fit for human society. He then introduced him to General Yehoshafat Harkabi, head of Aman, who recruited Kedar for Unit 131.

A short time after the 1956 Suez-Sinai campaign, Mordecai Kedar vanished. His wife, whom he abandoned together with their young son, began to receive postcards from him in various places around the world.

At the end of 1957, Kedar was summoned back to Israel. He flew first class on El Al from Paris, was taken to a small room at Tel Aviv's Lod airport, and asked to write a routine report about his activities. Then, unexpectedly, three armed policemen entered the room and arrested him.

For eighteen months, until May 1959, no one knew what had happened to him. He had simply disappeared, as if swallowed up by the earth. Even the prison guards did not know who he was and why he was kept in total isolation. Only after half a year of solitary confinement was he permitted to walk by himself in the exercise yard for half an hour a day. He was moved to another cell, which was larger, but he was unable to see any other prisoners. Rumours began to circulate, inside and outside Ramle Prison, about a Prisoner X known by no other name.

Avri El-Ad, the Unit 131 case officer in Egypt who survived the Lavon Affair but was then jailed in Ramle as a traitor, says he was known there only as 'X4'. In the adjoining cell – in shackles and unable to be heard through the thick walls – was Motke Kedar. They played chess, mentally, by tapping out their moves in Morse code on the wall. 'Don't let them drag you down!' Kedar once tapped. 'If you let them demoralize you, you're a broken man.'[22]

After several incomplete, censored references to him in the Israeli press, the government admitted that a man – understood by the newspapers to be Kedar – had been arrested for serious criminal offences. His trial was held behind closed doors and he was sentenced to seventeen years in prison. Kedar himself refused to confess to the crimes with which he had been charged. He was not broken. In prison, he maintained his physical fitness and became a student of Ayn Rand and her philosophy. In 1974, after he had served his entire sentence, Kedar was released from prison and demanded a new hearing. The police, the prosecution and the intelligence community all rejected his request.[23]

The Israeli government has continued its absolute silence about the Kedar case, which remains one of its best-kept secrets. What the authorities wish to conceal is the fact that Kedar was not sentenced for mere criminal acts, but for a severe violation of Israeli intelligence's unwritten codes of morals and methods.

While on his mission in Argentina in November 1957, he killed a Jewish businessman and stole his money. Most of the money was in Kedar's pockets when he flew into Tel Aviv. The murder victim was stabbed eighty times. He was Kedar's contact, the person who was meant to help construct the Israeli agent's cover story before he left for Egypt.

Thirty years after successfully prosecuting Kedar, Isser Harel disclosed that simply killing the renegade agent so as to cover up the crime had been considered in the intelligence community. 'I was insistent from the beginning,' Harel wrote, 'that we cannot take the law into our own hands. For this there are judges and courts. The British services may eliminate people. We do not.'

Harel proudly said: 'During my tenure as *Memuneh*, no traitor was ever executed.'

The only logic for not revealing any details is that it might expose some operational secrets, but the event occurred over thirty years ago. It seems that Israel is even more concerned that the irresponsibility of its intelligence chiefs would be exposed. It is they who agreed to recruit an unbridled adventurer such as Kedar. His recruiter, Harkabi, is now a professor in Jerusalem and stresses that 'people who are recruited for these operations are not uncomplicated people. There is always some type of story.'[24]

From Harel's viewpoint, the Kedar case supplied further proof for his old argument that running secret agents is too serious a business to be left to Aman. Harel wanted it all for the Mossad. Eventually, a deal was struck. Responsibility for operations in Arab countries remained in the hands of Military Intelligence, but Harel was permitted to establish his own operations department, with responsibility for the rest of the world.

Harel established the operations department with his typically uncompromising vigour. As he was, in practice, in charge of Shin Bet and the Mossad, he insisted that the department be available to both agencies and that it use the best human resources of both. Leading this department were Rafi Eitan and Avraham Shalom, previously named Bendor. They would feature later in various operations both brilliant and scandalous.[25]

In the years to come, Harel would act like a boy who had been given a new toy and could not wait to use it. His operations department became a department of show-off operations, with Harel nearly always in the vicinity and leading his men in what he considered the best interests of Israel. His agents suddenly began running all over the world: London, Paris, Rome, Antwerp, Johannesburg, New York and Geneva. And the mission? To look for an eight-year-old who had been kidnapped by his relatives. Such cases, it could be said, are a dime a dozen for any police force. For Harel, however, it was a matter of honour.

Yosef (Yossele) Schumacher was abducted in 1960 by his grandfather, an ultra-Orthodox Jew who feared that the boy's parents would give him a secular education. The old man was assisted by fellow members of *Neturei Karta*, the 'Guardians of the Citadel', who are violently opposed to Zionism, and Yossele was moved from one safe house to another in Europe and eventually to New York.

The entire State of Israel sang the refrain, 'Where is Yossele?' and jokes circulated about the authorities who were unable to track the child down. Harel, obsessed by the challenge, decided to prove that he could show everyone. He launched Operation Tiger. He gave it top priority and ordered all his senior agents to stop their other activities and find the boy. And they did.

Yossele Schumacher was located in July 1962 in an apartment occupied by Jewish zealots in Brooklyn, New York. Word was flashed to the FBI and Yossele was returned triumphantly to his parents in Israel. The publicity machine of the secret services was working overtime and Israel's clandestine defenders were basking in the praise.

A far more serious operation in 1960 brought Harel and his operations department half-way around the globe, in a manhunt of tremendous gravity. Acting on a tip from West Germany, Harel's men located Adolf Eichmann, one of the highest officials in the killing machine of the Nazi Holocaust. He was living in Buenos Aires, Argentina, under the name Ricardo Klement. On May 11, 1960, Eichmann was kidnapped by three members of the operations department: Eitan, Shalom and Zvi Malchin. Harel was in Buenos Aires to coordinate his team and they spirited the Nazi onto a flight to Israel without the local authorities noticing anything amiss. In Jerusalem the following year, judged guilty of crimes against humanity, Eichmann was hanged.

That was Harel's finest hour. To this very day, wherever he goes, he is identified as 'the kidnapper of Eichmann'. It was undoubtedly the most remarkable, bold and admired operation carried out by Harel and his intelligence agents. And it was pure *humint* – the human intelligence efforts at which Israel excelled, in this case without any technological gadgets.

Harel did not plan to rest on his laurels and continued to press for the capture of more Nazi war criminals. For him, it was a sacred mission, the payment of a debt owed to the six million who were killed. The secret agencies of other nations try to capture an enemy only when he poses an active, great danger to the state the agencies are defending. Harel would have the Mossad launch a massive, worldwide manhunt for criminals from other nations, who had acted in third or fourth nations against a whole people – rather than threatening the defence or security interests of the State of Israel, which had not even existed when the crimes were committed.

Harel came up with an original solution in a world which did nothing about the Nazis except indict them in court. The Israelis intended to find them. Harel set up a special coordinating unit, with the specific task of hunting for Nazis who had tortured and murdered Jews. He put Shmuel Toledano, code-named Amnon, in charge. Toledano joined the Mossad, from Military Intelligence, in 1954, and he worked under diplomatic cover at the Israeli embassy in Paris where he concentrated on the duty that was unique to the Mossad: protecting Jewish interests worldwide.

West German prosecutors helped the Israelis compile a list of the ten most wanted Nazis. Among others, the Toledano unit was searching for Dr Josef Mengele, the notorious medical 'experimenter' at the Auschwitz death camp; Hitler's deputy Martin Börmann; Heinrich Müller, the Gestapo chief; and Leon de Grelle, a Belgian who served enthusiastically as an officer in the Nazi SS storm troopers.

The hunt for de Grelle triggered a bizarre affair. A former Shin Bet operative, Zwy Aldouby, heard in early 1961 that the Mossad was searching for the Belgian Nazi and Aldouby dreamed of somehow stealing the glory. He approached Yigal Mossensohn, a famous Israeli writer and former captain in the police force, and recruited him for a kidnap operation – giving him the impression that it was an official mission for the government.

Aldouby was then a part-time journalist and used his contacts to recruit old friends in the French security service, including President de Gaulle's personal bodyguard. Hoping eventually to sell the story as a film script – and having received advance payments from major magazines – the oddly concocted team went into action in Spain. They followed de Grelle to his villa near Seville, planning to abduct him, Eichmann-style, and hand him over to the Belgian authorities who had already sentenced him to death *in absentia*. They even hoped that de Grelle would lead them eventually to Börmann, because they had intercepted letters between the two Nazis.

Their reconnaissance complete, Aldouby and a French partner named Jacques Finston were arrested on July 14, 1961, while crossing the border again from France into Spain for the kidnap itself. A few days later, Spanish detectives detained Mossensohn aboard a yacht which was intended to take de Grelle away. Mossensohn recalls: 'We were probably shadowed all the time, because Aldouby had a big mouth. He would speak about the operation by telephone, and all his girlfriends knew about it, and he had a lot of them.'

Aldouby and Finston were arrested and jailed by the Spanish, who tortured them and sentenced them to seven years in prison. Mossensohn was far luckier – released after just a few hours. More than twenty years later, he still did not know why he had been set free. A Mossad agent then told him that his good fortune had stemmed from the intervention of Prime Minister Ben-Gurion. He was told that because Ben-Gurion liked Mossensohn's writing, 'the Old Man' had phoned Generalissimo Franco and told him: 'Don't touch Mossensohn. Release him.'[26]

These odd events had definite and negative effects on Israel's intelligence community. Several countries in Western Europe were wary of Israeli agents after the rogue operation. Still, capturing Mengele continued to be a high priority – far higher than de Grelle – especially in the wake of Eichmann's abduction.

Shortly before Eichmann was flown out of Buenos Aires, one of his captors attempted to elicit information from the Nazi. 'Tell us where your friend Mengele is. You must know where he lives,' Malchin insisted. But Eichmann told him clearly that he had no idea. Malchin had to tell Harel: 'I tried everything. I believe that he has no idea where Mengele is, or that he is not willing to say a thing.'[27]

The attempts to capture Mengele nevertheless continued. To this day, there are contradictory versions as to how close Israeli agents got to the doctor of death. When the Brazilian authorities reported in 1985 that Mengele had died, after years of rumours, the Mossad secretly sent a pathologist to examine the skeleton and check that the quarry atop the manhunt list could now be crossed off once and for all.[28]

The massive search for Nazis was publicly seen only with Eichmann's capture, which gave Harel an image of being able to do anything, a reputation which he took pains to foster. The new focus on Nazis became – similar to his hunt for Communist moles – another one of Harel's obsessions, which in the end led to his downfall. The manhunt also co-incided with the arrival of German scientists in Egypt.

President Nasser wanted the Germans to help him develop ground-to-ground missiles which could be used in a future war against Israel. Harel genuinely believed that the Germans were again involved in a major effort to exterminate Jews. He responded with Operation Damocles, a sword hanging over the head of every German scientist who worked for the Eygptians.

Israeli agents sent booby-trapped letters to the German scientists involved in the missile project and to their families. Similar intimidation was being carried out throughout Europe. In this, Harel was reverting to a successful technique that had been used in 1956, when by the orders of General Harkabi, chief of Aman, letter bombs were sent to the Egyptian officers who had been responsible for infiltrating terrorists from the Gaza Strip into Israel. Two of the Eygptians were killed in those first, counter-terrorist assassinations by Israeli intelligence.

After initial successes, Operation Damocles came to an end in disastrous circumstances. Outside a Basel hotel on March 15, 1963, Swiss police arrested two Mossad agents – an Austrian adventurer, Dr Otto Joklik and an Israeli, Yosef Ben-Gal – as they left a meeting in which they had threatened Heidi, the daughter of Paul Görka, one of the German scientists working in Egypt on the development of missiles. The two Mossad men were sentenced to short terms in prison. If bad news comes in threes, this was the first.

Believing that the Germans and Egyptians were not being stopped, Harel decided to go public. He hoped to persuade the world, or at least the Israeli people, that the heirs to the Nazi generation were posing a mortal danger to the state built by Holocaust survivors. Mossad agents were sent on briefing missions to journalists in various European countries, and three leading Israeli newsmen – persuaded by Harel – undertook a special assignment, partly for their newspapers, and partly espionage, to learn more about the German scientists.[29] It was one of the few times, probably the first, that the Mossad used Israeli journalists as agents. This was Harel's second major mistake. The articles which were published, as a result of the semi-Mossad mission, caused panic among the Israeli public about the ballistic danger from Egypt. Ben-Gurion was furious. He rebuked Harel for his unauthorized leaks to the press and added that the developing ties between Israel and West Germany were being ruined.

Harel did not understand the diplomatic argument and how important West Germany was for Ben-Gurion's new foreign policy. 'The Old Man' was not going to allow anything to block better ties with Bonn. This was Harel's third major error.

Ben-Gurion demanded that Harel's private crusade come to an end. Harel refused and sought backing from other members of the Prime Minister's Mapai Party. He attempted to recruit Foreign Minister Meir and Finance Minister Levi Eshkol to his side. At the time, the political disputes over the Lavon Affair – cover-ups concerning sabotage in Egypt – were at the peak of their ferocity.

For the first time since 1948, Harel joined Ben-Gurion's opponents and found himself in the enemy camp. Harel was hoping to bypass his mentor's firm stand and to renew the 'holy war' against the Nazi scientists. In Ben-Gurion's eyes, that was tantamount to treason.

Behind the scenes, there was growing distrust between the Prime Minister and Harel over other issues. Ben-Gurion was not happy about Harel's zeal in pursuing Israel Beer, who had worked in the Prime Minister's bureau. His arrest had reflected on Ben-Gurion himself.

On the other side, Harel was not at all pleased with Ben-Gurion putting Peres in charge of the secret nuclear project and Lakam.

The Prime Minister began to worry about the excessive authority enjoyed by Harel. Now, because of the German scientists, large cracks appeared in the relationship between the two Israelis, and the flood waters rushed through into the breach.

On March 25, 1963, nine days after Joklik and Ben-Gal were arrested in Switzerland, Harel submitted a letter of resignation. Harel hoped that Ben-Gurion would not accept it and would ask him to remain as *Memuneh*. He believed that he was irreplaceable. Ben-Gurion thought otherwise.

It was the end of an era. The great crusader had fallen on his own sword.

6

Amit Cleans the Mossad Stable

'Contact the Prime Minister's office in Tel Aviv immediately,' read the message handed to Major General Meir Amit. It was March 26, 1963, and Amit was on an official tour of the Dead Sea area. He did as he was told – hurrying over to the nearest telephone and calling Ben-Gurion's office. 'The Old Man wants to see you immediately, so we're sending a plane for you,' Colonel Ben-David, the Prime Minister's military secretary, told him.

About three hours later, Amit arrived at the Prime Minister's office in Tel Aviv. A branch of the main bureau in Jerusalem, it is a small, three-storey building made of stone, with a red tile roof and a tiny front porch. The building is surrounded by trees and a garden, and is in the middle of a modest neighbourhood of similar houses. After the State of Israel was founded, it became a military zone – the *Kirya*, which included the offices of the general staff, the headquarters of the fledgling intelligence community and the Prime Minister's office.

Ben-Gurion placed a sheet of paper on the table in front of Amit. It was a copy of the letter he had sent a few hours earlier to Isser Harel, in which he notified him that his resignation had been accepted. Ben-Gurion did not ask Amit if he wanted a new job, but simply told him, 'You will be the next head of the Mossad.' It was a command, and Amit humbly accepted the verdict.[1] Ben-Gurion did not want another *Memuneh*. The Shin Bet job would go to someone else.

About a year earlier, Meir Amit had been appointed head of Aman – Military Intelligence – in what had seemed the crowning achievement of a long career in uniform. He was born in Tiberias in 1926. The family name was Slutzki, before he Hebraized it. Brought up with socialist views, Slutzki-Amit became a member of Kibbutz Alonim in the lower Galilee. He joined the Haganah there, and he was a company commander in the 1948 War of Independence. After the war he did a great deal of soul-searching and decided not to return to the kibbutz, despite his continued belief in its communal values. Instead, he remained in the army, as he was equally convinced that the Israel Defence Forces were absolutely essential to the young state.

In the following decade, Amit commanded infantry and tank units and he was one of the men who developed the principle of 'Follow me', which became the Israeli army's trademark throughout the world. The officer does not remain in the rear but leads his troops into battle. Amit became a good friend of General Moshe Dayan, served as his *aide-de-camp* in the 1956 Suez Campaign, and was considered to be his protegé. Amit also had a liberal arts education, including a degree in economics from New York's Columbia University.

When Amit was offered the opportunity to be the head of Aman at the beginning of 1962, perhaps he should have thought twice. The job had brought nothing but bad luck. Three of Aman's four commanders had been forced out after failing to avoid upheavals: Isser Beeri in 1949, Binyamin Gibli in 1954, and Yehoshaphat Harkabi in 1958 – the last case involving a fouled-up mobilization exercise of army reservists. After Harkabi, it had been decided that General Chaim Herzog would be returned to his former post, in order to restore the image of Military Intelligence.

Herzog accomplished this with the professionalism to be expected from a man who had obtained his education and experience as an intelligence officer in the British Army in World War II. There was one change, however, that Herzog was unable to accomplish: Aman continued to live in the shadow of a 'big brother', namely Harel, and in the shadow of the myth of the Mossad's ability.

The Chief of Staff, General Zvi Zur, painted a dismal picture to Amit of the situation in the army's intelligence branch. Aman was not functioning as it should and there was a need to rebuild and reorganize it from the ground up.

Harel expressed strong opposition to Amit's appointment, claiming he had no intelligence experience but perhaps also feeling threatened by Amit's reputation as a general with his own band of loyal followers. Harel's power was dwindling, however, and he was no longer able to stop Ben-Gurion from selecting whomever he wished.

Upon taking over at Aman headquarters in the *Kirya*, Amit first tried to lessen the traditional hostility and competition between the Mossad and Military Intelligence. He knew that rivalries were entirely out of place in any community entrusted with the defence of the state. Amit proposed to Harel that all the services should work in close cooperation.

Within a few weeks, however, after a few attempts to heal the breach, the hostility between the two was renewed and even intensified. There were not simply differences of opinion between the two men but two entirely separate mentalities. Harel was a virtuoso of operations, while Amit specialized in military strategy. Harel ran around Europe for months on end in the search for little Yossele Schumacher, working in the field and sleeping on cots alongside his most junior agents, grabbing a few hours of sleep in a safe house.

As in the disputes of the early 1950s between Guriel, Gibli and Shiloah, the army complained about the Mossad's poor productivity on the military capabilities of the Arab armed forces.

Army officers had great expectations when Amit – one of their own – was selected to be Mossad chief. He could improve efficiency and coordination, because he was the only person ever to serve as head of both the Mossad and Military Intelligence.

Furthermore, it was the first time that an outsider was appointed to be head of the Mossad. Amit had the additional handicap of replacing a man who had served as head of both the Mossad and Shin Bet for twelve years, who had shaped them in his own image. The Mossad could not and did not want to forget Harel. For most Mossad employees, Harel was a legend in his own time, the Great Father of the clandestine community.

When Amit walked into the Mossad on the first day of his tenure, March 26, 1963, in his general's uniform, the reception was distinctly cold. Harel was waiting for him, 'as sour as a lemon', as Amit recalled later. Harel said a few perfunctory words, read a few lines from a note in front of him and then he simply stood up and left. The *Memuneh*'s three secretaries burst into tears.[2]

The next day, an unwelcome letter arrived on the desk of the new head of the Mossad. It was from the senior Mossad agents in Europe and expressed distress at Harel's resignation. It also stressed that 'every effort must be made to return him.' The letter was signed, albeit using code names in order to observe secrecy in communications, by Shmuel Toledano, who organized the protest, Mordecai Almog, Yosef (Joe) Ra'anan and Yitzhak Shamir, who decades later would be Israel's prime minister.

Originally, some of the senior staffers had proposed that they all resign collectively. They decided, instead, to stay and simply write a letter. Their message was less severe than the revolt of the spies twenty-two years earlier against the Political Department of the foreign ministry, but the same atmosphere was created. Mossad operatives so admired Harel that in their eyes he not only symbolized the organization; he was the organization.[3]

Amit had no sympathy for letter-writers. He came from a different tradition. The military tradition believed in the division of responsibility and respect for the chain of command. If a commander is killed or departs, he must be replaced, and he can be replaced.

His response to the letter was a strong one. Amit knew that in order to stop the discontent from spreading, he had to strike while the iron was still hot. 'I do not accept your behaviour,' he wrote in his reply. 'I am not accustomed to collective protests.'

Within the next year, the four senior field agents who had signed the letter left the Mossad. They could not adapt to the work patterns of their new boss and they were disappointed in not being able to advance any higher within the agency. After Toledano left the service, he admitted that he had harboured hopes of leading the secret agency and had to settle for the post of Arab affairs adviser to Prime Minister Eshkol – appropriate for a fluent Arabic speaker, but not for a man accustomed to covert work.

The bad blood within the service led Amit to order that Harel's operation against the German scientists be investigated. Harel, for his part, continued to keep up to date with everything that was happening in the Mossad, and he even had informal but certain access to the most secret of documents, which he used in his testimony before a special committee of ministers which investigated the agency's internal troubles.[4]

The hostility between Amit and a number of the senior Mossad agents caused ripples and echoes outside the organization. It proved that hatred among spymasters never ends; it only intensifies with time. To this day, it is difficult to get Amit and Shamir to say a good word about one another. Amit and Ra'anan did not hide their enmity long after they had left the security services, when both headed giant economic enterprises in the 1970s. The strongest mutual repulsion, however, is between Amit and Harel, which, like old wine, only gains strength with each passing year.[5]

In any event, so as not to arouse the complete antagonism of the Mossad's top echelons and to create an atmosphere of reconciliation, Amit flew to Paris, where he invited Yaakov Karoz to be his deputy. Karoz was head of the Mossad's political action and liaison department, had been with the agency since its earliest days, and was known for his friendship with Harel. Karoz accepted Amit's offer.

Changes in Israel's government also helped reduce tensions, at least for a while. In June 1963, three months after Ben-Gurion forced Harel to quit, 'the Old Man' himself resigned as prime minister. He lacked the strength to keep fighting in the internal power struggles of the Mapai Party over the Lavon affair. A very short while later, Ben-Gurion left Mapai and founded a new, centrist party called Rafi, with the aid of his supporters, Moshe Dayan, and Shimon Peres. To replace Israel's first prime minister, Mapai appointed Levi Eshkol.

Eshkol showed great interest in intelligence. He was literally awed by the work of the Mossad. From time to time, he would compliment Amit on the work of his agents. In return, Amit made sure that Eshkol, who had previously been the minister of finance, would enlarge his budget, so that he could undertake a more speedy rehabilitation of the Mossad.

Until December 1963, Amit continued to appear in uniform and to serve in two capacities, moving between the Mossad and Aman offices in Tel Aviv. He utilized this period, until he left Aman and the army, to reorganize the Mossad structure. Almost as a dowry, Amit brought to the Mossad Unit 131, the élite operations arm of Aman, and integrated it with the two small operations units of the Mossad. This became possible because Shamir, one of the 'protesters', who headed one of the operations units in Paris, had resigned.[6]

Shamir regarded his work in the Mossad as a natural continuation of his underground days in the Stern Gang. Shamir was in the ascetic mould of highly committed fighting men. He was suspicious, could happily make do with very little, was not interested in creature comforts and was willing to do a prodigious amount of work. Just as during his time in Lehi when he had had no hesitation in passing sentence on enemies and traitors, he later had no qualms or doubts about carrying out tough intelligence work in the pursuit of victory.

'Shamir was an introvert, very dedicated, thorough and hard-working,' one of his Mossad colleagues observes. 'He taught himself French, hard as it was. You could always trust him, but he did not come forward with brilliant ideas. He came to work in the morning and at the end of the day returned to his wife Shulamit and their two children.'⁷ His daughter Gilada was attracted, from an early age, to her father's intelligence work. His son became an air force colonel.

After Shamir left the Mossad, he attempted to open a factory. When the business failed and he was left without employment, he decided in 1972, at the relatively late age of 55, to enter politics. This usually distant man, easily recognized by his moustache and lack of physical stature, also had the helpful ability to melt into a crowd. He had fond recollections of his days of drama and tension as a spy. 'My days in the Mossad were among the happiest in my life,' he said, 'and even politics and the premiership cannot compare to them.'⁸

To replace those who left, Amit installed his own men. He brought a number of people with him from Aman, led by Rehavam Vardi, who had been the head of the information-collecting department.⁹ Amit also arranged to raise the rank of the army's military attachés in the embassies overseas and he had some of them represent the Mossad as well. By doing so, Amit hinted at the path that he wished the Mossad to follow.

His first goal was to transform the agency into a serious

and modern intelligence organization that could deal with what Amit considered to be its major task: the collection of military and political data on the Arab states. He regarded the Mossad as an information-gathering body and not as one involved in operations for show. It appears that, influenced by his economics studies in the United States, he wished to imitate the American corporate mentality and style of management.

Amit moved the offices of the Mossad in Tel Aviv into modern premises, in a building in the middle of the city rather than in the defence ministry's compound. The other tenants – civilians working within steps of the top secret espionage agency – included lawyers and businessmen.

Mossad veterans were far from enthusiastic about these changes. They were upset by Amit's luxurious office, with its wood panelling and new furniture, which resembled a modern businessman's suite. These veterans, who were used to the modest, old quarters used by Harel, could not tolerate the change. Complaints about extravagance began flying, as they had about Ben-Natan's men in the Political Department a dozen years earlier.

Stories circulated about the allegedly luxuriant lives led by senior officials in the agency, who stayed in exclusive hotels and ate at the best restaurants abroad.[10]

Amit also changed the Mossad's methods of recruitment. Rather than relying on the recommendations of friends, along the lines of the British old boy network, he preferred to use more systematic methods than the mere luck of 'feeling' that a longtime acquaintance, who attended the correct school, was the right sort of fellow to be a spy.

Amit made an effort to spot potential candidates, not only in the army, but in the universities, in the business world and among new immigrants. Stress was placed on finding candidates who appeared European in manner and style of dress, qualities that Israeli society had generally scorned.

One of those who seemed to fit the bill to a T was Charlie Mayorkas. He was born in Istanbul, to a father who grew up in Switzerland and a mother of Austrian origin. At the age of 17, he left Turkey to avoid military service there. He travelled to France to study medicine, but a year later his academic field was commerce. In 1965 this Turkish Jew moved to Israel, not for ideological reasons, but because he discovered that the Jewish Agency was willing to finance his studies at the Hebrew University.

There, on the Jerusalem campus, Charlie Mayorkas caught the eye of the Mossad recruiters. They proposed that he join the agency. Mayorkas accepted the offer with enthusiasm and for three years underwent the required training. It was then, however, that his superiors discovered that Mayorkas was a homosexual. He was immediately dismissed from the Mossad.

'I wanted to serve the state and then they hit me with this. What other Israeli would have such a perfect cover, with my family background, with my knowledge of eight languages, with access to all of Europe?' he complained. Many Mossad colleagues sympathized, but they were unwilling to take what was universally considered – in the espionage world, always worried about sexual blackmail and compromising entanglements – an unnecessary risk.[11]

The situation of women in the Mossad was hardly any better. 'A woman cannot gather information in the Arab world,' one of the senior men in the Mossad explains. 'The different way that women are treated in Arab society prevents us from employing women as operatives or case officers. The Arabs wouldn't accept them. They would see a woman like that and jump out the window.'[12]

Most women in the Mossad are employed in administrative and service capacities. The Mossad has always been reluctant to send women on extended assignments overseas, even when these are the less dangerous jobs such as serving as liaison officers with the security services of other nations.

The inequality in who is sent abroad also affects promotions on the home front, because decision-making posts are generally reserved for those with experience in the field. For the Mossad's women, it is a vicious circle. Those who start out as secretaries may get to be managers – but office managers rather than captains of conspiracies and foreign plots.

To every rule, there are exceptions, however. For example, Lily Kastel was a living legend and years after her death in 1970 the men of the Mossad still speak of her extraordinary talent. She joined the agency in 1954, after previous experience in Shai.

Kastel spoke excellent Hebrew, English, French, German and Russian, and she had a working knowledge of Arabic and Italian. She is remembered as attractive, intelligent and trustworthy. Harel felt he was using both her brains and her looks, on various assignments in Europe.[13]

The changes in the agency under Amit did lead to some improvement in opportunities for women. The new boss's demand for proficiency and professionalism helped give women a fairer chance to be appointed to run 'desks' covering specific regions or subjects. These were women who had slowly made their way up through the ranks, until they were finally made responsible for a single area of expertise.

The formal job description of a 'desk' manager is that he or she is the contact point between the operatives and the head office, supplying the field agents with whatever they need for their assignments. The desk person transmits orders and receives whatever material is gathered in the field.[14]

Only when a specific assignment requires women, and even that is decided upon after all other avenues have been explored and dismissed, will a female be sent on an overseas mission. There can be the further advantage, when mounting surveillance with a male colleague, that married or courting couples attract less suspicion than single men.

The Mossad does use women for purposes of sexual entrapment. The intelligence chiefs prefer to use single women for such assignments. They are almost always used once and once only. The Mossad has always displayed great reluctance to order its agents, male or female, to engage personally in sexual relations for the sake of the mission. This may be a hangover from Harel's puritannical spirit.

When he saw a married staffer caressing female secretaries in Mossad headquarters, the agency chief was clearly annoyed and would rebuke the man.

The thinking on sex changed, however, and while there was no pressure on female agents to exploit their gender, it was expected of them to use sex as one of many weapons in the field.[15] If sexual blackmail or entrapment is an integral part of the mission, the Mossad employs actual prostitutes. Examples of that common practice in the intelligence world occur when Arab informants run by either Aman or the Mossad are smuggled across the border into Israel, are brought to the nearest town for a briefing, and then, as a reward for their work or in order to photograph them in compromising positions, they are supplied with prostitutes.

There was less hesitation about sending Mossad men abroad to the sexual hunting grounds. The appropriate agents would be chosen to befriend – and, usually, become intimate with – an international array of stewardesses, for they could provide much valuable information on airports and cities in Arab and other countries.

An Israeli case officer carried on a tempestuous relationship with the most important agent he was running, a young European woman. In addition to the meetings at which she handed him information, they would meet in hotels for sex. This had not been the original task assigned by Mossad headquarters. When a new case officer took over in Europe, his first report noted that 'the source' expressed amazement and even complained that he was not willing to go to bed with her. He found that there had been two generations of case officers using the woman in more ways than one, and that she believed that going to bed was part and parcel of her employment by the Israelis. Only because a number of years had passed was it decided not to bring disciplinary charges against the earlier case officers.

The use of sex and other Mossad working practices were not introduced for the first time by Meir Amit. The Amit era did, however, establish many of the structural and personnel principles which characterize the Mossad to this day.

The Mossad has eight sections, but four are by far the most significant: the Collection Department, the Operational Planning and Coordination Department, the Research Department and the Department of Political Action and Liaison. The other departments, namely Training, Finance and Manpower, Technology and Technical Operations, mainly provide assistance and support for the major sections.

There are 'desks' in the information-collecting and political departments, with responsibility for specific regions of the world. Mossad handles all data from abroad, except for some Arab military targets – on which Aman may spy.[16]

Mossad's *modus operandi* was shifting with time and personalities. Harel was a great believer in the power of human instinct. His was undoubtedly excellent and he preferred unexplained, but well trained inspiration to any dependence on cold, unfeeling technology. He did not hide his scorn for electronic gadgets, even though Israel was home to some of the world's greatest inventors.

Harel was always proud of the fact that his Mossad, unlike other intelligence organizations in the West, was an organization which relied on human resources. It was almost universally acknowledged by experts as the world's finest example of *humint* – the espionage analysts' term for human intelligence.

The Mossad, under Amit, continued to be primarily *humint*-oriented, but other strengths were also stressed. Advanced computers were introduced to the agency in large numbers, based on the earlier experiences at Aman, first under Herzog and afterwards under Amit and the head of his collection department, Colonel Aharon Yariv.[17]

Amit believed that all these changes were essential to improve the collection capability of the Mossad in its target countries, and especially in the Arab 'confrontation states' bordering Israel. This task became even more essential after a number of Israeli networks in Egypt collapsed, a failure which was yet another push towards the Mossad exit door for such senior operatives as Shamir and Ra'anan.

Between 1960 and 1963, the Egyptian press revealed the

existence of several Israeli spy rings, including 'the most dangerous and most important' network of Jack Thomas.

Jack Leon Thomas was an Armenian, brought up in Cairo. He was an educated young man, handsome, with jet-black hair and perfect command of Arabic, English, French and German. In 1956, he moved to Beirut and then on to West Germany, trying his hand at various commercial enterprises. In 1958, he met a young Lebanese man named Emil and they became close friends – enjoying the bars and restaurants of Cologne and Bonn. Emil, obviously wealthy, always picked up the tab. They talked about business and women and when the chat drifted into politics, Thomas made it quite clear that he could not stand President Nasser.

One evening, Emil offered Jack a huge amount of money and suggested that he return to Egypt and help overthrow the corrupt regime of his hated dictator. Thomas was told he would be working for one of the NATO countries. It is called 'false flag recruiting', and the Mossad is especially good at it. Israel was never mentioned and Thomas, who had always had a fondness for the West, swallowed the bait.

In a small apartment in Cologne, anonymous people taught him the basics of espionage: photographing documents and developing the film; hiding negatives in toothpaste tubes, shoe boxes or books; writing with invisible ink; and passing coded messages by leaving them in 'dead letter boxes' for unknown accomplices.

Full of enthusiasm, Thomas returned to Cairo in July 1958 and began recruiting informers into his network. From time to time, he would travel to West Germany for meetings with his operators, who continued to claim that they were 'senior officials in NATO'. In return for military information which he brought with him, his case officers gave him money and new orders.

On one of these trips, the young Armenian met a West German lady named Kathy Bendhof. After a whirlwind romance, they were married and Bendhof joined Thomas in Cairo. He added his wife to his network and she became his courier.

Thomas's case officer in Cologne eventually revealed the truth to him: 'I have been running you for Israeli intelligence.' The revelation did not come as a surprise to Thomas, nor did his lack of surprise entirely surprise his Israeli controllers. They knew they were dealing with an intelligent man and indeed, Thomas had suspected that he was working for Israel. Now that he knew for certain, it did not bother him a bit. He still hated Nasser and he returned to his espionage work in Cairo with even greater enthusiasm.

Gradually, his network expanded. Thomas recruited two Armenians and a Jewish nightclub performer. Another informer was a childhood friend of Thomas who had become an artillery officer. Kathy was sent to Amsterdam, where the Mossad taught her how to use a radio transmitter with great professionalism. The chosen code book was Pearl Buck's *The Good Earth*. The couple immediately received a pay raise and the money was sent through a Belgian bank, allegedly as 'help from relatives in Germany'.

Their network amassed its own espionage equipment: five cameras, a suitcase with a false bottom, an electric shaver with a secret compartment for hiding documents, a hollow cigarette lighter for film negatives and a sophisticated two-way radio, hidden in the bathroom of their comfortable apartment in the Garden City section of Cairo. Every few days, Kathy Bendhof-Thomas would contact Tel Aviv and pass on information, while at the same time picking up new orders.

In May 1960, the couple received an order which was designed to be a preview of a major project yet to come. They were to choose an Egyptian army officer whom they might later recruit into their network. The message warned them clearly to wait for further instructions, but they had already been infected by the most damaging of all occupational diseases faced by a spy: excessive self-confidence. They made overtures to a young officer of Coptic Christian extraction named Adiv Hanna Karolos.

Karolos appeared to have taken the bait, but he immediately informed his commanding officer of what had occurred. Egyptian counterespionage agents laid a trap for the Israeli network. At first, they fed false information to Thomas, who thought he was transmitting useful data to Tel Aviv.

Thomas evidently began to feel – with Isser Harel's favourite kind of instinct – that the ground was burning beneath his feet and prepared to disband the network and have everyone flee. He obtained false passports for himself and his wife. Kathy Thomas managed to escape together with the Jewish dancer, but Thomas and the other members of the network were arrested on January 6, 1961.

In a Cairo courtroom, Thomas claimed that he had been spying for Israel for a sense of adventure, for the money and because he hated the Nasserite regime. 'I am not a traitor,' he said. 'I never considered myself an Egyptian. We Armenians are oppressed in Egypt because we are a minority.' A military court convicted Thomas and two of his recruits of espionage and treason and the three men were hanged on December 20, 1962.

During the trial, prosecutors revealed that the Thomas network had made serious attempts to offer pilots in the Egyptian air force a million dollars if they would agree to defect to Israel or Cyprus with a Soviet-made MiG jet.[18]

Israel's intelligence chiefs did not give up. Spurred on by the air force commander, the hyper-energetic General Ezer Weizman, they pressed on with their efforts to acquire a Soviet-made warplane. A number of possible methods were considered: intercepting an aircraft in mid-flight and forcing it to land in Israel, planting an agent as a pilot in one of the Arab air forces, or bribing an Arab pilot. But how could they bribe a pilot, already living as luxurious a life as any that the Arab armed forces could offer?

The prevailing opinion was that, while difficult, this avenue offered Israel its best chances of success. Aman and the Mossad had already amassed a tremendous amount of information on the air forces of Egypt, Jordan, Syria and Iraq. Organized and stored by Aman and Amit's new computers, Israeli intelligence dossiers recorded every scrap of information on enemy pilots. The information was so comprehensive, that those in charge of the files felt as if they personally knew hundreds of Arab pilots.

That was why the Israelis were disappointed when an Egyptian pilot finally did defect to them in 1964. Captain Abbas Hilmi was indeed a pilot in Egypt's air force, and his plane was Soviet-made, but it was a Yak trainer of little interest to those who were dying to get their hands on a combat aircraft.

In spite of the disappointment felt in the Israeli intelligence community, Captain Hilmi was given a very warm reception. The information that he gave to the intelligence officers was an important addition to the data that had been painstakingly assembled about the Arab air forces. Hilmi was also used for other purposes. He publicly condemned Nasser's intervention in Yemen, where his army was trying to force another country into his sphere of radical Arab socialism and Hilmi further revealed that his country was using poison gas against the Yemeni royalists.

The Egyptian turncoat was given financial assistance and a good job in Israel, but he was not able to acclimatize himself to life in the Jewish state. Rejecting the strong advice of his intelligence handlers in Tel Aviv, Hilmi decided to move to South America. The Mossad furnished him with new identity documents and gave him a large sum of cash to help him begin a new life in Argentina.

As soon as he arrived in Buenos Aires, violating the instructions the Israelis had given him, Hilmi made a number of literally fatal errors. First, he sent a postcard to his mother in Egypt, where the secret police intercepted the card and found out where he was hiding. Later, he befriended an Egyptian woman whom he met in an Argentine nightclub. She promised him her favours and he agreed to go to her apartment. It was an Arab version of the 'honey trap' which the Israelis and other espionage agencies use. Egyptian agents were waiting for Hilmi in the woman's apartment. They subdued him, transported him in a crate to the

Egyptian embassy and from there smuggled him by cargo ship to Egypt. He was convicted by a court martial and shot for treason.[19]

Even though the Hilmi episode was not the fault of Israeli intelligence, its reputation was damaged by his capture. There were a lot of discussions on the matter, but Weizman continued to insist that obtaining and examining a MiG could be the key to winning a war. The efforts to snare a pilot continued.

A year later, at the beginning of 1966, another suitable target was found. This time it was an Iraqi pilot.[20]

Munir Redfa was a member of a wealthy Maronite Christian family in Iraq, where non-Moslems generally suffered discrimination. Trained by the Soviets, he was a pilot in a squadron of MiG-21s, the latest word in Soviet military aeronautics.

The Israelis, thanks to newspaper clippings, Iraqi communications they intercepted and agents on the ground in Baghdad, were aware of Redfa's background. They learned that Redfa had been dismayed and upset about his air force's bombing and strafing raids on Kurdish villages in the north, as part of the suppression of that minority.

The Israeli agents chosen for this mission were selected with great care and sent to Baghdad, by way of Europe, to make contact with the pilot and his family. Of all the agents dispatched for the Redfa project, and there were many for what rapidly became a high-priority objective, the most successful was a woman who had been born in the United States and carried an American passport.

She posed as a rich tourist who attended some high-powered parties in Baghdad and managed to enchant the Iraqi pilot, even though he was married and had two children. Taking a position commonly voiced by female Israeli spies over the years, the woman refused to have sex with Redfa in Iraq. He had to come to Europe with her, and then he could have his reward. The pilot agreed to accompany her to Paris, where romance would be in the air.

After two days in France, Redfa agreed to fly with the

enchantress to Israel, where she said she had 'some interesting friends'. The Iraqi pilot harboured certain suspicions,
but he did not seem to care very much and within twenty-
four hours, holding a false passport provided by the Mossad
in Paris, he was a passenger on an El Al flight to Tel Aviv.

In Israel, Redfa was treated as a VIP. He was taken on a
tour of an Israeli air base. It was there that he met officers
who offered him one million dollars and asylum for his
entire family if he would defect to Israel with one of the
new MiG-21s.

To demonstrate that their offer was authentic and authorized, the intelligence agents arranged a meeting for Redfa
with General Mordecai Hod, commander of the Israeli air
force, who had just taken over from Ezer Weizman. The
Iraqi was amazed at how well the Israelis knew his air force.
They knew the names of the Iraqi pilots and their Soviet
instructors. The Israelis described in great detail the air field
and its runways, control tower, operations room and living
quarters.

In coordination with Redfa and with his consent, a date
was set for his daring flight from Iraq non-stop to Israel.
Hod helped plan a flight route and arrangements for communications on the day of the coup.

A few days later, the pilot and the Israeli agent, who he
used to think was his American girlfriend, returned to
Baghdad by way of Paris. As agreed in Israel, a down
payment for Redfa was deposited in a Swiss bank account.
Redfa's family was smuggled out of the country into Iran,
with the help of Kurdish rebels who regularly worked for
Israeli agents. The Mossad station in Teheran then had the
family flown to Europe and on to Tel Aviv.

Amit, meantime, flew to Washington to inform the CIA
director, Richard Helms, that the United States would soon
be able to feast its eyes on a MiG-21. The Americans
had been trying for some time to examine this jet, with its
secret technology, in order to improve the US 'Top Gun'
fighter units and their simulations of Soviet–American
dogfights.

The planning was perfect. On August 15, 1966, Redfa flew the agreed route over Jordan, fleeing his homeland at high speed and landing his MiG-21 at an air base in southern Israel. This was the first time that such a sophisticated Soviet warplane had reached the West. Decades later, the air forces of the US and its NATO allies remained impressed by the feat accomplished by Israeli intelligence that day. Among Western military people, acquiring the MiG was one of the key events in building the Mossad's image into unassailable mythology. More than ever, Israel was seen as a master of *humint* methods.

The Redfa defection, known to some intelligence insiders by the amusing name of Operation 007, gave Meir Amit great pleasure. Unlike the Hilmi affair, this acquisition of an Arab aircraft had a happy ending. Munir Redfa and his family were given new identities, the promised cash and enjoyed happy lives in Israel. The American-born female agent left Iraq and turned to new duties for the Mossad.[21]

The Americans, NATO and other friends of Israel continued to heap praise on the Mossad, but Amit faced the reality of losing two top agents in a five week period: in Damascus on January 18, 1965, and in Cairo on February 22.

Until their capture, Eli Cohen and Wolfgang Lotz – not only in the two most important Arab capitals, but in the very heart of their political and military power centres – supplied Israeli intelligence with absolutely astounding information. They were extremely capable men and both penetrated the highest ranks of the leadership in their respective espionage posts. Cohen became a personal friend of the Syrian president and Lotz befriended many senior officers in the Egyptian Army.

The two spies sent huge volumes of information to Tel Aviv, but their most valuable contributions were the data on new weapons systems and general military preparations in Syria and Egypt. Cohen, unfortunately posthumously, and Lotz deserve Israel's thanks for making the six-day victory of 1967 possible.

Wolfgang Lotz was born in Mannheim, Germany, in 1921.

His mother was a Jewish actress, and his father was a Christian theatre manager in Berlin. It turned out that for his own perilous espionage act, it was lucky that Wolfgang was not circumcised.

His parents divorced and, following Adolf Hitler's rise to power the mother and son moved to Palestine in search of a safe life as Jews. Wolfgang changed his name to Ze'ev Gur-Aryeh, studied agriculture in the Ben Shemen agricultural school east of Tel Aviv, and developed a love of horses. Even though *Ze'ev* means wolf and therefore was a fitting equivalent for his German name, his Israeli friends nicknamed him Sus, Hebrew for horse.

After fighting for the British in World War II, behind German lines in North Africa, and then for Israel's independence in 1948, Lotz was recruited by Aman. He was asked if he could shed his Jewishness, pretend he had remained in Germany all these years and even convince others that he was a Nazi sympathizer.

As the daring assignment entered its advanced design stage, Lotz was ordered to forget he was Gur-Aryeh, to return to West Germany, and to start building a cover story – similar to that of Max Bennett a decade earlier. Lotz was now acting the part of a German businessman who had served in Hitler's army, the *Wehrmacht*.

In December 1960, his Aman handlers sent Lotz to Egypt with sufficient capital – a huge expense account, by Israeli standards – to establish a horse-breeding ranch. A convivial and charismatic sort of chap, Lotz played host at parties for senior army officers and all the 'right people' in Egyptian society. Using a small radio transmitter, he would send detailed reports to Tel Aviv.

In June 1962, during one of his trips to Europe to report to his case officer, Lotz met 'a tall, extremely pretty, blue-eyed blonde with the curvaceous figure I always have a weakness for' on a night train from Paris.[22] In just two weeks, Wolfgang married Waltraud and they travelled separately back to Egypt. It is almost unbelievable that a trained and otherwise reliable agent would do such a thing, but Lotz did not consult his Israeli controllers and simply took his bride to Cairo.

The new Frau Lotz soon realized what his real job was, but she liked the idea and began to help him in it. Some reports, never confirmed, claim that Lotz was aided in assembling his cover story by West Germany's BND and that the agency chief General Reinhard Gehlen himself – as part of his intelligence cooperation with Israel – assigned Waltraud, a BND agent, to work with Lotz in Egypt.[23] This possibility is reinforced by the little-known fact that Lotz was already married and had left his wife behind in Israel.

In Tel Aviv, meantime, the responsibility for running Lotz was transferred from Aman to the Mossad, and the latter did not quite know how to handle the secret second marriage of its agent. A long time passed before his wife in Israel was informed. The new case officers in the Mossad were also not pleased with their operative's habits: he drank to excess and was known for his great generosity. The bills, however, had to be covered by headquarters in Tel Aviv. The Mossad's accounting department called Lotz 'the champagne spy', based on the expense reports he filed when visiting Europe.

The information which he sent, however, was reliable and irreplaceable. Lotz was also used in Harel's ill-fated operation against the German scientists in Egypt. He supplied Mossad headquarters with the Cairo addresses of the rocket scientists and he sent them several anonymous letters warning them to quit the Egyptian rocket programme – for their own personal safety.

What was most amazing was that the Egyptian interrogators, after Lotz and his wife were arrested, were unable to crack his true identity. Even during his trial, he was viewed as a German who had been spying for Israel simply to make some money. His cover story was perfect.

Eli Cohen, the spy at the very heart of Syrian political power, also made women part of his operation. In his guise as Kamel Amin Taabeth, he had to make sure to supply lovely ladies to his friends among the Syrian leadership, and he had more than five hundred friends in the army, in the Ba'ath Party and in the government.

The easiest cover story that could be constructed for Cohen was that of an Egyptian merchant or businessman. After all, he had been born in the port city of Alexandria in 1924. His controllers in Unit 131 of Military Intelligence knew, however, that unlike other Arab countries, Egypt maintained registers of the civilian population and Aman feared that one day his real identity could be traced.

In addition, Cohen had been a member of the Israeli spy network in Egypt in the 1950s and it was purely a matter of luck that he had not been arrested with his friends when the network either fell or was denounced in 1954.

After the 1956 Suez Campaign, Cohen left Egypt and as soon as he arrived in Israel he contacted Israeli intelligence. He was put through the standard psychological tests and the results indicated disturbing signs. Cohen was found to possess a high intelligence quotient, great courage, a phenomenal memory and the abilities to adapt socially and to keep a secret; but the tests also showed that 'in spite of his modest appearance, he has an exaggerated sense of self-importance' and 'a lot of internal tension'. Cohen, the results indicated, 'does not always evaluate danger correctly, and is liable to assume risks beyond those which are necessary.'[24]

Only when the tension along the Israeli–Syrian border increased did Israeli intelligence decide to put Cohen on active service. It was May 1960 and Israel was in urgent need of a spy in Damascus. For two years, Cohen underwent rigorous training to memorize every facet of his new identity.

On February 3, 1961, Cohen left Israel for Argentina – by now a favourite, if out-of-the-way choice for building cover stories – and spent a year melting into the Syrian community of Buenos Aires as businessman Kamel Amin Taabeth. Just under a year later, Cohen/Taabeth flew to Damascus for the first time. In the three years which followed, he became

Israel's most important spy. He had managed to worm his way directly into the lion's den.

The information which he sent to Tel Aviv, mainly by tapping Morse dots and dashes on his telegraph key, covered all areas of life in Syria. Israel generally tells its agents abroad to report as fully and as frequently as their safety allows. As a result, Mossad and Aman headquarters have tended to receive much more information than just a narrow topic which immediately interests them.

Cohen's reports were always welcome. They contained vivid information on the internal squabbles and relations within the government leadership, as well as the kind of data on the Syrian military which Aman felt it badly needed for its computerized files.

Cohen/Taabeth was an invited guest at army bases and at Syria's Golan Heights fortifications confronting Israel. He was able to describe the troop deployments along the border in detail and he noted the locations of tank traps which might prevent the Israelis from advancing on land if war were to break out. He furnished Tel Aviv with a list of names of all the Syrian pilots, as well as accurate sketches of the weapons mounted on their warplanes.

If his Israeli controllers had only been more cautious and more vigilant, they might have been able to prevent his capture. In November 1964, just months before he was arrested by Syrian counterespionage agents, Cohen behaved as though he felt a noose tightening around his neck. He was on leave in Israel, waiting for his son to be born. He kept extending his leave, hinting to his operators that he may want to come in from the cold.

Cohen also mentioned that he did not feel comfortable in the company of Colonel Ahmad Suedani, head of the intelligence branch of the Syrian army. Unfortunately, Cohen's case officers – and this was just as the operation was being transferred from Aman to the Mossad – did not pay attention to the warning signs. There was renewed tension on the border and there were fears in Israel that a war could break out. It was vital to have reliable intelligence from Damascus and the Mossad applied pressure on Cohen to return to his espionage post as soon as possible.

In the next two months, Cohen forgot the rules of prudence. It is possible that the unbelievable ease with which he had befriended the highest echelons in the land had dulled his senses. In total violation of his orders, he immediately resumed his coded broadcasts – which meant a clever Syrian counter-intelligence agent could link their resumption with Taabeth's return from 'abroad'. The broadcasts increased in frequency and in the space of five weeks he sent thirty-one radio transmissions to Tel Aviv. Similarly, based on fatigue or some death wish, Cohen's espionage messages went out at the same time, 8.30 in the morning. This would make his transmitter easy to trace electronically.

Cohen sometimes even sent two transmissions in a single day. Thus, for example, Tel Aviv asked him one morning, 'What happened to the MiG-21 group that was on alert?' and that afternoon at four o'clock Cohen gave a detailed answer: 'One of their pilots was killed when his plane hit a small plane on the ground, after a training accident in the air, and the third was grounded because of disparaging remarks he had made about his commander.'

Cohen simply became something like a kamikaze pilot on the radio, as if he were deliberately trying to commit suicide. His case officers in Tel Aviv should have restrained him, but none of them did so. The material coming in was just too good.[25]

Apparently guided by radio direction-finding equipment, most likely operated by Soviet advisers, Colonel Suedani's Syrian intelligence men broke into Cohen/Taabeth's apartment in January 1965 and caught him red-handed, tapping his telegraph key in the middle of a transmission.

For a few days, Suedani attempted to deceive Israel by forcing Cohen to transmit fictitious information which had been encoded. After three days of this game, without response from Tel Aviv, the Syrians gave up and sent a final message – addressed to Prime Minister Levi Eshkol: 'Kamel and his comrades are being hosted by us for a limited period of time. We will let you know in the future of his fate.'

An investigation concluded that Cohen and Lotz had been caught under similar circumstances. In both cases, their radio transmissions had been discovered by means of advanced equipment operated in Cairo and Damascus by Russian personnel.[26] Soviet military intelligence, the GRU, apparently suspected that vital secrets of its two allies in the Middle East, especially regarding their Soviet weaponry, had been reaching Israel and the West.

There were differences between the two cases, however. While Lotz was sentenced to life imprisonment, he was released after three years in a swap of Six-Day War POWs – although only after Amit threatened to resign if Israel abandoned Lotz as it ignored other spies in Egypt after the 1956 Suez campaign. Cohen, however, was sentenced to death at the end of a sham trial. The Syrian interrogators mercilessly tortured him. Eli Cohen never broke and he was hanged on May 18, 1965.

Amit was terribly depressed by the fall of his two prized agents. The defeats, one after another, were almost too much to bear. He made superhuman efforts to prevent Cohen from being executed, even mobilizing international appeals on behalf of the Israeli spy. Despite repeated requests, the Syrians still refuse to allow Cohen's body to be brought to Israel for burial.

Amit learned a lesson: Israel would, from then on, do everything in its power to free its captured spies. Baruch Mizrahi benefited. On Mossad assignment, he was in Syria, working as a foreign-language school principal, at the time Cohen was arrested. His Mossad controllers immediately ordered him to leave Syria.

Later, he was sent to spy in Yemen, to monitor the Egyptian Army still involved in the civil war there, and to report on shipping traffic which came in and out of the Red Sea. The Yemeni authorities announced that he was captured there in May 1972, and although Egypt's army had left, Yemen sent Mizrahi to Cairo where he was charged with espionage on behalf of Israel. Matters did not turn out too badly for him because he was sent home in March 1974 in exchange for two Israeli Arabs who had been spying for Egyptian intelligence.[27]

Arab secret services have tried consistently to plant agents in Israel, to report first-hand on the military, politics and society. Mary Frances Hagen was an American journalist at the United Nations in New York who was fond of many Arabs and agreed to spy in Israel for her fiancé, Syrian diplomat Galab al-Khieli. In 1956, she went to Israel as a foreign correspondent and began sending reports to Syrian intelligence. She seemed unusually interested in Israel's borders, so Shin Bet began to watch her closely. She was convicted, in a trial behind closed doors, on August 27, 1956, and spent eight months in an Israeli prison. The naïve Hagen returned to New York and found that Khieli did not even want to see her.[28]

The Syrians and Egyptians pursued many different methods to penetrate Israel, including the use of the Jewish state's Arab citizens – far from ideal, as they are under suspicion – and sending in agents posing as tourists. The most daring technique was a mirror-image of Israel's *modus operandi*: an Arab agent would teach himself to be a Jew and would go to Israel as an immigrant, unnoticed in a wave of new Jewish arrivals.

So it was in the case of Kobruk Yaakovian, who would take on the false identity of Yitzhak Koshuk and move to Israel in December 1961 – ostensibly from Brazil. The Israeli consulate in Rio de Janeiro gave him his visa, not knowing that Egyptian intelligence had recruited Yaakovian/Koshuk, a photographer of Armenian parentage, while he was in a Cairo prison for a minor criminal offence. The Egyptians even circumcised Yaakovian, to make him a convincing Jew. As Koshuk, he worked on a kibbutz for a while, settled in Ashkelon and entered the Israeli army. Despite his desire to join the armoured corps, he rose no higher than a transportation unit. Even so, Shin Bet caught Yaakovian/

Koshuk in December 1963. After a few years in prison, he was sent back to Egypt.[29]

The Egyptians were much more successful in the late 1960s, when they sent a man they claim as 'one of the best' agents they had to Israel. He called himself Jacques Biton and opened a travel agency on Brenner Street in Tel Aviv. He, also, was an Arab posing as a Jew and similarly circumcised. Biton was never caught. Instead, he was a spy who chose to retire. The Egyptians allowed him to move to West Germany, where he settled with his wife and died peacefully.

Egypt's state television had a huge hit on the air, in 1988, when they broadcast a film of Biton's life story. At first, Israeli officials said it was 'Arab fiction', but when more details emerged in Cairo, Israel had to admit an enemy agent had got away scot-free, while insisting that he caused little or no harm.

The assumption that Biton had to have been harmless, that the Arabs could not run a successful operation within Israel, was a natural result of the traditional belief in total Arab fallibility. The Israelis became convinced that their enemies could not do anything right, especially after the Six-Day War of 1967.

The lightning victory was Meir Amit's triumph, made possible by his own 'obsessions'. Not the same as those of his predecessor Harel, Amit's dwelt on obtaining as much information as possible on the Arab armies, to prepare thoroughly for any military confrontation. The likelihood of a third Middle East war was one of Israel's major preoccupations in the first years of Amit's directorship of the Mossad. This concern to improve Israel's military posture also stood behind the tremendous efforts which Amit made to form ties with his counterparts throughout the world.

The Mossad's Political Action and Liaison Department, in Amit's years, became something of a second, secret Israeli foreign ministry, occasionally outmanoeuvring the genuine one. The Mossad was involved in areas which are not customarily handled by secret services. In Amit's time, the 'peripheral concept' gained terrific momentum. Israel's clandestine connections with Ethiopia, Turkey and Iran were strengthened. Both Israel and Iran aided the Kurdish revolt in Iraq. Israeli agents in South Yemen tried to help the royalists fight off the Egyptians. In southern Sudan, Israeli aircraft dropped supplies for Christian rebels; and as far afield as Uganda in East Africa, the Mossad and Aman helped Idi Amin depose President Milton Obote in October 1970.

The Mossad, in coordination with Shin Bet, also established ties with various foreign security services through membership in 'Kilowatt', a group formed to combat international terrorism. Its members were representatives of the espionage agencies of Italy, Belgium, West Germany, Britain, Luxembourg, Holland, Switzerland, Denmark, France, Canada, Ireland and Norway, in addition, of course, to Israel. The Mossad also has ties with other states in Europe, such as Portugal, Spain and Austria.

In most of these states, there are Mossad stations. The station generally operates under diplomatic cover within the Israeli embassy, but the head of the station does not inform the ambassador of his activities. Instead, he sends his reports directly to Tel Aviv. Every station has representatives of the two most important departments of the Mossad: collection and liaison. The agents abroad are strongly insistent on compartmentalization, so that the members of one department do not know, and should not know, about the work of the other. Their tasks include official liaison exchanges with the host country's secret services, but they also operate their own networks, without informing the host service.[30]

Amit's emphasis on quasi-diplomatic activities concentrated primarily on two continents: Africa and Asia.

The nascent, newly independent black African states of the 1960s opened their eyes to see Israel the beautiful: an example to copy. While the United States and the Soviet Union were regarded as expansionist superpowers, and Britain, France and the other European countries were still disliked as colonialists, Israel was a young nation which had mastered the process of rapid development in the modern age. Africa's leaders could see the pioneering spirit at work in Israel, with initiative and proven ability which they hoped might be contagious.

Over a dozen African states welcomed Israeli technicians and instructors in agriculture, industry, commerce and defence. Hundreds of experts started development projects and Israel's travelling politicians were not far behind. Foreign Minister Golda Meir toured the continent and Prime Minister Levi Eshkol was also an honoured guest in a number of African countries.

The number of Israeli advisers grew exponentially and naturally quite a few of them were Mossad agents. The governmental hosts in Africa were usually more than under-standing of this fact of life and Israel quickly developed excellent intelligence cooperation with Kenya, Zaire, Liberia and Ghana. In each country, espionage agencies or security services were trained or assisted by the Israelis.[31]

The Mossad's leading force in Africa was David (Dave) Kimche. Kimche, whose Eastern European family had moved from Switzerland to England, was a Zionist and he moved to Palestine in 1946. But he kept his British habits. He is quiet and cultured and wears thick, black-rimmed glasses. Kimche has the ability to blend into almost any crowd. He does not sound Israeli either, as he speaks English perfectly and with an accent which would lead anyone to believe he was an English gentleman.

Kimche was recruited by the Mossad in 1953, after a few years in academia, and quickly gained a reputation, in the intelligence community, for keen perception, excellent ana-lytical ability and a tendency to keep his feelings to himself. He is the true-life Israeli equivalent of John LeCarré's fic-tional British spy, George Smiley. His interests lay in forging relations with non-Arab or non-Moslem minorities in the Middle East, but his speciality was Africa.

He worked, all over the continent, under various guises including that of David Sharon, Israeli businessman. Kimche/Sharon was a reliable and friendly source for foreign journalists and he was always able to supply them with the latest gossip on African regimes in the oddest places.[32]

One of those was the small island of Zanzibar, off the East African coast. Until 1964 it was ruled by a sultan and the members of his court were descendants of Arabian slave traders. The rest of the population was black. A bloody revolution broke out that year in Zanzibar. The black majority seized the government from the Arab minority. The sultan and his family were killed or fled from the island.

In Israel, there were no tears shed over the departure of the sultan. Another Arab stronghold in Africa had fallen and another state had been opened to Israeli influence. Dave Kimche 'happened' to be in Zanzibar on the day of the revolution. His presence enhanced the reputation of the Mossad, among Western diplomats and intelligence analysts, as being able to do anything.

Amit also deserved the credit for the Mossad's achievements in Asia, where Israeli agents formed discreet ties with Indonesia, an Islamic state which refuses to recognize Israel, and with India. In both cases, there was cooperation based on common interests, which led to the exchange of information.

In the case of Indonesia, it faces the dangers of a revolt by minority groups and Communist subversion. As for India, the common potential enemy of New Delhi and Tel Aviv is Pakistan, where most of the population is Moslem and successive governments are believed to have been working hard to develop a nuclear bomb.

The Mossad was especially concerned upon learning that Libya's Colonel Qaddafi had offered to finance the construction of a nuclear reactor in Pakistan, in exchange for an 'Islamic bomb' over which he would have custody. Israeli agents even explored the possibility of acting together with Indian forces to destroy the Pakistani reactor.[33]

The ability of the Mossad to foster foreign relations on Israel's behalf is probably most striking in the unique relations Israel has with an Arab state, Morocco.

Morocco, as a Moslem country and leading member of the Arab League, has always offered vociferous support to the Palestinian cause. Secretly, however, it found ways to establish mutually beneficial ties with the Jewish state. King Hassan II has a personal pro-Western inclination and felt threatened, in the 1960s, by the radical and anti-royalist regime in neighbouring Algeria and by the extremist Nasser in Egypt.

Mossad experts helped Hassan establish a secret service and, in return, Israel received the king's assurance that he would protect the Jews in his country and would permit those who wished to emigrate to Israel to do so. The relations between the two nations were secret, but they were good – even ideal. Amit, however, soon found that there was a price to pay for all this bounty. The price was the head of Mehdi Ben-Barka.

The leading Moroccan dissident, Ben-Barka was a darling of the Third World and so-called progressives in the West. A powerful enemy of King Hassan, Ben-Barka was sentenced to death *in absentia*, and the king apparently decided to carry out the sentence wherever Ben-Barka might be.

Hassan assigned the task to his interior minister, who was responsible for domestic security, General Muhammad Oufkir. The Moroccan general asked for the assistance of his Israeli friend, General Amit.

Amit, concerned that refusing the request would adversely affect the Jews and Israel's ties with Morocco, agreed to help. The Mossad chief met Oufkir in France in the early autumn of 1965 and there they finalized the agreement. Amit insisted, however, that his agents would not take part in the assassination itself. They would only help set the trap for Ben-Barka.

On October 29, Mossad agents lured the Moroccan dissident into leaving Geneva for a bogus meeting with a film producer in Paris. There, just outside a fashionable brasserie on the Left Bank, three French security officers, who were cooperating with the Moroccans, 'arrested' Ben-Barka.

Oufkir and his men shot Ben-Barka dead and buried him in the garden of a villa outside Paris.

Amit and Oufkir believed that the secret had been buried together with the corpse. Who would pay attention to a disappearance – or even an isolated murder which was entirely within the norms of Middle Eastern politics? The two intelligence officers did not, however, take into account the reactions of two other people, of very different outlooks and temperaments – Isser Harel in Israel and General de Gaulle in France.

The French President immediately ordered an investigation as to how Ben-Barka could have vanished in the very heart of Paris. The investigation not only uncovered the Israeli–Moroccan connection, but also the involvement of the French equivalent of the Mossad, SDECE, *Service de Documentation Extérieure et de Contre-Espionage*.

De Gaulle, who suspected that his secret agency might be plotting against him, was absolutely furious. He immediately ordered that the secret service's house be put in order. He also directed his anger at Israel. How could France's allies, with whom de Gaulle had cooperated, work behind his back?[34]

As a reaction to the Ben-Barka killing, the French President ordered that the Mossad's European command be removed from Paris and he also ordered a cessation of all intelligence cooperation between the two nations. His decision simply sharpened the knives which had been drawn in Israel, where a scandal was brewing over the Mossad's involvement in murder.

There was already a major internal struggle in Israeli politics, as the election set for November 1965 approached. Labour was sure to win, as usual, but the Labour movement was bitterly divided between Ben-Gurion's Rafi Party and the Mapai Party of Levi Eshkol and Golda Meir.

Having learned lessons from the Lavon affair and wider scandals stemming from botched espionage operations in Egypt, Mapai leaders decided that, come what may, they would not permit the Ben-Barka affair to grow – or even to become public knowledge. Israeli involvement in the killing, which had led to a noisy scandal in France, was kept totally secret.

When a sex-oriented Israeli magazine called *Bul* hinted that there could be 'Israelis in the Ben-Barka case', Shin Bet impounded all 30,000 copies of the issue just before their scheduled distribution. Only five copies reached the news-stands. The editors of the magazine, Shmuel Mor and Maxim Gilan, were placed in administrative detention.[35] Article 23 of the Israeli security laws was invoked, even though this section had never been used before for anything other than espionage against the Jewish state. This was the first – and, at the time of writing, the only – occasion on which this law has been invoked against journalists in Israel.

As in the Lavon affair, the key question was: Who gave the orders? Amit claimed that he had been given the go-ahead by Levi Eshkol. The Prime Minister claimed that he had never done any such thing. A demand to set up a commission of inquiry began to gain momentum when Isser Harel joined in calling for one. His voice was authoritative, not only because of his past, but also because he had just been appointed to a new job, as Adviser to the Prime Minister on Intelligence.

Harel's surprising return to active duty came in September 1965, a month before Ben-Barka was killed. Eshkol may have been motivated by a desire for personal revenge against his constant rival, David Ben-Gurion. It was as if he were sending a message: I, Levi Eshkol, having filled the place of 'the Old Man', am returning to the Israeli secret services the person who had been considered to be Ben-Gurion's protegé, but who was thrown to the dogs.

Eshkol ignored Amit's protests and the dirty war between Amit and Harel was renewed from the first instant of the new arrangement. The intelligence community found itself being pulled in opposite directions. Amit refused to cooperate with Harel. Harel found ways to bypass Amit. Using his personal contacts and based on his experience, the former *Memuneh* withdrew secret files from the Mossad's safes.

Harel brought the heads of departments directly to Prime Minister Eshkol for meetings and that went against established policy. Furthermore, at these meetings, they discussed Amit's deficiencies and their own assessments of his ability.[36]

Proposals for secret operations, which were brought to Eshkol by Amit, were vetoed by Harel. That was also the fate of a bold plan put forward by Amit to travel to Cairo for a secret meeting with Field Marshall Hakim Amar, Nasser's deputy.

This proposal was brought to the Mossad by a Jewish businessman, who was close to senior officials in the Egyptian Government. Harel chimed in bluntly that it would be an insane and irresponsible act. He questioned the reliability of the source, saying the businessman had dubious connections. Harel seemed sincerely concerned that the proposed Cairo talks could be a trap. He pointed out that Amit knew all of Israel's security secrets, so the damage that would be caused if he were to be arrested in Egypt would be irreparable.

Eshkol, who was torn between the battle of the giants, again sided with Harel. The suggested negotiations with Egypt were dead.

It can never be known whether such a clandestine mission could have prevented the war which broke out in June 1967. Amit believes it could have. Tension along the borders with Egypt and Syria were beginning to increase sharply and the intelligence community had to devote all its resources to the new threat.

There was no time, then, for questions of who was in charge of Israeli intelligence – Harel or Amit. Even the suggestion of installing a cabinet minister, General Yigal Allon, a 1948 war hero, as the community's supervisor, did not get the attention it deserved. The questions about the Ben-Barka affair were swept under the rug. Dissatisfied in 1966 that an authoritative enquiry committee was not set up, Harel resigned after only nine months in his new job: his new crusade had got nowhere and he left public service for good.

Amit held on to his Mossad job by the skin of his teeth, in a way lucky that miscellaneous matters were shoved aside when all the community's resources were devoted to the real purpose of intelligence – war.[37]

One of the unknown heroes who helped Israel foresee and fight the 1967 war was Shaaltiel Ben-Yair. He was born into a family of Jewish settlers in Metullah on the Lebanese border. They were immigrants from the Russian Caucasian mountains, who converted to Judaism at the beginning of this century and moved to Palestine.

As a young man, Ben-Yair learned to be an Arab. He was a teenager in the Irgun, sent on underground missions into the Palestinian Arab community, pretending to be an Arab cattle merchant. Shaaltiel's father, hoping to keep his son safer, sent him off to a naval school in France. The young Ben-Yair ran off with an older woman.

His time abroad was not wasted. The experience made him tough and taught him a French accent and an in-depth knowledge of oysters and fish soups. Back in Palestine, he attended a Scottish school and learned that accent too.

In World War II, he fought in a British commando unit in Egypt, and then in the extremist Lehi underground before joining the Israeli army for the 1948 war. Unemployed except for bar-hopping in Tel Aviv, he noted in 1956 that Shamir and other Lehi colleagues had joined the Mossad. Ben-Yair was quite happy to join, too, and had no trouble assuming the cover identity of François Renancoeur, a Belgian national who was an international 'expert' on cattle. Ben-Yair/Renancoeur was invited to Egypt by the government as an adviser on livestock.

One day in the late 1950s, the telephone rang in the Parisian apartment of Israeli author Amos Kenan. *'Ici Charlie,'* said a far-off voice. That was one of Ben-Yair's codenames. Kenan went off to meet his friend in Paris –

on a tourist boat on the Seine, where he found that Ben-Yair no longer had a moustache and refused to speak anything but French.

'I am now an expert on cattle, and you must call me François from now on,' the shadowy Israeli confided to his old friend Kenan. 'Once a month, I come to Paris for one evening, going to Brussels the next day and from there to Cairo. I have no one to talk to. My work is difficult. I was trained and even if you shouted at me in the middle of the night in Hebrew, I would not wake up.

'Nobody in Egypt could imagine that I also understand Arabic. And in Belgium, they believe that I am Belgian. My French southern accent matches their own. Just for safety's sake, I also tell people that I spent part of the war in southern France.'

In Egypt, Ben-Yair/Renancoeur was one of Israel's most daring agents. He was in charge of mapping Egyptian airfields and providing details of military installations. He was one of the few Israeli agents who completed their missions and returned home – never caught, never causing a scandal. His most valuable attribute was that he was a natural lone wolf, a one-man spy network.

In 1962, Ben-Yair had trouble readjusting to life in Israel – a common malady among former field agents who miss the excitement. He simply found life too ordinary. After a while, he left the country and just disappeared. It was learned, many years later, that when the Six-Day War broke out, he was living in Canada with a new identity – far from the Middle East and its crises.[38]

Israel's air force guaranteed the six-day victory in less than six hours. The initial attack, on June 5, 1967, wiped out nearly all the Arab air forces on the ground. It was a preemptive strike and did not strictly mean that Israel started the war. President Nasser had moved the Egyptian army across the Sinai Peninsula towards the Israeli border; he ordered United Nations peacekeepers to leave, and he was trying to strangle Israel by blockading shipping from entering or leaving the Red Sea.

The first hours of the brief war were confusing. While Arab radio stations gloated over their imaginary victories, John Hadden, the CIA station chief in Israel, was able to report to his headquarters in Langley, Virginia, that 'the war is over'. He was on excellent terms with the Mossad and had access to the latest, honest battlefield reports.

Amit had been at the new CIA headquarters only a few days earlier, on a special assignment for Eshkol. His mission: to tell the Americans that war was inevitable, that Nasser was starting it, but that Israel would have to strike first in order to survive. CIA director Richard Helms heard him out, and then so did President Lyndon B. Johnson. The US understood, and this achievement – based on the international intelligence links which the Mossad had worked so hard to foster – was Amit's finest hour. The air force and army then did the rest.

Thanks largely to excellent intelligence, Israel scored a historic victory. Spies in Cairo, such as Ben-Yair and Lotz, had pinpointed targets and Egyptian weaknesses. Eli Cohen had scouted the Syrian lines. Israel's air force knew when and where to attack.

By June 11, Israel was the master of Jordan's West Bank, Egypt's Sinai and Gaza Strip, and Syria's Golan Heights. The capture of these huge territories erased forever the notion of a tiny Jewish state lucky to survive among the large and powerful Arab nations. The triumph marked a watershed in Israel's history, and the intelligence community was not immune to the sweeping changes which followed.

Shin Bet Has its Day

The bed was still warm, the sheets and blankets lay strewn all over the floor, the water had boiled in the kettle and the tea in the cups was still hot, but 'Abu Ammar' was not to be found. A few seconds before Israeli troops and security men broke into the two-storey villa in Ramallah, on the West Bank, the PLO leader – better known in the outside world as Yasser Arafat – had fled.

From his second-floor hiding place, he heard the voices of the Israelis as they surrounded the villa and began their search. Arafat leaped from a window and hid in a car parked nearby. When the men who were after his scalp left, he hurried eastwards and crossed the River Jordan for the last time. It was September 14, 1967, three months after Israel captured the area from Jordan. Since then, Arafat has never set foot on the West Bank.[1]

Even though Shin Bet was disappointed on that autumn night that its men did not ensnare the PLO leader, there were still reasons for the agency to feel satisfied. It had quickly managed to liquidate completely what the Palestinian organizations had dared to call a 'popular uprising'.

Most of the territories seized by Israel in June presented few difficulties in holding. Almost all of the Syrians in the Golan Heights, except for a few thousand Druze, had fled the area. The Sinai was almost uninhabited, except for a few wandering Bedouin tribes. The real problems, for Israel as an occupying power, were contained in the West Bank and the Gaza Strip. In other words, from the security point of view which naturally denies humanity, that is where the people were.

The West Bank, an area of less than 3,000 square miles, was home to around 600,000 Palestinians, while another 400,000 resided in the overcrowded poverty of the Gaza Strip, comprising barely 100 square miles. The Arab residents were terrified of the Israeli occupation and it was soon clear that they wanted, at the least, to return to King Hussein's Jordanian administration. Even the Gazans, who had done poorly under Egyptian rule, wanted the chance to throw in their political lot with the West Bankers – preferably, in their own Palestinian state.

Palestinian guerilla groups, influenced by Maoist, Cuban and other Communist ideology, tried to emulate the Viet Cong, who were successfully confronting the powerful American armed forces in Vietnam, and the FLN, which had driven the French from Algeria. They called upon the Palestinian population to rise against the Israeli–Zionist occupation.

Their plan, after the crushing defeat of 1967, was to dominate daily life in the 500 towns and villages of the West Bank and the Gaza Strip, and to install an independent, PLO-led administration. They were hoping then to achieve what they finally managed to accomplish in 1988, in the *intifada*, or uprising.

Arafat believed that a million Arabs under Israeli rule gave him the opportunity to realize his dream of a 'struggle for popular liberation'. Immediately after the Six-Day War, a PLO pamphlet urged: 'We must set up secret resistance in every street, village and neighbourhood. Each person is obliged to fight the enemy. Roll large rocks down from the heights of mountains, in order to block the enemy's traffic arteries. Try to cause the enemy's cars to burst into flames. We must impose a boycott on the economic and cultural institutions of the occupation forces.' The circular ended with instructions on how to prepare a Molotov cocktail.[2]

The guerilla groups, under the PLO umbrella, did not only borrow foreign concepts from Vietnam, Cuba and Algeria, but also tried to copy their operational tactics. The Palestinians had active assistance from Colonel Suedani, the head of Syrian military intelligence credited with catching Eli Cohen in Damascus. He was known for his enthusiastic support for the notion of 'popular struggle'. The militant organizations infiltrated dozens of their members, armed with weapons and explosives, into the occupied territories, set up command posts and declared the 'armed popular revolution' for 'the liberation of Palestine'.

Arafat was personally involved in recruiting commanders for various operations and he was apprised of almost every tiny detail. Guerilla cells were sent out on hit-and-run operations against army vehicles and patrols. The Palestinians staged ambushes on the narrow streets of West Bank towns. They placed time bombs in markets, cinemas and restaurants, and they planted cars packed with explosives in the central squares of Israeli population centres. To Arafat's men, it was a pure form of honourable armed struggle, whereas in the eyes of the Israelis and most of the outside world it was just bloody terrorism.

Shin Bet had no time to argue about terminology. Prime Minister Eshkol and Defence Minister Dayan – while putting the army in charge of the daily affairs of military and civil administration – assigned Shin Bet to fight subversion, preserve law and order and enable Israel to run a stable occupation. There were many, however, in both the government and the army, who doubted Shin Bet's ability to accomplish these aims.

At the time, Shin Bet was still a small and self-contained body working in the shadows, operating at home in Israel but barely known even to exist. The general public had not heard of its operations. The very mention of its name made headlines. The entire force numbered around five hundred people, and everyone knew everyone else, as in a close family.

It was also, however, a lacklustre body which was always overshadowed by the Mossad and by Aman. Only rarely were a few crumbs thrown to Shin Bet by the operations department which it shared with the Mossad. These were unusual overseas operations, such as finding little Yossele Schumacher or capturing Adolf Eichmann.

Only two years before the Six-Day War, the government abolished the military administration that had been in effect in Israeli Arab towns and villages ever since the War of Independence. While the Arab citizens of the Jewish state always enjoyed the right to vote for the Knesset, they were not governed by the same civilian system as the Jewish-dominated areas. The Arabs were closely watched by Shin Bet.

The recommendation to do away with military rule in specific regions of Israel came from former Mossad operative Shmuel Toledano, Eshkol's adviser on Arab affairs. Surprisingly, Shin Bet supported the proposal, not because the agency suddenly took a liking to Arabs and their civil rights, but because the interests of the state and its security could be served better.

The role of Shin Bet was to prevent the Arabs from acting as a Fifth Column which could help their brothers across the border. Abolishing military administration, Shin Bet claimed, would offer the Arabs an incentive to become integrated into Israeli society, to study in its universities, to set up businesses, to launch careers, to make money, and no longer to feel the discrimination, frustration, disappointment and hopelessness that fostered subversion. Shin Bet believed that lifting official restrictions on Israel's Arabs would calm that sector of society and would isolate the minority of extremists who claimed that life in Israel is bad.[3]

Once military rule was abolished in 1965, Shin Bet became involved almost exclusively in counterespionage, primarily against agents of the Soviet bloc. Shin Bet's success at catching spies demanded a great deal of sophistication. Interrogations were a type of intellectual challenge. There was an unceasing effort to identify human frailty and soft spots. The Shin Bet interrogator and the person being questioned – perhaps a suspected traitor or spy – would sit together drinking coffee, without violence and would engage in a battle of wits.[4]

It was no coincidence then that in 1964, the Shin Bet counterespionage chief, Yosef Harmelin, replaced Amos Manor as head of the entire agency. Harmelin personified the new priorities of Shin Bet in the years before the Six-Day War.

Harmelin, who was tall, with an expressionless face, was born in Vienna in 1922. After the *Anschluss* in 1938, when Austria was annexed by Nazi Germany, the family moved to Mexico and set up a factory there. The young Yosef, more Zionist than his parents, moved to Palestine instead. He studied at the Ben Shemen agricultural school, which produced such future political leaders as Shimon Peres and also the future spy Wolfgang Lotz. Similar to Harel and Amit, Harmelin joined a kibbutz, before enlisting in the British Army in World War II. After the war, he joined the Haganah, where he met Harel, and a few years after Israel's independence Harmelin was recruited by Shin Bet. He gradually worked his way up to the top.[5]

His relationship with Levi Eshkol, who appointed him to be head of Shin Bet, was very formal. Eshkol, who as Prime Minister was directly responsible for the Mossad and Shin Bet, tried to develop a close, almost paternal relationship with Harmelin – to contrast with the troubles he was having getting along with Meir Amit. Eshkol found Harmelin to be honest to a fault, sincere and a perfectionist. On the other hand, Harmelin was a 'square' and too dull for Eshkol, who was a canny politician, an expert manipulator of party intrigues and a compromiser. Eshkol was also known for his sense of humour, but this did not cut any ice with Harmelin – even when the Prime Minister, with his characteristic pungent wit, tried to crack jokes in his beloved Yiddish.

One day, after Shin Bet detected indications of an assassination threat, the guard around the Prime Minister was doubled. Almost every week, there were suggestions and threats that Eshkol might be killed. In general, these threats were ignored, because the Israelis have always believed that genuine assassins do not write warning letters. After President John F. Kennedy was murdered in Dallas, however, Shin Bet was not willing to take any unnecessary chances.

Harmelin, whose responsibilities included protecting the Prime Minister and other government officials, reported to Eshkol that from that time on there would be two bodyguards who would be with the Prime Minister constantly.[6] 'But you can trust their utter discretion,' the Shin Bet chief promised, remembering that Eshkol was a widower at the time and might have personal reasons for privacy. 'Even if you have any very intimate meetings, they won't breathe a word.'

Eshkol, with his typical chuckle, responded: 'On the contrary, let them tell.' Harmelin did not laugh at such jokes. He treated his work with complete seriousness. That was also how he behaved when he was given a new assignment: the occupied territories.

The decision to this effect was adopted on June 19, 1967, at a meeting of the *Va'adat*, the committee of intelligence chiefs. Mossad director Amit was chairman, and around the table in Tel Aviv sat Aman chief Aharon Yariv, Harmelin for Shin Bet, police chief superintendent Pinhas Koppel and the director-general of the foreign ministry, Aryeh Levavi.[7]

The Israeli government was finding it difficult to decide on a status and future plans for the territories captured in the Six-Day War. Were they 'liberated' portions of the biblical land of Israel, or 'occupied' pieces of hostile, foreign territory?

Lacking a political decision about the land, the *Va'adat* was forced to adopt an administrative policy of carrot and stick, designed to preserve the status quo while maintaining law and order as the highest priority. In an attempt to drive a wedge between the majority of the Palestinians and the dangerous, subversive minority, the intelligence chiefs decided that the inhabitants would be permitted to conduct their lives normally. That was the carrot.

The stick was the policy to punish, strongly and surely, anyone participating in subversion or outright violence. Palestinians who aided guerilla groups were punished by imprisonment and the destruction of their houses – usually by dynamite, in loud explosions meant to serve as examples to others. Losing one's home was severe punishment, but the most serious and decisive penalty available to Shin Bet was expulsion.

Transforming the carrot and stick theory into practice was no simple task. The Shin Bet agents were not prepared for it. The new territories in Israel's hands were to them *terra incognita*. Shin Bet had no men in the field – not in the West Bank and Gaza, anyway – and did not know the population. The agency had to start from scratch.

As a first step, Shin Bet personnel, with the help of Military Intelligence, used psychological warfare to spread rumours – more than accurate, they were chilling – of how tough the Israeli hard line would be.[8]

After it was clear that Israel's position was known to the inhabitants of the territories, Shin Bet prepared itself for the second and major stage: the struggle against the attempted Palestinian uprising and against terrorism. It was only natural that Harmelin assigned this task to Avraham Ahituv, the head of the small Arab affairs department of Shin Bet. This department ensured that the Israeli Arabs, under military administration and after its abolition, were not engaged in subversive acts, incitement or violence.

Ahituv, a lawyer by training, was able to establish a widespread network of informers among Israeli Arabs and almost nothing escaped his men's eyes. A secret report compiled about him by the CIA stated that he 'is extremely bright, hard-working, ambitious and thorough', but also 'headstrong, abrasive and arrogant'.[9]

Ahituv had also been in charge of the agency's operations in the Gaza Strip after Israel captured it in 1956. Now he was asked to use his talents to achieve – throughout the occupied territories – similar results to those he had achieved in Gaza and in Israel's Arab sector. Ahituv was aided in this by Yehudah Arbel.

Arbel, short, with prematurely greying hair, had hypnotic eyes. His eyes were the bluest of blue, but they were ice-cold. He was a romantic and an aesthete who loved music, art, beautiful women and good wine. His autobiography is similar to that of other employees in the Israeli intelligence community. He was born in Transylvania, then part of Hungary but now in Romania, moved to Palestine, served in the British Army, and fought for Israel's independence in 1948. Until he joined Shin Bet in 1955, he worked as a police officer. When the 1967 war broke out, Arbel was the Jerusalem district head of Shin Bet. It was a small, uneventful district, with relatively little work to do. Generally, since Israel's western sector of Jerusalem had very few Arabs until 1967, this work consisted of counterespionage and surveillance of foreign diplomats.

Arbel was so bored that for a time he considered resigning. Following the Six-Day War, however, he was given one of the most vital assignments in Israeli intelligence: fighting terrorism. It was like a sudden shot of adrenalin. It was as if he had been reborn. Arbel ran incessantly from one village to another in the West Bank, recruiting informers and coordinating the penetration of resistance cells.[10]

In no time at all, Shin Bet licked the problem facing Israel in the territories. There would be no popular uprising in the newly occupied lands. Shin Bet had good, inside information, and that is the essential weapon in waging a successful war against underground opposition. Within a short time, Ahituv and Arbel managed to envelop the entire West Bank and the Gaza Strip in networks of informers and secret agents. Most of them were Arabs, recruited either by bribery or intimidation, but there were also a few Israelis who were excellent Arabic-speakers. The agents often gave Shin Bet advance information of attacks planned by guerillas.[11] It was the continuous flow of information which had almost enabled Shin Bet to lay its hands on Arafat that night in the villa near Ramallah.

Shin Bet operatives, acting on tip-offs, were able to swoop down on subversive meetings and laid ambushes to capture Palestinian squads on their way to staging attacks. The system which permitted these successes became known as 'preventive intelligence', which is the main objective of every internal security service having to deal with violence and terrorism. The ultimate aim is not to have to search for the perpetrators after the crime, but to prevent the terrorists from carrying it out in the first place.

Within five months, before the end of 1967, Shin Bet had chalked up an amazing record of triumph: most of the PLO cells collapsed and their headquarters within the West Bank were forced to retreat to Jordan. Two hundred Palestinian guerillas were killed in battles with the army and Shin Bet units, and more than a thousand were arrested.

One cannot, however, claim that the failure of the attempted Palestinian uprising of 1967 was due solely to the efficiency of Israel's secret services. The Palestinians were also to blame to a large extent because of their lack of professionalism. They did not obey the rules of compart-mentalization in their operations. They organized in relatively large groups, knew one another and relied on the locals not to turn them in to the authorities. Arafat himself and his senior commanders, in total violation of the rules of a good conspiracy, knew most of the members of the cells. Their communications system was primitive and their codes were simple. No escape routes were planned. Their 'safe houses' were not really safe. Nor were the members of guerilla squads prepared for interrogation, when captured. As soon as they were picked up by Shin Bet, they would 'squeal', telling everything they knew.

Their codes were broken, their weapons and explosives were confiscated. Like dominoes, the cells fell one after another. Above all, failing to honour Mao Tse-tung's Chinese dictum that a guerilla fighter must have the support of the population and feel 'like a fish in the water', the Palestinian fighters could not 'swim' unnoticed among their neighbours, who swept them to the Shin Bet shore. Motivated by Israel's reward and punishment policy, the local populace preferred peace, quiet and prosperity – rather than collaboration with the underground.[12]

In any event, full credit for this success was given to Shin Bet and its case officers became known as the 'kings of the territory'. Almost as in a feudal society, each Israeli operative was given his own region, generally a village or a group of villages. He had to be Israel's eyes and ears, knowing everything that happened in his fiefdom. The operative was trained to know most of the villagers by name, while they knew him only by an alias – usually an invented Arabic name.

If a Palestinian wanted a building permit, the military government would check with the local Shin Bet case officer. An Arab merchant who wanted to export his citrus crop from Gaza or his olive oil from the West Bank was only able to obtain the necessary papers with the permission of Shin Bet. Almost every daily activity, almost every minute of the life of the local Palestinian, was supervised by Shin Bet. In many cases, the Israeli operative regarded his local network as a business partner. The Arabs supplied information and in return they were given security and fringe benefits.[13]

Success was achieved at a cost, however. The price was that Israeli society was judged in the outside world by what could be seen of its security policies. Even as Shin Bet cracked down on subversion, Israel's goodwill around the world was being squandered. Instead of being an admired favourite of international public opinion, the Jewish state became the Ugly Israel. The underdog of 1967 was now seen as a brutal occupier of another people's land.

Just as most intelligence agencies reflect their societies' ethics, values and morals, the change in Israel's image inflicted damage on Shin Bet. Until the Six-Day War, Shin Bet was a rare specimen in that its personnel were like a small family with much in common: they had served in the British Army or the Haganah, and were primarily from the European, Ashkenazi sector of the Jewish population.

After the war, Shin Bet was forced by circumstances to transform itself into an oppressive force, playing a central role in governing the conquered territories and their people. Suddenly, Shin Bet became the security service of an occupying power, self-confident and even arrogant. Having to cover a lot more ground, Shin Bet's perfectionism and meticulous work gave way to hasty improvisation.

In order to set up the large intelligence networks, there was an urgent need to expand Shin Bet's manpower. The recruiting criteria were made easier and less selective. There was no longer the emphasis on high standards.

Everything was done in a hurry. Shin Bet recruiters launched a frantic search for Arabic-speakers. The social profile of Shin Bet's personnel changed and quite obviously so. The Arabic-speakers who were now so essential were to be found among the Oriental, Sephardi sector of the Jewish populace.

Until then, most of those selected were men from élite combat units of the army. Unlike most countries, where the special forces or commandos are considered the most aggressive and bloodthirsty soldiers, over-eager for battle, Israel's élite fighting men were trained to be soul-searching and aware of morality. Now Shin Bet, to meet its urgent requirements, added to its ranks from mere support units, where soldiers were less inculcated with the finer aspects of morals and ethics.

Even senior Shin Bet commanders, who normally had a good eye for spotting problem applicants, made mistakes. Yossi Ginossar, who about twenty years later would feature in two of the worst scandals in the history of the Israeli intelligence community, was one of those 'errors'. Ginossar came from the adjutancy – a staff officer who assisted at the rear, rather than battling at the front.

The changed nature of the work also dictated new methods. At a time when 2,000 Arabs were being detained, when booby-trapped cars were exploding, and when hotels and airliners were terrorist targets, it was essential to extract information as fast as possible. The time factor became the most important element of preventive intelligence. When information is needed as quickly as possible, brutality is required without pausing for a second thought.

At first, Shin Bet found it difficult to adjust to this new reality. It hoped that it would be able to behave as it had in the past. When Yosef Harmelin once saw one of his young interrogators slap the face of a Palestinian suspect, the agency chief demanded that the man be dismissed. Harmelin did not understand why physical violence was necessary.[14]

The new circumstances, however, dominated. Shin Bet operatives learned, the hard way, what the occupation meant. Their work, after all, had to be dirty. Harmelin and his deputy Ahituv could take credit for suppressing terrorism, but they also had to take the blame for introducing 'the System'. It worked effectively and secretly, without the Israeli public knowing how it was being protected. Only the scandals of the late 1980s exposed the System.

Occupying the territories created a double standard of justice. One, democratic by nature, applied to Israeli citizens; and a totally different one, operating in the grey area between the permissible and the forbidden, was used against Palestinians.

The System and its double standard created a new frontier, 'Shin Bet country'. In Shin Bet country, there were special detention centres run by the agency and separate wings of Israeli prisons specially controlled by Shin Bet. Whenever Palestinian prisoners were arrested, they were brought directly to the special wings or detention centres. The police and the national prisons authority had no right to look at what was occurring in the cells behind those walls.

Arabs accused of terrorism faced brutal interrogation.

True, there were not necessarily physical blows, but there were other forms of coercion which left no marks. Once the gates of Shin Bet closed behind them, Palestinian prisoners found their heads covered by a black sack, reeking of urine, and then they were left, exposed to the hot Israeli sun or winter's cold, waiting for the interrogators. The questioning went on for hours. The suspects were usually deprived of sleep and sometimes soaked with cold water.

Some Shin Bet personnel did not like what they had to do, but they regarded it as necessary in the struggle for existence. They believed that they were defending Israel, which faced cruel terrorism. 'What do terrorists that kill women and children expect? That we should knock on their door and invite them for a cup of coffee?' said a Shin Bet veteran, known only as Pashosh, who headed the agency's interrogation department for many years.[15]

The military administration and intelligence community jointly engaged in other activities in the occupied territories. To counter the 'demographic problem', the danger that within a few years there would be an Arab majority in Israel and the territories, it was decided to encourage Palestinians to emigrate. This was a combined effort of psychological warfare and the work of a special unit formed by the intelligence community. The unit set up paper corporations in Europe, which bought land in Libya, Brazil and Paraguay. Palestinian inhabitants who agreed to emigrate were promised parcels of land in those countries, were given passports and were promised financial aid. The promises were not always kept, but around 20,000 West Bank and Gaza residents emigrated in the first four years after the 1967 war.

Despite these efforts, the special intelligence unit was unable to make significant progress. Over a million Palestinians stayed in their homes and the struggle only increased.[16]

After failing to ignite an uprising in the territories, Palestinian activists shifted their battle to other locales. Hijackings and bombings became a new norm, and the entire earth was transformed into a global terrorist village.

No target, especially if connected to Israel or Jews, was off limits. When the PLO moved abroad, Shin Bet followed accordingly. Shin Bet and the PLO became almost a symbiotic entity, like a cat and mouse that play hide-and-seek.

Despite inter-agency rivalries and its near monopoly over foreign operations, the Mossad accepted, although reluctantly, that Shin Bet had the legal and professional obligation to expand its activities abroad in the hot pursuit of terrorism. Therefore, Shin Bet officers and agents were either attached – on loan – to Mossad operatives, or operated independently. Theirs was a violent, dirty fight of innovation and improvisation.

The PLO, through its radical faction called the Popular Front for the Liberation of Palestine, or PFLP, caught Israel by surprise on July 22, 1968. In the first, memorable report of its kind, Harmelin informed Prime Minister Eshkol: 'An El Al Boeing 707 plane, on a flight from Rome to Tel Aviv, has been hijacked and landed in Algeria.'

Since the spring, Shin Bet had received fragmentary reports of tremendous efforts being made by some Palestinian groups, mainly the Marxist–Leninist PFLP led by Georges Habash, to attract volunteers from radical left-wing circles in Europe. Impatient emissaries, on behalf of Arafat, Habash and others, hopscotched across Italy, Holland, France and West Germany, using ideological comradeship and financial incentives to persuade young Europeans to come to the Middle East and fight 'the Zionist occupation' and 'its imperialist allies'. Dozens of highly motivated volunteers answered the PLO call, were brought to Jordan and Lebanon, were trained in guerilla camps, and went, in some cases, into battle as terrorists against Israel.

The passengers and crew of the Israeli airliner were held captive in Algiers for three weeks, and only when Israel agreed to free a dozen Arab guerillas from jail did the first Palestinian hijacking end with the release of the hostages.

The Israeli decision-makers drew their conclusions. They vowed never again to surrender to terrorist blackmail, but defiant statements of intent are insufficient in such matters.

Rather than words alone, Israel needed more stringent security measures.

Once again, Shin Bet had to build something formidable from nothing at all. 'We were on the verge of total desperation,' then-agency chief Harmelin recalls. 'The struggle against terrorism, especially aviation terror, seemed to us like mission impossible.'[17] Israel needed an effective and sophisticated defence system to protect its interests abroad: embassies, banks, tourism offices and the national airline. It was not only the fleet of airplanes but the ground facilities which had become terrorist targets. El Al reception counters and offices in all airports abroad had their defences 'hardened' and were given armed guards.

With an investment of hundreds of millions of dollars, El Al became the most secure airline in the world. Radical innovations included armed sky marshals on every flight, in plainclothes posing as ordinary travellers. There were young men who had served in élite army units, had learned to be quick on the draw, and were now being sent aboard El Al flights to protect the planes and their passengers.

The world only learned about it half a year later, when on February 18, 1969, Mordecai Rachamim, a young air marshal, drew a revolver and shot to death a Palestinian who had opened fire on an El Al plane that was on the tarmac of Kloten airport near Zurich. Swiss authorities arrested the Israeli guard and put him on trial. He was convicted and served a few months in jail, before returning to Israel as a national hero. Because he had been 'burned', with his photograph appearing in newspapers and on television throughout the world, Shin Bet assigned him to be personal bodyguard to the new Prime Minister, Golda Meir – a job which does not require undercover anonymity.

A key weapon in this foreign version of preventive intelligence was information from inside the terrorist organizations. In 1973, Shin Bet received excellent information about a plan to fire rockets at an El Al jet at Fiumicino airport in Rome. The information included precise details about the *modus operandi*, the exact date and the names of the attackers. Shin Bet issued a warning to the Italian security service, which set an ambush for the terrorists and captured five.

The joy felt by Israeli intelligence did not last long. Italy, under economic and diplomatic pressure from Libya's Colonel Muamar Qaddafi, used the first pretext which came its way to release the five Arabs. They were flown to Tripoli in an operation so low-key that the Italian air force used one of its oldest craft: a C-47 Dakota propeller plane.

On November 23, 1973, barely two weeks after returning from Libya, the same aircraft crashed near Venice. Four Italian military officers — the same men who had flown the terrorists to their Tripoli refuge — were killed. Sabotage was immediately suspected, but never proved.

Thirteen years later, the former head of Italy's counter-espionage service, General Ambrogio Viviani, charged that the Mossad had caused the crash. The Italian press said the Israelis were out to punish the government in Rome for being soft on terrorism.

Venice magistrate Carlo Mastelloni went further in 1989, by naming two Israeli suspects: Zvi Zamir, head of the Mossad from 1968 to 1974, and the Mossad station chief in Rome, identified by the judge as Asa Leven. Zamir strongly denied the accusations, calling them 'pure rubbish' and explaining that the combatants in an internal Italian dispute were wrongly dragging Israel into the picture.[18]

Each new threat by the PLO was met by a solution devised by Shin Bet. Four Palestinian terrorists hijacked a Belgian airliner on May 8, 1972. Sabena flight 571 was flying from Brussels to Tel Aviv, and indeed the hijackers had it land at Lod airport. They held nearly a hundred passengers and crew at gunpoint, demanding that Israel free 317 imprisoned guerillas. Aman's chief, General Yariv, negotiated with the two men and two women who had commandeered the airliner, demonstrating his talents as a talker while the Israel Defence Force prepared its true response.

On cabinet orders, an army commando unit, specially trained at storming airliners and rescuing hostages, went into action at 4.22 p.m. on May 9. The commandos, dressed in white overalls as airport maintenance men, broke into the Boeing 707 through every conceivable entrance and, with pinpoint markmanship, killed the two male terrorists, wounded the two females and freed 97 hostages. In the exchange of fire, one Israeli passenger died.

Theory quickly followed from practice and as Israel developed a new theory of war on terrorism, the rest of the world hurried to learn from the Israeli experience. West Germany, Britain and other states sent security agents and military commandos to Israel, in order to have them learn Israel's methods. Many nations then established commando units of their own, based on the Israeli model. In Britain, the hostage-rescue specialists were units of the SAS, the Special Air Services, while the West Germans formed a force called GSG-9.

When the PLO began to attack Israeli embassies and diplomats in Europe and Asia, Shin Bet was ready to respond. The embassies and consular offices were transformed into fortresses: double-thickness steel doors protected entrances, television cameras scrutinized all visitors, building perimeters were surrounded by electronic sensors and Shin Bet guards were assigned to keep watch over buildings and staff. The expanded 'protective security' department of Shin Bet did everything possible to defend Israeli facilities abroad, but the intelligence chiefs realized that to deter terrorism they needed stronger measures. From passive defence, they moved full speed ahead with active defences.

As early as 1968, the Israelis embarked on a new policy, after an Israeli passenger was killed on December 26 in a grenade attack on an El Al airliner at Athens airport. In Israel, the mood was one of frustration. The public seemed to believe that the Israeli security forces did not have any adequate response to the export of Palestinian terrorism from the Middle East to Europe.

It was with that dark mood dominating the country that Prime Minister Eshkol called a special meeting in his office with military and intelligence chiefs. Eshkol set the tone himself: 'We can't just ignore this,' he exclaimed. They decided to send the army on a retaliatory mission to Beirut, from where the Athens attackers had come.

Israeli special forces were landed by helicopter at the international airport just south of the Lebanese capital on December 28 at 9.15 p.m. Undeterred by a gun battle with Lebanese troops, the Israelis blew up thirteen empty civilian aircraft belonging to Lebanon's Middle East Airlines and other Arab companies. The world was shocked by the audacity of the move and condemned Israel for engaging in what was referred to as state terrorism. It emerged that as in the old days of the Lavon affair and the Ben-Barka murder, the Prime Minister was not told everything. Defence Minister Moshe Dayan had deceived Eshkol, by promising him that only four airplanes would be blown up in the action.[19]

Behind the condemnation, the world had to admire Israel's military prowess. The Beirut raid was a clear sign that Israel could strike with astonishing accuracy at the heart of the Arab world. The credit for the operation, which was commanded by Brigadier General Raphael (Raful) Eitan of the paratroops, went to the Israeli special forces. They form a category of units, each known as a *sayeret*. The word derives from the Hebrew for reconnaissance, but the soldiers in a *sayeret* are expert in many more areas. They have to undergo tough training, including guerilla warfare, night-time combat, parachute drops and the handling of a variety of firearms.

Almost every Israeli army brigade has its own *sayeret*. Thus the paratroops, the infantry, the navy and the tank brigades each have their own *sayeret*. Above all of these is another *sayeret* – the élite among élites – the name of which is not printed in Israel, due to censorship, but foreign publications have identified it as *sayeret matkal*.[20] *Matkal* is the Hebrew acronym for the general staff of the army, and this particular *sayeret* gets its instructions directly from the chief of staff, Israel's highest military officer.

These forces, which recruit volunteers from among newly

enlisted soldiers, hold a powerful attraction for Israeli youth, who are all subject to the draft at the age of 18. Israel does not have a military tradition as do other Western states, in which generations of the same family serve proudly in certain units or study in military academies such as America's West Point or Britain's Sandhurst. Israel does have, however, a tradition of personal and family contacts and *protektzia*, a term in both Russian and Hebrew for what Americans call using 'pull'. Often, such contacts are used for positive ends. The sons of celebrities or politicians when, highly qualified, are commonly accepted into a *sayeret*.

One example is Colonel Uzi Dayan, who took part in the raid on the Beirut airport. He is the nephew of General Moshe Dayan and was able, in spite of being seriously injured before joining the army, to be accepted into a very select *sayeret*.[21]

The ongoing war against terrorism took a turn for the uglier in 1972. On May 30, three gunmen of the Japanese Red Army slaughtered twenty-seven passengers, most of them Christian pilgrims from Puerto Rica, who had just arrived at Lod airport. After initial confusion, security guards fought back, leaving two terrorists dead and Kozo Okamoto captured. He confessed during his trial that he and his colleagues – to display solidarity – had acted on behalf of the PFLP. It was revenge for the failure of the Sabena hijack, on the Lod tarmac just a few hundred yards away from the carnage they caused in the terminal.

Five weeks later, it was Israel's turn to retaliate. A letter bomb which arrived in Beirut killed Ghassan Kanafani, a poet, writer and PFLP spokesman accused by the Israelis of planning the Lod massacre. Two days later, another letter exploded in the hands of PFLP official Bassam Abu Sherif, who lost an eye and several fingers. These attacks were in the old tradition of the parcel bombs which killed the Egyptian officers in the 1950s and the letter bombs sent to German scientists in Egypt in the early 1960s.

The vicious circle of violence and retaliation reached its peak at the Olympic Games in Munich on September 5,

1972. Under the cover of the shadowy Black September group, named for the month in 1970 when Jordan's King Hussein crushed the Palestinians, Arab terrorists seized eleven Israeli athletes in the Olympic village. The original aim of Black September, which was nothing but a secret branch of the PLO organized by Arafat, was to take revenge against Jordan, but it quickly turned its guns against Israel.

Similar to other hostage incidents, the seven terrorists demanded that Israel free 250 of their comrades from prison. The Israeli government, true to its firm policy, declined to cave in and refused to free any prisoners.

Israel immediately sent Mossad chief Zamir to Munich. He had replaced Meir Amit, who had asked Prime Minister Eshkol if he could serve another term after completing his five years in 1968. Eshkol rejected his request, in part because of continued bitterness over the Ben-Barka affair. But that was not the only obstacle. Eshkol greatly appreciated Amit's ability and his successes. In fact, Amit may have had to leave the Mossad because he was just too efficient. Eshkol, Golda Meir and other veteran leaders of the Labour Party began to fear the increasing power of Amit. Just as Ben-Gurion eventually became suspicious of the power accrued by Isser Harel, the new party leaders did not want to have an intelligence chief who was too strong and becoming arrogant.

Another cause of Eshkol's suspicion was a minor conspiracy by Amit with his long-time friend, Defence Minister Dayan. In March 1968, Dayan wanted to make a secret trip to Iran to see the Shah. He turned to Amit, because the Mossad was responsible for ties with Iran, to arrange the visit. When Eshkol found out, he was livid. He demanded an explanation from Amit.

'What's happening here?' Eshkol asked the head of the Mossad. 'How dare you do a thing like that? The Mossad and you are subordinate to me, and not to the defence ministry or Moshe Dayan.'[22]

Amit did not have a good answer and that was when his fate was sealed. When Amit asked to extend his tenure,

Eshkol explained to him politely that he had decided to appoint Major General Zvi Zamir to replace him at the Mossad.

There certainly were many who felt that Zamir should not have been given the job. The fact that he had no previous background in intelligence made him a surprise choice, even to himself.

So why was he selected for one of the most important and sensitive jobs in Israel? Because Zamir was considered 'one of us'. He was identified with the Labour movement. Like many Labour figures, he was born in Poland in 1925 and had arrived in Palestine at the age of seven months with his family, whose name was then Zarzevsky. At eighteen, he joined the *Palmach*, fought in the 1948 war and made his career in the Israeli army. He attained the rank of major-general, was placed in charge of the Southern Command, and, to cap off his career, was appointed in 1966 as Israel's military attaché in London.

There was another reason for Eshkol's decision: in a sense, Zamir's strength could be found in his weakness. After two decades of strong, overconfident master spies, the Prime Minister wanted to appoint a completely different character. Zvi Zamir fitted the bill. His London posting meant that he had missed the Six-Day War and the limelight of glory cast upon other Israeli generals. Nicknamed Zvika, Zamir lacked glamour and was one of those colourless, boring, expressionless faces of the Israeli military.[23]

Arriving in Munich and holding urgent discussions with West German security officials, Zamir had no time to display flashes of personality. It was right down to the business of saving the lives of the Israeli athletes. Under Prime Minister Meir's direct orders and armed with the experience of rescuing the hijacked Sabena passengers only four months earlier, Zamir pleaded with the West Germans to permit a specially trained Israeli *sayeret* to deal with the siege. But the German authorities refused.

Zamir, therefore, was left to watch helplessly from the control tower of Furstenbruck airbase as inexperienced and ill-equipped German sharpshooters failed to kill all the terrorists in the first volley. Three were still alive, and they fired their guns and detonated their grenades to kill the handcuffed hostages, who were slaughtered as they sat in helicopters on the tarmac.

Waves of shock reverberated around the world, with the massacre seen as both a human tragedy and a warning that terrorism was getting out of control. In Israel, an enquiry committee decided that the head of Shin Bet's protective security department, who had been responsible for guarding the Olympic athletes, should be dismissed. Agency chief Harmelin stood firmly against pinning the blame on the department head and for the only time in his career Harmelin threatened to resign. Prime Minister Meir insisted that the dismissal was a cheap bureaucratic price to pay and the man was fired.[24]

While the investigation continued, five days after the Munich massacre, Zadok Ofir received an urgent phone call at his desk in the Israeli embassy in Brussels. He rushed to the Café Prince, where an Arab carrying a Moroccan passport, who was a member of Black September, shot him at point-blank range. Later, it became clear that Ofir was a Shin Bet officer, working undercover as first secretary at the embassy. Ofir was wounded in the abdomen, but he survived. It also emerged that the Israeli knew his assailant. The Arab was a double agent and Ofir was his case officer. The embassy in Brussels was the centre of Israeli espionage activity in Europe and had been since de Gaulle expelled the Mossad from Paris after the Ben-Barka murder.[25]

The Brussels shooting should have lit huge warning lights in the Mossad and Shin Bet headquarters. For the first time, an Israeli intelligence officer on active duty abroad had been shot. The massacre at Munich, however, was overshadowing all other incidents and considerations. Even Zamir, returning from Munich, did not recognize the importance of the assault on Ofir.

Zamir landed at Lod airport and hurried to Jerusalem, where he told the Prime Minister of the disaster he had witnessed. There were tears in Golda Meir's eyes. Meir, a hardened politician but nevertheless a sensitive woman who was a typical Jewish mother, was torn between cool logic and a desire to avenge the lives of her murdered 'boys'. Before long, both converged in a cold, calculated decision to kill those who had killed.

Meir created the post of 'prime minister's adviser on counter-terrorism' and appointed General Aharon Yariv, who had just retired as Aman director, his place in history assured by the six-day victory of 1967. Also significantly, the Israeli cabinet formed a committee, chaired by Golda Meir and Moshe Dayan, to decide on the response to Munich. The panel was known only as Committee X so that even the other cabinet members and civil servants would not know of its purpose. Committee X decided to liquidate any Black September terrorists involved, directly or indirectly, in planning, assisting, or executing the attack on the Olympics.[26]

The responsibility for implementation was given to the Mossad. Zamir summoned Mike Harari, one of the senior agents in the operations department, and put him in charge of the assassination squads. Harari hand-picked a team of operatives, both men and women, and established his European command post in Paris. Using several false identities including a passport which identified him as French businessman Edouard Stanislas Laskier, Harari and Mossad operative Avraham Gehmer, whose cover was that of first secretary of the Israeli embassy in Paris, were in charge of planning.[27]

First, the Israelis compiled a list of Arabs who had been involved in the Munich operation. The team then began to trail the men on its wanted list, most of whom had remained in Europe engaged in various overt professions and covert terrorist activities. When Harari and his team felt ready to attack, they contacted Zamir in Tel Aviv, and he turned to Committee X for permission to give the go-ahead. Prime Minister Meir and her secret panel, in fact, had to approve each individual killing. The first to die, in October 1972, was Adel Wael Zwaiter, a Palestinian intellectual who worked for Black September. Within the space of ten months, Harari's men and women took the lives of twelve Palestinians. They were killed by guns with silencers, sometimes fired from cars and motorbikes in Paris and Rome, or by remote-controlled bombs, detonated by high-tech, high-pitched tones transmitted by telephone or radio in Nicosia and Paris.

Black September, which saw how its men were being killed, responded in kind. On November 13, 1972, a Syrian journalist in Paris, named Khader Kano, was shot dead. He had been an informer for the Israelis.

On January 26, 1973, Israeli businessman Hanan Yishai was killed as he stood in a doorway on the Gran Via, the main street of Madrid. After his death, it was revealed that his real name was Baruch Cohen and that he had come to Madrid from Brussels on a mission for Israeli intelligence.

Cohen was the black sheep of a well-known family in Haifa, most of whose members identified with right-wing political parties. One of his brothers, Meir Cohen, was deputy chairman of the Israeli parliament as a member of Menachem Begin's Likud Party. Only Baruch followed a different course. He lived on a kibbutz, identified with socialism and joined Shin Bet. Until the 1967 war, he worked in Avraham Ahituv's department of Arab affairs, mainly as a field agent in the upper Galilee.

Afterwards, because of his knowledge of Arabic, he was put to work in the West Bank. Although only a sergeant in the military reserves, Cohen was immediately promoted to captain in order to serve as military governor of the occupied territory's largest town, Nablus, where naturally he was to focus on suppressing terrorism. Almost as soon as he arrived, in July 1967, he nearly captured Yasser Arafat, who had to dress in women's clothing to escape Cohen and his men.

In 1972 he was involved in exposing a Jewish–Arab spy ring, which worked under Syrian intelligence orders, and later he was sent to Europe to operate a network of young Palestinian informers. One of his operatives was a double agent for Black September who had been instructed to shoot his Israeli operator. Zadok Ofir had survived a similar attack, but Cohen became the first Israeli intelligence man killed by a Palestinian.

Some members of Cohen's family claimed later that his death could have been prevented. Violating all security precautions, Cohen's photograph had been published – ironically, in an official army album celebrating the 1967 victory – and the snapshot showed Cohen, in military uniform, with his best friend, Zadok Ofir, also in uniform. The Arab enemy collects such clippings, and it is considered vital that intelligence operatives do not show their faces. Enemy agents can put two and two together. Even if Cohen concealed his identity as an Israeli when operating his Palestinian network, that photograph may have given him away.

The fact is that a few months before his death, Arab newspapers carried stories that Black September had sentenced an Israeli agent to death. Reading those reports should have alerted Shin Bet that Baruch Cohen's true identity may have been discovered, and his life should not have been endangered by sending him to Madrid. It is equally disturbing that while other Israeli agents were 'covering' Cohen by observing him, they did not spring into action when he was shot for fear that they themselves would be exposed.

Family members, who felt that Cohen was a victim of his superiors' failures, took no pleasure from indications that the Mossad was avenging the death of Baruch Cohen. His widow, Nurit, revealed: 'Occasionally, service officers would come to visit me and ask "Have you read in the newspaper that this-and-that guy has been killed or this-and-that-guy has been blown up?" What can I say, that it consoled me?'

Word spread that three members of Black September, who were involved in Cohen's murder, had been liquidated.[28]

Cohen's death should have served as another warning to Israel. The intelligence community should have linked the assassination of Cohen to the attempt on the life of Ofir and the murder of the Syrian double agent Kano. The Mossad should have concluded that its Palestinian enemy was displaying a degree of professionalism in penetrating the operational heart of Israeli intelligence overseas.

Instead, the intelligence community behaved as though still trapped by obsession. It had taken vengeance as its creed. The members of Black September were killed one after another in Europe. Booby-trapped envelopes were sent to other PLO officials and there were discussions about eliminating Yasser Arafat himself.

The Israelis actively attempted to capture PFLP leader Georges Habash. On August 10, 1973, their fighter planes forced a Lebanese civilian airliner to land at a military base in Israel. The passengers were led out single-file and individually questioned, but there was no terrorist chief among them, so everyone was set free – with considerable embarrassment to the Mossad.

A tip that Habash would be on the airliner had apparently come from one of Israel's best placed agents within the Palestinian terrorist hierarchy: a woman named Aminah al-Mufti. Born in 1935 to a Circassian Moslem family in Jordan, she was recruited by the Mossad in Vienna in 1972 – reportedly after she fell in love with an Israeli pilot visiting Austria, perhaps searching for a potential Arab agent – and set up a clinic in Beirut the following year. The Mossad was secretly financing medical care for Palestinians in Lebanon.

Mufti befriended top PLO officers, delivering reports and photographs to 'dead letter boxes' in Beirut – locations, such as hotel rooms where couriers whom she never met later picked up the documents – and transmitting by radio to Israel.

The flow of valuable information stopped in 1975, when Mufti was caught. She was tortured by PLO radicals and was reportedly questioned by Soviet KGB and East German intelligence agents during five years of imprisonment in a cave near the Lebanese port of Sidon. Working through the International Red Cross, Israel arranged a prisoner swap and freed two PLO terrorists – who had been sentenced to life in prison – in exchange for Mufti. After the Red Cross handed her to a Mossad team in Cyprus, she was given a new identity and a job as a doctor in northern Israel.[29]

In the end, Israel was unable to put its hands on either Arafat or Habash, but it did get to three other PLO leaders. Muhammad Najjar, Kamal Adwan and Kamal Nasser were all shot to death in their apartments in downtown Beirut, on April 9, 1973 by Israeli commando units. The army operation itself – the landing of members of the top *sayeret* on the Lebanese beach – was a masterpiece of precise military planning.

Even more impressive were the preparations by Israeli intelligence. This was shown by the fact that Israel had the addresses of all three leaders, that it was able to land men in places that were accessible to all three homes, and that there were rented Mercedes cars waiting for the men. It also showed an amazing degree of cooperation between Military Intelligence and the Mossad agents.

Israel again proved its military prowess. This second assault on Beirut in four and a half years was code-named *Aviv Ne'urim*, Hebrew for 'Spring of Youth'. The participants included young officers such as Ehud Barak and Amnon Lipkin-Shahak – who would later rise to the top of Aman.

The glow of a job well done lasted barely three months and was extinguished in a place called Lillehammer. At the beginning of July 1973, most of the members of Mike Harari's hit team, authorized by Committee X, gathered in that small town in northern Norway. They had come, from various locations in Europe, to settle a score with 'the red prince', the code name given by the Mossad to Ali Hassan Salameh.

Salameh was Black September's operations officer in Western Europe and he planned the attack on the Israeli athletes in Munich, as well as the assassination of Baruch Cohen. But he was more than that. Salameh, the son of a high-ranking Palestinian militia commander who had been killed in the war against Israel in 1948, was in reality the commander of Force 17, which was responsible for protecting Yasser Arafat.

Salameh was self-assured, a playboy and a womanizer, but a very difficult man to catch. After months of searching for him, the great enthusiasm of the Mossad agents who arrived in Norway was understandable. Mike Harari's gunslingers heard that Salameh was in Lillehammer, and after locating their quarry they tailed him before shooting him dead on July 21.

Only the next day did the Israeli agents discover that they had made a mistake. They had killed the wrong man, a Moroccan waiter named Ahmad Bouchiki who was married to a Norwegian – a pregnant woman who witnessed the shooting.

This murder might well have been ignored, had it not been for the stupid behaviour – which simply cannot be explained logically – of the Israeli support agents, the men and women who did the surveillance and some of the planning for the gunmen. They made every possible mistake, as if seeking to be caught by the Norwegian police.

The police were not even making any great efforts to capture the killers. The fact is that the Mossad agents – carefully trained, in Israel, to disappear at a moment's notice – left a clear trail at every step. They arrived in Lillehammer in cars which they had rented and, in trailing Bouchiki, had been as graceful as a herd of elephants in a china shop. They did not observe the rules of compartmentalization and instead, knew each other. It was only natural that within a few days they fell one after another into the hands of the Norwegian police, who were amazed at the amateurism displayed by the espionage agency considered to be the world's best. Harari and the actual gunmen managed to flee, but Avraham Gehmer and his colleagues were arrested.

The interrogations in Norway exposed the *modus operandi* of the other post-Olympic killings. It became clear that the Mossad was employing part-timers and freelancers, especially to handle logistics.

One example, and by far the most talkative when questioned in Oslo, was Dan Ert, a businessman of Danish extraction who lived in Herzliyya, north of Tel Aviv, under the name Arbel. He was called upon by the Mossad, from time to time, for various missions. Arbel broke immediately, as soon as he was placed by the Norwegians in a solitary, darkened room. His interrogators were unable to conceal their amazement when Ert/Arbel confessed that he suffered from claustrophobia. In return for being moved to a larger cell, he was willing to confess everything – not only about the Lillehammer operation, but also about his involvement in transferring the ship with uranium to Israel in 1968.

Another agent, Sylvia Raphael, was also arrested but showed far more professionalism. Under her cover name, Patricia Roxborough, she was a newspaper photographer with a forged Canadian passport. Raphael was born in South Africa and recruited by the Mossad after working as a volunteer in an Israeli kibbutz. Only in her case, incidentally, was there a happy end to the Lillehammer affair. She fell in love with her Norwegian lawyer and married him after she, like her comrades, had served a short prison term.

The Israelis were lucky that the Norwegians did not press very hard in their investigation of this complicated case, in a clear attempt not to embarrass Israel any more. Despite the information which did emerge from the trials in Norway, the French and Italian security services also displayed a great deal of solidarity with the Mossad. They ignored the PLO's demands to renew the investigations into the violent deaths of its men in those countries.

There were professional feelings of compassion for the Mossad being caught, as it were, 'with its pants down' – intelligence agents realized it could happen to anyone. There was also an element of the traditional sympathy felt for Israel, still strong in 1973. In addition, security services took the view that, despite its disastrous end, this had been an Israeli effort to show the world another way, not one of appeasement and submission, in the fight against terror.

This was small consolation for Israel. It could not even find pleasure when the Mossad finally did catch up with

Salameh and finished the job properly, five and a half years later. A large bomb was attached to his car, in Beirut, and was detonated by remote control. The CIA was not very pleased with that operation because Salameh, it became known after his death, had been helpful to the Americans. He had been the secret liaison between the PLO and American intelligence.[30]

Memories of that summer in Norway continue to haunt Israel to the present day. It is not surprising that the Israeli intelligence community refers to Lillehammer, in an unhappy pun, as *Leyl-ha-Mar*, Hebrew for the Night of Bitterness. Every time it is mentioned, Israeli secret agents cringe. They all agree that killing the wrong man – and then getting caught – was their greatest operational failure.

The obsession with revenge had made Israel misplace its keen judgment. It is true that there were a number of senior officials who claimed that it was not the duty of an intelligence organization to become a branch of 'Murder Incorporated'. They complained that significant human and technological resources were tied up in the manhunt rather than being involved in the more important and more traditional work of collecting information on the military ability of the Arab states.

The dissenters claimed that Israel was exaggerating the importance of Palestinian terror, for in the final analysis it was not this which would imperil the country's existence. At worst, it was like a pesky fly. Others stressed that there was no use in wiping out the heads of the Palestinian organizations. First of all, there was no guarantee that their replacements would be more moderate. Secondly, the Palestinians would always find successors who would be no less capable.

Zvi Zamir was in a very sensitive bind. The slaughter of Israel's Olympic athletes at the Munich airfield had affected him personally, and, in addition, he was greatly influenced by Golda Meir.

During the five and a half years that Zamir was in the Mossad, the emphasis had been on the struggle against terrorism. It was more than ironic – it was a powerful, painful symbol – that even three days before the outbreak of the Yom Kippur War, the most frightening military setback suffered by Israeli forces, the intelligence community was still obsessively investigating a terrorist incident, the PLO attack in Austria on a train from Moscow bringing Jewish emigrants to the West, bound for Israel.

To this day, although there is no concrete evidence, there are those who believe that the October 3 attack on the train near Vienna was one of the deceptions arranged by Egypt and Syria to heighten the surprise of their Ramadan War on October 6, 1973.

8

The Surprises of War and Peace

Syrian troops were knocking on the thick steel doors, but there is nothing polite about the explosion of hand grenades. The doors were built to withstand such an attack, and for a few hours, at least, the Israeli soldiers inside the Mount Hermon bunkers were beyond the reach of their rapidly advancing enemies.

The soldiers worked for Aman. They were not fighters. They were Military Intelligence professionals, posted on the snow-capped mountain in the occupied Golan Heights to spy on Syria.

The Aman men were working, despite it being Yom Kippur, the holiest day of the Jewish calendar, when Israel normally stands still. It was Saturday, October 6, 1973, at two o'clock in the afternoon.

The Hermon post commander, young Lieutenant Amos Levinberg, had just been on the radio-telephone to his superior officer to report incoming artillery fire. Levinberg recalls: 'I told him I wasn't worried, that everything was under control, and once the shelling stopped we would repair the damaged aerials outside tomorrow.' But the next day, Levinberg and the survivors of his unit were in the hands of the Syrians.

They were Syria's best troops, commandos who landed from helicopters. It took them around twelve hours to break in, kill eighteen of the Israeli guards, wound others and capture thirty-one soldiers – with all their Western- and Israeli-made electronic equipment, which Syrian and Soviet experts would later examine in minute detail. This, without regard to the setbacks suffered on the wider fronts, was a major blow to the Jewish state's defences. Mount Hermon – with its tall antennae, dish aerials, telescopes, ultra-modern binoculars and night-vision devices – had been Israel's top secret eyes and ears in the north.

The post was one of Aman's eavesdropping units which monitored all radio traffic in the region, and from the mountain on a clear day you could watch the full deployment of Syrian forces all the way back to Damascus, twenty-five miles away.[1] It was the latest word in *sigint*, signals intelligence and *comint*, communications intelligence: high-technology means of detection and interception of every audio source ranging from radio transmissions to telephone conversations.

The sophisticated listening post was supposed to see and hear everything the enemy was doing. The system had failed. Levinberg's tale – his complacency, his failure to detect the danger and the shock of being taken captive – illustrates the humiliation shared by the entire country that day.

The armies of Egypt and Syria, in a carefully planned attack, totally surprised the Israeli defensive positions in the territories lost by the two Arab states six years earlier. Israel's intelligence community failed for the first time, in its primary mission: giving the advance warning of war. It was Aman's responsibility, above all, but the blame – and the nation's feeling of having been let down – extended to all the espionage agencies.

The intelligence chiefs in the *Va'adat* had every reason,

even five months before Yom Kippur, to know of the preparations for war on 'the other side'.

They simply did not believe what some of their junior agents and analysts were seeing. Everyone, it seems, had their brains manacled by what strategic experts in Israel called *ha-Konseptzia*, 'the Concept'. This informal but forceful doctrine developed rapidly in the euphoria which followed the stunning six-day victory of 1967. It held that the Arabs would never launch an all-out war, since it was so clear that they could not win. In the unlikely event of war, the Israelis were utterly convinced that they could smash the enemy lines and march on the Egyptian and Syrian capitals, Cairo and Damascus.

The intelligence agencies were, as always, amassing detailed information on military movements in Egypt and Syria, but 'the Concept' dictated that these were just exercises or, at most, empty attempts to prod Israel into ordering an expensive and disruptive mobilization of the army reserves.

'The Concept' spread, like an illness, up and down the military, intelligence and political chains of command. 'There was a general acceptance of the inherent inferiority of the Arabs,' says Brigadier General Yoel Ben-Porat, who was then commander of Aman's eavesdropping units. 'A single Israeli tank platoon could hold back a battalion, three times as large. Of course it was nonsense. Aman was ignorant regarding the Arabs, their history, culture, religion and literature. Aman people did not speak Arabic and they looked with contempt on the need to learn the language. If you want to be an intelligence analyst, you need to touch and understand Arab affairs in their own language.'[2]

No one clung to 'the Concept' more, in 1973, than the head of Aman, Major General Eli Zeira. He was, from a bureaucratic point of view, on top of the world. Military intelligence, after all, had made the triumph of the Six-Day War possible. The unanimous praise of the political and defence establishments went to Aman chief Aharon Yariv, but Zeira shared in the warm glow, as he was Yariv's deputy until inheriting the top job in 1972.

The agency is part of the army's general staff, reporting to the chief of staff and the defence minister. Although it has been overshadowed by the headline-making exploits of the Mossad and Shin Bet, Aman is the largest and most important intelligence agency in the defence of the Jewish state. In that way – and not only in its responsibilities for electronic and radio monitoring – Aman resembled the US National Security Agency. Dubbed 'the Puzzle Palace', by one author, the huge NSA lives in the CIA's shadow while laying the groundwork for American intelligence successes.[3]

Aman has six departments, dominated by the two called Collection and Production.

The Collection Department is responsible for *sigint*, for the *humint* running of agents and informers just over the borders, and often for plugging into the telephone systems of the Arab countries to eavesdrop and record 'landline' conversations. Part of the 1967 success was the quick interception and efficient distribution of Arab planning sessions, including a telephone call between Egypt's President Nasser and Jordan's King Hussein.

Aman works closely with the air force in the area of electronic warfare, known to intelligence analysts as *elint*. Radar and even more sophisticated signals are sent to disturb and deceive enemy forces.

The Production Department is the largest, employing nearly 3,000 of the 7,000 men and women involved in Aman. They receive and analyse the information which has been collected. They are organized into 'desks', and as in the Mossad these are divided along geographical and functional lines: the western area for Egypt, Sudan, and Libya; the eastern area for Iraq, Syria and Lebanon; a separate desk for Jordan and the Arabian peninsula; a Palestinian desk to track guerilla groups; analysts of inter-Arab relations; and a desk for Middle East economics.

Aman is also responsible for sending military attachés to Israel's overseas embassies, for administering the military

censorship of the press and for 'field security' to prevent
secrets from leaking. There is a small research and development department which comes up with hardware and
software to help in the collection of intelligence, and the
navy and the air force have their own, tiny and specialized
intelligence units.[4]

This structure provided the Prime Minister and the cabinet with an annual National Intelligence Estimate – signed
by the Aman chief – designed to review and predict the
wide range of military, economic, and political factors which
add up to war or peace. In the years after 1967, these
Estimates were riddled with the bias of 'the Concept'.

Such was the high-flying reputation of Aman that when
Zeira said, in 1973, that Egypt was far too distracted and
disorganized to attack Israel, it was taken as modern-day
Jewish gospel in Jerusalem. He said it in May of that year,
when the Egyptian Army went on alert and prepared its
units along the Suez Canal for a possible offensive. When
nothing further happened, Zeira and 'the Concept' were
again seen to be right.

Similar Arab moves were noted in late September, but
the omnipotent 'Concept' said these had to be harmless.
Even in the United States, the CIA, according to then-
President Richard M. Nixon, reported that 'war in the
Middle East was unlikely' on October 5, 'dismissing as
annual maneuvers the massive and unusual troop movements' by Egypt and Syria.[5]

Unfortunately, the CIA was getting much of its data on
Middle East events from Israeli intelligence – through the
long-standing direct link from the Agency headquarters in
Virginia to the Mossad building in Tel Aviv. In other words,
the Americans had been taught 'the Concept' and it blinded
them, too.

Egypt's President Anwar Sadat gave an overt hint of his
intentions in a string of bellicose speeches. On the third
anniversary of his predecessor Nasser's death, September 28,
Sadat told his nation: 'We shall spare no efforts or sacrifices
to fulfil our objective. I shall not discuss any details, but the

liberation of the land is the first and main task facing us.'⁶

Zeira and his Aman analysts had decided long ago to ignore the flood of Arabic hyperbole heard from politicians such as Sadat – even when covert sources seemed to confirm Egypt's plans for war. Aman chiefs considered but rejected a startling report by an intelligence officer who was attached to Israel's Southern Command and monitoring the occupied Sinai all the way to the Bar-Lev Line along the Suez Canal. Lieutenant Binyamin Siman-Tov reported on October 1, in detail, that Egypt was preparing to launch an attack across the Suez within days. Zeira was unmoved.

The Mossad, on the other hand, was more alert. More than two days before the Egyptian and Syrian attack, a Mossad agent in Cairo reported that war was on the immediate horizon. Mossad chief Zvi Zamir took it seriously, but he did not fight for his point of view.

Precisely how the Israeli intelligence bureaucracy handled – or mishandled – the signals of war remains a mystery, with retired officials still vehemently defending their honour. According to the system as it then stood, Zamir – as the Prime Minister's chief intelligence officer – was supposed to report such information both to Golda Meir and, in writing, to Aman.

The charge is that Zamir, although he was convinced that war was imminent, merely told Zeira by telephone and left an assistant to report to the Prime Minister's office. The Mossad assistant believed that all he had to do was verbally transmit the information to Meir's office, yet he was unable to reach the appropriate official by phone.

The information did not reach its intended destination. Zamir left the country, probably to meet and evaluate the Mossad source – brought briefly out of Egypt – in person. Prime Minister Meir could not find him on Friday, October 5. And only on Saturday morning did the mighty Israeli intelligence community reach its conclusion that a war would start that day. But it was too late.

True, Israel could still have used its air force for a pre-emptive strike, on the 1967 pattern, but Meir and Defence

Minister Dayan decided not to do it. They knew that the US would disapprove and for the sake of American support they sadly concluded that Israel would have to absorb the first blow.[7]

The surprise was similar to Pearl Harbor. The information was there, but intelligence chiefs either chose to ignore it, or wrongly analysed it.

The Israeli foot soldiers in Sinai and the Golan Heights had to compensate with their lives for the complacency of their leaders and the mistakes of the intelligence community. In fierce battles, the Syrians recaptured part of the Golan Heights, the Egyptians crossed the Suez canal and gained a foothold in Sinai, and Dayan – the hero of the 1967 war – panicked. He was so gloomy that on the third day of the 1973 war, he muttered darkly about the possible destruction of 'the Third Temple' of Israel.[8] Jewish history counts two periods of independence, until the first temple was destroyed by the Babylonians in 586 BC and the second by the Romans in the year AD 70. The third is the state of Israel.

General Rehavam Zeevi tried to persuade his army colleagues that Israel should use unconventional weapons.[9] Indeed, serious consideration was given for the first time, that week, to the possible need to use Israel's nuclear bomb as a last act of almost suicidal defence. The secret arsenal, which Lakam had worked so hard to acquire, was then untested and still 'dirty', in the view of scientific analysts. On Dayan's orders, Jericho missiles and special bomb racks on Phantom aircraft were prepared for the possible launch of atomic weapons.[10]

The defence minister's despair weighed heavily on Golda Meir's mind and spirit. She even considered suicide, as her confidante Lou Kaddar recalls: 'I never saw her so grey, her face as in mourning. She told me, "Dayan wants us to discuss terms of surrender." I thought that a woman such as she would never want to live in such circumstances. So I prepared it for both of us. I went to see a doctor, a friend of mine who would agree to give me the necessary pills so that we both – she and I – would go together.'[11]

Meir pulled herself together, and with her army Chief of Staff Lieutenant General David (Dado) Elazar, who was strong as a rock, she directed the counterattacks which eventually brought victory. The short-term result was a heavy price for Israel: 2,700 soldiers killed – the equivalent, by proportion of population, to 170,000 dead Americans. In a nation with just over three million people, the losses were traumatic.

The long-term result: the entire State of Israel lost confidence in its once legendary intelligence community. It was not just a feeling. It was in writing. Prime Minister Meir commissioned an official enquiry into the Yom Kippur War and the *Mechdal*, or Omission – the instantly coined euphemism for the intelligence blunder which made the war a total surprise. The investigators were known as the Agranat Commission, and they were led by the Chief Justice of Israel's Supreme Court, Shimon Agranat.

As usual, the politicians escaped the full brunt of the investigation – for which they themselves set the terms of reference – and the blame was placed on the military and on the intelligence community. The commission cleared Meir and Dayan of 'direct responsibility' for the *Mechdal*. Instead, Agranat's panel made Chief of Staff Elazar and his Southern Command General, Shmuel Gorodish-Gonen, the scapegoats, and the official report scathingly destroyed the careers of Aman chief Zeira and three of his assistants. They were replaced by new officers, led by Major General Shlomo Gazit. Under public pressure, Meir and Dayan resigned within months.

In the intelligence community, Agranat recommended – as investigative commissions always do, usually to little lasting effect – a structural reorganization. It insisted that a new intelligence unit be formed, and the tiny nucleus of the foreign ministry's Research and Political Planning Centre – which existed only on paper – was brought to life. Its mission was not to collect intelligence but to provide a further, independent assessment. It has its own office, in a separately fenced-in compound within the ministry of foreign affairs in Jerusalem. This is not because it has secret agents, but due to the raw intelligence material it receives from the Mossad and Aman.[12]

Other changes included enlargement of the tiny research department of the Mossad, so as not to depend solely on Aman's analytical powers. The Mossad would now have a hand in assembling the National Intelligence Estimate prepared each year for the Prime Minister.

Yitzhak Rabin became Israel's new leader in May 1974. As army chief of staff in the 1967 war and ambassador in Washington, he was no stranger to intelligence reports. As the Prime Minister, he asked to see much of the raw data collected by the secret agencies rather than the digested summaries favoured by many civilian politicians. This was not only because of Rabin's military background. The CIA, in a secret profile, considered him 'introspective' and 'having a tendency to worry'.[13] He had the distinct personal habit of not trusting others, and Rabin was certainly not going to trust the judgment of intelligence agencies after the total failure of their powers of analysis in 1973. He was simply acting within the new spirit.

Aman's morale was at its nadir. The Mossad, on the other hand, because Zamir had known the October war was coming, escaped almost unscathed from the Yom Kippur débâcle and the investigations which followed. Rabin, naturally, turned to the Mossad – very much in fashion, now – to coordinate the most sensitive and secret aspect of Israel's foreign policy: the clandestine relations with Jordan's King Hussein.

Even though the Israelis were occupying his former West Bank, the monarch had stayed out of the Yom Kippur War. He had been having face-to-face meetings with the leaders of Israel since 1963, aimed at hammering out a peace treaty, but the two sides had settled instead for *de facto* peace. The Mossad, in its contacts with the CIA to arrange the details, referred to the project by a code name – 'Operation Lift'.[14] Hussein happened to be on the CIA payroll as an 'asset' in the Middle East.[15] The Mossad's role followed in the old footprints of Shiloah, who conducted the talks with Hussein's grandfather King Abdullah until 1951.

Rabin and Hussein intensified the relationship and the Jordanian monarch even went so far as to visit the Israeli Prime Minister in Tel Aviv – a secret never disclosed, even in the memoirs of the few officials who knew of the clandestine diplomacy. The king felt high and mighty, after his Arab Legion defeated Yasser Arafat's PLO in the 1970 civil war. The Israelis had indirectly helped Hussein, by making military moves coordinated by the US.

One of the results was a top secret but highly useful intelligence exchange between the Mossad and Jordanian intelligence, the *Mukhabarat*, Arabic for intelligence. Their common enemies were the Palestinian terrorist organizations and the Israelis happily informed Hussein of PLO plots against him and his cabinet ministers. There were quite a few. Jordan's secret police, meantime, provided the Mossad with a window on the politics and the dangerous radicals of the Arab world. They did not give each other everything and the Israelis were especially careful not to put their own agents and informers in any danger, but senior officials of the two agencies met frequently – on both sides of the River Jordan and on neutral ground in Europe.

When Hussein met Rabin in a Mossad-operated guest house to the north of Tel Aviv, the Mossad recorded the talks with hidden cameras and microphones, but the official tapes and files have been locked away in Israel's government archives with absolutely no plan ever to release them.

The Mossad also had the pleasure of arranging a secret visit by Rabin to another Arab state, Morocco. Rabin was hoping to break the Middle East deadlock, after finding that Jordan would not sign an overt peace treaty and deciding that a more permanent arrangement with Egypt was needed than a mere disengagement of forces.

The Prime Minister flew to Rabat in 1976, by way of Paris, wearing a wig as his disguise. Rabin asked King Hassan II to try and persuade Egypt's Sadat to come to the negotiating table. There were no political gains, but the clandestine cooperation between Israel and Morocco was reaffirmed. Both the Mossad and the CIA had the freedom to roam Morocco, making contact with other potentially useful Arabs, running eavesdropping posts to keep an electronic ear on North Africa, and advising the king and his people on internal security.[16]

The failure to sign any peace treaties, but the achievement of limited military-restriction agreements with Egypt and Syria, reflected the nature of the twilight between peace and war during Rabin's period as Prime Minister. In that sense, his selection of a new Mossad chief made no real difference. One army general left the post and a new one came in.

After serving five years as Mossad chief, just as his predecessor Meir Amit had done, Zvi Zamir retired from the agency – as colourless and unnoticed as he was when he joined it. His term, ending in 1974, was dominated by two failures: the Lillehammer disaster and the Yom Kippur War, even though he was not besmirched.

Rabin chose an old acquaintance, Major General Yitzhak (Haka) Hofi. The choice reflected the lingering memories of the 1973 intelligence failure. Hofi, in charge of the army's Northern Command, was probably the only general who urged his superiors, in the weeks before the Yom Kippur War, to take notice of Syria's threatening troop movements. He asked that his tanks and artillery units be reinforced, but his pleas were ignored. During the war, Hofi and his soldiers fought well and recaptured Mount Hermon and the Golan Heights and even advanced deeper into Syria.

Born in 1927, Hofi became the first *Sabra* Mossad chief. *Sabra*, Hebrew for cactus fruit, is the term used for Israeli-born people, because they, too, are said to be prickly on the outside but have sweet and soft centres. Like many of his generation, Hofi joined the Palmach special forces, fought in the 1948 war, and – as did Amit and Zamir – decided to stay in the army. As a paratroop commander, he was involved in several daring Israeli operations in the Sinai and Gaza Strip before the 1956 war, and ten years later he was a planning officer in the preparations for the Six-Day War. In

July 1974, the heavy-set, round-faced Hofi left the army and simply disappeared. Israel did not announce his whereabouts, but he soon landed in Mossad headquarters in Tel Aviv.[17]

He was no intelligence genius, but Hofi had always been highly respected by his men and he was hard-working and serious. He was also helped by the fact that his youth had been spent in the same wing of the Labour movement as Yitzhak Rabin.

While the Mossad continued to pursue the traditional Israeli policy of surrounding the hostile Arab states with 'peripheral' friends, it became clear under Hofi that Israel had an even greater need to come to terms with the Arab nations themselves. After Jordan, Morocco and initial contacts with Egypt, Lebanon came into play.

The main motive was still the old peripheral notion of ties with the Maronite Christian minority in Lebanon, but the connections in Beirut gave the Mossad another channel of communications with the Moslem world as well.

At the same time, the Mossad's secret diplomacy dovetailed with the war against terrorism – reaching the pinnacle of success as far south as the heart of Africa. A special effort was required at the end of June 1976, when a combined team of Palestinians and West German urban guerillas – heirs to the notorious Baader-Meinhof Gang – hijacked an Air France jet to Entebbe, Uganda.

Ugandan President Idi Amin had abandoned his friendship with Israel, as did most African leaders, after the 1973 war and the murderous madman – a former British army sergeant and boxer – had realigned his mercurial policies in favour of the Arabs.

On July 3, 1976, Israel's air force flew several *sayeret* commando units well over 2,000 miles to end the hijack – deceiving the Entebbe airport control tower by silently landing Hercules transport planes full of troops, weapons and a field hospital. Some of the troops even deplaned in a duplicate of Amin's black Mercedes limousine, as the assault force burst into the old passenger terminal and killed the terrorists within minutes. Lieutenant Colonel Netanyahu, leading his élite *sayeret*, was the only soldier lost, when a Ugandan sniper in the control tower cut him down.

Israel's famous success, in rescuing over one hundred hostages at Entebbe – a bold, long-distance version of the Sabena hijack assault four years earlier – is part of the Jewish state's non-fictional folklore. Even in the United States on that July 4, it nearly overshadowed the celebrations of America's Bicentennial.

Not celebrated publicly, in fact untold amid the rejoicing which followed in Israel, was the excellent preparatory legwork by anonymous Mossad agents. The Israeli cabinet instructed its intelligence community to devise possible responses, from the moment that the French Airbus was hijacked – loaded with Israelis on their way to Paris, after a stop in Athens where anti-terrorism security was lax.

The Mossad immediately knew that the man to contact was Bruce Mackenzie. A British businessman and farmer who had settled in Kenya and was the only white man to attain cabinet rank there, Mackenzie was a good friend of President Jomo Kenyatta. Mackenzie had a role in his adopted country's defence and security, and as a British expatriate he was in close contact with MI6. He also knew the Israelis very well.

The Mossad, through its station in Nairobi, maintains excellent ties with the Kenyan security service.[18] The interest for Israel is that Nairobi, not far from the Horn of Africa, is one of the most important capitals on the continent, with diplomats and spies at offices of the United Nations and the Organization of African Unity.

On January 18, 1976, less than half a year before the hijack drama at Entebbe, Kenyan police arrested three Palestinians on the edge of Nairobi airport with two Soviet-made, shoulder-fired SAM-7 rocket launchers. They were planning to shoot down an El Al airliner, with 110 people aboard, which was due to land in an hour. Based on their interrogation, Kenya's secret police arrested a West German couple, Thomas Reuter and Brigitte Schulz, both 23 years old, when

they arrived in Nairobi three days later. All five suspects –
the three Palestinians and the two Germans who were
another example of cooperation between Arab terrorists and
European radical youth – then vanished.

Schulz's family tried to discover her whereabouts, but the
Kenyan Government denied holding any foreign prisoners.
Eventually, Israel confirmed that it was holding the five.
The Kenyan authorities had handed them over to the
Mossad. They were secretly tried, convicted and jailed.[19]

At the end of June, with Israelis among the hijacked
passengers in Entebbe, the Mossad turned to Mackenzie
with a need for even greater assistance. He secured President
Kenyatta's approval for the use of Kenya by Israeli intelligence. Within a few hours, ten Mossad and Aman agents
flew to Nairobi and set up a planning centre, laying the
ground for intelligence and military operatives. The Israelis,
some posing as businessmen, crossed the border into the
Entebbe area – just across Lake Victoria from Kenya – on
reconnaissance.

Kenya also allowed the Israeli aircraft, which served as a
field hospital, to stop in Nairobi after the successful rescue
raid. Israel gave the world a demonstration of its talents in
combating terrorism. The Jewish state also showed, as was
the case with the CIA's James Angleton, that it could honour
its clandestine friends. Two years after the Entebbe assault,
Mackenzie was killed when Libyan agents working for
Uganda's dictator planted a bomb in his private jet as
revenge for his aid to Israel. The Association of Israeli
Intelligence Veterans, headed by former Mossad chief Meir
Amit, raised money to plant a forest of 10,000 trees in the
hills of lower Galilee in memory of their British–Kenyan
ally.[20]

The Entebbe success was, quite naturally, a morale-
booster for Aman, three years after its Yom Kippur humiliation, but it was not enough to keep Yitzhak Rabin in
power. In May 1977, the Israeli electorate unexpectedly
rejected Rabin and his Labour Party. All the failures and
scandals, ranging from the Lavon affair to the *Mechdal*,

with the further spice of corruption, finally caught up with Labour. The right-wing Likud bloc won the election and Menachem Begin was the new Prime Minister.

As much as other Israelis, senior members of the intelligence community were shocked by Begin's victory. The secret agencies had become accustomed to working with the famous faces of Labour and most intelligence officials came from the Labour movement's ranks. Although their objectives were meant to be non-partisan, the top echelons of the community had established familiar, almost intimate relations over the years with their political masters.

Now, there was uncertainty and even fear that the lust for power, which they naturally expected of a party which had been in the political wilderness for twenty-nine years, would lead to a purge of the Labour-appointed civil service. The intelligence chiefs had no reason to believe that they would be excepted. Their fears were not without foundation, because there were indeed Likud leaders who urged Begin to launch just such a purge.

Both Mossad chief Haka Hofi and Shin Bet chief Avraham Ahituv conveyed almost identical messages to the new Prime Minister: if he wanted them to, they would resign. Although both were civil servants who could retain their jobs, they recognized the right of the new leader to appoint his own people to these sensitive positions.

Begin, however, told them to stay. He did not wish to cause any unnecessary disturbances or discontent in government agencies. In fact, Begin very quickly fostered close relations with Hofi and Ahituv. The two men, and especially the Mossad chief, were often in the Prime Minister's office.

Begin was fascinated by the Mossad's secret operations, which apparently reminded him of his past as head of the Irgun underground in the 1940s. With an almost boyish enthusiasm, he frequently asked Hofi to tell him 'everything' – not to spare any details. Haka Hofi showed great patience, even though he was astounded time and again by Begin's ignorance of intelligence and military matters. As the ultimate outsider since 1948, he had not acquired the background information gained by Labour Party insiders. As Hofi later put it, Begin's lack of knowledge forced him and the Aman chief to go into great detail in their explanations, so that the Prime Minister would get the full picture.[21]

Begin loved the glamour of the intelligence agencies and he enjoyed being their new boss.

There were also other reasons for his intense interest. Begin was out to change history and he was going to use Israeli intelligence to do it. Begin had his own vision for his first years in office. His political enemies in the Labour Party had portrayed him as a demon, as a satanic figure 'who would devour Arabs', and as a warmonger who would bring about a terrible conflict with Israel's neighbours.

Begin was aware of his image problem and tried with all his might to prove everyone wrong: he would be a great peacemaker. One step was to make Moshe Dayan, until then a Labour stalwart, his foreign minister. Another step was to send Hofi to Morocco.

The Mossad chief, accompanied by his assistant Dave Kimche, arrived at King Hassan's secluded Ifran palace within weeks of Begin taking office. The new Prime Minister was hoping to achieve what Rabin had failed to do in his trip to Morocco the previous year: to make peace with Israel's major enemy, Egypt. Hofi had secured Hassan's agreement to play host to a unique encounter. The head of the Mossad, hated and feared throughout the Arab world, was about to meet senior Egyptians to pave the way for future negotiations.

The same day, two top officials from Egypt arrived in Morocco. They were General Kamal Hassan Ali, head of the Egyptian equivalent of the Mossad and Hassan Tohami, the religious deputy prime minister known for his spiritual visions. Years later, General Ali would recall how his President, Sadat, instructed him by telephone to fly with Tohami on an unspecified mission. All through the flight, Tohami was absolutely silent.

The two Egyptians entered Ifran palace and shook hands with the two Israelis, but Ali was not told who they were and was then astonished to be dismissed from the room by Tohami. Ali, the head of Egyptian foreign intelligence, did not know what his own government was doing under his own nose, while the King of Morocco did.

When the meeting ended, Ali waved an angry finger at Tohami and said that he would not have come if he had known he would be excluded. Tohami replied that the two strangers were French and the talks were about arms deals.

General Ali was even more offended: 'I am a military man. There is no reason why I should not take part in such talks.'

When they returned to Egypt, Ali complained to Sadat about Tohami's mysteries. 'The President laughed as I've never seen him before,' Ali recalled, 'and then he told me the real purpose of the trip.'[22]

Hofi's purpose was to convince the Egyptians that Begin was sincere about making peace and was strong enough to pull it off. Hofi and Tohami agreed that there should be more secret meetings. On September 16, 1977, Tohami flew again to Morocco to meet this time with Moshe Dayan – the new Israeli Foreign Minister, but also the long-feared general who was a living symbol for the Arabs of Israel's military superiority.[23]

Dayan, with the Mossad's Kimche at his side, gave Tohami the impression that in return for a peace treaty, Begin – quite unexpectedly, for a man known publicly as an ultra-nationalist – would be willing to withdraw from the entire Sinai, with its valuable oil fields, airbases and settlements.

That meeting paved the way for the historic visit of President Sadat to Jerusalem, just two months later.

Even though Israel's intelligence chiefs were in on the process from the beginning, they were sceptical about its chances of success. Hofi had returned from Rabat, still suspicious about the real intentions of the unpredictable Egyptian President.

As for Aman, its annual National Intelligence Estimate predicted that Sadat would again resort to war – not peace.

Aman explained later that it had been unable to foresee the personal decision of an individual man. Intelligence, in such circumstances, had very little to go on. Sadat made 'a decision that was not considered beforehand or decided by any forum of the senior government echelon in Cairo,' said Aman chief General Gazit, trying to excuse his agency's being surprised – this time, by peace.[24]

The army Chief of Staff, Lieutenant General Mordecai Gur, was advised by Aman that Sadat's short flight from Cairo could be a decoy for a military assault. Israel's army was placed on alert as the Jewish Sabbath ended that Saturday evening, November 19, 1977.[25] Gur even embarrassed Begin by publicly doubting Sadat and stressing that Israel was ready for war. Sadat was not embarrassed and just after coming down the steps of his airplane at Ben-Gurion airport he remarked to Gur with a smile: 'I come for peace, not war.'

Aman, still suffering the shellshock of its 1973 failure in prediction, was ultra-cautious to the last moment. Paralysed by the past failure and the fear of failing again, Aman's staff had become paranoid. Suffering obsessions, which used to be the Mossad's institutional disease, it was now Aman's turn to see war behind every door. But this did not become a new 'Concept'.

On the contrary, the concept was now not to have a 'Concept'. This psychology led to a worst-case analysis of almost everything; but unlike insubstantial thoughts, their *modus operandi* on solid ground had been corrected. There was a new emphasis on long-distance military monitoring, using technological advances such as the unmanned drones which could transmit live television pictures from above the enemy lines.

In any event, the failure in 1977 to predict peace was not so bad as the intelligence *Mechdal* which had cost the Israelis thousands of lives. At least it was peace and not war.

Three years later, after the Camp David peace treaty was signed, a strange scene was played on the fringes of another Sadat visit to Israel. In 1980, he was in Haifa, and Deputy

Prime Minister Tohami was waiting to enter an official banquet. Six feet away stood Mossad chief Hofi and his wife. Tohami and Hofi pretended not to know each other – not a handshake or a nod of the head.

An Israeli television reporter, who knew that the two men had launched the peace process, nudged Tohami: 'Enough of the play-acting. It's already in the history books.'[26]

For the Good of the Jews

'Yehiel, please invite Harry Hurwitz in,' the Prime Minister asked his dedicated political secretary, Yehiel Kadishai. Menachem Begin, in July 1977, was leader of Israel and determined to become champion of the Jewish people everywhere.

Kadishai had been Begin's private secretary since their underground days in the Irgun. Now, after the frustration of opposition to an unbroken string of Labour-led governments, Begin and his men were more than eager for real action.

Kadishai picked up the internal telephone, dialled extension 211, and invited Hurwitz to come to the Prime Minister's office immediately.

In the short time that the South African-born Hurwitz, dark-haired, bespectacled and heavy-set, had been working for Begin as his adviser on Jewish affairs, he had learned to understand his boss. Begin would only rarely invite him to his office and this was usually when he needed Hurwitz's skill in wording letters and sensitive documents in English.

Begin, although born and educated in Poland, had little trouble with the English language, which he sharpened daily by listening to the BBC World Service – an odd, private tribute from the man who was a wanted terrorist during the British Mandate in Palestine, but Begin believed that Israel should be a British-style democracy.

'Harry,' the Prime Minister greeted him as he entered Begin's office on the second floor, 'I would like you to write a letter which is not only important, but is dear to my heart.' The letter was addressed to the new Marxist president of Ethiopia, Colonel Mengistu Haile Mariam, and in exceptionally polite language Begin asked Mengistu to permit the Jews of Ethiopia to move to Israel. Begin framed his request as a humanitarian plea to the leader of the Provisional Military Administrative Council which had overthrown Israel's secret peripheral ally Emperor Haile Selassie.[1]

A short while earlier, Jerusalem had received a request from Colonel Mengistu to renew arms sales to Ethiopia, and to try to persuade the United States to aid him in his wars against neighbouring Somalia and against the rebels of the Eritrean Liberation Front. This appeared to offer an opening to Begin and his special interest in liberating the Jews of the world.

In fact, on his very first visit to Washington in July to discuss prospects for peace, the first question Begin raised with President Jimmy Carter had to do with Ethiopia and the yearning of the Jews there to realize their ancient dream of moving to the land of their forefathers.[2]

In Africa and elsewhere, the Begin government brought about a sweeping change in Israel's perception of the Jewish diaspora – the majority of the world's Jews dispersed around the globe, residing outside the biblical homeland of their people.

The new Prime Minister summoned the Mossad chief, Yitzhak Hofi, and explained to him that he regarded immigration to Israel as no less important than peace with Egypt, combating terrorism, or issuing military assessments – normally the highest priorities of the intelligence community.

On the surface, this seemed surprising. What should the intelligence services have to do with a Jewish problem? Hofi knew that Israel's secret agents had always been involved in Jewish affairs. But he also understood that Begin wanted more.

Israel regards itself as the national and natural home for the entire Jewish people, and as the home of each individual Jew wherever he or she may be. This is a matter of clear and unequivocal ideology, which has been cardinal to the Zionist movement since its inception.

Behind the doctrine, however, lies a certain degree of self-interest. As a state which absorbs immigrants and has a serious demographic problem – surrounded by far more numerous Arabs – Israel constantly needs new immigrants. They serve not only as a human reservoir, but also as justification for the state's existence.

Israel therefore feels an obligation to help every Jew or Jewish community in distress. The responsibility most definitely extends to the secret agencies. When Israel believes that there are Jewish problems, its intelligence community becomes a 'Jewish intelligence' service.

Israel's policy, enunciated publicly but not fully, holds that everything possible must be done to protect Jewish communities abroad, and also to bring them to the Jewish state as new immigrants. This should preferably, but not necessarily, be done by open and legal means. Where that has not been possible, Zionist organizations and Israel itself have rarely hesitated to use illegal means. That was the *raison d'être* of the Institute for Aliyah B, and the basis for the massive wave of Jewish immigration from Yemen, Iraq and the Soviet bloc countries during Israel's first years.

After most of the Jews who wished to move to the Promised Land had done so, there was no further need for Aliyah B and its duties were reassigned to the Mossad.[3]

After a few years of inactivity in Jewish affairs, there was a reawakening in 1953 of ethnic consciousness in the two great Jewish communities which are traditionally the focus of Israel's secret immigration agents: the Soviet bloc and the Arab world.

Veteran Aliyah B chief Shaul Avigur found himself without a job. He returned to his kibbutz Kinneret, by the Sea of Galilee, and felt frustrated after so many years active in secret service to his nation. Prime Minister Moshe Sharett, who happened to be Avigur's brother-in-law, hastened to help him. Sharett telephoned Isser Harel and asked the *Memuneh* to do Avigur a favour: 'Bring Shaul back into business.' Avigur certainly had the necessary experience.

Harel was reluctant, but because he wished to maintain cordial relations with the Prime Minister he gave in, and Israel silently set up a new unit to focus on Jewish immigration from Eastern Europe. Ambiguity surrounded details such as to whom the new unit was subordinate. Avigur was simply the 'assistant for special matters' to the defence minister. The unit's offices were in the *Kirya* compound in Tel Aviv and administratively, it was part of the Prime Minister's office. It was known by various names, including 'The Liaison Office of the Foreign Ministry' and, simply, 'The Advisory Body to the Prime Minister'.

Its original duties were to direct the struggle, within and outside Israel, for Jews to be permitted to leave the Soviet Union. The new unit would ensure that all efforts towards that aim were housed under one roof.[4]

It was not a coincidence that the special office was set up at this time. As long as Israel had maintained good relations with Moscow and its satellite states, Jerusalem did not want to irritate the Soviet bloc and attempted to play down the Jewish question. After the Korean War, however, Israel's leaders decided to adopt a clearly pro-Western orientation and they felt that they had nothing to lose. This was especially true when immigration from Hungary, Romania and Poland ceased and disturbing reports of anti-Semitism under Stalin emerged.

To carry out its assignment of keeping in contact with Jews, the unit sent its own 'special' diplomats to the Soviet Union, which had the world's second-largest Jewish community, three million strong, second only to the United States.

Avigur chose his representatives extremely carefully. Firstly, they had to be volunteers who demonstrated 'high Zionist motivation'. They had to know Jewish traditions and customs because much of their work consisted of meeting Jews in synagogues, and Israel could not be disgraced by having representatives who were not qualified for Orthodox prayer.

The diplomats had to be relatively young, in order to withstand the physical and mental ordeals of their assignments. Being in Moscow could be uncomfortable enough, but these men and women had to travel to all corners of the Soviet Union by various exhausting, long-distance routes. Married couples with families were preferred. Israel did not want to have any singles in its embassies, for it felt they would be more vulnerable to subversion by sexual temptation. The candidates had to speak Russian, at least to some elementary spoken proficiency.[5]

One of Avigur's men in Moscow was Lova Eliav who had wide experience as a clandestine emissary. He was sent to Russia in the summer of 1958 as the Israeli embassy's second secretary. In addition to his duties as a member of the consular team, dealing with property and other bilateral issues, Eliav admits in his memoirs that his work included slipping pocket-sized Jewish calendars or miniature Hebrew-Russian dictionaries into the jackets of Jews in synagogues. The diplomats also distributed prayer books, Bibles, the Psalms, Israeli newspapers and books in Hebrew, even though they knew that the Soviet authorities considered these to be anti-state propaganda.

The KGB knew who Eliav was and in due course arranged to have him seduced. One day, when travelling from Moscow to the University of Leningrad, Eliav noticed a remarkably attractive young woman at one of the capital's railway stations. She had the kind of European style which was all too rare in Moscow and it was hard to resist looking at her. Simply 'by chance', he met her that night in his hotel in Leningrad. Although quite certain that the young woman had been sent to seduce him and thus put him into the blackmailing clutches of the KGB, Eliav decided that he could not be hurt if he merely befriended her and trusted himself to withstand further temptation.

Eliav asked the mystery woman for a dance and she responded enthusiastically. The Israeli had never danced the kind of tango he experienced that night. He felt her warmth as she clung to him. Hot kisses on his lips were but an invitation to further pleasures.

At this point, Eliav decided that matters had gone far enough and that the game might become dangerous. He fled the woman's embrace and found solitary shelter in his own hotel bedroom. He locked the door until morning. He knew that if he were caught with that lady, the theatrics to follow could involve a 'deceived husband' threatening to kill him, the mediation of 'hotel employees', and finally a happy 'arrangement' which would require Eliav to become a KGB plant in his embassy.[6]

Another Soviet technique was to use hidden cameras to film espionage targets making love and to use the film for blackmail. According to a story which circulated among Israeli and other diplomats, President Sukarno of Indonesia had a passionate love affair with a KGB plant, but when Soviet agents came and showed him incriminating photographs, Sukarno did not give a damn. He is said to have told them nonchalantly: 'I would like six of this picture and a dozen of that one.'[7]

The special attention paid by Soviet intelligence to the special units diplomats stemmed from the KGB's belief that these Israelis were spies, and the Soviets thus tried to obtain as much information about them before they left Israel on their missions.

In March 1958, Israel informed the Soviet embassy in Tel Aviv that Lieutenant Colonel Moshe Gat was being sent to serve as the second secretary at Israel's embassy in Moscow. The Liaison Office requested the visa. A Soviet diplomat, who was a secret agent, asked one of his Israeli informers to check on Gat's background. Unfortunately for the KGB man, the Israeli whom he asked was a double agent and he immediately told all to his true case officers in Shin Bet's counterespionage department.[8]

When Israeli diplomats arrived in the Soviet Union, the authorities imposed especially strict travel limitations and tried to prevent them from meeting Jews. 'KGB men followed us twenty-four hours a day, including when we came and left, even within our homes and rooms,' Eliav recalls. 'Open surveillance, hidden surveillance, electronic surveillance, optical surveillance – all of these were constantly available to the KGB. But in addition, there was almost no member of our staff who had not been subject to more drastic measures: starting with staged "scandals" against us by "enraged citizens", and including attacks and threats of imprisonment.' The Soviet authorities realized that synagogues, in the absence of any other Jewish institution, became much more than merely a house of prayer and they attempted to keep the Israeli diplomats away from the few Jews who went to synagogue.[9]

In another case, the KGB trailed Eliyahu Hazan, yet another second secretary at the embassy in Moscow. The maid who worked in his house turned out to be a KGB agent. When Hazan and his wife arrived in Odessa, on the Black Sea, in September 1955, he hurried to meet a Jewish contact. Ruth Hazan, meantime, suddenly had an attack of food poisoning and was rushed to hospital. When he returned from his meeting, Hazan was stopped by KGB men who asked him to accompany them. He protested his detention and claimed that he had diplomatic immunity, but the Soviets ignored him. They accused him of having been involved in anti-Soviet activity and claimed that he had been arrested for giving a Soviet citizen forbidden propaganda material. Hazan was interrogated for many hours and the questioning concentrated on his meetings with Jews.

The Soviets then stepped up the pressure and demanded that Hazan work for them. He was told that the maid in his house was pregnant with his child – physiologically impossible, from the Israeli's point of view – and the Soviets threatened to publicize the scandal unless he signed a statement that he had volunteered to spy for them. They tellingly added that if he did not cooperate, 'your wife will not recover from her stomach troubles.' By then, it had become clear that she had been poisoned.

Hazan broke and agreed to be a Soviet agent. The KGB gave him three days of briefings, a first payment of 1,500 rubles for 'expenses' and his freedom. Ruth Hazan was feeling better and they returned to Moscow from Odessa. For two days, Hazan suffered terrible pangs of conscience. His colleagues in the embassy sensed that he was terribly frightened and that something was wrong. Ambassador Yosef Avidar invited him in for a chat and Hazan finally broke down and confessed what he had done.

Accompanied by a fellow diplomat, Hazan was placed on the first flight to Israel, where he was quickly dismissed from the foreign ministry. No disciplinary action was taken against him, however. Foreign Minister Moshe Sharett simply noted in his private diary: 'It is shameful that one of our men could not resist, but caved in to threats and was broken. This is a blot on us.'[10]

When the Soviet Union severed diplomatic relations with Israel in 1967, the special unit had to seek roundabout routes by which to continue its work. Now the cloak of secrecy would have to be airtight. Nehemiah Levanon replaced the ageing Avigur as head of the unit in 1970. Levanon was an experienced diplomat-agent in Moscow, expelled from there with two other Israelis in the 1950s for their Jewish intelligence work.[11]

Levanon, following the pattern of his predecessor, believed in quiet activity. In Israel and in the diaspora, however, various militant organizations had sprung up that rejected hidden methods and called instead for a vociferous campaign 'to free Soviet Jewry'. These groups forced Golda Meir's government to change its policy and from the beginning of the 1970s the Israelis began taking a different tack.

This coincided with the diplomacy of détente between the Soviet Union and the United States, in which Soviet party chief Leonid Brezhnev permitted about 250,000 Jews to leave the country. Around 160,000 of them settled in Israel.

These new immigration waves rekindled the problem that Shin Bet had had to deal with in the early 1950s: fear that the Soviet Union was exploiting the massive immigration wave to plant secret agents in Israel, or was using it as a springboard for getting its agents into the West.

The use of such techniques was confirmed by Ayala Grigorowitz Dzhirkalov, a senior KGB official who defected to the West. He told British interrogators in 1987 that the Soviet secret police examined the lists of all Jews who asked to emigrate, looking for a few who might spy for Mother Russia. These Jews were recruited only if they had a specific talent and the right personality for espionage. Several were instructed to act immediately as agents. Others were planted as 'sleepers' who would do nothing for a few years and then be 'reawakened' by Soviet controllers. The KGB set up a special department to recruit Jewish agents, to train them and to run them.[12] Further confirmation of the extent of Soviet penetration of Israel came in 1982 in Court Number One of London's Old Bailey – a few minutes, by coincidence, after the end of the trial of Rhona Ritchie, who had betrayed British diplomatic codes to her Egyptian lover in Israel.

It was in that same courtroom that an economics professor holding dual Canadian–British citizenship, Hugh Hambleton, was tried for espionage. The KGB had recruited him in the late 1940s and his clandestine career had taken him to a job in Paris as an economist for NATO. British prosecutors said the professor caused 'exceptionally grave damage' to the interests of the West.

As evidence of how much the Soviets valued Hambleton, Yuri Andropov, the head of the KGB who would later become leader of the Soviet Union, personally invited him to Moscow. At a festive banquet, they discussed Western

defences and specific assignments the professor had undertaken – notably, in Israel.

Hambleton visited Israel three times, in 1970, 1975 and
1978, entirely at the Soviet Union's expense. He did some
legitimate research, but he had a lot of extra homework
assigned by his KGB masters. During his first visit,
Hambleton was instructed by his Soviet case officer in
Austria, known only as 'Paul', to find out whether Israel
had produced atom bombs and to investigate the extent of
Israel's relations with South Africa.

Hambleton was also asked to prepare reports dealing with
his field of expertise, economics. His Soviet controllers asked
him for details on the costs incurred by a Jewish immigrant
in Israel: education, setting up a new business, acquiring
a new home and other specific topics. He gave his report
to 'Paul' in Vienna. In this case, as Hambleton told his
British MI5 interrogators, it was clear to him that he had
been paving the way for the planting of a Soviet agent in
Israel.[13]

It is difficult to know to what extent Hambleton's report
influenced the KGB, but only on January 10, 1988, did it
become clear that another Soviet agent had been planted in
Israel and had been financed generously by Moscow. This
emerged when Shabtai Kalmanovitch was charged in Tel
Aviv District Court with spying for the Russians. He had
been arrested by Shin Bet, three weeks earlier, on his return
from a visit to the Soviet Union.

When Kalmanovitch first left Russia for Israel in 1971, he
was 23 years old and had already been recruited by the KGB.
His case officers ordered him to become fully integrated in
Israeli society, to build himself a strong economic base and
to befriend political and military leaders. Using Soviet funds,
he acquired a reputation as a world-class businessman.
His financial interests extended from Monte Carlo to
Africa.

The seductive powers of wealth attracted friends with
great influence in the Israeli army and government. One of
them was Brigadier General Dov Tamari. Kalmanovitch

invited Tamari, a former commander of a top *sayeret* unit, to visit Sierra Leone at Kalmanovitch's expense for some consulting work on domestic security.

Kalmanovitch also fostered other ties with high-ranking politicians. At first, he served as an adviser to junior Knesset member Samuel Flatto-Sharon, himself a refugee from criminal charges in France. He helped Flatto-Sharon and New York congressman Benjamin Gilman, together with East Berlin lawyer Wolfgang Vogel, to arrange a bizarre international prisoner exchange involving an American in East Germany, an Israeli in Mozambique and a Russian in Pennsylvania.

Developing an appetite for bigger fry to befriend, Kalmanovitch invited cabinet ministers to lavish parties and business receptions at his ostentatious villa in a posh suburb of Tel Aviv. Many of his neighbours, intentionally or not, were senior men in the intelligence community. He even boasted that Golda Meir's door was open to him.

Kalmanovitch also worked for a short time for the East European department of Israel's Labour Party. He was assigned to ensure that new immigrants from the Soviet Union showed their gratitude to their new homeland by supporting Labour.

As a rule, the intelligence community sidestepped Israeli politics, but a few significant pockets of partisan bias remained in the mid-1970s. One of them was the Liaison Office. The unit was considered an important political fortress, as it brought new citizens into the country, who were always sized up by all the parties for their electoral potential. Nehemiah Levanon, head of the unit, happened to be a professional who dealt with the Jews of the Soviet Union, but he was also known for his loyalty to the Labour Party and the socialist movement.

Especially when Labour was in power, until 1977, Kalmanovitch was in all the right places. He continued to flutter around the edges of Israel's power centres, until Shin Bet spotted him delivering secrets to known Communist agents in Eastern Europe. After a closed-door trial in Tel Aviv, Kalmanovitch was sent to prison for nine years.

Kalmanovitch's excellent connections and his ability to make friends in high places pose serious questions about Shin Bet's failure to spot him earlier. The damage he caused, however, was not severe. He was not able to gain access to secret installations, to scientific institutes, or to army bases.[14] He could tell his Russian masters what leading members of the Israeli establishment were thinking, but could supply few details on what Israel was doing to protect itself. This is in sharp contrast to another Soviet spy – also planted as an immigrant – who was far more successful.

When he was 20 years old, in 1948, Marcus Klingberg arrived in Israel as a new immigrant from Eastern Europe. He studied the natural sciences, and at the end of the 1960s was appointed deputy director of the government's Biological Institute in the town of Nes Ziona, about ten miles south of Tel Aviv. As he seemed to be sickly, Klingberg would often travel to Switzerland for 'therapy'.

In 1983, Klingberg suddenly disappeared. Mysterious men came to the institute and took everything that had been left in his files. For a number of months, rumours flew that the high-ranking Professor Klingberg had defected to the Soviet Union. His wife told enquiring reporters that he was in Europe for the sake of his health. The truth finally emerged, that he had been a Soviet agent all along.

Klingberg had been arrested by Shin Bet, charged with espionage, convicted in a secret trial and sentenced to life in prison – with absolutely no publicity.

His trips to Switzerland had served as cover for meetings with his Soviet case officer. The damage which Klingberg caused was extensive because he had been working on top secret projects. He is assumed to have told the Soviets about research projects touching on potential biological warfare in the Middle East.[15]

Israel knew that being penetrated by Soviet agents was damaging, but it was willing to pay that price to fulfil its self-proclaimed strategic goal of acting for the good of the Jews.

The increased immigration from the Soviet Union in the 1970s forced the Liaison Office to expand. The unit began to appoint consuls to various Israeli embassies in European capitals and it sent liaison personnel to maintain ties with Jewish organizations throughout the world. It is still very active. Through the low-key, if not quite undercover, special unit, letters of support are sent to Soviet Jews, as are packages and Hebrew books.

Israelis and even some foreign Jews who travel to the Soviet Union are briefed beforehand by the unit's officials or consuls abroad and are given detailed instructions of what to do and what not to do. They are told which Jews to meet and which to avoid, and how to behave if detained by the authorities.[16]

In giving this advice and trying to coordinate the international campaign for Soviet Jewry, the special unit sometimes steps on a few toes. In late 1980, Israeli operatives sent young, dedicated British Jews – equipped with Jewish books, records, and cassettes – to the Soviet Union. Their parents and the local Jewish organizations did not know the true aim of these mysterious trips and they angrily complained to Levanon through his representatives at the Israeli embassy in London.

Levanon replied: 'Don't get involved. This doesn't concern you. We know better what we are doing.' In the course of this power struggle, the Israeli government has collected names and addresses of Soviet Jews and has planned operations, which it wants the worldwide Jewish organizations to finance while behaving like disciplined schoolchildren.[17]

The disputes have even included the bestowing of titles and financial compensation. It is the special unit which grants the label 'Prisoner of Zion' on any Soviet Jew who actively promotes the Zionist movement, Jewish culture, or both, and is arrested for those activities. Israel draws a distinction between Jews who are simply dissidents fighting for Soviet human rights, and Jews who are active

Zionists and suffering because of their love for Israel.

Anatoli (Natan) Shcharansky, one of the most famous Prisoners of Zion, did not even qualify at first. He was imprisoned on charges of spying for the CIA and was considered a human rights activist. Only later did he declare himself a Zionist and become a living symbol of the co-ordinated Israeli–Jewish fight for the right of Soviet Jews to emigrate. Shcharansky moved to Israel in 1986, when released as part of a spy swap.

The tensions began to fade with the emergence of President Mikhail Gorbachev and his policy of *glasnost*, or openness, and the astonishing number of Jews who were granted the right to emigrate, but chose to go to other Western countries rather than Israel.[18]

The concern over the fate of Soviet Jews, occasionally seen as exaggerated, resulted in a wave of bitter Israeli humour in the 1970s and it was suggested that the new immigrants were motivated more by materialism than by ideology. One joke told of the Russian Jews who came down an airliner's steps at Tel Aviv with their fingers flashing the traditional V sign. But theirs was not a V for victory. It was a demand for a villa and a Volvo.

There were also more serious charges of racial discrimination, as Israelis whose families had come from Iraq, Yemen and other Arab nations recalled the dusty tents and other poor conditions they had had to endure after arriving in the Jewish state in the 1950s and 1960s. They claimed that the Ashkenazi élite, with roots in Europe, continued to favour Russians and others of their own kind.

At least one common factor, however, can be found in the immigration of the Sephardi Jews from the Arab world and the later influx of Jews from Communist Eastern Europe. In both cases, Israeli intelligence acted under extremely dangerous conditions to arrange the emigration. But, even greater efforts were made and bigger dangers risked to arrange the departure of Jews from the Arab lands.

After the electrifying operations to bring out the Jews of

Iraq and Yemen, the next Sephardi exodus to Israel was to come from Egypt in November 1956.

At the beginning of the Suez–Sinai campaign, Aliyah B chief Avigur sent a small team of operatives to Egypt. Their mission was to establish contact with the Jewish community there and arrange their clandestine departure for Israel. On November 9, Lova Eliav and Avraham Dar, who had been the handler of the 1951 Israeli espionage network, and an Aman radio operator left for Egypt – wearing French uniforms and flying a French military aircraft to Port Said, at the entrance of the Suez Canal.

Operation *Tushia*, or 'Cunning', began with the hope that the intelligence operatives would be able to contact Egypt's Jews and persuade most of them to leave for Israel. The plan was for Eliav, Dar and their radio man to advance alongside the British and French forces as they marched on Cairo and Alexandria, which had large Jewish communities. When the Anglo-French force halted its invasion, the three Israelis found themselves stuck, however, in Port Said, where there were only 200, mostly elderly, Jews.

All that was left for Eliav and Dar was to go to the local synagogue, where they hid their true identities but offered to arrange safe passage out of Egypt. The Port Said Jews realized that the two 'Frenchmen' with whom they had spoken were Israeli secret agents and 65 of them packed their bags. They were taken to the dock, where they boarded two landing craft belonging to the French navy.

The two small vessels sailed a few miles into the Mediterranean, where they rendezvoused with two ships of the tiny Israeli navy which – with the cooperation of French secret agents – were camouflaged as two Italian fishing vessels, the *Aphrodite* and the *Castello del Mare*. French sailors carried the old people and the women from the landing boats to the Israeli ships, where they were greeted by a veteran agent of Jewish intelligence operations in Iraq, Shlomo Hillel. A day later, they docked in Haifa. Eliav, Dar and the radio man returned to Israel two days later, the same way they had gone to Egypt, with the aid of French intelligence.[19]

The mini-exodus from Port Said was only a small-scale venture and an easy one to execute, thanks to French assistance, but it does serve as a solid example of the intentions, planning and methods of operation of Israel's Jewish intelligence. It also reflects the supreme importance which Israel attaches to the immigration of Jews, in any manner and at any price. In order to bring out a small number of Jews, Israeli intelligence was willing to endanger three valuable operatives in a hostile country and to invest relatively large sums of money in means of transportation – all the while incurring a political debt by using the facilities of a foreign power.

It is obvious that all the preparations and assets which are needed increase geometrically, when instead of dozens, Israel plans the clandestine emigration of tens of thousands of Jews – as it did from other nations, beginning with Morocco.

On March 2, 1956, the French occupation ended and Morocco gained its independence. Until then, for eight years, its exit gates had been open and about 100,000 Moroccan Jews had gone to Israel. In the early days of Moroccan independence, however, the new government gave in to the pressures of fellow Arab states and forbade the departure of Jews.

The fate of the remaining 100,000 Jews in Morocco was naturally the subject of great concern in Israel. Isser Harel, *Memuneh* of the intelligence community, had foreseen this two years earlier, when Morocco was still under French rule. To prepare for unexpected disruptions of the emigration campaign, Harel had established a secret infrastructure for Zionist activity in Morocco. The Mossad recruited a team of kibbutz members and reserve officers of Moroccan origin who spoke Arabic and French. All had to have been in combat units, and preferably they had experience in clandestine activities.

The head of the Israeli network in Morocco was Shlomo Havilio and his immediate superior was Shmuel Toledano. The original aim of the unit, which had the code name

'Framework', was to organize young, local Jews to defend their community, if, as they feared, their Arab neighbours launched pogroms or other disturbances. When the legal emigration under French auspices ended, however, Framework was assigned to find a way to renew it by illegal means.

This was, probably unconsciously on Harel's part, a repeat of the pattern which had worked in Iraq until the network there had fallen. This time, though, the Mossad agents were able to learn from the mistakes of the past and they were better equipped for the venture. Along the pattern devised by Shiloah in 1952, the responsibility for operating Framework was shared between the Mossad and the Jewish Agency. Once complaints began, Harel cut them short – not wanting to fall into the Iraqi-style trap of dissension – by firing Havilio in February 1960. The new Framework commander was Alex Gatmon.

Up until that point, about 18,000 Jews had clandestinely left Morocco for Israel. The Mossad representatives had established headquarters in the large cities of the new North African state and they started using forged documents and other deceptions to arrange the departure of Jews willing to leave for their ancient Promised Land.

To the religious North African Jews, the young Israeli agents seemed to be envoys from the Messiah. The Jews were instructed to gather at various meeting places in the large cities and from there they were taken by taxi or truck to the border. To smooth the way, the Mossad paid half a million dollars in bribes to Moroccan officials. A favourite route out was through Tangier, which at the time was an international city, and from there on to Israel. Later, two towns in Spain were used as bases for the project, which had the full cooperation of Generalissimo Franco – acting, so the Mossad believed, out of guilt feelings over Spain's close ties with Hitler and Mussolini and even the expulsion of Spanish Jews in 1492, the year that Columbus discovered America.

The Mossad also purchased an army camp near the Spanish towns of the Costa del Sol, but actually inside the British Crown Colony of Gibraltar. The grounds and barracks were converted into an absorption camp for Moroccan immigrants. The British authorities knew, of course, the true purpose of the former military base but agreed to look the other way. From the time that the Jewish refugees arrived in the camp, the Jewish Agency had the responsibility for putting them up, sailing them to the French port of Marseilles and then aboard larger ships to Israel.

Tragedy struck on January 11, 1961. A ship flying a Honduran flag of convenience sank, not far from the Moroccan coast. Forty-four men, women and children, together with the Mossad radio operator, drowned. The disaster aroused sympathy worldwide, but it also triggered a sharp response from the Moroccan authorities. They uncovered the underground network, arrested scores of Zionist activists and placed the entire operation in jeopardy.

Israel asked the governments of France and the United States, as well as international welfare organizations, to apply pressure on Morocco. Luckily, King Hassan II was crowned in early March and had a keen interest in gaining Western support, and no interest at all in being seen as the persecutor of a Jewish minority.

Paradoxically, however, it was the sinking of the ship which accelerated the Jewish emigration from Morocco and made the entire project better organized. At first, a Jewish welfare organization had the responsibility for helping the Moroccan Jews, but in 1964 direct ties were established between the Mossad, headed by Meir Amit, and the Moroccan security services. Their relationship was based on a tacit understanding – Jews in exchange for technical and military aid – which led to the Ben-Barka murder fiasco in Paris the next year.

The renewed operation to relocate Moroccan Jewry was codenamed 'Yakhin', that being the name of one of the two central pillars that supported the Holy Temple built in Jerusalem by King Solomon. Israel regarded immigration as a major pillar, which supported the existence of the Jewish state.

Operation Yakhin was, in reality, a joint project of Morocco, Israel and France. Mossad agents fanned out to almost every Jewish neighbourhood in Morocco. They invited the people to come and live in their ancient homeland and were overwhelmed by the positive response. The Mossad men gave instructions for reaching the rendezvous points and transported the Jews by bus and truck to Moroccan ports, where ships and planes picked them up.

By the use of these methods, more than 80,000 Jews left Morocco. The Israeli–Moroccan cooperation also yielded an unusual by-product in Tunisia, less than a thousand miles to the east. In the summer of 1961, the Tunisian Government demanded that the former colonial ruler, France, shut down its naval base at Bizerta. In the crisis which followed, the Tunisians arrested some French citizens, as well as a few dozen Jews in Bizerta.

The Mossad agents in Morocco began to fear for Tunisia's Jews and arranged for French warships – following the pattern of Port Said – to sail off the North African coast and take on 1,000 Jews from the coast at Bizerta. They were transported first to France and then on to Israel.[20]

In the middle of the Yakhin–Bizerta operation, Shmuel Toledano was suddenly given another assignment by Harel – in another field for Jewish intelligence action, South America. The capture of Adolf Eichmann in Buenos Aires in 1960 had earned kudos for the Mossad around the world, but the exploit also gave a boost to anti-Semitism in Argentina and endangered the half a million Jews there. There was a marked increase in the number of attacks on Jews, organized by *Tacuara*, the Argentine fascist 'Reed', which had many children of prominent police and military officers among its members.

On July 1, 1962, a Jewish student named Garcia Sirota was kidnapped by Tacuara members and they tattooed a Nazi swastika on her breast. The incident sent shock waves through the Jewish communities of Argentina and in Israel, newspapers published editorials urging their government to send assistance to 'our Jewish brethren' in South America.

Harel hardly needed any encouragement. Young Jewish activists from Argentina and nearby countries were brought to Israel and trained in self-defence.

By the 1970s, Israel was finding new ways to defend the continent's Jews. When, in Chile and Argentina, military juntas with strong anti-Semitic tendencies came to power, Israel sold weapons and military know-how to both governments. In return, the Israelis obtained pledges from the Santiago and Buenos Aires dictators to protect the Jews and to permit them to leave – with their cash and property.

A similar policy was adopted with Romania, the only Soviet-bloc state which preserved its diplomatic relations with Israel after all the other Communist countries severed their ties following the 1967 war. The special relationship surfaced in January 1985, a few months after Shimon Peres became Prime Minister of Israel, when he flew to Bucharest to meet President Nicolae Ceausescu. On the official airplane with Peres was an old, white-haired man.

His name was Yeshayahu (Shaike) Trachtenberg-Dan, a figure both mysterious and heroic. In World War II he had volunteered for the British Army and had been parachuted, together with other young Palestinian Jews, behind the Nazi lines in the Balkans. He was one of the survivors who returned to Israel and joined the organization led by Avigur and Levanon.[21]

Dan's activities made him a target for several Eastern European services, but an American paid the price.

On August 14, 1967, Charles Jordan, a senior officer of the American Joint Distribution Committee, a Jewish welfare organization known as Joint, arrived in Prague, the Czechoslovakian capital. Two days later, he left his hotel and disappeared. When he failed to return, his wife reported his disappearance to the police. Four days later, his body was lifted out of the Moldau river. The authorities said that Jordan must have somehow fallen into the water and might even have committed suicide.

The secret services of the Soviet bloc always suspected that the Joint representatives were nothing but CIA operatives and they were aware of the ties between Joint and the Israeli government. Jordan attracted quite a bit of attention from Communist operatives, especially as he had arrived in Prague from Jerusalem.

It has since become clear that Charles Jordan was murdered – in a case of mistaken identity – by agents of Czech intelligence. They believed that their victim was Yeshayahu Dan.[22]

Dan, undeterred, continued to operate in Eastern Europe and he won President Ceausescu's agreement to permit the departure of his Jewish citizens. In return, Israeli experts serviced Romanian tanks and other military equipment, while the Jewish state imported far more Romanian goods that it truly needed – there is a limit to how much prune jam a country can use. With the help of Jewish welfare organizations in the West, Israel specifically agreed to pay three thousand dollars for each Jew permitted to leave. Officials said Romania was simply being compensated for the cost of educating its citizens, but it was clear to all sides that ransom was being paid. Dan used to fly to Bucharest once a year with a suitcase full of cash to make the payments. Israel also endorsed Romania's request for 'most favoured nation' trading status with the United States.

The only condition set by Ceausescu, which Israel accepted, was that these agreements be kept secret to spare him any embarrassment. This was not simply to protect his friendships with his sister Communist states or the Arab countries. Romania's president feared that other minorities, especially those of German origin, would press similar demands upon his government.

The financial *quid pro quo* remained secret. In obvious contrast to the noisy policy adopted by Israel in demanding the freedom of emigration for Soviet Jews, Jerusalem maintained a low profile and absolute silence with regard to the Romanian Jews. Different circumstances called for different methods. The departures for Israel were therefore described officially as 'reunification of families' and not as emigration.

Shaike Dan became a leading Western conduit to the

Romanian leadership. As an intelligence community expert on the status of the Eastern Europe Jewish 'family', Dan gave briefings to every Israeli leader, from Golda Meir through to Menachem Begin.[23]

In Begin's eyes the Jewish family had no borders and had to be reunified whenever and wherever opportunities could be found. Under him, the intelligence community became equally family-minded.

Ethiopia's Jews, while considered unique because their skins were dark, had the same strong desire as their Jewish brethren in Morocco, Romania and the rest of the Arab world and Eastern Europe. The Jewish world knew nothing about the existence of the Ethiopian or 'black Jews' until the end of the 18th century. The Jews of that troubled African land, however, never stopped dreaming of the Bible's Promised Land. They called themselves *Beta Israel* 'the House of Israel', even though their non-Jewish neighbours labelled them with the derogatory *Falashas*, which means strangers in the worst sense of the word – akin to bastards who belong nowhere.

In the distant past, they had been a mighty tribe of fighters who had had their own kingdom in the northern Ethiopian mountains. Gradually, after a series of setbacks in battles with other tribes, *Beta Israel*'s power dwindled, to the extent that by the middle of the 20th century they numbered around 20,000 people, concentrated primarily in Gondar and other districts. The Christian Ethiopians who controlled the surrounding regions prohibited purchases of land by Falashas, and as a result the Jews became artisans and sharecroppers in a country where owning your own field provides the only real chance of having enough to eat.

In the early 1950s, a handful of young Ethiopian Jews managed to reach Israel and they applied pressure on the Israeli Government to bring the rest of the Jews out. Despite excellent ties with Israel, the government of Emperor Haile Selassie refused to allow the Jews to emigrate. It was a matter of national pride: a respected emperor could not be seen to be losing his subjects.

The Labour-dominated Israeli Government, on the other hand, did not go out of its way to help Ethiopian Jewry. Reuven Merhav, who worked in the Mossad station in Addis Ababa, recalls: 'The Jews banged on the doors of our embassy. Their leaders begged us to get them out. But we sent them away crestfallen.'[24]

The Israelis feared that merely bringing up the issue could ruin the strategic ties with Ethiopia – one of the key countries in the peripheral strategy of diplomatically outmanoeuvring the Arab countries.

It was also significant that the Orthodox religious authorities in Israel stated darkly that they did not recognize the 'black Jews' and that added to Israel's reluctance to help. The Ethiopian Jews continued to wait for a sign from Zion, but the sign was delayed. Only when Menachem Begin and his Likud won the 1977 election was there a dramatic change in Israel's approach and for a few months in 1978 it appeared that the Ethiopian Jews would realize their dream.

US President Jimmy Carter refused, in his meeting with Menachem Begin in July 1977, to change allegiances in the Horn of Africa and to supply Ethiopia, rather than Somalia, with arms. In President Carter's eyes, Colonel Mengistu's regime was tyrannical, Marxist and unworthy of US support. Begin's letter to the colonel, worded by his adviser Hurwitz, informed the colonel that Israel itself would offer the aid.

The resulting situation included two strange coalitions in northeastern Africa which can only be explained by the aphorism – politics makes strange bedfellows. It could be added that international politics makes even stranger ones. Marxist Ethiopia was supported in 1977 by the Soviet Union, East Germany and Israel; while Somalia had the support of the United States, Saudi Arabia and Egypt.

In return, the Ethiopian Government agreed to permit the departure of small numbers of Jews. Up until February 1978, two groups, totalling 220 Jews, were flown directly from Addis Ababa to Israel, in Israeli cargo planes which secretly brought weapons to Ethiopia. Foreign Minister

Dayan inexplicably uttered a careless remark, however, which cut short the honeymoon – and the long marriage – between Ethiopia and Israel. Dayan admitted, in a news conference, that Israel was supplying uniforms to the Ethiopian army. Everyone knew he meant weapons and that was enough to prompt Mengistu to cut the covert relations. His Jews would no longer be allowed to leave.

Begin, while angry at his foreign minister, was at least slightly comforted by Mossad chief Hofi's enthusiasm about finding alternative routes. While Hofi worked on his plans, Begin protected the security of the operation by not saying a word. He even had to tolerate the abuse being heaped upon him without responding.

Jewish organizations led the attacks on Begin – claiming he was doing nothing, in the face of reports that Ethiopia's Jews were being persecuted by their government, rebel groups and gangs of robbers. The critics suggested that Israel might be apathetic because of the black skin of the Falashas.

'Mr Begin, you have to respond,' Yehiel Kadishai begged the Prime Minister, as Kadishai could not stand the attacks on the leader he revered. Begin, however, refused to budge, absolutely unwilling to reveal that action was, in fact, being taken on.[25]

The Israeli Prime Minister knew in 1979 that the rescue operation was already in full swing. Young Ethiopians, who had moved to Israel earlier, were recruited to work for the Jewish state. Just as young Moroccan Jews had been sent on assignment to their native land twenty years earlier, the Ethiopians underwent a brief training period and were sent back from where they had come – now as secret agents of Israel.

The inexperienced Israeli team travelled to Jewish communities and proposed that whoever was able to leave should make their way, by a long and dangerous route, to neighbouring Sudan. Agents briefed the leaders of the Jewish villages and in some cases accompanied them on the perilous journey. Entire villages began to trek along almost non-existent paths. In many instances they were caught, tortured and forced back to their villages.

Those who managed to reach southern Sudan – and thousands did not make it, dying along the way – were lodged in a camp established twenty miles from the border. It was a cesspool of humanity – overcrowding, insufficient food, and no clean drinking water – administered, as best they could, by personnel of the United Nations High Commission for Refugees.

The only consolation for these Ethiopian Jews was that their condition was better than that of other refugees in the camp. At least in their case, Mossad agents were in the area to ensure that they received the best possible treatment. Some of the Mossad men were black, but others assumed various cover identities – as relief workers from Europe, for example.

The next objective was to gain the clandestine cooperation of Sudan. The US Government helped apply pressure on President Gaafar Numeiri, a member of the Arab League and officially at war with Israel, by offering financial assistance. This, inevitably, amounted to little more than a bribe to swell Numeiri's own bank accounts. Egypt also helped, because Anwar Sadat was a personal friend of Numeiri and, at Begin's request, urged Sudan to help the Ethiopian Jews escape. Begin had thus found a valuable side benefit to his peace treaty with Egypt.

General Numeiri promised to turn a blind eye, as long as everything was kept secret. In order to work out the details, the Mossad sent a senior operative to Khartoum at the beginning of 1980 and he coordinated the operation with Abu Tayeb, the head of the Sudanese security services. The most convenient and effective method was to transfer the Jewish refugees by the shortest possible route – by sea to the port of Eilat – but Numeiri did not want his own shoreline to be used and demanded that, in any event, the Jews be moved via a third country and not directly from Sudan to Israel.

The Mossad and Sudan finally hammered out an arrangement whereby the Ethiopian Jews were moved through camps in southern Sudan, in coordination with UN field workers, across the border into Kenya. The Kenyans were, of course, old allies of Israel and were parties to the secret agreement. This escape route, too, was closed, however, after a small private airplane belonging to an American charity crossed the border from Sudan and had to make an emergency landing in Kenya. The occupants, including five Ethiopian Jews as the smuggled cargo, were arrested and a Nairobi newspaper published details of the clandestine operation – including information on the Mossad station in Kenya. The Kenyan Government insisted on shutting down the flow of Falashas rather than risk the hostility of Arab and other African nations.

With no alternative immediately available, the Mossad was forced, once more, to use its talent for improvisation. The agency again needed some foreign assistance, however, and this time Israel's operatives turned to the US. The chief Mossad representative in Washington asked the CIA to help liberate Ethiopia's Jews and the Americans agreed with surprising alacrity. With the new Reagan administration in office, the military and intelligence ties between the two nations were at their strongest.

The Mossad and the CIA established a dummy corporation named Navco, which leased land by the Red Sea shore in Sudan with the stated intention of constructing a holiday village for undersea divers. Indeed, within a short time, foreign divers did arrive in the area, but not the amateur variety who enjoy looking at coral reefs. These were members of Israel's naval commando force.

The frogmen received Ethiopian Jews who were sent to the Navco village by Mossad operatives inland, and under the cover of nighttime darkness they took the refugees in small boats to Israeli vessels anchored offshore. The ships then sailed the Red Sea to Sharm el-Sheikh, the southern tip of the Sinai Peninsula then still occupied by Israel. The Ethiopians, soon to be Israelis, were then flown in cargo airplanes to air force bases in central Israel.

The Mossad assigned a team of photographers to record the final stages of the exodus for posterity. These films and videotapes were intended only for the archives of the secret agency and they were considered extremely sensitive. An Israeli Government cabinet meeting, however, was treated to a private showing and several ministers – including Begin – could barely hold back their tears as the amazing saga unfolded on the screen. It made no difference that the faces of these Jews were black. The sufferings and struggles which they had survived were clear, as was the joy they felt when finally reaching the soil of Israel.

Some of the ministers recalled the daring operations in which Jewish refugees from Nazi-ravaged Europe arrived in pre-Israel Palestine. Now that the Jewish people had their own state, it seemed absurd that the techniques of illegal immigration had to be used again. But when no one wanted to go on record as aiding the Jews to escape the horrors of Ethiopia, the State of Israel had to resort to clandestine methods. The Red Sea route, through the bogus holiday village on the Sudanese coast, brought some 2,000 Ethiopian Jews to Israel.

The operation's planners were concerned that the pace could not be stepped up. Thousands more Jewish refugees, having crossed the desert from Ethiopia despite difficulties of biblical proportions, were waiting for their chance to reach the Promised Land. President Numeiri, meantime, knew that the Mossad and the CIA were using his country as a conduit and he became increasingly concerned that the operation might be exposed. Numeiri could never explain to the anti-Zionist, fervently Moslem majority of Sudan why he was helping Israel. He was also afraid that radical Arab regimes, especially his neighbour and enemy, Libya, would discover his involvement with the Israelis and would brand him a traitor.

The Sudanese President took a firmer stand, insisting that the exodus from Ethiopia to Israel be reduced to a trickle, just when the number of Jews leaving their villages and risking their lives to walk to Sudan had increased tremendously. Prime Minister Begin and his Mossad chief, Hofi, knew that time was running out. They decided on a grandiose operation which hoped to bring 20,000 Jewish refugees to Israel in a very short period of time. Thus Operation Moses was born.

The first step was to refurbish an old runway near the Sudanese town of Shubak. Then, one night in March 1984, two Hercules transport planes landed, speedily took on board 200 Jews who had been brought by truck and took off into the invisibility of the night sky. The operation, using unmarked aircraft belonging to Israel's air force, was repeated a number of times that month. The Mossad made sure not to leave anything on the ground which might indicate Israel's involvement, not even an empty cigarette packet or a matchbook.

A few Ethiopian Jews were flown out of Khartoum airport on commercial flights to Europe, to catch connections to Israel. The Mossad wanted to make more use of the airport, knowing it was far safer than the desert landing strip being used by Israeli crews, but President Numeiri would have to agree. His own troops would have to guard the airport and keep curious onlookers away whenever special, unscheduled flights were about to leave.

At Israel's request, the United States promised further economic aid, $200 million, to Sudan, in return for a promise by Numeiri that he would allow Jews to fly out of Khartoum. The key negotiator was George Weber of the US embassy in Khartoum, working under the title 'refugee coordinator'.

To grease the wheels and to ensure Numeiri's final approval, the Mossad deposited $60 million in European banks, primarily in Switzerland and London, to the accounts of Numeiri and a number of his aides. Much of the money was specially collected by Jewish fundraisers worldwide, who only knew that it was to 'help the Falashas'.

The Mossad also persuaded George Mittelman, a Belgian

millionaire who was also a religious Jew, to help the secret project. Mittclman was ideal, simply because he owned an airline – the little known Trans Europe Airlines. Even better, TEA pilots and crews had plenty of experience at Khartoum airport as they regularly flew devout Moslems from Sudan to Mecca in Saudi Arabia, during the annual *hajj* pilgrimage. Mittelman immediately agreed to place his airplanes at Israel's disposal and to keep his mouth shut. He did consult Belgium's Prime Minister Wilfried Martens and Justice Minister Jean Gol, who was responsible for the Belgian secret service and just happened to be Jewish. They both gave Mittelman the nod to help the Israelis.

From November 21, 1984, until the first week of 1985, thirty-five flights left Khartoum's international airport, carrying 7,000 immigrants to Brussels. After a two-hour refuelling stop at TEA's home base, the airplanes headed back towards the Southeast – but this time to Israel. The operation worked with clockwork precision and it always took a day off on Saturdays because the Ethiopian Jews devoutly honoured the Jewish Sabbath.

Even though hundreds of people in Israel and abroad knew about Operation Moses, the secret leaked no further. The editors of the Israeli newspapers agreed not to publish any reports that Ethiopian Jews were arriving and even the foreign correspondents based in Israel who heard about it displayed sufficient responsibility not to file any dispatches which might jeopardize the operation.

Instead, it was an Israeli official who was unable to hold his tongue. Operation Moses met a premature death because of the indiscretion of Yehuda Dominitz, a senior official in the Jewish Agency. His office had become an active participant in the arrival and accommodation of the Ethiopian Jews and in fundraising. At the beginning of January 1985, Dominitz was interviewed by an obscure Hebrew-language journal, *Nekudah*, or 'Point', published by Jewish settlers on the occupied West Bank. He unnecessarily gave details of the amazing project to rescue Ethiopian Jewry and the 400 foreign correspondents saw this as a signal to quote the journal and report fully on the entire operation.

The cat was out of the bag and there was nothing for Israel's leaders to do but celebrate the success – so far – of their formerly secret project in Africa. The new Prime Minister, Peres, had been in his job for only three months. He hurriedly convened a press conference and answered any and all questions on how Israel had brought some 10,000 Ethiopian Jews to their historic homeland. Peres, the Labour Party leader, apparently wanted to take credit for an operation which had begun at the initiative of Begin and his Likud.

The story was big news around the world. As President Numeiri had feared, the Arab states and the PLO's Yasser Arafat condemned him as a traitor, for having helped the Zionists recruit added manpower for their army. On January 5, two days after Peres's press conference, the Sudanese Government informed Washington that the exodus of the Ethiopians, through Khartoum, would have to stop at once. Ethiopia followed suit, by closing its border with Sudan and accusing both Numeiri and the Israelis of 'kidnapping' Ethiopian citizens.

In Sudan itself, there still remained over a thousand so-called Falashas, mainly young people, because Israel's policy had been to evacuate the sick, the old and the women first. Under further pressure from the United States, with the personal intervention of then-Vice President George Bush, Numeiri agreed that six US Air Force Hercules planes could land on a deserted airfield near one of the refugee camps on March 28, 1985. The remaining Jews were picked up there and flown directly, by the Americans, to Israel.

Numeiri's days were numbered. A short while later, he was deposed by a military coup. He and other government leaders, including secret service chief Abu Tayeb, were tried *in absentia*. They were accused of corruption, accepting bribes from the Mossad and the CIA, and collaborating with the Israeli enemy. Numeiri found asylum in Cairo, by courtesy of his friend, Hosni Mubarak, successor of the slain

Sadat. The worst part of the matter was that 15,000 Jews still remained in Ethiopia. They continue to suffer there, along with nearly all the people of that arid land.[26]

An interim summary of this amazing operation, possibly the most remarkable epic in the history of Israel's Jewish intelligence – in many ways a greater achievement than Iraq, Yemen and Morocco combined – can be given in a single sentence: Begin initiated, Sadat mediated, Dayan botched, Hofi rectified, Reagan paid, Peres talked and Numeiri was ruined.[27]

The tragic and unexpected end of Operation Moses exposed, for the first time, matters that had remained happily hidden for the sake of the Ethiopian refugees. Begin had achieved his twin goal of writing his place in history as a peacemaker, while ensuring that Israel would act for the good of the Jews. But he also embarked on a third path and this was the start of a new period in the history of Israeli intelligence, the era of adventurism and of major failures.

10

The Age of Adventurism

The stillness of the hot morning was shattered in the West Bank by three explosions before eight o'clock on June 2, 1980, and so were the bodies of three Palestinian mayors. The fiery and popular Bassam Shaka of Nablus, the elegant English-style gentleman Karim Khalaf of Ramallah and the quiet Muhammad Tawil of El-Bireh were victims of bombs planted in their cars outside their homes.

Outrage and sympathy were expressed around the world for the politicians who lost limbs and barely concealed their 'feeling' that the Israeli authorities were responsible.

Prime Minister Begin might have been expected to do everything possible to capture the bombers and prove there was no link to the government. All that Begin and Shin Bet director Ahituv – remaining anonymous, as always – did, however, was issue a public denial, on August 8, that they had in any way been responsible for the attempted killings.

Right-wingers in Israel suggested openly that the mayors were probably attacked by fellow Palestinians and there certainly were many precedents for radical factions killing Arabs who were considered too moderate or too close to the Israelis.

Officials in Jerusalem could hardly deny, on the other hand, that the trail, if pursued, would be likely to lead to the controversial Jewish settlements on the West Bank. Ultranationalist settlers had the means and the motive to terrorize the Arab mayors. That was known to be the suspicion, if not the certain knowledge, of Ahituv. Based on the sophistication of the car bombs and the absence of fingerprints and other physical clues, there was reason for the Israeli authorities to believe that the underground group responsible had to be taken very seriously – as a law enforcement challenge, without regard to political considerations.

Ahituv met Begin and asked for permission to plant Shin Bet agents as spies among the Jewish settlers. In the 1950s, '60s and '70s, networks of wiretaps and informants had been used effectively against extreme left-wing Jews in Israel and Shin Bet found it easy to keep tabs on them. Intelligence chiefs believed that the Left was susceptible to subversion from outside, whether by Soviet intelligence or by Arab interests.

As the occupation of the territories captured by Israel in 1967 became more entrenched, however, the extreme right-wing became a growing source of concern. This fringe had developed a Messianic complex – an explosive mixture of religious fanaticism, extreme nationalism and hatred of the Palestinians.

Shin Bet had a free hand in surveillance with Rabbi Meir Kahane's Israeli political party, Kach, which acted as extremist successor to the Jewish Defence League he had founded in the United States. Shin Bet agents infiltrated Kach, filing full reports on what was happening within, so there would be advance warning if a maniacal member embarked on a campaign of murder or mayhem.[1] Kach activists, including Kahane, were arrested from time to time and held in administrative detention based on tips received from informers.

Over the years, a number of other people belonging to tiny, naïve, mentally unstable, or ephemeral groups had been arrested for planning to attack Arab civilians or blow up the sacred mosques on the Temple Mount in Jerusalem. Many devout Jews believed that the Moslem places of worship would have to be flattened before the Messiah could come, build a Third Temple for the Jews in place of the gold and silver domes of the Omar and el-Aqsa mosques, and proceed to save the world.

Shin Bet had a much more delicate task when it came to West Bank settlers. Most of them were widely considered to be extremely patriotic and nationalistic and they had excellent and obvious ties to Begin and his Likud establishment.

As Ahituv had feared, the Prime Minister rejected his request to plant spies among the settlers. Begin put aside the professionalism required for security and intelligence, in favour of emotional and political considerations which dictated extreme caution.

This was a different Begin from the one who took office in 1977. After securing his role as a peacemaker, by making compromises for a peace treaty with Egypt, the 'real' Menachem Begin — the highly nationalistic demagogue, as depicted by his opponents — was yearning to break out of his moderate shell. Now, he started to become an enchanted Begin, falling under the spell of General Ariel Sharon.

Ariel Scheinerman, later to change his name to Sharon, was born in 1928 on a farm to the north of Tel Aviv and was raised on socialist dogma. He remained in the embrace of Zionism's dominant Labour movement. First, however, came the army, where he showed great courage and skill. He was wounded in the 1948 war, but in the 1950s he helped set up Israel's special forces as head of the famed commando platoon — responsible for stern retaliation against Palestinian guerilla attacks — known as Unit 101. It was the forerunner of the Israeli *sayeret* forces. Sharon was promoted to commander of the paratroops and hoped to become the army chief of staff.

He certainly commanded the respect and loyalty of many lifelong friends, but he also rubbed up many other people the wrong way. Various internal feuds prevented Sharon's rise to the top military job. Disappointed, Sharon resigned from the army, by coincidence a mere three months before the Yom Kippur War of 1973.[2]

He returned to duty to help reverse Israel's early setbacks in the war, daringly driving west of the Suez Canal into the Egyptian mainland to force a ceasefire. Sharon then channelled his ambitions and tactical genius into politics. The Labour Party already had plenty of generals in starring roles and he could do better in a political party where he could play first fiddle. Sharon thus found his way into the Liberal Party, a right-wing group despite its name. Within a short time, Sharon, with his limitless energy, managed to persuade several parties, in what was then a right-wing opposition, to merge under the umbrella of a single organization which named itself Likud, a Hebrew word for consolidation or unity. In less than four years, Sharon would see his creation win control of the nation.

After Likud's election victory in 1977, Sharon plotted tactics on the battlefield of government bureaucracy. With his military background, he understood the importance of controlling and supervising the intelligence community. Intelligence means information and information means power. In many ways, Israeli intelligence acted as a state within a state – conducting its own foreign policy, influencing defence policy and becoming involved in almost every decision of internal policy. Sharon took a keen interest in such autonomy, so as better to serve his view of national security.

Knowing that Begin was planning to give the defence ministry to General Ezer Weizman, the former air force commander who ran the Likud election campaign, Sharon nominated himself to head a new ministry of intelligence. Similar suggestions had been made a dozen years earlier, when another general – Yigal Allon – had been considered for such a post, which in the end was never created. In Sharon's vision, the ministry would be in charge of all the intelligence agencies and could even take Aman away from the defence ministry.

Begin rejected Arik Sharon's proposal and instead gave him the agriculture ministry – where the retired general oversaw the building of Jewish settlements in the occupied territories and waited for bigger opportunities to arise. When the quarrel between the Prime Minister and Shin Bet chief Ahituv broke out over the 1980 bombings, Sharon was nearing his goal.

Ahituv had considered resigning over his demand for a tougher investigation of the apparent outbreak of Jewish terrorism. He knew that such a step, however, would jolt Shin Bet severely and would lead to a huge political storm. He therefore decided to swallow his professional pride and for the agency's sake soldier on for another year.

When Ahituv finally left Shin Bet in 1981 and was replaced by his deputy, Avraham Shalom, intelligence community insiders who were asked to deliver a critique said that Ahituv had made a mistake by requesting Begin's permission to spy on the settlers. If the Shin Bet chief believed there was subversion and violence in Israeli society, they said, then he should have used his own judgment and authority to plant a network of informers among the Jews of the West Bank.

In the absence of information on the car bombers, Israel's security authorities were not in any position to stop the Jewish underground from continuing along the path of violence. In July 1983, three students at the Islamic University in Hebron were killed in a gun and grenade attack and that crime, too, remained unsolved until May 1984.

A further expansion of anti-Palestinian violence was stopped in Jerusalem in May, just in time, when twelve bombs were discovered by police hours before an intended bloodbath. They were Israeli army munitions and they were attached to Arab buses in East Jerusalem, carrying passengers including children. The police found the bombs and Shin Bet rounded up the Jewish terrorist cell, only because Begin had retired and Shalom had managed to plant agents in a group of more than twenty Jewish settlers dedicated to killing and intimidating Palestinian civilians. The Jews were treated somewhat more gently than Arab terrorists are by Shin Bet, but still the suspects confessed all and were tried, convicted and imprisoned.[3]

Begin, as Prime Minister, showed no patience or mercy towards threats from abroad. Peace with Egypt did not mean he had gone soft, as Begin proved with a bold decision in 1981. On June 4, fourteen F-16 and F-15 fighter-bombers of the Israeli air force destroyed the Iraqi nuclear reactor in Baghdad. Militarily, it was a singularly successful operation, which showed great accuracy and exceptional intelligence over an unprecedented distance from Israel.

The background to the attack shows the key role of the intelligence community in Begin's bold foreign policy. The Mossad and Aman had been watching and waiting from the first moment that Iraq's intention to purchase a nuclear reactor from France became known. The possibility that any Arab state – and especially radical Iraq – could obtain nuclear weapons which would threaten the Jewish state kept Israeli leaders awake at night.

It was in November 1975 that France formally agreed to supply Iraq with two nuclear reactors, a small one for research and a larger one with a capacity of 70 megawatts. The Iraqis dubbed the project *Tammuz*, based on the name of a Canaanite god and a reference to the Arabic month in which the Ba'ath Socialist party came to power in 1968.[4]

Until Begin became Prime Minister, the Israeli government had used quiet diplomacy in attempts to dissuade France and certain other countries, such as Italy and Brazil, from supplying Iraq with the equipment, uranium and technical know-how which they had agreed to furnish for Project Tammuz. Israel also asked the US to intervene, hoping that President Carter's campaign to prevent the proliferation of nuclear weapons might influence France. The quiet approaches were fruitless, however. The construction of the nuclear reactors at a secret location near Baghdad continued apace.

Begin decided to adopt an entirely new policy. He called

in his intelligence chiefs and declared that henceforth the destruction of the larger Iraqi reactor, with its potential weapons-producing capability, would be considered one of Israel's supreme national goals. Begin ordered them to make every possible effort to obtain information on the Tammuz One reactor: how quickly it was being built and the extent of cooperation between Iraq and other nations.

More than any other Israeli leader, Begin was haunted by the Nazi Holocaust. He regarded the extermination of six million Jews as not only a terrible event in history, but as a clear warning of present dangers. The Prime Minister, as a result, established a new doctrine: Israel would not permit any Arab state to develop an offensive nuclear capability.

Begin's secret battalions went quickly into action. A team of agents arrived in Toulon, France, by various routes in the first week of April, 1979. Their objective: a large storehouse, in the seaside town of La Seyne-sur-Mer, containing two cores for the Iraqi nuclear reactors. French authorities later said it was an extremely professional job: explosives attached to the cores themselves, timers set for three o'clock in the morning and not a trace of the attackers when the blast occurred.

A French ecology group claimed responsibility for the bombing but this was not taken seriously. The destruction of these important components was believed to have been on behalf of Israel – either by the Mossad or by sympathetic French secret service agents.[5]

Begin and the Israeli intelligence community hoped that France would use the explosion as an excuse to terminate its aid to Iraq, but within a very short time their hopes were dashed. The French Government announced that it would honour its agreements with Iraq and would supply it with new cores.

Begin turned to what he considered Israel's last remaining course of action: the military option. In coordination with the Chief of Staff, Raful Eitan, Begin ordered the Mossad to investigate the possibility of a direct attack by ground forces – whether army commandos or some sort of irregulars

– on the Iraqi reactor. At the same time, General Eitan ordered the air force to build a full-scale model of the reactor, based on Mossad and Aman espionage reports, and to practice bombing it.[6]

As the preparations for an attack began, major differences emerged among Israel's decision makers. The raid, after several delays, was finally executed only three days before the general election of June 7, 1981. Not surprisingly, Labour Party leader Peres opposed the attack on the nuclear reactor, after he and former generals in his party learned of the planned bombing raid from friends and ex-colleagues in the military and intelligence establishment. Peres told Begin, beforehand, that it was a bad idea. Privately, Labour leaders feared that attacking the reactor would enhance the popularity of the Likud and Begin on election day.

Perhaps it was surprising that some of the leaders of the intelligence community also opposed the overt military option. Mossad chief Hofi and Shlomo Gazit, head of Aman until Yehoshua Saguy replaced him in February 1979, believed that there was still a long time to go before the reactor would be 'hot', the operational stage at which it could begin to pose a real danger. These intelligence men, perhaps even representing a majority, suggested a firmer diplomatic initiative and expressed the fear that bombing Baghdad might prompt Iraq and Iran to call off their Gulf War and unite against Israel – just when the war which began in 1979 seemed to be serving Israel's interests – and would certainly trigger a tidal wave of international condemnation.[7]

On the other hand, a strong coalition of Likud cabinet members, led by Ariel Sharon who was then Minister of Agriculture, rallied around General Eitan in supporting the raid. The Begin–Sharon–Eitan view proved correct. The intelligence chiefs were wrong in their predictions of great diplomatic damage to be inflicted on Israel. Obviously satisfied that Iraq's nuclear Tower of Babylon was flattened, the superpowers said little. Furthermore, the French Government, under the new Socialist President François

Mitterrand, did this time use the attack as an excuse to scale down nuclear cooperation with Iraq. France decided not to replace the reactor which Israel had demolished.

The attack on Baghdad was the launching pad for the Begin government's new approach to problems on the foreign front, after Likud's re-election in 1981. The Prime Minister was adopting an aggressive and adventurous line, wherever he thought it necessary, and he was willing to take great risks.

A clear expression of the second-term policy tone was the appointment of Sharon as Minister of Defence. For more than a year, Begin had withstood strong pressure by Sharon and his supporters to grant him the defence portfolio, after Ezer Weizman left the government to protest the new, militant approach. Begin expressed resistance, even remarking – only half in jest – that 'the day that Sharon is appointed Minister of Defence, he will surround the Prime Minister's office with tanks.'

Sharon's conquest of the defence ministry was, for him, the realization of a cherished dream. However, believing national security is best united under one roof, he still wished to take control of the intelligence community.

He had already persuaded Begin to appoint Rafi Eitan, an old Sharon crony, as counter-terrorism adviser to the Prime Minister. Not to be confused with the army Chief of Staff, Raful Eitan, Rafi Eitan had been a senior intelligence operative who scored his greatest coup with the kidnap team which captured Adolf Eichmann. Later, however, he had sharp operational and political disagreements with Mossad chiefs Zamir and Hofi. Eitan naturally drifted into Sharon's camp.

At age 55 in 1981, Eitan still wished to be promoted – possibly even to head the Mossad. When his advancement was barred, he had no choice but to leave. He tried various businesses, from raising tropical fish to dealing in West Bank land. But, as many others before him who had attempted to exchange their cloak and dagger for civilian clothes, Eitan was unable to make a success of it. Sharon saved his old friend from sinking into further boredom and returned him to government service, as the prime minister's adviser: a coordinating job with little authority, however, on the edge of the intelligence community.

Sharon also discovered within the defence ministry the intelligence treasure of Lakam – the Science Liaison Bureau – the existence of which was known to very few people. Sharon, unlike his predecessor Weizman, paid attention to the complaints that kept coming to the defence minister's office against Binyamin Blumberg, the head of Lakam. These focused on his links with the Labour Party, which was out of favour since Begin's election in 1977.

Sharon did not need complaints to dismiss Blumberg from his position. He had planned to do so, anyway, but now he had an excuse. The complaints spread as rumours and grew into slander, but although no persuasive evidence was ever presented, they made it easier to dismiss Blumberg, who had spent more than thirty years working in the intelligence community and more than twenty years as head of Lakam. There was a tremendous storm over his departure, but only within the community, with nary a whisper in the Israeli press. Sharon quickly put his friend Rafi Eitan in charge of Lakam.

For the first time since the days of Reuven Shiloah and the nine months of Meir Amit's overlapping jobs, a senior official in the intelligence community not only wore two hats but was subordinate to two bosses. In his position as counter-terrorism adviser to the Prime Minister, Eitan was under Begin; whereas as head of Lakam, he was under Sharon.

The coup in Lakam was an important step in Sharon's efforts to become the dominant figure in the security/intelligence establishment, but there were still two independent organizations which stood in his way, and which were in no way subservient to him: Shin Bet and the Mossad. Sharon knew that no prime minister would agree to forego his direct ministerial supervision over these two agencies, but he did hope to persuade Begin to replace their two chiefs. He was especially interested in removing Yitzhak Hofi from the Mossad.

The enmity between Sharon and Hofi stemmed not only from basic differences in their political and defence outlooks and on the role of intelligence. It also included an undercurrent of mutual hostility extending back many years. Following the Suez war in 1956, four battalion commanders in the paratroop brigade rose up and rebelled against their brigadier, Colonel Ariel Sharon. The head of the rebels was his deputy, Lieutenant Colonel Yitzhak Hofi. They harshly criticized Sharon's tactics and judgment.

Sharon and the rebels turned to two neutral officers to settle their dispute, but the arbitrators contradicted each other and were unable to reach a decision. This strange episode had been kept secret for many years, but Sharon is credited with having the memory of an elephant and did not forget Hofi's mutiny.[8]

The personality clash persisted a quarter of a century later. In any event, Hofi displeased Begin by counselling against the raid on the Baghdad nuclear reactor.

The Mossad chief was not, however, cowed in any way by Sharon. Hofi was no doubt aware that within twelve months, he would be completing eight years in the Mossad, the longest that any person had remained at the helm since Isser Harel. In any event, rather than assume a bureaucratically defensive posture, Hofi embarked on a vehement and unprecedented attack.

On June 18, 1981, on his own initiative and without seeking Begin's permission, Hofi was interviewed by the Israeli newspaper *Ha'aretz* – as the anonymous 'chief of the Mossad' – and warned that politicians should stop boasting publicly about the air raid on the Iraqi reactor.

While he could not be named, under Israeli law, Hofi's statements marked the first time that the head of the Mossad had been interviewed on the record. He claimed that, because of the numerous leaks to the Israeli press and to overseas media, 'tremendous damage is being caused, and it is liable to affect sources of information and ties with parties outside Israel.'

By the nature of things, this interview invited interpretations and guesses as to whom exactly the Mossad chief had in mind. A number of journalists who were close friends of Hofi gave the answer: they said that he had been referring to Sharon and newspaper columnist Uri Dan, one of Sharon's closest friends.

As could be expected, Sharon responded to Hofi in kind. Dan himself published a vitriolic attack in the afternoon newspaper *Ma'ariv*, against the unnamed Mossad chief, claiming that the interview had supplied the Labour opposition with ammunition and that the intelligence chief had intended that precise goal: to serve the Labour Party which had appointed him to his position.

Dan also claimed that Hofi was in constant contact with the leaders of the opposition, had leaked secret information to them and had misled the Prime Minister by not supplying him with accurate information on the Iraqi nuclear reactor. The *Ma'ariv* columnist explicitly called upon Begin to dismiss the head of the Mossad immediately.

The Prime Minister refused to respond to Dan's call, even though it was well known that the man behind the article was Sharon, and even though Begin himself had been angered by Hofi's unauthorized interview.[9] Dan's column was considered too angry, too biased and too politically divisive by the editors of the newspaper, and a short time later he left *Ma'ariv*. He immediately and easily landed a new job: media adviser to Ariel Sharon and spokesman for the defence ministry.

As a good general, when it became apparent to Sharon that he would be unable to attain his objective by direct strategy through a frontal attack, he changed his approach and adopted an indirect strategy. This was expressed in the establishment of various 'forums', some of them unofficial, composed of government officials and private individuals. Political opponents referred to these meetings in the defence minister's office, on the third floor of the defence ministry in Tel Aviv, as 'the war room' or 'Arik's court', Arik being Ariel Sharon's nickname.

The participants in what rapidly became an influential tool included Rafi Eitan; the former Mossad operative, Rehaviah Vardi, whom Sharon had appointed as the government 'coordinator' in the occupied territories; Major General Avraham Tamir, who was his assistant for planning and strategy; private arms merchant and Mossad veteran Yaakov Nimrodi; and, from time to time, David Kimche, the former Mossad number two who was director-general of the foreign ministry.

For a quarter of a century, from the day that he joined the Mossad, as a British-born academic in 1953, Kimche dreamed of heading the agency. At the end of the 1970s, Kimche believed that he had an excellent chance, when Begin considered him Hofi's natural successor. Hofi had entirely different ideas, however, strongly resenting Kimche for acting as though he were a one-man organization. Kimche vanished frequently on mysterious missions which no one, including the agency chief, knew about. In the Mossad, the globe-trotter was known as 'the man with the suitcase'. Hofi accused Kimche of not reporting properly. Kimche denied all the charges, but finally was unwilling to stay where he was unwanted.

Kimche left the intelligence world in 1980 and his former Mossad colleague and respected elder Foreign Minister, Yitzhak Shamir, quickly invited him to direct his ministry. Kimche did not, however, give up on his ambition to become the Mossad chief one day and that was why he maintained contact with his old colleagues and continued to keep up-to-date with what was happening within the agency.

Rafi Eitan, the Mossad veteran with similar ambitions, began to expand the activities of Lakam. The shadowy agency's concerns did not simply stop at science liaison, as its name might suggest. Compared with Blumberg's tenure, Eitan increased productivity tenfold. If the Lakam people had laid their hands on 200 documents a year in the old days, the figure under Eitan reached 2,000 per year. Gradually, Lakam began to enter grey areas overseas, an operational no-man's land which should have been the sole province of the Mossad. As the Prime Minister's adviser on terrorism, Eitan also found himself, whether deliberately or not, in incessant confrontations and disputes with the Mossad.

Eitan's independent operations were resented tremendously by Hofi, who repeatedly complained to Begin and raised the issue at the *Va'adat* meetings of the secret service chiefs.

Sharon, himself, could also feel encouraged when Avraham Ahituv was replaced as head of Shin Bet by Avraham Shalom, an old friend of Rafi Eitan and also a participant in the capture of Eichmann in 1960. Sharon and Shalom were on the same wavelength on many issues.

There was a very good chance, too, that Major General Yekutiel (Kuti) Adam, a military man who had worked for the Mossad for a number of years, would replace Yitzhak Hofi. Adam was considered an old friend of Sharon's, going back to their paratrooper days.

Sharon's self-confidence, which kept growing, also found expression in his attempt to reformulate Israel's foreign and defence policies. In November 1981, the new defence minister delivered an astonishing speech which declared that Israel's security interests lay beyond the areas of its direct confrontation with the Arab states and included Pakistan, the North African states and even more distant parts of Africa.[10]

Sharon did not limit himself to words. Faithful to his views, he attempted to implement them. He undertook various political, strategic and intelligence projects.

The Mossad soon found itself confronted by the independent activities of Sharon's arms-dealing friend, the former Mossad agent Nimrodi, and Nimrodi's business partner Al Schwimmer, former chief executive of Israel Aircraft Industries, IAI. Their wheeling and dealing often brought them into contact with Arab merchants and politicians, and their policy adviser and conduit to Israeli power centres was Sharon.

Nimrodi, who had lost millions of dollars when Ayatollah Khomeini's Islamic legions overthrew the Shah of Iran, was especially eager to regain his lost investments. With Sharon's strategic ambitions, Nimrodi felt that commercial contacts with Iran might be revived and expanded to other countries. While considering himself a supreme patriot, the line which separated Nimrodi's own interests from those of the State of Israel was constantly blurred.

Thanks to business connections with the Saudi billionaire, Adnan Khashoggi, Nimrodi made contact with members of the Saudi royal family. He hoped to use them to advance his business dealings, believing this would also be good for Israel. He and Khashoggi repeatedly plotted breakthroughs towards peace between Israel and the Arabs, and Nimrodi obtained a secret political document drawn up by the crown prince and heir-apparent to the Saudi throne, Prince Fahd. It was quite a coup for Nimrodi and that naturally rankled the Mossad, which accused him of 'running around under-foot' and disturbing their work.[11]

The document, since referred to as the Fahd Plan, spoke for the first time of Saudi recognition of the State of Israel and Nimrodi brought it to Israel even before it was published in Riyadh. Nimrodi was excited and clearly liked Fahd's proposal that the Saudi flag should fly over the Moslem holy places in East Jerusalem, as a symbol of guardianship over those shrines along with those in Mecca and Medina. In exchange, the Saudis would work for peace and mutual recognition.

Prime Minister Begin was, however, angry at Nimrodi for even attempting to portray the document as moderate. Begin would not consider any whittling away of Israeli sovereignty over the whole of Jerusalem and he did not care to examine the niceties of the document. In his view, Fahd's words were a mere reformulation of the old Arab extremism, reflecting an attempt to force Israel to surrender what Begin considered the soil of the Jewish homeland.

The Saudi affair was nothing, however, compared with the almost mind-boggling plans cooked up during a series of secret trips in late 1981 and 1982. Nimrodi and Schwimmer, as Khashoggi's guests aboard his luxurious DC-8, flew from Europe to Morocco for detailed discussions with senior Iranian army officers who had been living in exile since the Shah was toppled. They also met there with the late Shah's son, Prince Reza Pahlavi – known to insiders as the 'Baby Shah'. He was a weak character, but Western intelligence agencies were interested in Reza as someone they could influence. The CIA helped him broadcast clandestine radio and television messages to Iran, where his words fell on deaf ears.

The Baby Shah had taken up residence in Morocco, with a coterie of servants and military men, plotting an almost impossible return to power in Teheran. They told Nimrodi, Schwimmer and Khashoggi that all that was required was financial support, to buy arms and pay the salaries of a mercenary force to overthrow the ayatollahs.

The two Israelis seriously believed such a coup could succeed and they hurried home to tell Sharon. The Baby Shah's dreams could fit in conveniently with Sharon's wider geostrategic aspirations. After a series of excited international telephone calls and meetings, a larger group of plotters came together in Africa.

There they were, perhaps the most incongruous assembly imaginable, standing on the green and manicured lawns of a Safari Club in Kenya. It was May 13, 1982. In the welcome seclusion of the exclusive resort owned by Khashoggi – near the Tanzanian border, distanced from Nairobi by some one hundred miles of grazing land where wildlife runs free – six Israelis, two Sudanese and a Saudi shook hands among the flowers and fruit-laden trees.

The gathering was always intended to remain a secret, but it was so relaxed that one of the group even took snapshots of the others as they chatted. There was Arik Sharon, with his wife Lily – whom he took on almost all his secret missions – laying on the charm with foreigners who were officially his enemies.

The business was deeply serious, however. The Sudanese were the President, Gaafar Numeiri, and his intelligence chief, Abu Tayeb. They were in the process of being persuaded to go far beyond their cooperation, which had already begun, with Israeli intelligence's project to rescue Ethiopian Jewry. Now the Israelis – in the persons of Sharon and his 'court' – had far greater plans for Numeiri and his territory.

The defence minister was there with Nimrodi, Schwimmer, Kimche and Tamir, and their master plan was to turn Sudan into a gigantic arms cache for 'special projects'. Saudi Arabia would provide the finance: Khashoggi told his guests that he had won King Fahd's agreement to sign cheques up to $800 million – 'and if necessary,' he smiled, 'perhaps even one billion dollars!' Israel would come up with the weapons, either home-produced or captured surplus. The arsenal would go far beyond rifles, mortars and bullets. It was to include tanks, airplanes and even missiles.

The carrot for Numeiri, as far as the Israeli's could tell, was the money to be paid both to his country and into his own pocket. As middlemen, Nimrodi, Schwimmer and Khashoggi would be instrumental in buying and selling the weapons, profiting from fat commissions.

For Sharon, there was the opportunity to win a sizeable export order, which could easily include arms captured from PLO guerillas and Arab armies over the years. The plan offered the welcome irony that the Saudis could be made to pay Israel for guns and ammunition which were originally purchased by the PLO and Arab states using Saudi financial aid.

For whom was all this firepower intended? Iran was high on the agenda and the Baby Shah and his exiled generals would have received the weapons they wanted. Instead of the insignificant opposition they had become, Reza and his followers could suddenly pose a genuine threat to the Islamic

Republic and bring Iran back into the arms of the West.

Weapons would also be supplied, from the depot in northeast Africa, to guerilla forces which were fighting governments inimical to Israel, Sudan and Western interests. These civil wars might be waged in Africa, Asia or even in the Arab world. For such a project, the sky was the limit.

The Mossad was excluded from the safari club meeting in Kenya but insisted on receiving a full report. Kimche, from his foreign ministry office, informed the agency that President Numeiri had agreed to permit the Mossad to open a permanent station in Khartoum. The report also said that Sharon had ensured that Numeiri would continue to cooperate in the exodus of Ethiopian Jews.

Yitzhak Hofi was, naturally, pleased to have a new Mossad station in an Arab capital, but he resented being left out of the meeting with Numeiri. Furthermore, Khashoggi had never been a favourite of the Mossad, and now the Israelis who had established the closest links with the Saudi tycoons were embarking on a major covert operation – without the Mossad. 'Arik's court' was threatening to encroach into Hofi's territory.

In addition to considerations of internal politics and bureaucratic territoriality, the Mossad's analysts had genuine concerns about the Sudan 'special projects' proposal. When it came to Iran, the Mossad believed that the Baby Shah and his powerless generals were men whose days had passed. A small-scale invasion of Iran, which was successfully holding back the huge army of Iraq since September 1980, would be extremely unlikely to triumph. It would more likely lead to a huge embarrassment and, perhaps, exposure of the plotters behind the coup.

As for the wider, geostrategic goals of the proposed Sudanese arsenal, Hofi and the Mossad simply believed that Sharon was overstretching the abilities and interests of the State of Israel. The agency had concluded, in this and other cases, that it was not a good idea to trust Arabs – certainly not to the extent of putting Israeli lives, limbs, money and prestige at risk based on the cooperation and goodwill of nations such as Saudi Arabia and Sudan.

Foreign Minister Shamir, a Mossad veteran, was also inculcated in the faith of not having too much faith in Arab partners. In assessing the Sudan project, he sided with the Mossad and was not swayed by the director-general of his ministry, Kimche. Prime Minister Begin did not take a definite stand, telling Sharon and his friends that they would have to present more convincing evidence that a coup in Iran could succeed – as a first step in the wider, more ambitious plan.

The Mossad was not about to let the plan proceed one step further. It was a bad idea for Israel and clearly bad for the Mossad. Hofi sent one of his top deputies on a secret flight to Morocco, by way of Europe, to see the Baby Shah. The senior Israeli spy made his identity, aside from his real name, quite clear to Reza and told the young prince: 'I am authorized by the highest circles in Israel to tell you that the Israelis with whom you have met are not our authorized representatives. They would only draw you into trouble. Please coordinate directly with us in the future, although this plan involving Sudan does not interest us.'

The Mossad envoy flew back to Tel Aviv, again careful to disguise himself on his transit through Europe. His mission was accomplished. The colossal project developed by Sharon, Nimrodi, Kimche and the others was dead.[12]

The arms cached in Sudan were also to be used in Chad, where Sharon welcomed the opportunity to deliver a punch in the nose to Libya's Colonel Qaddafi. Chad, Sudan's western neighbour in central Africa, was being torn apart by a civil war, and Libya was actively supporting the anti-government rebels.

Sudan's Numeiri had a clear interest in aiding the pro-Western President of Chad, Hassan Habre. The United States also had motives to support Chad, and so did France, the former colonial ruler of this poor nation.

As for Israel's interest, it was finding that its energetic

efforts in the early 1980s to restore the influence it had lost in Africa were met at every turn by Qaddafi, who threatened, blackmailed and bribed fellow African states not to restore diplomatic relations with the Jewish state. Qaddafi's support for Palestinian and European terrorist groups strengthened the goal shared by Israel and the US: to weaken the Libyan leader wherever possible, in the hope that he might eventually be overthrown.

Calculating the odds for his boss Sharon, General Tamir believed that Qaddafi would not tolerate the defeat of his allies in Chad and would send the Libyan army southward into Chad to check President Habre's advances. Tamir also believed that France would then dispatch troops with the support of friendly central African states led by Zaire. Because of this, the Israeli general wished to establish a military presence, even if only a symbolic one, in Chad. Tamir was seeking the best of all worlds: that France would bear the burden of saving Habre's government, while Israel could take at least partial credit for causing Qaddafi a setback. And that is what happened.

At the beginning of 1983, Sharon visited a number of African states to propose that they renew diplomatic relations with Israel in exchange for military assistance. Dozens of nations had abided by a decision of the Organization of African Unity in late 1973 to cut their ties with Israel, as a reaction to the Yom Kippur War and the consequent oil embargo which had made Arab petrodollars more valuable than ever. While visiting Zaire, Sharon met not only his host, President Mobutu Sese Seko, but also Chad's President Habre. Habre and Sharon agreed in principle that Libyan subversion in Africa had to be halted and that contacts on the subject would be maintained.

The breakthrough came the previous November, when General Tamir disappeared from Israel, as was his frequent habit as a clandestine diplomat. Authorized only by Sharon, the general flew to Paris for a meeting with a Chadian government minister. They agreed that Tamir could visit N'djamena, the capital of Chad and details of a secret communications link with Israel were finalized.

Two weeks later, the awaited signal from Chad was received and Tamir donned civilian clothes and clutched a false passport for a flight to Paris. From there, he took a long, tiring flight to N'djamena. Many houses in the capital of half a million residents had been destroyed, the roads were pitted and the debris of war could be seen all around.

The word N'djamena means 'the city where one rests', in one of the local dialects, but the Israeli general was given no rest. Immediately after arriving, he was rushed to the presidential palace to meet Habre. Their talks lasted all night and in the morning the general was taken for a tour of the desert front lines. At the end, it was agreed that Israel would send military experts to Chad to help its army in both the civil war and the war against Libya.

Tamir returned to Israel, by way of Paris, and reported to Sharon. Within a very short time, the Israeli army sent a delegation of fifteen advisers to N'djamena from a secret contingent already posted in Zaire.

When the Mossad found out about Tamir's secret mission, Hofi was furious. The entire operation had been carried out behind his back and Sharon showed no apparent intention to inform the Mossad. Hofi complained to Prime Minister Begin and made strenuous efforts to end the contacts with Chad. The Mossad warned that it was highly perilous to station Israeli army officers in a country with an unstable regime, where rebels could gain the upper hand at any time. The dangers were even greater, because Israel's military advisers might be taken prisoner by Libya's frontline troops.

Sharon and Tamir defended their diplomatic foray, stressing to Begin the advantages of helping a moderate African state to defeat Colonel Qaddafi. The Prime Minister, however, decided to side with the Mossad. The fifteen Israeli officers were ordered to return home from Chad.[13]

The Chad episode, and the attempt to sidestep both the foreign ministry's conventional diplomats and the alternative diplomacy of the Mossad, marked the collapse of the grand, strategic schemes of Ariel Sharon as defence minister. From June 6, 1982, most of his attention had to be devoted to the invasion of Lebanon which he launched that day in a quest to destroy the PLO.

The Palestinians had built a formidable military infrastructure in southern Lebanon – 'a terrorist state within a state', in the words of Israel's policy makers. After a series of painful guerilla raids and rocket attacks against Israeli towns and farms in the northern Galilee, followed by Israeli retaliation in the form of air raids or artillery fire, Begin reluctantly agreed in July 1981 to an American-sponsored cease-fire with the PLO. It was clear, however, that this was a weak and temporary accord.

Begin and Sharon both felt a visceral hatred for the PLO, which they regarded as a group of murderers out to destroy Israel. The Prime Minister openly likened Yasser Arafat to Adolf Hitler. It was evidently only a matter of time until Israel would attack the Palestinian strongholds in Lebanon. The only questions were when the Israelis would strike, and how large and ambitious their operation would be.

In an attempt to clarify the possibilities, Sharon and Tamir met secretly in Geneva in January 1982 with General Rifa'at Assad, the brother of the President of Syria. It is quite astounding that Israel's most militant government minister managed to arrange a meeting with a senior representative of its most threatening enemy, but in the world of clandestine diplomacy in the Middle East anything is possible. Israel and Syria, in spite of their hostility, had at least two common interests: to weaken the PLO and to stabilize Lebanon by partitioning it. Merely holding the meeting was an achievement, although nothing, not even a tacit understanding, emerged from it. It is probable, if unconfirmed, that Rifa'at Assad, a colourful, controversial character, but also a cruel military man and hedonist who pursued wealth and women, had met his Israeli enemies with the approval of his brother, the president.

In any event, when the chance of reaching an understanding with Syria failed, Sharon decided to gamble for the whole pot. Using the June 1982 shooting of Israeli ambassador Shlomo Argov in London as a pretext – ignoring the fact that the gunmen were from the renegade Abu Nidal faction rather than the PLO mainstream – Sharon launched an invasion of Lebanon.

The defence minister and his Chief of Staff, Eitan, promised Prime Minister Begin an easy, quick victory. The goal of wiping out the PLO's military and political infrastructure in southern Lebanon was also supported by the opposition Labour Party and by the intelligence community.

The Israeli hope was that a clear PLO defeat would undermine the allegiance to the organization felt by the Palestinians of the West Bank and Gaza Strip. Planning to exploit the peace treaty he had achieved with Egypt, Begin wished to strengthen Israel's hold on the occupied territories, while offering limited autonomy to their Arab inhabitants. The PLO absolutely rejected autonomy, insisting on winning outright statehood, and Begin wanted to encourage alternative Palestinian leaders who would be willing to work with the Israelis.

Sharon had more ambitious plans. He was interested in reaching the gates of Beirut, to link up with Christian forces there and together to impose a 'new order' on Lebanon. They would bring about the election of Bashir Gemayel, the Maronite Christian militia leader, as president. His Phalangist forces would help the Israelis expel the Syrians from Lebanon. Beirut and Jerusalem would have a peace treaty. Gemayel could be counted on to expel the Palestinians either by sea or by road to Syria.

For eight years, the Mossad and Aman had kept in close contact with the Christian forces in Lebanon. The first contacts had been made in 1974, when the Christian leaders feared that they were losing the dominance they had enjoyed in their country. Rising in power and influence was a coalition of the local Moslems and the Palestinians, demanding a greater slice of the political pie. The Christian leaders stubbornly rejected any reforms in a system which had suited them nicely.

It was Jordan's King Hussein, himself involved in secret diplomacy with Israel, who persuaded the Christian militia chiefs of Lebanon, Camille Chamoun and Pierre Gemayel, to enter into contacts with the Jewish state. Chamoun, a former Lebanese president, and Gemayel, a government minister, held long discussions with Israel's Prime Minister Rabin. It was agreed that Israel would help the Phalangist militia, which, ironically, had begun as an admiring model of European fascism in the 1930s.

On the Israeli side, the Mossad had responsibility for contacts with the Phalangists and took an especially keen interest in Pierre Gemayel's son Bashir. The young Gemayel was a lawyer, but in a country of lawlessness he was known to be bold, sly and murderous. He showed no hesitation in killing his Christian 'allies' – members of the Chamoun and Franjieh families – in order to be sole ruler of the militias.

When he was working for a law firm in Washington, DC in the 1970s, the CIA recruited Bashir Gemayel as a source of information – adding, in effect, another Arab leader to King Hussein and King Hassan as CIA 'assets' in the region. The Americans paid Gemayel thousands of dollars and were proved to have chosen well, when, despite being the youngest of Pierre's six children, Bashir took charge of the country's largest Christian militia in 1976.[14]

The Mossad opened a new station, including a powerful radio transmitter, in the port city of Jounieh, just north of Beirut, where the Christians had absolute control – although officially, Lebanon was in a state of war with Israel. In addition, Israeli army officers travelled to the capital itself and set up a formal liaison system with Gemayel's Phalangists.

At the same time, the Israelis formed their own Lebanese militia in southern Lebanon, to combat the growing PLO presence in the area and to help protect Israel's northern border. The force was called the South Lebanese Army, and the SLA was dominated by local Christians in and around the town of Marjayoun. The SLA men quite clearly wore Israeli uniforms, which were simply stripped of their Israeli Defence Forces markings, and drove tanks and jeeps which did not even have all their Hebrew labels removed.

Aman was responsible for training, equipping, financing and clothing the SLA. Phalangist combatants from northern Lebanon also underwent training by the Israeli army, as well as by Mossad and Shin Bet experts when it came to intelligence and interrogation methods. The head of the small security and intelligence service which the Phalangists had established with Israeli help was Eli Hobeika.

Aman and the Mossad wholeheartedly supported the contacts with the Phalangists, believing that they gave Israel two important advantages. They enabled Israel to set up a broad network of informers that supplied up-to-date information on Palestinian guerilla groups, the Syrian army and political developments in that part of the Arab world. The secret links with Lebanon also fitted into the traditional 'peripheral' concept of Israeli intelligence. The Christians of Lebanon could naturally be friends of Israel, because they were the enemies of the Moslems.

Until 1981, Israel went no further with the Phalangists than helping them to help themselves. Kimche, then in charge of the Mossad project in Lebanon, says the Israeli liaison officers in Jounieh always made it clear to the Christians that Israel would not fight their battles for them. Begin, when re-elected, ordered Hofi to expand and deepen the contacts with the Phalangists. Sharon took them even further.

The Christian leaders, who were aware of Begin's moral vulnerabilities, began to apply pressure on him to increase Israeli aid to them. They bawled that they were in danger of annihilation by the Syrians and they cunningly staged provocations and issued false reports to back up their version of reality. Begin, sympathetic to oppressed minorities – especially when Moslem Arabs were the oppressors – tended to believe the Phalangists.

Sharon knew the truth, but he believed that Bashir

Gemayel was a man after his own heart, who would be willing and perhaps able to implement the Sharon strategy to bring about a new order in the Middle East.

On the night of January 12, 1982, a small and powerful group gathered at a military airport near Tel Aviv. They included Ariel Sharon, General Tamir, representatives of the Mossad, Aman chief General Saguy and other senior Israeli army officers. They were given a short briefing on how to behave should anything go wrong and how to escape from enemy territory if necessary. They then took off in a military helicopter.

It was a strange flight into the unknown for these men who were entrusted with the security of Israel. They looked down on the blinking lights of the Lebanese shoreline, trying to identify the places they were flying over, until they saw the brighter lights of Beirut. The helicopter proceeded northward to a landing strip in Jounieh, where Sharon and his colleagues were met by the local Mossad station chief.

Bashir Gemayel had only been told that 'a senior Israeli official' planned to come, but he had already guessed who it would be. Smiling at the sight of the burly Sharon, the young Phalangist leader said: 'I knew that you would come. We waited for you.'

Over a string of sumptuous meals, interspersed with tours of various parts of Beirut, the two sides worked intensively to reach a broad and basic understanding. When he returned to Israel, Sharon crowed to his friends: 'I have finalized the plan with the Christians. Now we can carry it out. I tied their feet.'[15]

Sharon's claim of a convincing and all-encompassing alliance with the Phalangists triggered off a fierce debate in Israel's intelligence community. Aman insisted vehemently that Israel could not trust the Christians enough so as to base a military operation on their support. The director of military intelligence, General Saguy, noted that Gemayel also had ties with the Syrian leadership and to some extent with the PLO.

The Aman analysts wondered how the Phalangists could

be considered trustworthy when some of the arms they had received from Israel later found their way to the PLO. Some of the Christian leaders evidently engaged in private deals involving arms and drugs. Aman also opposed embarking on a military venture which would bring the Israeli army into confrontation with the Syrian forces in Lebanon.

Sharon was adamant, however, that the time had come to carry out his plan to change the course of history. To everyone's surprise, he found an ally in the Mossad, an organization which he generally treated with extreme suspicion.

It appears that this time the Mossad forgot one of the most sacred rules of intelligence: never have too intimate or familiar a relationship with your sources. It is difficult to know what was the immediate cause of this sudden faith in the Christians. Was it the lavish meals and the nightclubs that the Mossad men had enjoyed in Beirut in the company of their Phalangist hosts? Or was it Bashir Gemayel's charm and eloquence?

On June 6, 1982, Sharon sent his troops out to a war that Israel had initiated, for only the second time in her history – the first having been in 1956. It turned out to be Sharon's Waterloo. Just as Aman had warned Sharon, the Christian forces did not abide by their word. They did not help the Israelis fight the PLO and Gemayel later refused to sign a peace treaty with Israel. Sharon sank deep into the Lebanese mud, blaming what he could only see as bad luck.

On the fifth day of the war, General 'Kuti' Adam was killed in battle. He had been a friend of Sharon and was also the heir apparent to the top job in the Mossad. Adam was gone, but after eight years it was time to replace Yitzhak Hofi. Begin turned to Hofi for advice, and on June 27 the Prime Minister recommended to the full cabinet that Hofi's deputy, Nahum Admoni, be appointed head of the Mossad.

It was the first time ever that the man chosen to lead the agency in Israel's secret battles was himself a career officer in the Mossad. In keeping with traditional security restrictions, Admoni was not publicly named. Insiders described him, however, as a 'nondescript' and 'average' man, 'a manager', a bureaucrat without any sparkle, but one who was stable and deliberate. Fifty-three years old, he was American-educated and had already served the Mossad for twenty-eight years in posts ranging from Washington to Ethiopia. Admoni had, quite simply, worked his way up through the ranks. He was not an adventurer; he was not a killer; he was solid.

As the Lebanese war unfolded along bloodier and increasingly unpleasant lines, Sharon's initial promises of a rapid *blitzkrieg* gave way to the reality of an occupied territory between Israel's northern border and Beirut. It was an area full of refugees and turmoil and it had to be controlled.

Shin Bet was given the unsavoury assignment of entering Lebanon to find friends and fight enemies. Shi'ite Moslem villages, which at first welcomed the advancing Israeli troops because the hated PLO was being forced out, now became centres of anti-Israeli terrorism – inspired by the image, and some active agents, of Iran's Ayatollah Khomeini. Suicide truck bombers, long before killing more than 250 US Marines and French troops in Beirut in 1983, started by attacking Israeli units in the South. Fanatical Shi'ites willingly drove and detonated vehicles packed with explosives, entering heaven's gates by pushing the Jews back to their border.

Shin Bet was in no way ready for this type of confrontation. The Palestinians of the West Bank and Gaza were never happy living under Israeli occupation, but they had never volunteered to blow themselves up to make their point.

Meantime, a bureaucratic second front was opened in the seemingly unending Lebanon war, when Shin Bet agents came across a rival Israeli – Rafi Eitan – touring the area in his capacity as the Prime Minister's adviser on terrorism.

The final blow to Sharon's plans for Lebanon came on

September 14, 1982, when the two-way radio in his luxury car suddenly came alive with an urgent message to contact the chief of the Mossad immediately. Being driven at the time to his farm in southern Israel, Sharon turned off the road at an army base and telephoned Tel Aviv.

Yitzhak Hofi, on the verge of leaving, told Sharon that Bashir Gemayel had been killed by a powerful bomb at his party headquarters in Beirut and first indications were that Syrian agents were responsible. The process that Sharon had counted on, the establishment of normal relations between Israel and Lebanon which he believed would vindicate the controversial war, had now reached an explosive end. Gemayel was assassinated only a few days before he was due to have been sworn in as the elected president of Lebanon.

The next day, September 15, Sharon flew to the Gemayel family farm in Lebanon, accompanied by Nahik Navot, the Mossad representative who served as chief liaison officer with the Phalangists. Sharon expressed his condolences to Bashir's father, the veteran militia leader Pierre Gemayel. Navot acted as notetaker in the conversation, which took on a surprisingly formal character. The meeting, in short, was important – even vital to the next turn of events – and Navot's handwritten minutes have been preserved in the Mossad's safes. Those minutes would later become a key factor in a huge libel trial in New York. Sharon was able to establish that *Time* magazine falsely reported that he had suggested to the Gemayels that they exact revenge on the Palestinians remaining in Beirut. Sharon only lost the case because the Court did not find that the magazine published its story with malice.

In any event, the Phalangist leaders were busy on September 16. They decided that Amin Gemayel, Bashir's brother, would be their candidate for president, and they sent their gunmen on a vengeance mission into the Palestinian refugee camps called Sabra and Chatila in Beirut's southern suburbs. The units which entered, under the command of Eli Hobeika, simply walked past the Israeli military forces which surrounded the camps. The Phalangists' aim was to 'clean up' the Palestinian guerillas lodged in the camps.

Instead, the militiamen engaged in an orgy of blood-letting which continued for twenty-four hours. It was a heartfelt response to the murder of their beloved Bashir, and the shootings and stabbings killed over 700 unarmed Palestinians under the direct gaze of the Israeli enlisted men and officers, who manned their observation posts, but did not seem to care what was happening.

The entire world saw this as the final word on Israel's invasion of Lebanon. It had been a disaster.

The Syrians were not expelled from Lebanon. Lebanon did not sign a peace treaty with Israel. It is true that Sharon managed to expel the PLO military infrastructure, but the Israelis failed to cultivate any alternative leadership among the Palestinians in the occupied territories and the PLO's acknowledged leadership persisted.

Within Israel's defence establishment, the intelligence community was considered to have performed very badly. The Mossad failed in its most basic function of evaluation by placing its bets on the benefits of an alliance with the Phalangists, now seen worldwide as a gang of bloodthirsty murderers.

Word also leaked out that the Mossad and Aman, although asked repeatedly by Begin and Sharon, had been unable to furnish precise details of Yasser Arafat's move-ments. Several attempts by Israeli forces to kill the PLO leader, during the war, took many other lives instead. The booby-trapped cars and precision air raids simply missed Arafat, the man whom Begin had dubbed 'an animal on two legs'.

The warfare unleashed by the Israelis in an already violent country killed thousands of Lebanese and Palestinian civ-ilians, and the Israeli casualties, too, were far greater than the army had anticipated: more than 600 soldiers killed and thousands wounded.

A special commission of inquiry, led by former Supreme

Court Justice Yitzhak Kahan, decreed that Israel would have to accept 'indirect responsibility' for the slaughter in Sabra and Chatila, and the report also specified that Ariel Sharon should be excluded from the post of defence minister. When the commission's report was published in February 1983, Sharon was forced to resign.

Half a year later, Menachem Begin himself astonished his cabinet ministers when he told them, 'I have no more strength' and also resigned.

Foreign Minister Yitzhak Shamir became the new Prime Minister and Begin withdrew into almost total seclusion in his modest home at 1 Zemach Street in Jerusalem. Although one of Israel's great historical figures, Begin refuses to explain his motives for either war or peace. His few confidants say that he is tortured by the fact that he was led astray by Generals Sharon and Eitan and in place of the jubilation of victory that was promised to him, he has the deaths of more than 600 young men on his conscience.

Nine months after Begin's dramatic departure from the political stage, a new Israeli government was elected – or, rather, not elected in voting which produced a deadlocked division of the Knesset between Likud and Labour. After months of wrangling in the summer of 1984, party leaders Shamir and Peres decided to share power in a unique government of national unity. The cabinet was made up of both major political blocs, and while Peres would be Prime Minister for the first twenty-five months, he would hand the job back to Shamir in an unprecedented 'rotation' for the second half of the government's term.

There were great hopes for change in many facets of Israeli life. The reluctant coalition managed to agree on an economic plan which reined in the galloping three-digit inflation. Israeli forces withdrew from almost all of Lebanon, patrolling only a 'security belt' in the south alongside their SLA surrogates.

Sharon himself was merely the minister for trade and industry in the coalition government, but he continued to cast an influential shadow on the nation's strategic outlook.

Meantime, his friends in the intelligence community – Shalom, Eitan and Nimrodi – would stir up an incredible amount of trouble in the next few years.

Killings and Cover-Ups

'Mr Prime Minister,' one of Yitzhak Shamir's bodyguards whispered to him, 'there is an urgent message for you to contact the head of Shin Bet.'

Anything but that, Shamir thought to himself, as he quickened his pace, his bodyguards at his heels, to a side room in the international convention centre in north Tel Aviv. Short and stolidly built, with bushy eyebrows as his hallmark, Shamir glanced at his watch.

It was 7.30 pm on April 13, 1984, and in a few hours the results of the internal elections of his Likud Party would be known. Shamir had been preoccupied for weeks by the battle of the Titans that had been raging in Likud for the top posts on the list of Knesset candidates. A full eight months after Menachem Begin's dramatic resignation bequeathed the premiership to Shamir, party rivals David Levy and Arik Sharon refused to recognize him as the leader of Likud. Shamir knew that the results of the internal elections would decide the struggle.

The Prime Minister was aware, at the back of his mind, that Shin Bet was on the verge of solving one of the most important mysteries in Israel in recent years: exposing the Jewish terrorist organization that had killed Palestinian students and attempted to murder the three West Bank mayors.

Unlike his predecessor, Shamir did permit Shin Bet to plant informers among the Jewish settlers in the occupied territories, and, at the last briefing he had been given by agency chief Avraham Shalom, the Prime Minister had been told that more than twenty suspects would be arrested in the near future, all of them settlers.

Shamir did not attempt to intervene in the investigation, but privately he dreaded the inevitable findings. He hoped that the indictments would come after the internal Likud voting, and even after the general election which was due a month later. Arresting Jewish settlers would place him and his party under tremendous pressure from the extreme right-wing and nationalist parties, who would accuse the Likud of being unpatriotic and would attract some of Likud's traditional voters.

'Mr Prime Minister, I have already spoken to the head of Shin Bet,' Colonel Azriel Nevo, the Prime Minister's military aide, said as Shamir entered the room. 'He reported that Arab terrorists have hijacked a bus along the Number 300 line, after it left the central bus station in Tel Aviv on its way to Ashkelon in the south. Military and police forces are on alert and orders have been given to stop the bus. There is fear that the terrorists will try to cross into Egypt and take the passengers along as hostages. We have no further information, not even regarding casualties. Avraham Shalom promised to keep us posted.'

In spite of the seriousness of the incident and his natural concern for the bus passengers, Shamir felt a small measure of relief. He was confident that the security forces – the army and Shin Bet – would defeat the terrorists. The hostages, he had to hope, would be rescued. The political fallout would favour Likud. The incident would illustrate Shamir's belief that concessions should not be made to Israel's Arab neighbours, and certainly not to the PLO because this would only encourage terrorism. Most opinion polls had Shimon Peres's Labour Party in the lead, but Shamir could portray Peres as soft on the Arabs.

The information that a bus had been hijacked could not be kept secret for long and rumours quickly began to fly among the thousands of delegates at the Likud conference. The news then spread to the scores of reporters and photographers covering the political gathering. Most of the latter made a mad dash for their cars and began driving southwards in search of a hot story.

Soldiers at a roadblock, meantime, had managed to shoot out the tyres of the bus, bringing it to a halt near the town of Dir al-Balah in the Gaza Strip, less than six miles from the Egyptian border. The bus was surrounded by large forces of police, army and Shin Bet personnel. Avraham Shalom himself arrived on the scene.

Shalom had joined Shin Bet after short stints as a kibbutz member and as a soldier. He had always wanted to belong to Israel's cream of the crop – the pioneers who could perceive life in terms of power, politics, voluntarism and complete identification with the State of Israel and its struggles. He was born in 1929 as Avraham Bendor, to parents who had moved to Palestine from Germany after Hitler's rise to power. In Tel Aviv, as in Berlin, his parents attempted to give him a bourgeois education, along the lines of a prosperous, German Jewish businessman. But Avraham Bendor-Shalom preferred socialist values and joined a kibbutz. When he joined the army in the 1948 war, he was sent to a patrol unit and Isser Harel then recruited him into Shin Bet.

Shalom had the soul of a dedicated soldier and was known for putting his all into any mission – even training exercises. Among his valuable talents, he spoke English and German. He was also quiet, ascetic and exuded coldness; he always appeared to be angry or upset.

In three and a half decades with Shin Bet, Shalom had

participated in most of its major operations, including the joint mission with the Mossad to kidnap Adolf Eichmann in Argentina. Shalom was always a field and operations man. He developed a close working relationship with Yehuda Arbel and together they conducted many secret attacks against Palestinian terrorists. This remained Shalom's focus of interest after he was appointed head of Shin Bet in 1981, replacing Ahituv.[1]

The sandy terrain, close to the road, where the Bus Number 300 had been halted, was a beehive of anti-terrorist activity. Giant searchlights turned the nighttime into day, as armed soldiers mingled with uniformed police and Shin Bet men in their civilian clothes. Walkie-talkies echoed back and forth and dozens of press photographers provided even more light with their flashes. A short distance away stood the Israeli bus, under the control of four Palestinian gunmen.

Shalom, senior army officials, and Defence Minister Moshe Arens were on the scene in the pre-dawn hours of tensions, but they could not dispel the feeling that there was a lack of order and control. It was typical of any major event in Israel: there were clearly too many people milling around for the job at hand, but the gossiping crowd and the curious officials and operatives, who were not needed, were there anyway.

The Israeli forces gathered as much precise information as possible about the hijackers, the weapons they had and the location of any explosives on board the bus.

Not for an instant was there any intention of knuckling under to the terrorists' demands. They wanted fellow Palestinian guerillas released from Israeli prisons; but they would not succeed. Once all the necessary data had been assembled, using night-vision and audio eavesdropping equipment, the Israeli forces knew that the hijackers had only light side arms – not even a machine gun. They were amateurs.

Israel's professional army commandos were ready and the signal was given for the rescue assault to begin. Soldiers of the top *sayeret*, specially trained for such missions, broke several windows at once and clambered aboard the bus within instants. They opened fire immediately, killing two of the terrorists and wounding the other two. The hostages were free, although a 20-year-old woman was killed in her seat and other passengers were slightly wounded.

The men of the *sayeret* returned to their base after handing over the two wounded terrorists to another army unit and to Shin Bet interrogators. It appeared that Israel's soldiers had swiftly accomplished yet another dazzling rescue – after some two dozen similar feats since 1967 – making it look easy to do what other nations could hardly ever manage.

'But that can't be,' Alex Libak, a photographer for the new tabloid newspaper *Hadashot*, said to himself, when he heard the official army spokesman's announcements on the radio a few hours later. The spokesman first announced that two terrorists had been killed and two wounded. An hour later, the announcement was corrected, now saying that all four bus hijackers had been killed by the army.

'The army spokesman is lying,' Libak said to himself, for he remembered quite clearly the somewhat charred bodies of two hijackers – the bus had caught fire in the gunfight – but had also seen how soldiers and men in civilian clothes were pummelling two wounded terrorists with their fists and rifle butts. He even remembered the terrified eyes of the Palestinians, as he hurried to the *Hadashot* photograph laboratory to develop his rolls of film. Libak did not have to make too great an effort to find the picture he was looking for. It clearly showed security men leading away one of the terrorists for questioning.[2]

'You're sure?' said Yossi Klein, the newspaper's young but balding editor. He was simply amazed when Libak showed him the photo and told him what he had seen with his own eyes.

'Yes, a thousand per cent,' the photographer answered.

What was odd was that the defence ministry itself seemed unsure of what precisely had happened on the night between

April 13 and 14. Arens appointed an internal commission of inquiry, headed by a reserve major general, Meir Zorea, an honourable man with an impeccable record.

Arens's spokesman, Nahman Shai, called the military censors' office and asked them to prevent the publication of any reports on the topic. The censors and Shai himself contacted all the newspapers and foreign reporters in Israel and told them that any article on Bus 300 would have to be submitted for censorship. The implication was clear: any article, report, or radio or television dispatch would be turned down. The reason given to the media for this decision was that any publication, even a mere hint, that the two terrorists had been caught alive and subsequently killed while in captivity could cause the deaths of Israeli prisoners held by Palestinian guerilla groups.

Klein suspected that behind this reason, there were other factors at play, meant to deprive the Israeli public of the truth. In direct violation of the military censor's ban, he splashed Libak's dramatic photo across *Hadashot*'s front page, with a brief news item that the defence ministry had established a commission of inquiry to examine the circumstances surrounding the incident.

Following *Hadashot*, which was no doubt motivated in part by its appetite for a sensational scoop and added sales, the other newspapers soon published details of the case. Defence Minister Arens reacted extremely vigorously, using his legal authority to punish *Hadashot* by closing it down for four days. Excluding administrative actions against Arab newspapers in East Jerusalem and the occupied West Bank, this was the first time an Israeli newspaper had been shut down since the Communist Party's *Kol Ha'am* in 1952. The stern reaction against *Hadashot* strengthened suspicions that its story was accurate.

The next month, on May 24, 1984, the Zorea Commission submitted its report to the defence minister, stating clearly that two of the terrorists had been taken alive off the bus. It was now necessary to investigate, to find out who had killed them. The Zorea report was classified and not released to the press; but it was sent to the police, Attorney General Yitzhak Zamir and the state prosecutors, and the military police for further attention.

The general election in June produced a stalemate: a dead heat between Likud and Labour and neither were able to woo enough small parties into a coalition. The two political behemoths were forced to create a strange new creature, the government of national unity, with a peculiar characteristic called 'rotation'. Peres would be Prime Minister for twenty-five months and then swap jobs with Shamir, who in the meantime would be Foreign Minister.

The new government was busy, from the start, with power struggles over Peres's efforts to halt the galloping inflation rate, which had jumped the 600 per cent hurdle, and his insistence that Israel's troops be brought home from their disastrous adventure in Lebanon. Nothing was being said about the hijacking of the bus in April.

Only a small minority in Israel was moved by the fate of the two Palestinians, who were, after all, terrorists. Even as Bus 300 faded from public memory, a battle royal was being waged behind the scenes.

Shin Bet's men had testified to the Zorea Commission that they had received the two terrorists from the army so badly beaten up that they were not even able to interrogate them. This Shin Bet version said that the two hijackers died a short time later from the blows previously inflicted on them – obviously pointing the finger of blame at the army.

The investigative team working for the state prosecutor, Yona Blattman, was inclined to go along with Shin Bet's story. In July 1985, Blattman charged Brigadier General Yitzhak Mordecai, who was the commander in charge of the army's rescue operation, with responsibility for the two deaths. General Mordecai was court martialled and did not deny that he had hit the terrorists with the butt of his revolver, but he explained that he had done so 'for the needs of operational intelligence' – to find out, immediately, if bombs had been planted aboard the bus. In any event, he added in his defence, 'When I received them, they were already in bad shape.'[3] The military court accepted his claim that by the time the hijackers were forcibly taken off the bus they were already pathologically dead. The general was acquitted of all charges.

Based on all the testimony available, Blattman and Attorney General Zamir recommended that two Shin Bet operatives be tried for having beaten the terrorists. These two Israelis were also acquitted – but they had faced only an internal Shin Bet court.

Shin Bet has always had its own disciplinary court, consisting of three members: one from Shin Bet, one from the Mossad and a district court judge who is president of the special, secret tribunal. The court is convened when a Shin Bet operative is accused of violating orders or the agency's code of conduct.[4]

The internal court is known for the severity with which it treats even the most minor infractions. Shin Bet personnel who are caught exploiting their position for private purposes are dismissed. For example, operatives who used their official missions abroad as an excuse to smuggle a television or video tape recorder into Israel were tried and dismissed, forfeiting all their rights to severance pay or a pension. Those found lying or not giving full reports to their superiors were also dismissed.

The aim was to create – and in this it was successful – labour relations based on mutual trust and accurate reports. The reports would not always be pleasant and everyone in Shin Bet knew that the agency had to be involved in questionable endeavours and dirty tricks. How else could the state be protected, considering the challenges and dangers of the Middle East?

The heads of Shin Bet always attempted to explain to their personnel that, regardless of how serious or disturbing the circumstances were, they had to report the complete truth to headquarters. By this, Shin Bet wished to adopt as sacrosanct the principle that, while the nature of the work would often entail lying to the outside world, operatives would report only the truth to their superiors.

The bus case proved that this was an impossible expectation. Sooner or later, a person who has been given permission to lie in certain circumstances will permit himself to lie in other circumstances as well. So it was with three of the highest-ranking men in Shin Bet: Reuven Hazak, Avraham Shalom's deputy; Peleg Radai, head of the security branch; and Rafi Malka.[5] Even though they were in their 40s, while Shalom was in his 50s, they were all considered part of 'the Arbel kids' who acted in the spirit of Yehuda Arbel's daring operations against terrorism. After so many outrages by Arab attackers and so many successes in combating them, the 'kids' broke apart completely over a single bus hijack.

Hazak, Radai and Malka revealed that, following orders from the head of Shin Bet, they had presented false testimony and forged papers to the agency's internal court. They were willing to do anything for Shin Bet – to lie, to fabricate documents and to conceal evidence – but this deliberate deception of the disciplinary tribunal proved too much for them. They had done it, but now they wanted to come clean.

The three men went to the head of Shin Bet and asked him for a full explanation of why they had been ordered to act as they did. When Shalom's explanations failed to satisfy them, they demanded that he resign.

Shalom refused to quit, but he permitted Reuven Hazak to meet Prime Minister Peres. The meeting was short and frosty. Peres did not want to believe what he was hearing from Hazak. The Prime Minister had been warned that Hazak's true intention was to have Shalom dismissed so that he could take over.

Peres was concerned about the political implications. After all, this was a case which related to the period when Yitzhak Shamir had been Prime Minister and Moshe Arens Defence Minister. Now, when all were together in the national unity government, a decision by Peres to side with Hazak could blow the coalition apart. Peres could only imagine, after all, that Shin Bet's Shalom must have acted in accordance with orders from, or at least the knowledge of, Shamir.

Peres accepted Shalom's version and claimed that Hazak had a hidden agenda – to stage an internal revolt in Shin Bet. Bolstered by the Prime Minister's backing, Shalom felt sufficiently strong to suspend all three of his opponents. He was kicking out his former protegés.

If Shalom thought that he was thus closing the Pandora's box which had come ajar, he was deeply mistaken. The three Shin Bet officers pressed forward with their struggle. Even though the agency chief specifically forbade them to do so, they went to Attorney General Zamir and gave him further, hair-raising details at the end of 1985.

Shin Bet was immediately split into two camps: those who supported Shalom and the others who backed the three rebels. It was impossible to remain aloof, with such a struggle touching nearly everyone in the secret agency. The clashes between morals and expedience, between emotion and logic, and between loyalty and a higher patriotism were coming to the surface.

Rafi Malka filed a suit in Israel's supreme court, charging that Shalom had wrongly suspended him and demanding that he be reinstated. At Shin Bet headquarters in Tel Aviv, all that everyone discussed – the secretaries who typed the reports, the technicians who invented the counter-intelligence equipment, the mechanics who maintained the counter-terrorism systems, the operatives checking in from their posts in the occupied territories and right up to the heads of departments – was 'the case', as if they had no other work to do.

All manner of wild rumour flew around, with the most absurd accusations being made. All the resentments and grudges bottled up for years were being voiced, even to journalists who could not possibly publish them in the light of press censorship.

Among others, it was hinted that somewhere behind the scandal stood a woman. It was claimed that one of the three rebels was on intimate terms with a senior Israeli attorney and that she had pushed them into complaining to the attorney general. This was not merely a debate as to how to treat hijackers once they are captured. Shin Bet had never known an internal war of such ferocity.

Yitzhak Zamir, who had been dean of the law faculty at Jerusalem's Hebrew University before being appointed in 1981 as attorney general and legal adviser to the government, was deeply shaken by the seriousness of the accusations being made. He went to Prime Minister Peres and told him everything he had heard. Zamir said he intended to hand all the evidence, hearsay and documentary to the police for a formal investigation.

Peres was shocked – not by the evidence he heard, but by the attorney general's plans to pursue it in the way of all perjury and cover-up allegations. The Prime Minister tried to explain to Zamir that a police investigation of Shin Bet would seriously harm national security.

Zamir suggested, as a compromise, that Avraham Shalom resign immediately. Shalom and Peres rejected the proposal out of hand. Peres then convened an urgent meeting with Shamir, formally deputy premier, and Defence Minister Yitzhak Rabin. These three men, who made up 'the Prime Minister's club' in the national unity coalition because all had experience in the top job, decided to do whatever they could to stop Zamir.

The three 'club' members knew that the attorney general had already asked, months earlier, to be relieved of his position. However, Zamir's wish to retire from government was in no way connected with the Bus 300 incident and the Shin Bet mess. Peres, Shamir and Rabin concluded that they should be able to make Zamir's resignation immediate, with a minimum of fuss. They could then have an attorney general and legal adviser who would be more amenable.

The club, accustomed to acting almost as a government within the government – three politicians, making all the toughest decisions on their own – was not going to have its way so easily this time. They were simply too late.

Zamir preferred to postpone his intended departure, so he could pursue his own view of the Shin Bet situation. He saw no contradiction between the democratic rule of law and national security. On the contrary: as he saw it, an attempt to cover up and obscure matters could only harm Israel.

On May 18, 1986, Zamir lodged a formal complaint with the police, which was thus compelled to investigate the charges and counter-charges within Shin Bet. By now, in private talks and even in the public media, the subtle, censored hints had changed from 'the bus case' to 'the Shin Bet affair'.

A few days after the police investigation began, Israel's state-owned television news broadcast an item on the case. Because of the censorship system operated by Aman, the TV newscast was not able to use the names of the Shin Bet officers concerned. Instead, it referred to 'a senior official' and to 'the case', which brought to mind a similar scandal thirty years earlier – the Lavon Affair regarding sabotage in Egypt. Once again, only Israelis already in the know could understand their own nightly TV news. The general public was left in the semi-dark.

The cork finally flew out of the bottle when the censorship system proved how ineffective it had become. An American television network violated censorship by naming Avraham Shalom as the 'senior official'. ABC News reported that he was suspected of having ordered the killings of the two bus hijackers and that the government was trying to cover up the entire case despite the stand adopted by its attorney general. Because the American people had been told rather more about the case, the censor now had to allow the Israeli newspapers to repeat what had been broadcast in the US. At the very least, Shalom's name was out. A Shin Bet chief had been unmasked in public.

The investigation took shape at an ever-increasingly dizzy pace. The police reluctantly questioned the Shin Bet personnel involved, including Shalom, plus the ministers in power at the time of the hijack, Shamir and Arens.

Shalom, who had decided to defend himself, hinted that he had been acting 'with the authority' of Prime Minister Shamir. But once he saw that the evidence was mounting against him and that there were real chances of his being charged with murder or manslaughter, Shalom engineered a clandestine, late-night meeting of the entire cabinet on June 23. Like a thief in the night, the government passed an unprecedented resolution: the head of Shin Bet and his three rebellious operatives would all be dismissed and as part of the deal, a total of eleven members of Shin Bet would be granted a blanket pardon – so that they could not be brought to trial. The cabinet also appointed a commission of enquiry, made up of three government attorneys, headed by Yehudit Karp, to investigate the Shin Bet case in detail.

The Karp Commission presented its report at the end of December 1986 and it exposed a number of illegalities. It praised the testimony of Hazak, Radai and Malka and it stated its firm conclusion that the three rebels had told the truth. The commission said that the head of Shin Bet had lied, had ordered his aides to lie and had altogether pulled the wool over the eyes of three prior investigations – by Zorea, by Blattman and by the Shin Bet disciplinary court.

Karp and her panel also ruled that Hazak, Radai and Malka had known of Shalom's decision to lie to the Zorea and Blattman investigations. As part of the cover-up, the Shin Bet chief had demanded the right to put one of his own men onto the Zorea enquiry panel. At the time, the demand had appeared to be strange, but only when the Karp Commission issued its report did the true intent of Shalom's demand become clear.

The report revealed that the Shin Bet representatives on the Zorea Commission, Yossi Ginossar, had acted like a Trojan horse or a Fifth Column, informing his boss of the direction being taken by the investigation and influencing the commission to reach conclusions which favoured the Shin Bet chief.

Ginossar carried out his task with complete loyalty to Shalom. He changed some evidence, suppressed other statements and documents and did everything possible to make sure that the cover-up would be complete. Before each meeting of the commission, he would meet the Shin Bet operatives who were due to appear before the panel. Ginossar would brief them and he would make sure that their testimony did not conflict with that of others.

The result of all these meetings was that Zorea placed the blame for the killing of the two terrorists on General Mordecai.

The attempt at whitewashing involved blackening the name of a prestigious military officer. In order to save his own skin and by invoking a phony claim of national security and secrecy, the Shin Bet chief was willing to see General Mordecai convicted, when the person who had given the orders to kill the terrorists was none other than Avraham Shalom himself.

The truth, as it emerged through Karp's report, was that the two wounded bus hijackers were brought to a Shin Bet interrogation facility near the site of the gunbattle and there, they were killed in cold blood. Shin Bet's staff attorneys, who were involved in the cover-up, rationalized their behaviour by claiming that they had attempted to protect what, in their opinion, was 'one of the greatest secrets of Shin Bet'. The Karp Commission condemned the agency's in-house lawyers.

In his defence, Shalom continued to claim that he had merely acted on the basis of authority granted to him by the Prime Minister. According to Shalom, he had had a meeting with Yitzhak Shamir in November 1983 – five months before the bus hijack – in which the question of how to deal with captured terrorists was dealt with in a general manner, without referring to any specific event. Afterwards, Shalom claimed, Defence Minister Arens had authorized having the two terrorists killed. Arens denied this completely and while Shamir admitted to having had such a conversation with Shalom, Shamir denied that he had ordered the Shin Bet head 'not to take prisoners'.

The Karp Commission preferred to believe the Prime Minister and the Defence Minister and not the head of Shin Bet. The commission also stated clearly that on the night of the bus hijack itself, the Shin Bet chief had not received any orders from the Prime Minister as to how to treat the terrorists.[6]

As a result of the report, it was decided that the practice at the time of Prime Ministers Golda Meir and Yitzhak Rabin would be revived, whereby there would be a notetaker present at any meeting between the Prime Minister and the heads of the secret services. No one had attended the Shamir–Shalom talk in 1983, so there were no memoranda or minutes.

The State of Israel was completely shaken. The head of the security service in a democratic country had acted in a manner which might be characteristic of the worst dictatorship. He had behaved as if he were above the law. In the eyes of many Israelis, Shalom could have been forgiven if he had 'only' been guilty of killing two Palestinian terrorists. But the battle ethic of the intelligence community must be free of any taint of any kind.

Dirty security services are dangerous, first of all, to the regime which they are supposed to defend. As in the Lavon Affair and America's Watergate scandal, the true dynamite was not in the deed itself, but in the cover-up which followed. The top people in Shin Bet – the most sensitive branch in the intelligence community because its actions can affect every single Israeli – had conspired against their political superiors and the public they were meant to serve.

Had any one of the central characters in the case stood up at any stage and admitted, 'I gave the order,' there would have been a chance to contain the fire. But it is clear that at a time of crisis and pressure, people have a tendency to shift the responsibility elsewhere, usually downward through the bureaucracy. The secret services are no exception.

The question which was widely asked was: What happened to the head of Shin Bet? Avraham Shalom took a vow of silence, although even this he would not confirm. Prime Minister Peres recommended Shalom for a job with Shaul Eisenberg, an Israel-based international merchant of aircraft, arms, goods and services of all sorts. Shalom was sent to New York, but to avoid the glare of unfavourable publicity he went under his old name, Avraham Bendor.

In the United States, Shalom/Bendor exploited his professional experience and information learned while in the Israeli secret services to procure defence-related contracts for Eisenberg. He had always appeared to be an unhappy man, but now he genuinely seemed displeased with his lot. New York was exile for him and the work was far from fascinating. He even had to take care of the kind of details which he had delegated to his Shin Bet subordinates for many years.

He had few alternatives. The Shin Bet killings and cover-up were too fresh, too embarrassing and too painful for anyone to give him a decent job in Israel. Shalom/Bendor's homeland had rejected him.

He found it hard to act freely outside the country, too. The Port Authority of New York and New Jersey cancelled a $75,000 contract with an Israeli company called Atwell Security, when it learned that the firm's president was Bendor and who he really was. The Port Authority said simply it was 'no longer satisfied with the agreement' it had signed for security advice at the New York-area airports from the Eisenberg-owned firm of consultants.[7]

In the absence of an explanation by Shalom himself of his decision to liquidate the two terrorists, his friends in and around Shin Bet attempted to come up with their own justifications. One claimed that it was a cold-blooded and 'professional' move – quite right in terrorist warfare because the bus hijackers were amateurs who acted on their own initiative and could not provide any intelligence on any enemy organization. Unable to supply information, they represented no value to Shin Bet. Even a trial, in this view, was too good for them.

There were others who explained that the decision was based on the cumulative effect of Shin Bet's involvement in Lebanon between 1982 and 1985, until the national unity government withdrew the Israeli troops. Lebanon was Shin Bet's Wild West. Yossi Ginossar went around acting like a sheriff. There were cases of smuggling and other breaches of army and secret-agency regulations, and reports to Shin Bet headquarters were incomplete at best. The agency's operatives knew that while certain norms and rules of behaviour applied in the West Bank and Gaza, there was nothing but barely controlled anarchy in Lebanon. The misbehaviour which had been learned there spread to the occupied territories.[8]

Everything that was published about Shin Bet and its problems was read avidly, and possibly nowhere more than in one of the cells of a military prison in central Israel. As he sat engrossed in his thoughts and longing for his family in Kafr Kama, the afternoon papers arrived in Izat Nafsu's cell, just as they had been arriving for the previous seven and a half years.

He was suddenly overcome by emotion and turned pale. In one of the newspapers, he saw a photograph of Yossi Ginossar – one of the Shin Bet officers who had just been pardoned by President Chaim Herzog. The news was that Ginossar had now been given a job in Ariel Sharon's ministry of trade and industry.

'That's the man who interrogated me and set me up!' Nafsu exclaimed and he hurriedly scribbled a letter to his lawyer, Zvi Hadar. 'I said to myself that even if a hundred years pass, I will not forget Ginossar's smile, a mocking smile, and how he told me to strip, spat at me, and afterwards, when I was on the floor, stomped on me and pulled out my hair.'[9]

That was the beginning of a new case, no less severe than the first, in which Shin Bet's once-good name was sullied. This case, too, was related to the Lebanon.

No one could have expected a security scandal to emerge from a clean and prosperous town such as Kafr Kama, in the rural hills near the Sea of Galilee. Most of the members of Israel's tiniest minority live there: a few thousand Circassians, non-Arab Moslems whose origins are in the Caucasus mountains of the Soviet Union.

Like almost all the other young men of his community, Nafsu volunteered to serve in the Israeli army and was proud that he had attained the rank of lieutenant. In 1976, well before the Israeli invasions of Lebanon in 1978 and 1982, he was sent to serve in the south of that country – a mere thirty miles from his home in Kafr Kama, but across the Lebanese border.

'I did not have a specific assignment,' Nafsu wrote in his diary. 'It was in the first days of Israel's involvement in the region. I was involved in all types of intelligence assignments, without being given any type of real briefing. I was not given specialized training or warned of any specific precautions to take. My assignment required me to live among the Lebanese, many of whom were informers.'

Nafsu used the word 'shtinker' in his diary, a Hebrew corruption of the English word 'stinker', to describe relatively unimportant collaborators and informers whom Israeli intelligence employs from among the Arabs in Israel and outside the nation's borders. The young lieutenant wrote that his job was to provide arms, ammunition and medical supplies to Christian and Shi'ite Moslem Lebanese who would oppose the Palestinians.

Obviously sensitive to the complex historical and religious enmities in Lebanon, Nafsu called it 'a place which destroys souls'. He wrote: 'It was easier for me to liquidate a person there than it is for the Mafia in New York. All around me, the cruelty of jungle law prevailed. Everywhere we looked, we saw events taking place which, in our terms, were utterly appalling – murder, revenge. Human life was cheap.'

The diary records many incidents of Israeli soldiers and operatives becoming rich by smuggling cigarettes, watches, televisions and even drugs into Israel. 'For me,' Nafsu added, 'Abu Kassem was the symbol of all these things. He was a *shtinker* who worked for all sides. He was the Zorba of southern Lebanon. He was as sly as a snake. He was the Lord of Survival and it was he who decreed my fate.'[10]

On the rainy night of January 4, according to the diary, a knock on his door in Kafr Kama awakened him. Nafsu was still three-quarters asleep, when he blindly asked, in the Circassian language, 'Who's there?' There was no reply. Only when he repeated the question in Hebrew did he receive an answer and he opened the door to find one of his friends, Danny Snir – an officer in his army unit. Snir told Nafsu to accompany him immediately on a secret mission into Lebanon, promising that he could return home in a day or two.

Nafsu agreed immediately. He went up to the second floor, took a bundle of clothes he kept ready, kissed his wife Siahm, whom he had only married three weeks earlier, and accompanied Snir. The next time Nafsu would see his home would be seven and a half years later.

Rather than being taken to his military unit, Nafsu was brought to a hotel suite in the port city of Haifa and that is where he first made the acquaintance of Yossi Ginossar. At the time, Nafsu did not know the man's real name, but as he was being treated so well he believed that Shin Bet was out to recruit him.

As the conversation continued, however, he realized that he was under investigation. The anonymous questioner kept asking about a certain PLO man who, according to Shin Bet, had been in contact with Nafsu. Only then did the Circassian officer begin to be afraid.

The Shin Bet man told him: 'Confess that you were a double agent for the PLO. You can't play around with us; we know everything. We have been following you for months.' Nafsu denied all the charges vehemently and he continued to do so after being transferred to the Kishon prison in Haifa, where Shin Bet maintains its own cells.

'Days and nights of investigation, threats and intimidation

began,' Nafsu wrote, adding that the then unnamed Ginossar had a superior who called himself only 'Pashosh'.

'Once "Pashosh" came into the room and claimed that he was the deputy head of Shin Bet and head of its investigations branch. He threatened to send me to a facility used to investigate terrorists and that they would inject me with a substance which would render me impotent. This threat of an injection was repeated constantly throughout the investigation. Someone would open a drawer, as if he were taking out the hypodermic.'

Nafsu's diary says the Shin Bet interrogators also threatened to detain his wife and strip her naked. 'They would sometimes bring *Playboy* magazine with its pictures of nude women, so that I would get the message. They also threatened to bring my wife and tell her that I had had homosexual relations with Abu Kassem, and that they would spread rumours in my village that I was a homo.'[11]

Nafsu understood that the evidence against him was based on Abu Kassem's testimony and that the alleged motive for his working with the PLO was sexual blackmail. Ginossar claimed that he had witnesses, including Abu Kassem who had seen Nafsu go to bed with a PLO man and with a Lebanese Christian. After the threats, other Shin Bet investigators came to Nafsu's cell and played the role of the good guys. They promised him that if he cooperated and told everything he knew, they would give him a furlough so that he could visit his wife.

The speciality of any intelligence agency, and Israel's Shin Bet is especially talented in this area, is discovering the weaknesses of the people it contacts. In the case of Nafsu, his weak points were his wife and his masculinity. As a member of the Circassian community, with its clearly defined status for the male, he was afraid of the humiliation that he would suffer if these rumours were circulated.

After forty days of continuous interrogation, he finally broke. He confessed to all the crimes attributed to him, including treason and espionage against Israel through contacts with the PLO.

But when the trial began before a military tribunal, Nafsu retracted his confession and claimed that it had been obtained through pressure and threats. The Shin Bet investigators denied this, of course, and the judge – as in most cases regarding the security agency – believed them.

The trial was conducted behind closed doors and even the accused's family was denied access to it. After hearings and deliberations which dragged on for two years, Nafsu was convicted. At the end of 1982, he was sentenced to eighteen years in prison and demoted to the rank of private.

Only Nafsu, his family and his lawyer – who had previously been chief military prosecutor with the rank of colonel – continued to believe in his innocence. Even after his appeals had been denied, Nafsu refused to entertain suggestions, from Shin Bet among others, that he request a pardon. 'I wanted an acquittal, not a pardon,' he explained.

Nafsu got what he wanted – but after long suffering – on May 24, 1987, when the Israeli supreme court acquitted him of the charges of espionage and treason and annulled his eighteen-year sentence. Nafsu was freed, promoted to the rank of sergeant and was paid all the salary due since his arrest. The justices did, however, sentence him to two years in prison for failure to report meetings with PLO members in the Lebanon. But the focus of the ruling was harsh criticism of Shin Bet, its interrogators and the methods they used to extract confessions.

The secret agency's actions were merely part of a wider, hostile environment. Shin Bet was like the bogey man, with which parents threaten their children if they do not behave. So it was in the case of Daniel Shoshan. He was a private in the Israeli army, sentenced in October 1986 to ten years in prison for 'transferring information to the enemy'. He allegedly, as an army mail courier, handed documents to an Arab in the West Bank who had PLO connections. The military police interrogators intimidated Shoshan by warning him that if he did not confess to the charges, they would turn him over to Shin Bet – and that would, no doubt, be much worse for him. Based on what he had heard about Shin Bet, he succumbed to the pressure and confessed to a crime he did not commit.

Two years later, after a re-trial, Shoshan was completely cleared. The appeal judges ruled that the military police had used physical force and other coercion to obtain the young soldier's confession, and that they had concealed evidence from the court.[12]

The Israeli public was shocked. Barely a decade earlier, it had been practically forbidden to utter the name of Shin Bet and absolutely unacceptable to criticize the secret services. Now, in less than a year, the veil of secrecy had lifted twice to show Shin Bet sullied by its two worst scandals. The agency's judgment, piety of purpose and *modus operandi* were now under widespread suspicion. The people of Israel were seeing their domestic security agency for the first time and they did not like what they saw.

President Chaim Herzog, who had consented to the deal whereby he had pardoned the senior officers of Shin Bet, now declared that the case had made him feel 'ashamed'. The new attorney general, Yosef Harish, defied the wishes of the Prime Minister's club and of Shin Bet itself, by ordering an investigation of Nafsu's interrogators. The official intention was to press criminal charges, even though it was clear that Ginossar could not be touched because of the blanket pardon he had received.

Following pressure by public opinion, as represented by Israel's newspapers and magazines, the government appointed a commission of inquiry on May 31, 1987, headed by Justice Moshe Landau who had retired from the supreme court. The other two investigators were former Mossad chief Yitzhak Hofi and the state comptroller, Yaakov Maltz. For half a year, the Landau Commission heard testimony from prime ministers, heads of Shin Bet, its operatives and legal advisers, those who had been interrogated, representatives of the Israeli Association for Civil Rights and even foreign attorneys from Amnesty International.

In the meantime, yet another disturbing case came to light. Awad Hamdan, a 23-year-old resident of a small village near the town of Tulkarem on the West Bank, was arrested on July 19, 1987, by Shin Bet men. He was suspected of membership in a Palestinian terrorist organization. Two days later, he died in his cell. His interrogators claimed that he had died of a heart attack, but his family stated that his corpse showed signs of physical brutality.[13]

The suspicions of torture swirled about the 'Hamdan Affair' and they even tainted the government's pathological institute, where forensic experts were in charge of determining the cause of death of all who expire under suspicious circumstances in Israel. Until the Landau report, the institute had the reputation of being reliable, professional and trustworthy. It then became clear that, in the interests of security, a number of the doctors there had distorted the facts. They had readily determined the cause of death of the two terrorists killed in the Bus 300 affair – in Shin Bet's favour as far as was possible – and, equally readily, agreed to state that Hamdan had died as the result of a heart attack.[14]

In late November, the Landau report was published. It was simply devastating: a printed record of how deeply the rot had penetrated inside Shin Bet. It said that as early as 1971, the then-chief of the agency Yosef Harmelin had agreed to let his men lie in court. The report noted that Harmelin did not order his men to lie, but simply accepted it as a fact of life.

Landau, Hofi and Maltz exposed the fact that Shin Bet operatives lied to Israeli courts, as a matter of course and habit, even though Israeli law imposes a penalty of seven years in prison for perjury. Shin Bet employees placed themselves above the law.

The decision to lie stemmed from the drastic upsurge in terrorist acts which followed Israel's capture of the West Bank and Gaza Strip. As the terrorism increased, Shin Bet investigators felt they had to use psychological pressures and some forms of torture – 'physical pressure', in the words of the commission – to extract confessions from the guilty.

Shin Bet took on the assignment of obtaining preventive intelligence, to give the earliest possible warning of Palestinian attacks. Its methods, however, went beyond Israeli law. Hundreds of terrorist trials were little more than summary court martials, in which military prosecutors would simply read aloud the confessions obtained by Shin Bet. When defendants claimed that they had been tortured or otherwise coerced into making false statements, the military judges – without any jury in the process – accepted Shin Bet's denials.

This pattern of perjury continued for sixteen years, including the terms of Avraham Ahituv and Avraham Shalom at the top of the agency. The Landau report said that 'Shalom "found a norm based on false testimony", so we were told, which "was transferred from one generation to the next."

'"When I think of the war against terrorists," so he told us, "I do not think in the context of the Israeli court." He did not even understand that there is something wrong with this norm. The commission regards him as one of those responsible for the existence of this defective method.'

The report deplored the entire Shin Bet leadership, 'which failed to understand that no security consideration, important or vital as it may be, can place those involved above the law. The leadership did not understand that it had been entrusted with an essential mission which might possibly justify certain means, but not all means, and certainly not that of giving false testimony.'

Landau's conclusions were written with more crystal clarity than most government documents, when he noted that within Shin Bet, it was mandatory that operatives tell the truth. 'Whoever was found not to have reported the truth within the service was punished in the most severe fashion and there were even cases of dismissal from the service. This approach created a type of double bookkeeping: insistence on truth within the service on the one hand, and false testimony in court on the other. This dual message evidently did not disturb anyone for sixteen years.'

At the same time, because the commission stressed the complexity of Shin Bet's struggle against terrorism, it explicitly stated that the agency's interrogators have the right to use a certain degree of 'pressure' on people – meaning Arabs – being questioned, without actually defining what the limits should be. The report cautioned, however, that each Shin Bet operative should not 'make his own rules for himself, arbitrarily, in applying pressure upon the person being interrogated.'

The report continued: 'In such circumstances, Israel's image as a law-abiding state, which observes civil rights, might be irreparably destroyed and it might come to resemble those regimes which grant their security services unlimited powers. In order to prevent this danger, one may not use excessive pressure upon a person being interrogated. The pressure may not reach the stage of physical affliction or of brutality against the person under investigation, or of any serious infringement of his honour which denies his dignity as a man.'

Hoping to offer some sort of guideline, Landau wrote: 'The degree to which these means are employed must be weighed against the degree of expected danger. The means of physical and psychological pressure must be defined and limited in advance. Every departure from the permissible must be met by a reaction from the commanders which is forceful and unhesitating.'[15]

The commission thus chose a middle course between the view that the law must be supreme, regardless of the terrorist threat, and the opinion that fighting terrorism requires departures from the strict rule of law. But even while Justice Landau and his colleagues were concerned about Shin Bet running wild, they did not attempt to uproot overnight the unlawful norms to which the agency had become accustomed.

Even before the ink on the report had dried, it became clear that three Shin Bet interrogators had lied to the commission itself. As soon as the new head of Shin Bet found out about the false testimony, he suspended all three. The irony was that the new agency chief was none other than Yosef Harmelin – coaxed out of retirement for a second term twelve years after leaving Shin Bet, and seven years after flying aboard a United States evacuation aircraft out of Teheran, where he was Israel's unofficial ambassador until the Islamic revolution in 1979.

It was during Harmelin's original term, from 1964 to 1974, that the habit of lying to the courts had developed. Harmelin was an established and respected veteran, however, and welcomed as an interim Shin Bet chief to fill in at a time of crisis. His assignment in 1986 was to reintroduce order, trust and hope in the agency, which had been torn apart by the various scandals and inquiries.

There was grave fear that Shin Bet's efficiency would be seriously impaired. Morale was certainly terrible. After the Karp and Landau reports, many Shin Bet operatives felt that they had been abandoned, as usual, by the politicians who expected the secret service to take care of the dirty work in the cruel war against terror.

In Shin Bet, the signs of discontent continued to grow. Operatives barely concealed their disgust with investigators and journalists who expected some sort of pure warfare against terrorism, when it was the politicians who should have faced the pressure to make long-term decisions on the status of the occupied West Bank and Gaza Strip and law enforcement there. 'We are the scapegoats of the occupation,' was how many in Shin Bet felt. More than thirty-five years after the original revolt of the spies who abhorred the formation of the Mossad, it appeared that another mini-revolt might break out inside the Israeli intelligence community.

Harmelin, in his quiet way, managed to stabilize the Shin Bet ranks and to calm down his employees. He was unable, however, to rectify the damage caused to the reputation of Shin Bet, in particular, and of the entire intelligence community. For the first time in Israel's history, the secret services ceased to be sacred cows which need not face questions about their methods of operation.

In the 1980s, the community faced unprecedented questions and painful truths.

A Spy in America

When Jonathan Jay Pollard burst into the Israeli embassy compound in Washington, DC, on November 21, 1985, it marked the end of the Jewish state's lifelong relationship of trust with its most vital ally, the United States, one of the key sources of its strength.

Jay Pollard was sitting, that Thursday morning, in his five-year-old Ford Mustang, sweating profusely. He was at the wheel; his wife Anne Henderson-Pollard sat on his right; they had their birth certificates, marriage certificate, family photographs, their cat and their cat's vaccination papers with them. The Pollards were ready to flee America; their engine was running; and they were just outside the gates of the embassy compound, near Connecticut Avenue and Van Ness Street in Northwest Washington.

The heavy steel doors swung open to let another car in. Pollard stepped onto the accelerator, swerving around the other vehicle, to bring his vehicle into the parking lot at the front of the embassy building which was new, but built in the traditional style of Jerusalem stone and arched windows. An Israeli security guard was about to pull a gun out of his concealed shoulder holster, when the pudgy, balding 31-year-old driver blurted out something about being a Jew seeking asylum. 'The FBI is onto me, I need help,' he told the puzzled Israelis.

Within moments, FBI agents who had followed Pollard were telling the Israeli security team, through the intercom at the gate, that the man who had just entered the compound in a Mustang was wanted for questioning. Armed with diplomatic immunity, the Israelis could have done almost anything – although sheltering a fugitive would surely lead to a damaging diplomatic incident. The front gate made a quick internal telephone call to the top floor of the six-storey building, where the intelligence agencies had their Washington representatives.

The embassy's chief security officer had heard from Pollard himself the previous day, reciting the names of Eitan and his other handlers and demanding help. On a second call, the security man told the American to come to the embassy if he could shake off the FBI. But here was the FBI, right behind the Pollard couple, still waiting in the parking lot out front, surrounded by Israeli plainclothes guards.

'Sorry,' the Pollards were told, as the Israeli security men escorted them back out the front gate. The FBI men arrested Pollard and they drove his wife home to 1733 20th Street, in Northwest Washington. Jonathan Jay Pollard was on his way to life imprisonment.

Pollard was a civilian who had worked for the US Navy for six years, most of that time in various intelligence and counter-terrorism units. Lest that sound too swashbuckling, Pollard was only a desk man. But he was a man whose desk included a computer, with access to almost every secret collected and stored by America's huge intelligence network. And while he considered himself a loyal American, he was also a fervent supporter of Israel.

Pollard was born on August 7, 1954, to a Jewish family in

Galveston, Texas, and he spent most of his youth in South Bend, Indiana. These were not America's strongest centres of Jewish culture or Zionist activism, but Pollard was a loner, anyway, as well as a zealot.

Pollard studied at Stanford University, one of the nation's finest, where his international relations professors found that he had an overactive imagination. He claimed to be a colonel in the Israeli army, although at other times he said he was a captain, and he even told acquaintances that the Mossad was grooming him to be a spy within the US Government.[1]

He was both 'very troubled and very shadowy' and once was so agitated about a group of Israelis supposedly trying to kill him, that he showed friends a revolver and locked himself in his dormitory room. He also told them that once, on guard duty on a kibbutz, he had killed an Arab.[2]

His friends and classmates recalled that Pollard's stories always involved Israel and many believed that his tuition was being paid by the Mossad. While the tales did not all seem to be credible, they were told with such conviction that it was hard to believe they were totally false. They were.

After receiving a Bachelor's degree from Stanford in 1976, it was cross-country for Pollard to the Fletcher School of Law and Diplomacy at Tufts University, near Boston. His graduate courses did not yield a degree, but the United States Navy hired him as a civilian intelligence analyst in the autumn of 1979. His Washington-area navy jobs were in agencies with names such as the Naval Operational Surveillance and Intelligence Center, the Naval Intelligence Support Center and the Naval Investigative Service or NIS.

He was one of the chosen few brought into a new Anti-Terrorism Alert Center in NIS headquarters in Suitland, Maryland, when all the American armed forces greatly expanded their effort to detect early signs of a terrorist threat. That was in June 1984, in reaction to the suicide truck bombing which killed 241 US servicemen in Beirut the previous October. A serious attempt to bring together all available facts, clues and rumours in this shadowy field

He could even borrow reconnaissance photographs taken by American spy satellites, but because these could not be reproduced by his computer terminal, he would have to borrow the photos for a day or two. Sella was thrilled. He knew how valuable the spy-in-the-sky could be. Just over three years earlier, before leading his squadron of pilots in the raid on the Baghdad reactor, Sella had studied US satellite photos which pinpointed the target. Such access was rare, however. Only infrequently did CIA director William Casey share such gems with Israel, as part of the strategic cooperation accords.

Sella, meantime, completed the computer science courses he was taking at New York University and returned to Israel. Pollard waited for a new case officer.

Eitan was so pleased with the results to date that he decided to launch a new phase. Pollard and Anne Henderson, then his fiancée, were flown to Paris at Lakam's expense in November. There, a little surprise awaited them. Avi Sella was again on the scene and he wined and dined them in the City of Lights. They were puzzled as to why they had been brought to France for a pleasant reunion. The mystery was cleared up when Sella introduced the couple to Yossi Yagur, their new case officer.

Yagur was Lakam's science consul at the Israeli consulate in New York. His official, but vague, career record speaks of several unspecified jobs, earlier, in the defence ministry. In case the worst should happen, Yagur was protected by diplomatic immunity.

As consul since 1980, Yagur was accustomed to attending academic conferences, forging friendships with American scientists in the defence and other industries, and sending huge files of clippings from newspapers and professional journals to Lakam's analysts in Tel Aviv.

What Pollard and Henderson did not know was that the true purpose of their trip to Paris was to be ensnared – eliminating their last possibility of escape. Rafi Eitan was waiting for them at their hotel and with his wide experience in the intelligence craft, Eitan knew perfectly well that there was a great difference between running a volunteer spy and a paid one.

Sella encouraged Jay and Anne to admire the windows of some of the French capital's most elegant jewellery shops. When she fell in love with a large sapphire and diamond ring, Sella said: 'Go ahead and buy it.' He would pay, on condition that they made it their engagement ring.

It cost around 10,000 dollars and in many ways it was the tangible mark of the Pollards' engagement by Israel. Sella even gave them a handwritten note which spoke of the jewellery as a gift from 'Uncle Joe', just in case someone in Washington should ask them how they could afford such a thing. Jay and Anne would marry the following August, and not only was their three-week honeymoon in Venice paid for by Israel, but it included a detour to Tel Aviv in order to meet Eitan again.

In compensation for necessary expenses and as a token of Israel's appreciation, Eitan told Pollard that he would be paid $1,500 a month. In addition to Anne's ring, Pollard was immediately given $10,000 in cash, and Eitan told him that a Swiss bank account – numbered and anonymous – had been opened for him. His fees would be deposited directly for use after Pollard retired. Then, the American replied, he hoped to live in Israel. Eitan showed him an Israeli passport already prepared for Pollard with his photograph and the false name Danny Cohen. He would be welcome in Israel at any time, as an unsung and unseen hero.

What Eitan did not tell Pollard was that the money was part of a classic technique to ensnare a secret agent and keep him. The spy who tells his controllers he is acting voluntarily, out of ideological affection for the country he is helping – or disgruntled hatred of the nation he is betraying – can easily be overcome by fear or change his mind. Being a volunteer, he feels he can withdraw at any time.

A paid agent cannot. He feels obliged to deliver and in the background lies the threat of blackmail. By establishing this implied contract, the employer can feel certain of having hired an agent.

Pollard's motivation was a combination of Zionism and excitement. The thrill of being a spy was enhanced by exotic trips, secret payments and numbered Swiss bank accounts.

As soon as he returned home from Europe, Pollard got right to work. He brought an entire suitcase full of documents – and the fabled satellite photographs of the Middle East – to a house in Maryland, where he met Yagur. The case officer taught Pollard some code words to be used in case communication or cancellation of an expected meeting were absolutely necessary. Yagur told Pollard that he would be expected and most welcome, every other Friday, at a special photocopying facility being prepared in a Washington apartment building where Irit Erb resided. She worked as a secretary for the Lakam man in the Israeli embassy.

The photocopying flat had been purchased by Harold Katz, an American Jew working as a lawyer in Israel who did not know how the property was to be used. It contained so much high-speed and high-quality copying equipment that a special electronic defence system was installed to prevent any electromagnetic interference being noticed by other residents of the block watching their television sets.

The Israeli handlers knew how to keep Pollard interested in his work: stroking his ego. Yagur frequently told Pollard that he was extremely valuable and that various parts of Israel's intelligence and defence communities were using the information he had provided. Pollard, however, was in the business of analysing such matters and he was not satisfied by generous but general platitudes. He insisted that Yagur find out, line by line, agency by agency, who in Israel was using the secret documents from Washington and how.

The various agency chiefs must have known that Eitan's scoops were coming from Washington. After all, only an American source could have provided satellite photographs. No one asked Eitan who his agent was. A military man? A Jew? An Israeli planted in the US armed forces or secret agencies? Men such as Admoni of the Mossad and the new

Aman chief Ehud Barak must have wondered. The quality of the 'product' was so good that the nature and risks of the espionage operation could not be ignored.

It is inherent in the system, however, that such questions are never asked. Revealing details would violate compartmentalization. Internal rivalries, also, would have stopped them from insisting that their counterparts reveal their sources.

Pollard was bringing huge piles of files to Irit Erb in fortnightly instalments. At first, he did the selecting. But Yagur then made it a habit to choose certain documents in advance – as though he were ordering from a menu, in this case, apparently, a catalogue of documents compiled by the Pentagon's Defense Intelligence Agency, the DIA. How could such a catalogue, itself a classified document, fall into the hands of foreigners? The Israeli embassy in Washington has a huge number of friends in the Pentagon, even when the Secretary of Defense is antagonistic towards Israel, as was the case with Caspar Weinberger during Pollard's illicit activities.

American investigators later suggested there may have been another spy working for Israel in the US administration, probably at an even higher level than Pollard. They called him 'Mr X' and incessantly but fruitlessly asked Pollard to name any American accomplices. Mr X supposedly gave the Israelis the reference numbers of DIA and other documents.

Using his 'courier card', Pollard was able to borrow secret documents from six restricted archives: the CIA, the FBI, the State Department, the DIA, his own NIS, and even the National Security Agency with its tight controls.[5] If it involved the Middle East, even peripherally, Pollard believed that Israel should know about it. He felt strongly that Secretary Weinberger and the US intelligence community were not sharing with Israel everything that they knew about potential threats to the Jewish state.

Thanks to their eccentric but effective spy, the Israelis received CIA analyses, copies of messages exchanged be-

A Spy in America

tween American facilities in the region, details of Soviet arms shipments to Syria and other allies, as spotted by US secret agents or spy-in-the-sky satellites, and actual photographs from those satellites.

While much in the way of raw data and polished analysis was regularly shared between Washington and Tel Aviv, satellite photos had always been a particular problem. Out of a purported fear that information on the methods and capabilities of US 'technical' reconnaissance would leak out, the Americans usually rejected – or sometimes considered at length, until they were no longer relevant – Israeli requests for specific photographs. The US had indefinitely delayed a reply on a more ambitious request by Israel to be given its own ground station and satellite dish to receive and decode the photographs taken from orbit.

The photographs and analyses provided by Pollard allowed the Israelis, for nearly a year until he was caught, to monitor in detail the movement of various navies' vessels in the Mediterranean. There was a CIA file on Pakistan's efforts to build a nuclear weapon, an 'Islamic bomb' project which was of concern to Israel as the greatest threat of its kind after the destruction of Iraq's reactor in 1981. There were details on chemical weapons stockpiled by Iraq and Syria, two of Israel's implacable enemies where information was difficult to obtain.

The most valuable pieces of purloined intelligence, in terms of enabling the Israelis to carry out a specific mission, were the aerial photographs of PLO headquarters in Tunis. There were also reports on the air defence systems of the North African states on the way to Tunisia, including Colonel Qaddafi's Libya. The attack, on October 1, 1985, was the most distant bombing raid ever undertaken by Israel's air force. It flattened much of Yasser Arafat's base and Pollard took pleasure in knowing he had helped make it happen.

In Washington, Pollard was driving himself too hard. His overenthusiasm gave way to fatigue, and the navy's Anti-Terrorism Alert Center noted that his job performance had markedly declined. He was doing a full-time job, analysing data and computerized intelligence reports for the navy, and then another full-time job as a spy obtaining many more documents for his Israeli handlers.

Pollard began to deliver thousands of pages dealing with terrorist threats, Soviet arms shipments, electronic communications intercepts and weapons systems in the Arab nations. Eitan and the few analysts at his disposal in Lakam could barely keep up. Even at Stanford, one of Pollard's professors had found that he 'tended to overdo things; if you gave him an assignment to write a paper, it would come in elegantly, but much longer than was assigned.'[6]

America's intelligence community should have known Pollard was unreliable, based on his background and quirky behaviour. His boss at ATAC was Commander Jerry Agee, who began to have doubts about Pollard's reliability after catching him lying twice about some trivial matters. Agee kept his eyes open and noticed 'huge stacks' of top secret material on Pollard's desk, not related to his assigned tasks. On Friday afternoon, October 25, a colleague reported that Pollard left work with a large package of material in computer centre wrapping. The authorities found that he had just 'accessed' Middle East message traffic.

Agee checked again on the following two Fridays, November 1 and 8, and noted that Pollard was collecting additional top secret data. So worried that he was losing sleep, Agee came into the office at 4.30 one morning and found even more Middle East material in Pollard's workspace. The navy commander said to himself: 'I've got a fucking spy!'[7]

Agee could not persuade the FBI to put Pollard under surveillance – as the agency had its hands full with a rash of foreign espionage rings – but naval counter-intelligence did plant hidden TV cameras around Pollard's workplace. They watched him and they felt certain that he was amassing his own personal intelligence library. He was detained for questioning on November 18.

Naval intelligence agents questioned Pollard for three

days, on and off, but they did not hold him incommunicado. Experienced at telling tales of fantasy rather than fact, he told the agents that he would help them uncover a multi-national espionage plot of which he was aware.

They were too lax and even during the first session the interrogators permitted Pollard to call his wife. While ostensibly explaining that he would be coming home late that evening, he also told Anne to 'take the cactus to friends'. It was a code they had developed earlier, indicating he was in trouble and any secret documents at home should be removed at once.

Ironically, the Pollards were scheduled to have dinner that evening, the 18th, with Aviem Sella and his wife, who were on a visit to the US. Sella had told the Pollards that the air force had promoted him to brigadier general and they ought to go out to celebrate. Instead, as Anne left for the dinner date, she was in a state of panic.

On her way out, she tried to get rid of a suitcase which, for the Pollards, was as explosive as dynamite. It contained a fifteen-inch-thick stack of secret US documents; it was in their apartment; and it was the 'cactus' to which Jay had referred. Anne frantically turned to their friendly neighbours, the Esfandiaris, for help. She asked Christine Esfandiari to take the suitcase, which she said was filled with documents from Jay's work, and to deliver it to Anne at Washington's Four Seasons Hotel. She was extremely nervous and also gave Mrs Esfandiari the Pollards' wedding album for safekeeping.

The Pollards had been good to the Esfandiaris, even lending them their Mustang on occasion, but a request to smuggle a suitcase out of the apartment building seemed too weird for Christine. She happened to be the daughter of a US Navy career officer and the next morning she telephoned the Naval Investigative Service, saying: 'I have some classified information that may be of help to you.'

Mrs Esfandiari later recalled: 'It was very hard because we cared so much about them, but in good conscience we couldn't let something like that go. I couldn't believe that was our Anne and Jay. I was mad. I was hurt. I felt deceived and betrayed.'

Asking a neighbour for a favour was certainly not a professionally planned way to get rid of incriminating evidence. Among other things, the suitcase had Pollard's name on it. Even if it had made its way to the DC dump, it could have landed him in trouble.

Anne had a nervous dinner with Aviem Sella, saying Jay was in trouble. Sella sensed severe danger and nervously told Anne not to admit they had ever met. They never saw each other again.[8]

Anne Henderson-Pollard returned home and found that Jay was back from his first questioning session. Both were extremely agitated – Pollard telling his wife of the horrors of being questioned – and they decided to call their case officer. Pollard got through to Yagur and demanded asylum and transport to Israel.

Yagur, to warn Pollard but also to calm him, replied: 'You're probably being followed. If you shake your surveillance, come in and we'll try to help.' The remark was unexpectedly amateurish for an espionage handler: if Yagur believed that his agent was being followed, he should have known Pollard's telephone was being wiretapped, too.

Israel and the Pollards would all pay for their lack of professionalism in this most delicate and dangerous operation. The Israelis were in an unseemly race to see who could flee the fastest. Within three days, Yagur and Sella flew home from New York; Irit Erb and her boss, deputy Lakam attaché at the Washington embassy, Ilan Ravid, also left the capital. The news, that an American had been arrested for espionage, had broken – although, amid much confusion and with only moderate impact.

When Pollard's handlers arrived in Israel, intelligence officials and politicians there already knew that media reports of his being brought from the embassy gates to FBI headquarters would be bound to harm Israel's relations with the United States – more specifically, with the CIA and the defence establishment.

When Israel first admitted the possibility of involvement with Pollard – a full three days after his arrest – there was general shock that Israeli intelligence could have been so stupid as to have allowed an agent to be arrested at Israel's embassy. With foreign espionage activities always assumed to be in the Mossad's purview, the public was surprised that the Mossad could be so amateurish and foolish.

Within a few days, it was revealed that Lakam – its existence never even mentioned before – was responsible. But this did not offer much comfort to the people of Israel.

There was puzzlement on the American side, too. President Ronald Reagan first heard of the case when he was flying back to Washington from his first summit with Soviet leader Mikhail Gorbachev in Geneva. Of the Israelis, whom he had nourished with juicy financial and military aid, promoting them into major allies of the United States, Reagan said: 'I don't understand why they are doing it.'9

On the other hand, the Americans should have known better. The CIA, for one, always assumed that Israeli spies were busy in the US. A secret agency study declared that after gathering intelligence on its Arab neighbours, the second and third priorities of Israeli intelligence were the 'collection of information on secret US policy or decisions, if any, concerning Israel,' and the 'collection of scientific intelligence in the United States and other developed countries.'10

They also should have known more about Pollard and his unstable history, as it unfolded during his interrogation. It became clear that he should never have been in the intelligence community. The CIA had rejected Pollard, but the agency never advised naval intelligence when he started working there.

Anne Henderson-Pollard, for her part, did not reject her husband's espionage. She actually enjoyed the fact that he had so much information at his fingertips and she even benefited by using some of it in her public relations work. She was arrested, too.

Federal prosecutors told the court that 'this defendant

has admitted that he sold to Israel a volume of classified documents, 10 feet by 6 feet by 6 feet' if all gathered into one huge pile. Defense Secretary Caspar Weinberger wrote his own letter to federal judge Aubrey Robinson: 'It is difficult for me to conceive of a greater harm to national security than that caused by the defendant.' Weinberger said privately that Pollard deserved to be hanged or shot, adding that repairing the damage he had caused could cost the US a billion dollars.

On March 4, 1987, nine months after pleading guilty in a bargain that was supposed to mean he would not have to spend the rest of his days in prison, Pollard was given a life sentence. Weinberger's letter had swayed Robinson.

Pollard was 32 years old. His wife, at age 26, had pleaded guilty to lesser charges of handling classified documents and was sentenced to five years in prison. Anne fell to the floor and screamed: 'No! No!' More composed, she said: 'I pray to God every single day I'll be reunited with my husband. That's all I live for.'[11]

Pollard had made the mistake of boasting in court that he had been 'quite literally, Israel's eyes and ears over an immense geographic area stretching from the Atlantic to the Indian Ocean.'

The spy also offered his own analysis that the information he purloined 'was so unique' that Israel's political leaders must 'have known about the existence of an agent working in the American intelligence establishment'. The way the Israeli handlers had 'tasked' him indicated, he said, 'a highly coordinated effort between the naval, army and air force intelligence services.'[12]

Inflating the importance of his undercover work could hardly strengthen Pollard's case before Judge Robinson. But the spy felt abandoned by his spymasters and implicating top Israelis was his bit of revenge.

US investigators rushed to Israel to test the government's assertion that the Pollard affair had been merely 'a rogue operation' – that the Jewish state's leaders had not known they had a spy in American intelligence.

To show their goodwill, they set up a liaison team to give US investigators all possible assistance. Their choice, to lead that mission, seemed perfect: Shin Bet chief Avraham Shalom was considered to be a man of integrity, known to his American counterparts. In retrospect, he was indeed the right man in the right place. Anyone, no doubt, with the talents displayed by Shalom would have been suitable to 'handle' the investigation.

Even as Shalom was supposed to be assisting the US investigators, he was sinking deeply into the web of his own Shin Bet scandal. After hiding the truth from his own government ministers, it was very easy for him to lie to representatives of a foreign power.

While prosecutor Joseph DiGenova and State Department lawyer Abraham Sofaer believed that they were questioning all the Israelis involved in running Pollard, they were not told about Aviem Sella. His role was completely covered up.

When, on top of that, the Americans were told that every single document provided by Pollard was being returned to them, they flew home to Washington to find that they had received only 163 out of over 1,000 separate items they had expected. The sleight of hand angered the US investigators, even though the point was purely symbolic: the Israelis obviously could keep copies of their photocopies and Pollard had never given them any original documents or photographs to keep.[13]

The FBI director, William Webster, was openly critical. He accused the Israelis of giving only 'selective cooperation'. Webster's attitude, as an antagonized and frustrated crime-solver, would haunt Israel's intelligence community for a long time to come because barely a year later he was appointed the Director of Central Intelligence, head of the CIA.

With such a reputation for falsehoods, it was hard to believe Israel when it gave 'inside' information on the workings of its intelligence community, to 'prove' that the political leadership had not known about Pollard.

With their eyes on the American practice of setting up

investigative commissions, the Israelis reluctantly formed two inquiry bodies. One probe would be by the Knesset's foreign affairs and defence committee. The other, cabinet-appointed commission ran into early trouble when a former chief justice of the supreme court, Moshe Landau, refused to serve because the two-man panel would not have the power to compel witnesses to testify and its findings would not be binding. At age 74, Landau had retired after an honourable career and did not want to be used as part of a cover-up.

The government, however, found two other men who had solid, establishment connections and believed they could do an honest job in the cause of justice: attorney Yehoshua Rotenstreich, who was a consultant to the intelligence community, and former army Chief of Staff Zvi Zur – who two decades earlier had been soft on Lakam, under Blumberg.

Israel's national unity government agreed that the two parallel investigations should look into everything, including the role of top politicians in the Pollard affair. The cabinet's leading trio played a concerted tune. Shimon Peres as Prime Minister, his Foreign Minister Yitzhak Shamir and Defence Minister Yitzhak Rabin promised to cooperate with Abba Eban's Knesset committee, but they contributed little.

As long as the investigators dealt with the operational side – how Pollard was run, rather than who was behind it – they felt safe. Both inquiries agreed that Pollard was recruited by Rafi Eitan's Lakam and that Aviem Sella played the role of middleman and seducer, with the full consent of his military superiors.

Where the two committees differed was in the question of political responsibility. The government-appointed commission did not find – or at least mention – any connection with the political echelon; it considered the Pollard affair only as an intelligence operation in isolation. The parliamentary panel, before disintegrating due to divisions between Likud and Labour members, did drop some hints.

Pollard was recruited when Moshe Arens was Defence Minister, responsible for Lakam, and Shamir was Prime Minister. The American spy continued to provide information when Rabin replaced Arens and Peres replaced Shamir. The four politicians concerned did concede that they had received some of the data provided by Pollard, but in keeping with normal practice they had never asked the identity of the source. If they had known, they claimed, they would immediately have cancelled the operation.

Rafi Eitan, on the other hand, told the committees that his conscience was completely clear. 'All my actions, including Pollard, were done with the knowledge of those in charge. I do not intend to be used as a scapegoat to cover up the knowledge and responsibility of others.'[14]

The veteran spymaster's hints seemed to suggest that the political leaders knew more than they were admitting. It was in no way surprising that they did not know the name of Jonathan Jay Pollard and his specific job, but some appreciation of where the intelligence 'product' must have come from could be expected from politicians with such deep experience in military affairs: Rabin as a former Chief of Staff, Shamir as a senior Mossad operative, Peres as the Deputy Defence Minister who created Lakam and even Arens with his military aeronautical engineering background.

If the US administration and the American people were astonished by the lack of accountability in democratic Israel, they were further flummoxed when the Israeli culprits not only escaped punishment, but enjoyed promotions.

Shortly after returning from the US, Brigadier General Sella was put in command of the Tel Nof airbase, south of Tel Aviv, the biggest in Israel. American military attachés were often there, debriefing Israeli pilots on their missions in US-made warplanes as part of the bilateral defence and intelligence cooperation.[15]

It hit home when Sella became the third and last person – after the Pollards – to be indicted on criminal charges in the conspiracy. For the first time, a high-ranking military

or civilian official of a US ally was formally accused of
espionage against the United States.[16]

When the Americans learned that the air base commander
was the case officer of the American spy, Washington
decreed that no US official would set foot inside Tel Nof
so long as Sella was in charge. US embassy officials in
Tel Aviv were annoyed when they learned about Sella's
promotion only when they were invited to his installation
ceremony. Then-Vice President Bush refused to visit Sella's
base while visiting Israel in 1986.[17] The pressure worked.
Israel's political and defence leaders sacrificed the young
general on the altar of Israeli–American relations. Sella left
his command and the air force.

The same Israeli leaders found it more difficult to remove
Eitan. They were faced with the heavy wall of Arik Sharon.
As Minister for Trade and Industry, Sharon once again
rushed to the rescue of his old protegé. Just as other intelligence veterans had discovered shelter in Sharon's fiefdom,
Eitan was given the chairmanship of Israel Chemicals, the
largest state-owned industrial company.

Israel's complex military-industrial requirements have obviously not changed, even after the Pollard scandal. The state
still needs its spies in Lakam's field of science, technology
and industry. This, after all, has always been one of the
specialities of the Israeli intelligence community.

Despite the government's firm declaration, soon after
Pollard was arrested, that the 'rogue' unit had been disbanded, Israeli intelligence is getting along without Lakam.
The American authorities are not bothered by this, it being
accepted that Israel still has to meet its defence requirements
by using technological espionage.

The Israeli intelligence community, for many years, had
been careful not to confront Jews in other lands with the
painful question of dual loyalty. The Pollard case shattered
that pattern and the US Jewish community was deeply
disturbed that its Gentile neighbours might believe that it
owed its ultimate allegiance to another nation.

So why did Israel confront the six million American Jews

with this dilemma by using Pollard? Stupidity? Arrogance? Carelessness?

These were not the only questions left unanswered. A former CIA director says: 'I've never understood why the Israelis ran Pollard. They get everything for free here in the US. The Israelis based at their embassy in Washington aren't just strumming their guitars. They're out there, doing legwork, meeting people. But they don't have to steal much, because ninety per cent of what they get, they are purposely given by friendly and cooperative Americans.'[18]

The shadow of distrust cast by Pollard between US and Israeli intelligence would never quite be removed, but hurt feelings gave way to strategic realities and national interests. When the two nations needed each other, in coping with sensitive issues such as Iran and hostages, they found new, unorthodox channels for cooperation.

13

The Chaos of Irangate

The Iranian Prime Minister's voice could be heard from the other end of the Swiss hotel suite. Mir Hossein Musavi was speaking from Teheran, shouting down the telephone line at his intelligence chief, Mohsen Kangarlu. Kangarlu, in turn, glared at the Israeli who was with him in the elegant room. The Mossad, the Iranian thought, had just played a nasty trick.

Kangarlu, an important behind-the-scenes figure in Iran but hardly known in the West, was in Geneva's Noga Hilton Hotel with part-time Iranian intelligence operative and weapons dealer Manucher Ghorbanifar, and an Israeli who was selling arms in the hope of liberating American hostages held by pro-Iranian Shi'ite Moslems in Lebanon. The Israeli was Yaakov Nimrodi and the Iranians felt certain that he was a Mossad agent. Nimrodi was, in fact, only an ex-Mossad man. Disturbingly, from the point of view of Israel's intelligence community, the Mossad knew nothing about what was going on.

It was November 25, 1985, only four days after Jonathan Jay Pollard's arrest in Washington had triggered off a dangerous loss of faith between the United States and Israel. Yet here was Nimrodi, authorized by Prime Minister Shimon Peres to join two other Israelis in close cooperation with US officials in the effort to trade arms for hostages.

For both Israel and the US, it was vital that the contacts with Iran be kept secret. The Israelis and Americans who were involved deceived even the Mossad and the CIA.

The Iranian Prime Minister certainly felt deceived that day, because he was at Teheran airport with senior military men examining air-to-ground missiles which had arrived on a clandestine flight from Israel. Musavi dialled Kangarlu's suite and screamed: 'Who is trying to treat us as fools? I am standing here with the Hawk missile expert of our army, and he sees that these are old Hawks – totally out of date and worthless to us!'

The Iranian officer had a list of military specification numbers – US 'milspecs' – and could see that the anti-aircraft missiles had been manufactured before the US improved the Hawk's speed and accuracy.

Nimrodi, who worked for decades in Iran for the Mossad, for Aman, and finally for himself, sensed that something was seriously wrong. He had not been trying to fool the Iranians. They had already paid him nearly $24 million for eighty Hawk missiles and the Americans had helped to arrange the delivery from Israel, with a promised replenishment from US stocks. It all made sense. It was a good deal for Israeli military exports. It would help establish contact with the relative moderates in Iran's radical hierarchy. And perhaps five more Americans, in addition to the US hostage already released in exchange for armaments, would soon be free as a pleasant dividend.

From his long experience, Nimrodi knew that Iranians were unsurpassed in their ability to invent difficulties, but he had a feeling that the 'milspecs' dispute was a genuine problem and that its source could well be in Israel.

Nimrodi tiptoed down the hall to his own hotel room

and telephoned his close friend and business partner, Adolph (Al) Schwimmer, who held both US and Israeli citizenship.

Schwimmer was at home in Tel Aviv and he was exhausted. He could scarcely believe what he had gone through to get those Hawk missiles flown out of Israel. And here was Nimrodi phoning from Geneva, but not to say that the Iranians were delighted and an American hostage was on his way to freedom. Instead, Nimrodi said that the Iranians were livid and the crew of the chartered airliner was now held prisoner.

Schwimmer had suffered the ordeal, the previous night, of finding a fistful of cash for the West German captain of the Boeing 707 who was about to leave Ben-Gurion airport with those Hawks. Schwimmer was muttering curses all day at 'those American crooks', because Lieutenant Colonel Oliver North of the US National Security Council, the NSC had sent an aeroplane but no money for aviation fuel. The Israeli had only about $500 in his pocket and he quickly drove to the homes of wealthy friends to borrow the rest of the $9,000 which the pilot said he needed.

North was the main White House operative in the attempt to win freedom for half a dozen American hostages held in Lebanon by pro-Iranian Shi'ite Moslems. The Vietnam war veteran was fond of complicated covert operations. Now he was President Reagan's most active operative, in the most secret project of the administration – to barter arms for hostages despite Reagan's strong public stand against making deals with terrorists.

Why did Colonel North have to deal with two private Israeli businessmen in a clandestine mission, involving a third country and delicate national interests? And why were not the Mossad and its intelligence soul brother, the CIA, running the show, as could have been expected?

Like President Reagan, Israel's Prime Minister Peres had reached the conclusion that this operation could be run more smoothly through these new channels, rather than the conventional ones. Peres hoped that the use of private Israelis would not only free hostages, but would help the

Jewish state profit from arms sales to its traditional market in Iran. The complex deal could also repair the damage in US–Israeli relations.

But who were these Israelis, these three musketeers?

The first was Al Schwimmer, who was born in 1917 in the US and decided in his youth to learn all there was to know about aviation, and he mastered the field – from piloting small aircraft to selling aeroplane parts to Third World nations. He worked as an engineer for Lockheed and for TWA, served in the US Air Force and after World War II rediscovered his Jewish roots when he met Holocaust survivors in Europe. Schwimmer became a secret agent of sorts in Czechoslovakia, where he amassed arms sold by Western dealers and from the Soviet bloc. His own cargo airline transported the guns and ammunition to Israel before and after statehood in 1948.

An unknown hero who had helped the newborn state to win its War of Independence, Schwimmer was commissioned as an officer in the Israeli Air Force. He returned to the US in 1949, hoping to help his new homeland from afar, but first the American authorities charged him with the illegal export of aeroplanes and spare parts to Israel, Czechoslovakia, Italy and Panama. Schwimmer and his company, Service Airways, were convicted in a federal court in Los Angeles in 1950 and fined $10,000. The FBI believed that in exchange for using the Czech airfield at Zatek, Schwimmer had supplied the Communist government with a training plane and a miniature radar unit.[1]

His next project was Intercontinental Airways, which did not fly passengers but served instead as a renovation and repair centre in the US for aeroplanes of the Israeli Air Force and El Al Israel Airlines. Prime Minister Ben-Gurion and his young defence aide Peres persuaded Schwimmer to return to Israel in 1951 and set up an aircraft industry, known first as Bedek and later as IAI.[2] It was a proud moment in 1975 when Schwimmer presented the air force with the Kfir, based on the plans Lakam had obtained from its Swiss agent Frauenknecht.

After his retirement from the state-owned aircraft manufacturer, Schwimmer became a special adviser to Peres and
a partner in various businesses with Nimrodi. From 1984
to 1987, Schwimmer drew a token salary from the Prime
Minister's office of one shekel a year – less than one dollar.

The second Israeli was Yaakov Nimrodi, who was born
in Iraq in 1926 but brought up in Jerusalem, one of ten
children of a poor family. His intelligence career began just
before Israel's statehood in 1948, when Nimrodi joined the
Palmach. After the War of Independence, he was a junior
field officer in Aman.

In 1956, he was sent to Teheran on behalf of Israeli
intelligence, working for both Aman and the Mossad in the
early stages of the developing 'peripheral' strategy. In the
formal role of military attaché, Colonel Nimrodi spent most
of the 1960s doing what he could to make Iran dependent
on Israel.

He was instrumental and efficient in selling $250 million
a year of Israeli defence equipment to Iran. He arranged
demonstrations in Iran of new Israeli weapons and he always
made sure that Farsi-speaking Israelis were used as military
trainers. Years later, hundreds of Iranian officers, who were
secretly trained in Israel, are still fighting in Iran's army.
Nimrodi can also take credit for building Iran's military
intelligence corps into a respectable body.

Seeking his reward within the Israeli defence system,
Nimrodi returned home in 1969 and lobbied for the job
of military commander on the West Bank, captured from
Jordan only two years earlier. He was rejected, however,
and left the army.

After a short time in Israel, he returned to what he knew
best: selling goods in Iran. He became a private merchant
of arms and other Israeli products, acting as a 'Mr Fix-it' to
arrange exports to the large Iranian market. Nimrodi, with
his wife Rivka and their young children, returned to
Teheran. All the sales of Israeli goods which he had previously arranged as part of his low-salary job as an Aman
man were now handled by Nimrodi as a private import-

export agent. The commissions were huge – millions of dollars in some years.

In the unique way that flamboyant, wealthy men are mutually attracted, Nimrodi met the Saudi tycoon Adnan Khashoggi, a man of great ambitions in both business and clandestine diplomacy.

Nimrodi, Schwimmer and Khashoggi invested millions in the Shah's Iran, but all that was swept away in the 1979 Islamic revolution. Nimrodi, having banked wisely in Europe, settled in London to be near his old Iranian friends, now exiles.

The third Israeli was Dave Kimche. He was not a private operator; he was director-general of Israel's foreign ministry and represented the Israeli Government in its secret deals with Iran. Kimche, who had been longing to return to the clandestine wheeling and dealing of his Mossad days, did not find the methods – including convoluted air transport arrangements – strange in the least.

On that long night of November 24th, Nimrodi, Schwimmer and Kimche were struggling to score an arms for hostages triumph by keeping the Boeing 707 on its flight path from Tel Aviv, via Cyprus, to Teheran. An Israeli army crew had barely squeezed the first eighteen of the eighty missiles aboard. Then, six hours after the plane's 9 pm departure – with the refuelling funds Schwimmer had scurried to obtain – Schwimmer was awakened by a telephone call. A man, obviously speaking from abroad, said he was the owner of the Boeing and was phoning from Brazil.

A bleary-eyed Schwimmer wondered: 'What, money again?'

'No,' said the chartered aircraft owner, 'our pilot has been arrested, after arriving on Cyprus, because of irregular documents.'

It was mere luck that the Cypriot authorities had not opened the packing crates for inspection. Within hours, they might do so, and in any event the press – Middle East correspondents from the world's leading media based themselves on Cyprus – would quickly learn of the mystery jet standing in a corner of Larnaca airport with its pilot under arrest.

Schwimmer telephoned Colonel North in Washington, where it was still Sunday evening, and North then partially lifted the veil of ignorance he had placed on the CIA by asking the agency for assistance. At North's request, a CIA agent on Cyprus pulled some strings with the local authorities to have the pilot released quietly. The Boeing took off again, now refuelled, at six o'clock Monday morning.

Obviously too excited to sleep, North called Schwimmer a few hours later to say that the plane had landed in Teheran. Fully convinced that one or more American hostages would now be freed by Iran's friends in Lebanon, Colonel North told the Israeli: 'God bless you.'

When Schwimmer then heard from Nimrodi that the Iranian Prime Minister himself was at Teheran airport and furious about having been sent the wrong goods, he immediately telephoned the deputy director-general of the defence ministry in Tel Aviv, Chaim Carmon, who told him: 'Don't worry. Tell them the Hawks were modified in Israel and are better than the original missiles.'

This reassuring message was passed from Tel Aviv to Teheran, by way of Geneva, where the telephone soon rang again. This time it was the Iranian colonel who was, with Prime Minister Musavi, bending over the crates filled with Hawks. The officer said he and a technician were examining the missiles, but he demanded to know: 'What modifications?'

By now, Ghorbanifar was staring at Nimrodi with hurt in his eyes, as though the Israelis, who had always seemed so serious and sincere, had betrayed him at the climax of their seven-month relationship. Kangarlu was agitated and insisted that Nimrodi get the answers for the colonel in Teheran 'at once!'

An urgent question was put by telephone from Geneva to Tel Aviv: 'What modifications?' Nimrodi asked Schwimmer, who in turn telephoned his defence ministry contact. Carmon said he would check and call back. Within minutes he was speaking slowly and calmly as he finally told

Schwimmer the truth: 'Listen. Those missiles did not undergo modification.' Someone thought Iran could be cheated.

Schwimmer realized that a seemingly well controlled operation had become quite absurd. He called Nimrodi with the bad news: 'They're right. They are the old Hawks.'

Nimrodi told Kangarlu just as the Iranian's boss, Prime Minister Musavi, came on the line again from Teheran. Kangarlu stuttered nervously as he told Musavi that he had indeed received an outmoded model of missile.

Musavi yelled on and Kangarlu turned white as a sheet and fell to the ground. He had fainted from the pressure. His bodyguards feared it was a heart attack and began pounding on Kangarlu's chest.

Nimrodi, meanwhile, fearing that the entire project was disintegrating before his eyes, grabbed the telephone and picked up the conversation with Musavi in the Iranian's own language, Farsi.

Nimrodi explained to Musavi, knowing not to offend the Iranian leader by identifying himself as an Israeli, that Kangarlu had just collapsed and that there had to be a calm, reasonable way to settle the 'misunderstanding'. Musavi kept on shouting, threatening to keep the transport plane and put the chartered crew on trial, until Nimrodi offered to return to Iran the bulk of the payment already made.

The precise arrangements were made through Ghorbanifar, even as an ambulance took Kangarlu to a Swiss hospital, and the next morning Nimrodi was accompanied by burly Iranian bodyguards to a branch of Credit Suisse to transfer $18 million back to Iran's account.

The Hawk missile incident was a disaster for the arms for hostages deal, as engineered by Nimrodi and his small Israeli team. Nearly a year more would pass before the existence of the complex, three-sided negotiations would become public knowledge. At that time, US officials would say they entered into the transaction because they trusted 'the Israelis' and their superior knowledge of Iran.

The ultimate failure and the embarrassment caused to the

White House by the Irangate scandal were due to the mind-boggling link between Iran and Central America. Colonel North tied the Iran operation to his secret programme for sending aid to the anti-Communist Contra rebels of Nicaragua – hiding the Reagan Administration's actions from Congress and the public, while skimming off profits from the Ayatollah's money to pay for bullets in America's backyard. Kimche had little interest in the Contras, but great interest in Israel's frontyard, Iran.

Kimche was one of the great advocates of the 'peripheral' strategy, both when he was in the Mossad and when he surfaced from the black hole of a clandestine career and joined the foreign ministry. He never abandoned the idea that Israel should collaborate with the Iranians. Despite the takeover by the ayatollahs, he believed that there must be a core of moderates – either in the army, or elsewhere in society – who would be willing to cooperate with Israel and the West.

Within two years of starting his second, public career, Kimche did not stop short at mere dreaming. He was well aware that Israel was selling arms to Iran, to expand its exports, to help the Jews of Iran and to maintain a link with Teheran. In 1982, he took part in the complex plot of 'Arik's court'. With Nimrodi, Schwimmer, and Khashoggi, in Morocco, Kenya and Sudan, plans were laid for a *coup d'état* against Ayatollah Khomeini.

Kimche was so confident that he permitted himself to go on the record, as the British-style gentleman on British television in February 1982, publicly urging that Israel and the West should encourage a coup in Iran. It was no coincidence that Nimrodi appeared on the same programme, filling the screen with his round face and plumes of cigar smoke, saying in heavily accented English that a coup was a simple matter and quite essential.[3]

In many ways, the earlier plot was a preview of Irangate. The difference was that in 1982, by sending its special emissary to the Baby Shah in Morocco, the Mossad was able to kill the conspiracy.

It would not, therefore, have been surprising if, in 1985, secret service veterans Nimrodi and Kimche had decided to ignore the Mossad completely when Khashoggi proposed a new initiative towards Iran. It was still important, however, to adhere to the bare minimum of intelligence community etiquette and the Mossad was given a chance to express its opinion.

Khashoggi contacted Nimrodi and Schwimmer at the beginning of April 1985 and invited them to come urgently to London to meet him and several Iranians 'who are worth meeting'. Khashoggi added to the importance by indicating that King Fahd of Saudi Arabia had himself approved the plan he was about to propose.

Schwimmer, officially employed by Peres, told his old friend about the invitation and received the Prime Minister's permission to see what was on offer in London. Thus it was that the Irangate scandal began.

In a $600 a night suite in London's Hyde Park Hotel, Adnan Khashoggi introduced Nimrodi and Schwimmer to an Iranian named Cyrus Hashemi. The Saudi said that Hashemi was a man of influence and a cousin of Ali Akbar Hashemi Rafsanjani, the Speaker of the Iranian parliament who was second only to Ayatollah Khomeini in political power in Teheran.

Suddenly, instead of overthrowing the Khomeini regime, Khashoggi was recommending that the Israelis join in making friendly overtures to specific elements of that regime.

Hashemi said he was authorized by senior Iranian government officials to look into the possibility of renewing contacts with the West. He said his aim was to restore contacts between Washington and Teheran, cut off nearly six years earlier when the US embassy was seized by Iranian radicals, but Khashoggi had advised him to begin with the Israelis. What did Iran want? A renewal, Hashemi said, of the arms sales which Israel had stopped – at America's demand – and which Iran needed in the prolonged Gulf War against Iraq.

A short while later, Khashoggi similarly introduced Nimrodi and Schwimmer to Manucher Ghorbanifar, whom he identified as a Hamburg-based Iranian business-man who had been authorized by Iran's Prime Minister to pursue better relations with the West – again, through Israel.

Intrigued, Schwimmer persuaded Peres to permit brief visits to Israel by Hashemi and Ghorbanifar to be 'tested'. Indeed, in the course of April, using false passports, the two Iranians separately flew from Europe to Tel Aviv.

'Ghorba', as he was immediately dubbed by the Israelis, travelled in the guise of a Greek citizen 'Nicholas Kralis'. To avoid the Border Police at Ben-Gurion Airport, who are excellent at spotting forged documents, the two Iranian but nominally non-Iranian gentlemen were escorted by Israeli agents through Passport Control without questions or visa stamps.

Peres was also intrigued at the possibility of renewing relations with Iran. Instead of protesting Israeli arms sales to Iran, this time the Americans might endorse them. The Prime Minister ordered the Mossad to interview Hashemi and Ghorbanifar carefully and give a quick and comprehensive report. Mossad involvement was quite natural, since Kimche and his fellow musketeers gave the agency a chance to take part.

Hashemi was simply full of talk, obviously willing to make some deals to arm Iran and line his own pockets, but lacking any political sophistication which might impress his Israeli hosts. The Mossad also checked its computerized files and found that Hashemi had a bad reputation for selling himself and his information to the highest bidder, without regard for any particular strategy. All the European security services, East and West, had used Cyrus Hashemi. The Mossad did not want him at all.

The Mossad was not enamoured of 'Ghorba', either, but all the Israelis who met him had to admit he was interesting. Both the Mossad and Aman interviewed him, as did the foreign and defence ministries. He told an impressive tale of having gone to Riyadh, the Saudi capital, and – in an audience arranged by Khashoggi – having warned King

Fahd of Iranian plots to attack the sacred Moslem shrines in Mecca.

While the Mossad reserved judgment on Ghorbanifar, the defence ministry was delighted to say yes to a relatively simple deal suggested by him. It would be a further test of the Iranian's credibility and an easy $40 million of revenue for Israel. Ghorbanifar telephoned Teheran, from Israel, and drew up a shopping list of artillery pieces, mortars and ammunition which the Israeli ministry experts considered old junk.

Within days that April, the Israelis chartered a cargo ship and prepared it to sail from Eilat to Bandar Abbas, Iran. The arms were loaded aboard and Ghorbanifar seemed to prove himself again when a lieutenant colonel from Iran's army flew into Tel Aviv – out of uniform and, again, on a false passport – to sail home aboard the ship.

In the meantime, however, another telephone call from Ghorbanifar to Prime Minister Musavi's office in Teheran produced a totally different shopping list. The Iranians cancelled the $40 million purchase and began to demand TOW missiles which their troops could use to destroy Iraqi tanks during a Gulf War offensive which was expected to start soon. Iran needed TOWs, and that was all it wanted from the Israelis. The ship never sailed. The lieutenant colonel flew home.

In a nutshell, that was the problem with Ghorbanifar and whoever his contacts might be in Iran. Agreements might not be honoured and Israel could be sucked in ever deeper, until it was providing the Iranians with whatever they wanted while receiving nothing in return except – at best – money. This problem made the Mossad more reluctant to participate, but the agency was still in the picture.

Ghorbanifar was now seeking hundreds of TOW missiles. The price of around $10,000 each presented certain attractions, but the fact that TOWs are strictly 'Made in the USA' and would have to be re-supplied from there presented many problems.

On a second visit to Israel, Ghorbanifar could see that his

new, simple, but lucrative shopping list was being met by doubt and hesitation. He stepped up the pressure – and the possible rewards for Israeli intelligence – by sitting down, in the large Mossad guest house just north of Tel Aviv, and writing a long report on the political scene inside Iran.

Dated May 2, 1985, Ghorbanifar marked it 'Strictly Confidential – For Your Eyes Only'. It was highly professional, from an intelligence man's point of view, and it revealed a well organized mind – which impressed the musketeers, who had found Ghorbanifar to be so calculating and confusing that conversing with him was 'a real challenge'.[4]

His report was written for the Mossad, but surely designed by Ghorbanifar to be passed on to Washington – at that point, completely out of the picture. He had tried several times to develop links with the CIA, offering information and various deals to the Americans, who used lie detectors to conclude that he was unreliable.

The detailed study began with the obvious. Professionals in the intelligence community learn not to exclude the facts which 'everybody knows', because they could be inadvertently forgotten in a final analysis. Therefore, the Iranian visitor in Tel Aviv wrote: 'The Imam Khomeini is Iran's sole ruler,' adding that the most powerful politicians and Shi'ite mullahs at any time are those who have Ayatollah Khomeini's support.

Ghorbanifar's secret report introduced the notion of three 'lines' of politicians and clerics standing in the wings, competing for power below the supreme Ayatollah's exalted level and awaiting his death. This was the kind of detailed analysis which both the US and Israel knew they had been missing without good sources inside Iran.

Line One, Ghorbanifar wrote, was 'Rightist', finding its strength in the army, the police, the parliament known as the Majlis, most merchants and even some Revolutionary Guards. They favoured free trade and were strongly anti-Soviet. They opposed exporting the Shi'ite revolution by force and they wanted friendly relations with both the West and other Moslem countries.

Line Two, he wrote, was 'Leftist' and included both the President and the Prime Minister. Ghorbanifar described this group as 'hardline at home and abroad', supporting terrorism and the export of an armed Shi'ite revolution. He blamed Line Two for the ordeal of the fifty-two American hostages in their Teheran embassy.

Line Three was described by Ghorbanifar as a 'middle, balancing line' with great strength in the Majlis, in the supreme court and scattered among revolutionary foundations.

He was able to name names – dozens of Iranians, some prominent and others hardly known in 1985 – and he placed them neatly into the three political 'lines'. He quoted Khomeini as saying: 'Stop the line-playing.' But Ghorbanifar also predicted that after the Ayatollah's death, one of the political groupings would win the struggle and 'eliminate the other two'.

His advice to his Israeli and, he hoped, American readers was: 'We must support Line One, eliminate Line Two, and absorb Line Three.'[5]

It was politics by numbers and Kimche now felt he had something to tell the Americans about. The three musketeers had always intended to bring the US into their scheme and they now believed they held the bait to bring the huge fish into the net. The best possible bait would be the hostages in Lebanon and the Israelis knew how desperate Reagan and his White House were to liberate their countrymen. Kimche's team informed Washington that there was an attractive contact, well worth examining.

Even before receiving Ghorbanifar's three-line analysis, President Reagan's national security adviser Robert (Bud) McFarlane reacted to what he heard from his old friend Kimche. McFarlane sent a part-time consultant on terrorism and the Middle East, Michael Ledeen, to Israel to discuss the possibilities of joint, covert efforts to gain contacts in Iran. Ledeen met Prime Minister Peres, whom he knew from meetings of labour movement leaders worldwide known as the Socialist International.

When Peres gently mentioned the possibility of selling weapons to moderate elements in Iran, it was only natural for Ledeen to take this as a mere rationalization for previous Israeli arms sales – which were mostly intended to help fearful Jews flee from Iran without hindrance. Mossad operatives had helped smuggle Jewish Iranians across the border into Pakistan and Turkey, with authorities looking the other way.

This time, there was the more complex and attractive motivation of attempting to help one political line emerge victorious from Iran's inevitable power struggle.

Peres decided to proceed with the three musketeers. He ignored the Mossad, which finally – at the delicate stage of drawing in the Americans – decided not to take part. The Mossad did not believe in the scheme and saw no real opportunities in radical Iran.

The situation was truly abnormal. In other times, if the Mossad said no, a proposal could be cancelled. Now, after thirty years of dominating intelligence operations on Israel's foreign horizons, here was the Mossad locked out completely from a covert project abroad.

More puzzling is the fact that the Mossad was cold-shouldered by Peres – a Prime Minister with a reputation for being balanced and moderate in his actions. He was not Begin, in his era of adventurism, or Sharon, who sought changes in the Mossad. But Admoni was not nearly so strong an agency chief as Hofi had been in 1982 when he stamped out the Sharon–Nimrodi scheme of staging a coup in Iran from Sudanese bases.

In 1985, Admoni merely registered his objection but retreated in the face of the Prime Minister's wishes. Peres was strongly in favour of the Iran project and he preferred to press on with an ex-Mossad official and two businessmen, rather than cancel a project with potential political benefits which could include President Reagan's lasting gratitude.

The Prime Minister did make a minimal effort to put an intelligence professional in charge of the threesome. He asked former Aman chief Shlomo Gazit to oversee the musketeers, but Gazit quit within weeks 'because the Mossad is not completely in the picture' and he refused to take orders from arms dealers, pursuing profit from political affairs.[6]

The Prime Minister sent Kimche to Washington, to supplement what McFarlane had already heard from his aide, Ledeen. It was automatic, almost a reflex by both Americans and Israelis, to connect the word 'Iran' with the thought of 'hostages'. And Ghorbanifar was dangling the possibility of freeing William Buckley, the CIA station chief in Beirut who had been kidnapped by pro-Iranian Lebanese Shi'ites and was under severe torture. The notion of swapping arms for hostages was off and running.

The musketeers attempted to organize themselves along professional divisions of duty. Kimche was liaison officer with the Americans, Nimrodi was in Geneva and London as financier and Schwimmer was the operations officer who had to solve transportation problems.

On the American side, the circle of people who knew about the secret deals widened. Defense Secretary Weinberger did not like the operation, but was brought into the picture. His Pentagon had to replenish the Israeli arsenals missile-for-missile after every Israeli shipment to Iran. That had been the price demanded by Defence Minister Rabin for his cooperation.

A jet chartered by Schwimmer brought 508 TOW missiles to Iran – which paid $5 million – on two flights, in August and September, 1985. The Reverend Benjamin Weir was released, after sixteen months in captivity, and the trade in weapons for human beings was in full gear, with great expectations.

Kimche would be back in the thick of covert operations, in search of peripheral alliances. Nimrodi would make money and return to his old stomping ground, Iran. Schwimmer would be fulfilling his view of serving Zionism, while exercising his abilities to manoeuvre aeroplanes. Peres would be a key statesman who pulled off a clandestine coup.

All of them would be thanked by Reagan for bringing back his beloved US citizens.

All the aspirations of the Israeli musketeers were crushed by the ill-fated flight of the Hawks in November. The Iranians were furious, but more importantly the Americans lost all confidence in the three Israelis. The project itself, however, seemed too tempting to be abandoned. The Americans wanted to keep going and Peres was equally eager. Rabin, though, was insistent that someone else be put in charge of the Israeli side, but the Mossad was angrier than ever about the entire affair and refused to lift a finger.

A new conduit through the darkness had to be found. Peres, as a master politician, did not hesitate to ditch the musketeers – even his old friend Schwimmer. The light at the end of the tunnel would now be Amiram Nir.

At the age of 35, Nir may have looked too young for such worldwide wheeling and dealing, but his ambitions knew no borders. As the Prime Minister's adviser on counter-terrorism, he represented a new generation of Israeli operatives. He was born as Amiram Nisker in 1950, after the State of Israel was established, so he did not have the traditional background as a pre-state underground fighter.

Unfortunately for Nir, he did not even have a military background. He served his country's cause as a reporter for the Israel Defence Forces' radio station and lost an eye in a car accident. For a while, he wore a Moshe Dayan-type black eyepatch before a false eye was inserted.

Nir excelled as a journalist and became a well informed defence correspondent for Israeli television. The golden boy also married one of the daughters of the Moses family, the leading newspaper proprietors in the country.

Feeling keenly his lack of military experience in a nation of warriors, Nir volunteered for a one-year hitch in the army and became a lieutenant colonel in a reserve tank battalion. Now satisfied, he turned his career in a new direction and became an aide to Shimon Peres when he was opposition leader.

While researching for his PhD at the strategic studies

centre at Tel Aviv University, he was swept into the Prime Minister's office – as the expert on terrorism – when Peres led the new national unity government which was formed in 1984.

The intelligence community rejected Nir, however. He was an outsider, lacked the right background and espionage men never like journalists, anyway. The secret services were also resentful that Peres ousted veteran spy Rafi Eitan, in favour of Nir. Nir's father-in-law was powerful publisher Noah Moses.

Nir desperately tried to convince the intelligence chiefs that he was a man to be trusted. As a first step, he hoped to acquire Eitan's other hat – as chief of Lakam – not knowing that Eitan was busy running Jonathan Jay Pollard in the US. Nir was also interested in the top job at Shin Bet, once Yosef Harmelin completed his post-scandal interim term, and Nir's long-term ambitions extended to the Mossad as well. First, to be taken seriously, Nir settled into the dark shadows of his current post.

The prime minister's adviser on counter-terrorism was a position created when Golda Meir wanted her own close counsel during the post-Olympics revenge killings of Palestinian terrorists and endorsed a year later in the wake of the 1973 war and the *Mechdal*.

The adviser was to give the prime minister the tools for improved decision-making in the war against terrorism. Nir, with his analytical mind, took easily to coordinating the activities of the intelligence and security agencies and used a terrorist attack in 1985 as the model to prove that his work was needed.

An Arab ship, with Palestinian guerillas aboard, left Yemen. Detecting and tracking a vessel near an Arab country was Aman's responsibility.

When the ship approached Israel's territorial waters, it entered the jurisdiction of the Israeli navy.

The terrorists planned to land on the beach in Tel Aviv. That would be a job for the police.

The attackers then hoped to break their way into the

Kirya and the headquarters of the general staff. It was up to the army to prevent this.

Next to the headquarters is the defence ministry itself, with Yitzhak Rabin on the first floor. The Palestinians planned to take him hostage. Protecting a minister is Shin Bet's business.

Someone in authority had to prevent such an assault from falling between the bureaucratic cracks. In this particular case, the navy stopped the terrorists before they reached the beach, torpedoing the Arab vessel and taking several Palestinian prisoners. Nir showed the intelligence community that his job was vital.

The final proof that he could be a leader among intelligence men was that Nir abandoned his old, talkative habits as a journalist. The media veteran ignored his friends in the media.

When Nir was given the chance to exercise his co-ordination skills in the Iran affair, he sensed a once-in-a-lifetime opportunity to expand his one-man organization into a new, secret intelligence unit. He found a soulmate in Oliver North. North and Nir were both lieutenant colonels, they were both great fans of secrecy and good organization and they got to know each other – by scrambled telephone – when the Israelis assisted the US in tracking the hijacked *Achille Lauro* cruise liner in October 1985.

It was Nir, as counter-terrorism coordinator, who informed the Americans that Israel was intercepting and recording every word spoken by radio between the Palestinian hijackers and their PLO controller, Abul Abbas, on shore in Egypt. Aman chief Ehud Barak, whose agency intercepted the conversations, went on American television – targeting the US audience, even before talking to Israeli TV – to play some of the tapes on a small recorder held in his hand.

Now, with the backing of the 'Prime Minister's club', Peres, Shamir and Rabin, Nir felt he could start laying plans with North for an around-the-world crusade against international terrorism. His first assignment, in December 1985, was to revive the Iran affair.

Nir had little trouble gaining the confidence of the White House – North being his biggest booster in Washington. Elbowing his way into the Iranians' hearts required stunts, such as a meeting in a London casino which had two objects: to prove that the three musketeers were ousted from the scene and to impress the Iranians that he was now Peres's man.

Nir originally planned to use his leader's visit to see Prime Minister Mrs Thatcher in January 1986 as an opportunity to introduce Peres himself to North and Ghorbanifar. The Iranian, however, leaked word of the plan to his old buddy Nimrodi. Nimrodi informed Schwimmer, who immediately flew from Tel Aviv to London to confront Peres and demanded to know why they had been sacked in favour of Nir. The Prime Minister denied there was to be any such meeting and he did not meet Ghorbanifar.

To demonstrate his close relationship with Israel's leader, Nir instead tricked a senior Peres aide, Colonel Azriel Nevo, into accompanying him to the casino. There, he showed Ghorbanifar the photograph in that day's newspaper which showed Nevo standing alongside Peres. If Peres was with Nevo, and Nevo was now with Nir, it stood to reason that Nir was the Prime Minister's personal delegate.

North was there, too, confirming that Ledeen – in an American parallel of the Israeli manipulations – had been ousted. If Nimrodi and company had been out to out-Mossad the Mossad, Nir had just out-Nimrodi'd Nimrodi.

Nir also managed to persuade the White House to renew the arms deliveries to Teheran. He even joined McFarlane, North and a team of American intelligence men – all on false Irish passports – on a secret visit to Teheran in May for talks that were not only fruitless, but completely ridiculous. Trying to rescue US hostages, they all could have been taken hostage by Revolutionary Guards. Nir and the Americans were tempting fate, in the lion's den.

Two more hostages, Father Lawrence Jenco and David Jacobsen, were freed by Iran's allies in Lebanon. Even as they were received in America and at the White House with all of Reagan's favourite hoopla, the seeds of failure planted in Teheran were yielding fruit. The story of the McFarlane-Nir trip was leaked to the world press, by domestic foes of the Iranians who had spoken to 'the Great Satan' – killing the arms for hostages deal in November 1986.

As a scandal, it was not dead. The secret and illegal actions of McFarlane, North and the NSC were unravelled in public and the trail led directly back to the Oval Office. The American press and public demanded to know about President Reagan's involvement. Did he authorize trading arms for hostages? Did he permit North to violate the Congressional ban on aid to the Contras, by using Israeli arms dealers and their Swiss bank accounts to divert the profits made out of the Iranians? The media and official investigators could only find that Reagan had delegated responsibility to a host of aides, who were forced to resign.

One man who survived all the questions, the probe by Senator John Tower's commission and the Congressional hearings was Vice President George Bush. Refusing to reveal what he had known, thought, felt or done during the Iran affair, Bush was elected President in November 1988.

The only person who could perhaps have buried Bush politically died in a plane crash three weeks after the election. Amiram Nir perished, just short of his 38th birthday, in a small Cessna T-210 bound for Mexico City from a tiny airport in Uruapan. It crashed in bad weather 110 miles west of the capital.

Two and a half years earlier, in the plush and traditional surroundings of the King David Hotel in Jerusalem, Nir had met Bush and had given him a briefing on the ongoing deal with Iran. The new President would never talk about it.

The chaos of Irangate ruined Nir's career. He remained in the Prime Minister's office for some eighteen months, but as an embarrassment, not assigned any real duties. Upon resigning in the spring of 1988, he moved to London with the total silence which had become his adopted trademark. No one knew the precise nature of his work, though there are hints that he might have been preparing his cover for a new espionage mission.

The Mexican police said the Israeli, whose body they found, hired the Cessna under the name 'Pat Weber'. It was Nir, but the only explanation offered for his presence in Mexico was a sudden interest in avocados.[7]

Amiram Nir took to his grave, in Israel, the remaining secrets of Irangate.[8]

Business at All Costs

'When we demonstrated our Galil rifle in the Philippines,' said an Israeli arms dealer at the end of the summer of 1982, 'we brought over the rifle's designer. First, he dropped it in a tank of water. Then he rubbed it in the dirt. Then he started firing it. The Filipinos were greatly impressed.'[1]

They did not, however, buy any of the guns – standard army issue and Israeli-made, based on an earlier Soviet Kalashnikov. The buyers could not overcome the reluctance they felt to deal with Israel, target of a concerted Arab campaign to brand the Jewish state a 'pariah state'. The Galil is only one of the many Israeli weapons which are considered among the best in the world, but the drive for foreign sales often runs into political brick walls as it did in the Philippines.

Israel is therefore forced to search actively for lucrative markets and to sell its military hardware to regimes with dubious reputations, such as South Africa, Iran and dictatorships in Latin America.

The sale of arms is considered by Israel to be a vital national interest. It is not only a source of foreign currency and a useful means of projecting influence overseas. Israel believes that to have its own defence industry – which it is convinced it requires, so as not to be dependent on the kindness of other nations – it must achieve economies of scale. The Israeli arms industry must manufacture far more guns, bullets, shells, tanks, missile boats and more sophisticated equipment than Israel itself can use. Foreign sales cover the price of research and development and the costs of having a military industry can be met by revenues from abroad.

It is no wonder, then, that the intelligence community is involved in protecting this vital interest by promoting the products. Mossad men, when abroad on missions as unofficial ambassadors, and Shin Bet operatives, acting as clandestine counter-terrorism advisers, spread the word about the excellence of Israeli products. The guns and other material became part of a package deal: good advice from the Israelis went hand-in-hand with battle-proved weapons.

This is a relatively new phenomenon, which began after the 1973 war. Until then, Israel's arms exports amounted to about $50 million a year. In the first stage, the sales were handled directly by Sibat, a Hebrew acronym for *Siyua Bitchoni*, Security Assistance, a small department in the defence ministry in Tel Aviv.

When selling to countries which were especially anxious to conceal their business links with Israel, Sibat made sure that the source was kept secret. This was not pure intelligence work, and Sibat's director did not take part in *Va'adat* committee meetings, but he was usually a retired senior military officer whose recommendations carried great weight in the alternative diplomacy practised by Israel's intelligence community.

Secrecy was relatively easy to maintain when official state agencies were both vendor and customer, such as when old Skyhawk jets from the Israeli air force were sold to

Indonesia, a Moslem nation which was overtly hostile to the Jewish state.[2] Sibat occasionally employed middlemen, mainly for the purpose of concealing Israeli involvement in a transaction.

A few years later, as military exports expanded, a second phase began. Israeli middlemen started to take the initiative, actively knocking on doors and opening them for Sibat and the growing military-industrial complex. These were the golden years for Yaakov Nimrodi, as an Israeli sales agent during his Iran days. When the Iranian market was shut down by Ayatollah Khomeini's takeover in 1979, Israel was anxious to find another buyer for its products and it discovered China. The explorer who made it possible was Shaul Eisenberg.

Israel's wealthiest businessman, Eisenberg was born in Europe and found refuge during World War II in the Far East. He settled in Japan where he married a Japanese woman and made his fortune selling war surplus and scrap metal.

Eisenberg quickly established himself as one of the leading middlemen in the region. He never lost his awareness of being a Jew, however, and his emotional ties led him to set up businesses in Israel and then to move his family there. He also retained his interests in the Far East and in the late 1970s was able to pave the way to Beijing for Israeli military exports.

His most formidable tool was his private jet, on which he could ignore the official hostility and fly high-level Israelis directly to China. Eisenberg made dozens of trips, carrying Sibat officials, army advisers, financiers and military salesmen for what the Israelis described as their 'toughest negotiations ever'.

After making a solid, initial contact, Eisenberg would leave the coordinating role to the Mossad, which acted in its traditional role as Israel's secret, alternative foreign ministry. He would later send his bill, for a hefty commission, to Sibat and the Israeli defence contractors who would actually make the sale.

Israeli defence exports to China in the 1980s were esti-
mated to total nearly three billion dollars for the entire
decade.[3]

Within fifteen years, Israel's arms exports grew, although
the figures are not published officially, to over one and
a half billion dollars a year.[4] With the mushrooming exports, the Israeli arms industry reached its third stage.
Israeli middlemen started not just knocking on doors, but
actively pulling and dragging their government into
doorways which they claimed to have opened. There was
an abrupt change: the middlemen were attempting to
dictate Israeli foreign policy, based on their own financial
expectations.

Israel has an entirely new class of Mossad, Shin Bet and
senior army veterans working to persuade their own country
to sell while convincing foreigners to buy. These former
intelligence and military men are part of a social network –
which can be called the 'formers' – as self-centred and
protective of its members as any élite in the world. Their
family backgrounds, education and lifestyles might vary,
but they have one desire in common: to do business at all
costs.

The environment was right in many ways for these
men to put profit before everything else. Israeli society
had undergone a transformation during the 1970s and
1980s. In part, there was the fatigue brought about by
war after war. The idealism and pioneering spirit of
Israel's first quarter-century had largely given way to self-
interest and materialism. In the early days, people were
ashamed to discuss money and it was considered 'coarse' to
concentrate on making it. It was thought 'rude' to profit
from business deals, especially when they involved national
interests.

In today's Israel, however, making money has become a
Golden Calf, before which most of the society – including
its mirror image in intelligence and military circles – kneels.

The 'formers' find that their careers end early and their
pensions approximate the civil service average of $12,000 a

year. They feel they have few marketable talents, after working even harder than their international counterparts, and they particularly envy CIA agents for their fat salaries and generous pensions. They tend to forget that the same comparison could be made for any profession in low-wage Israel.

As soon as they leave their intelligence or army work and sometimes while they are still employed by the state, many individuals make connections which they will find useful for making a living – often a very nice living – in private life.

Some are genuine heroes. Others will leave you with that impression, and who can check with their former employers? They exploit the reputation which the Israelis have built up in counter-terrorism, military expertise, airline and office security and personal protection.

Countries such as Iran, when it was at war with Iraq, or some of the South American juntas became utterly convinced that Israel could provide them with anything and everything. Israel sold complete weapons systems to South Africa and licensed companies there to manufacture the Israeli-designed Kfir fighter jet as the renamed 'Cheetah', Reshef missile boats, and sea-to-sea Gabriel missiles under the new label 'Scorpion'.

Ostensibly private Israeli arms dealers have occasionally been used by their government to sidestep political barriers – even when they are raised by Israel's chief benefactor, the United States. Although forbidden by Washington, Israel permitted a former official dealer, Norman Shkolnick, to negotiate the sale of a dozen American-made Skyhawk bombers to Argentina's navy. This was in the Spring of 1982, just as Great Britain sent its naval task force to recapture the Falkland Islands. The Reagan administration clamped an arms embargo on the Argentines and sternly told the Israelis to stop the Shkolnick deal. The sale of the aircraft was cancelled, but US officials have remained deeply suspicious of both Sibat and 'private' Israeli merchants.

On the other hand, some of the private brokers who

happen to come from Israel are only bluffing when they suggest that they represent their government. It was just that impression of omnipotence that Brigadier General Avraham Bar-Am tried to convey.

Bar-Am, a thirty-year army veteran in the infantry and armoured brigades, left the army in 1978. He had been disciplined for having provided guns to alleged Israeli under-world figures. As an unemployed veteran, he looked around him and saw how well a number of his good friends were doing in private business.

Former senior officers of the air force, including its com-mander in the 1973 war, Major General Mordecai Hod, had set up agencies which represented large Israeli suppliers and giant American manufacturers. The officers, who had dealt with these corporations during their military careers, con-tinued to maintain these ties after leaving the military and entering civilian life. Bar-Am was especially impressed with the wealth amassed by Nimrodi in Iran and figured that he could do the same.

Along with about 1,000 other retired senior officers, Bar-Am applied for, and was issued, an apparently routine defence ministry document authorizing the holder to go forth and prospect for sales of Israeli arms. The permit, however, specifically bans participation in actual nego-tiations.

At the end of April 1986, General Bar-Am, two other Israeli businessmen and fourteen other men, were arrested by American customs officers. All were the victims of a four-month sting operation, in which Iranian arms dealer Cyrus Hashemi – who had visited Israel the previous year, in the first act of the Irangate drama – was a United States government informant. All seventeen defendants were in-dicted in New York for involvement in an alleged conspiracy to sell Phantom fighter planes, tanks, missiles and an array of other sophisticated weapons to the Iranians.

The shopping list was sheer megalomania, and it is diffi-cult to believe that Bar-Am and his colleagues would have been able to obtain so much to sell to Iran. Hashemi, however, had been in Israel with Nimrodi, had even met CIA director William Casey on his own in 1985 to suggest a huge arms for hostages deal, and was able to persuade Bar-Am that the entire package would be welcomed by all governments concerned.

Hashemi's true motives were blurred, once the customs service used him to frame Bar-Am and the others. Even the White House was left confused. In a discussion with President Reagan in November 1986, his closest advisers wondered whether Israel had an official role in the Bar-Am arms-dealing ring.

Vice President George Bush asked, at that meeting: 'Is that a case of private or public endeavour to sell arms for Israel?'

One of the aides, not identified in official White House notes, replied: 'Probably private with government knowledge.'

Bush felt that the arrests could lead to further problems. 'Israel may try to squeeze us,' he said.[5]

The Israeli Government emphatically denied that it was involved in the alleged scheme, but Bar-Am phoned the Israeli military attaché in Washington after his arrest and insisted that friends in the Mossad had checked out the participants in the arms deal.[6]

By 1988, amid the embarrassment of Irangate and the revelation of US weapons sales to the ayatollahs, the American authorities dropped their criminal charges against Bar-Am. He was one of those defence and intelligence veterans who, while perfectly patriotic when in official service, ignored Israel's interests once their income depended on supply and demand market realities. When an opportunity arose to sell some jeeps, rifles, ammunition, mortars, spare parts and other 'small junk' which Israel did not want anyway, the privateers had few hesitations. They did not even check whether Jerusalem might object.

Sibat claimed in 1989 that it was tightening up its system of oversight, now requiring anyone selling Israeli military equipment to apply for permission regarding every nut, bolt and bullet. Many of the privateers seem undeterred, however. In the world of covert operations, all these former operatives had had drilled into them that many missions are not worthwhile because of the damage which might result from exposure. When they become private business-men, they hardly seem to care about such niceties. But when they make mistakes, the Jewish state is invariably blamed.

Worse still, some of the intelligence veterans come to believe that everything they might do automatically becomes Israel's national interest. The self-righteousness has at times been stunning and the grey areas are blinding. Do they lobby for a particular political step because it would be good for Israel? Or is that just an excuse, when their only concern is the good of their bank balances?

Israel occasionally ends up involved with some of the ugliest regimes in the world. A private intelligence veteran might find some opportunity, say, in an African dictatorship such as Idi Amin's Uganda or Mobutu's Zaire, and before long other former operatives and army veterans are training the security services of these countries. The defence ministry in Tel Aviv generally applauds the profitable export deals initiated by the 'formers'. Word leaks out through diplomats and journalists. Inevitably, Israel's unfortunate image as a pariah state in league with other international untouchables is reinforced.

Mike Harari also had friends in high places and his actions, too, added no lustre to Israel's name. Harari, the son of a customs official, was born in Tel Aviv in 1927. His career was similar to that of many of his generation in Israeli intelligence. He served in the Palmach and Shai and when the state was proclaimed he joined its intelligence com-munity.

His Shin Bet job in the 1950s was as security officer in the foreign ministry and he then spent the next twenty years in the anonymity of the Mossad. He was always a field operat-ive on special missions, with a reputation for extreme thoroughness. In 1972 and 1973, he was in charge of the assassination squads hunting Palestinian terrorists in Western Europe, until the Lillehammer fiasco. Only Harari, his girlfriend Tamar who served as his female assistant, and the two gunmen managed to escape from Norway. The other members of the hit team were arrested.

Harari returned to Tel Aviv and continued to work for the Mossad for a number of years, even though he was implicated in the most serious blunder in the history of Israel's secret services up until that time. In Israel of the 1970s, no one dared to voice public criticism of the intelligence community, or to demand a public inquiry or dismissals. Harari eventually left the Mossad in 1978, when he launched a new career as an insurance man.

Two years later, Harari moved his base of operations to Central America and befriended General Omar Torrijos, the strong man of Panama, who took an instant liking to the strong man from Israel. When Torrijos died in a mysterious plane crash late in 1980, General Manuel Noriega inherited both the country and the friendship with Harari.

Harari, quietly but surely, became the indispensable right-hand man to Noriega, a former secret services chief who appreciated Harari's special talents. His greatest achievement, which is testimony to his manipulative ability, was to persuade the general to dismiss Shaul Eisenberg from the post of honorary Panamanian consul in Israel. Harari took the honour for himself.

He sent Israeli bodyguards to Panama and also trained local men to protect General Noriega, whose mansion in Panama City benefited from the classic Israeli perimeter security of barbed wire and electronic sensors. Through Harari, Israel also sold light arms to the Panamanian civil guard. Before long, all commercial deals between Israel and Panama, not only weapons, began to go through Harari's hands. His profit lay in the commissions.

Harari was self-contained and seemingly immune to having his name appear in the press. Only twice was his photograph published in Israeli newspapers, when he ac-

companied General Noriega on an official visit to Israel in
1985. A third attempt to photograph him failed. That was
in June 1988 at a large garden party in Savyon to honour a
professor on the publication of his new book.

As Harari feasted at the party, a young photographer
from one of the Israeli dailies steadied her camera for a shot.
Harari recoiled. He then strolled over to the photographer
and politely demanded that she hand over her exposed film.
He promised to develop all the prints and return them to
her within a day or two – except for the picture she had
taken of him.

When she refused, Harari grabbed the camera from her,
pulled out the film and burned it before the astounded eyes
of hundreds of guests. 'No one dares to photograph Mike
Harari,' he declared and continued to mingle as if nothing
had happened.

The line between national interest and personal riches
became blurred, with huge sums of money floating around
and ready to be plucked. In the United States, after Noriega
was indicted for alleged drug smuggling in 1988, officials
whispered about the mysterious Israeli who helped to protect the general.

Harari had, at times, done Israeli intelligence some
favours during his years in Panama, but he eventually became more of a liability than an asset. Did Harari represent
the State of Israel? 'He is a private party,' the foreign ministry in Jerusalem replied. But his past in the Mossad, even
if the Mossad itself cut off contacts with Harari, always
raised the suspicion that he was still an Israeli agent in the
Americas.[7]

Pessach Ben-Or, too, would be constantly regarded as an
'Israeli agent', even if he was just a young former sergeant
who represented another type of Israeli arms merchant.
Ben-Or did not have an illustrious military past or the
old 'formers' ties with the political and defence establishment.

Born in Lod in 1948 as Pessach Spiegler, he was an
ambitious lad from his earliest days. After he completed his

compulsory army service, he joined his father as an employee at Israel Aircraft Industries. There he met Marcus Katz, a Jewish arms dealer and middleman from Mexico who represented IAI in Latin America.

Spiegler-Ben-Or moved to Mexico as chauffeur and body-guard to Katz. Soon, the young Israeli had learned all the tricks of the arms trade. Ben-Or waited for the right opportunity and it came in 1980 when the United States imposed an arms embargo against Guatemala. That country's regime was also locked in a dispute with Katz, so Ben-Or made his move, elbowing his employer aside to fill the vacuum and become chief arms supplier to one of the most notorious juntas in the region. By selling to a government brutally suppressing human rights, he became a millionaire.[8]

Ben-Or purchased a luxurious home, secured like a fortress, in a suburban area in central Israel and invested his money in restaurants. His name was mentioned in connection with various shady arms transactions in Latin America, including the sale of weapons to the Nicaraguan Contras.[9]

Above all, Ben-Or, Harari, Bar-Am, Nimrodi and many others became symbols of 'the ugly Israeli'.

Israelis seem to be making secret deals everywhere. A visitor to one of the privateer 'formers' in Europe is likely to be met by the bizarre sight of a wealthy Saudi or other Arab sitting comfortably, drinking, laughing and doing business with Israelis.

The privateers are also to be found in Africa, Asia and Latin America, pursuing their own policies in the twilight zone between the legal and the banned. Some of them remain in touch with intelligence agencies and regularly send reports to Tel Aviv on their activities and what they have observed in far-flung foreign parts.

The authorities in Israel make no efforts to rein in their former operatives and soldiers. The damage they have done, however, is tremendous. They give Israel, its armed forces and its intelligence community a bad name. Almost every

nasty or mysterious act in the world is blamed by the press
and even by foreign government ministers on the Israeli
secret services.

In courts around the world, 'Israeli intelligence' or 'Mossad' was put forward as a defence, as though all would be
forgiven by judges if they believed a criminal had been
working for Israel. The reputation of Israel's intelligence
community had sunk sufficiently low to be dragged through
the mud by gun-runners, drug dealers and kidnappers in
courtrooms from the Caribbean islands to the capital cities
of Europe.

On July 5, 1984, the obvious nervousness of the Nigerian
shipping clerks at Stansted airport, northeast of London,
alerted the British customs officers. They were familiar with
the faces of the Nigerian Airways crew and the usual type
of diplomatic bags sent home by the Nigerian embassy in
London. This time, the customs men were confronted with
two large wooden crates. And one of them smelled, somehow, like a hospital ward.

They asked what was inside and the Nigerians refused to
say, hiding immediately behind their diplomatic immunity.
Undeterred, the British officers grabbed a hammer and
crowbars and prised open the boxes.

In one sat two white men, looking hot and guilty, who
did not put up a struggle when they were arrested by
the Essex police. In the other crate, a white man who
immediately shouted 'I'm a doctor!' had an intravenous drip
running into a black man, in a business suit, unconscious
and rolled into a ball at the bottom of the box.

That was the first episode in what would become known
as the Dikko affair. Umaru Dikko was a former senior
minister in the government of Nigeria, topping the
'most wanted' list there after a military coup. The Lagos
regime said he had fled to London with millions of dollars
in public funds. The Nigerians wanted him for a show
trial and they found three Israelis to do the dirty work for
them.

Alexander Barak was the brain and he and his assistant

Felix Abutbul – sharing a crate that day – came from similar backgrounds on the criminal edge of Netanya, Israel. After they left the country in the early 1980s, their precise where-abouts were difficult to trace.

The third man was Dr Lev Shapira, a Soviet-born emi-grant to Israel with an excellent reputation as an anaesthetist in a small hospital near Tel Aviv. He was in the crate with Dikko and had drugged him.

After their arrest, the three Israelis lodged the by now common claim that they had done it for Israel. Their English lawyers said the Mossad had issued the orders. Israel's government denied it completely.

Even after they were sentenced to prison terms ranging from ten to fourteen years, a cloud of mystery lingered over the Dikko affair. Few facts were definitely established: the Nigerian Security Organization, acting out of its embassy in London, ran the operation. The Nigerians committed amateurish errors, such as introducing their ambassador to the kidnap team. The three Israelis, however, were quite professional and efficient, as were two others who fled from Britain after grabbing Dikko outside his home and stuffing him into a van.

Some links were found with Jewish and Israeli business-men who had lost heavy investments in Nigeria after the *coup d'état*. For whom were the five Israeli kidnappers work-ing? For the businessmen? For Nigerian intelligence? For the Mossad? For the Israeli foreign ministry? For a combi-nation of them? One thing is certain: if the operation had been successful and the crate containing Dikko had not been opened until it arrived in Lagos, the Nigerian Government would have owed a huge debt of thanks to someone in Israel – either to the five kidnappers, or to a higher power behind them.[10]

Possibly worse than the damage to Israel's image, there is reason to fear that Israel's essential interests and secrets are being leaked abroad and are even reaching its enemies.

Perhaps Israel was unable to avoid the security breach in the case of Ulrich Wegener, a West German police officer who had established his nation's special counter-terrorism unit, GSG-9. He and his men gained instant fame when, on October 17, 1979, they used stun grenades and machine pistols to assault a hijacked Lufthansa airliner on the ground at Mogadishu, Somalia – liberating ninety passengers and crew, killing three hijackers and wounding one in a mixed team of German and Arab terrorists. The Germans were using the tactics pioneered by the *sayeret* commando units of Israel in the Sabena hijack of 1972.

No wonder. Wegener learned his craft from the same teachers. He was trained in hostage-rescue techniques in Israel. In June 1988, however, Wegener took these professional secrets to Saudi Arabia, when he went there to train special forces.[11]

Israel could not stop the German from going to the Saudis, still officially at war with the Jewish state. But what should it do when its own security men, such as Danny Yissacharov and Yitzhak Yefet, sell the know-how which they acquired while working for the state?

Yissacharov was a senior officer in charge of security for El Al, the Israeli airline. After he left the agency, he joined a number of other intelligence community 'formers' to set up their own company offering consultant services in the field of security and anti-terrorism. Do you want to protect your office? Your mansion? Your airport? Call the Israelis. Yissacharov and his colleagues gained some lucrative contracts and what he used to do for El Al he now did for American airlines.

Yefet was chief security officer of El Al, but after taking early retirement he ran a worldwide security-consultancy empire from a luxury flat in New Jersey, overlooking the Hudson River and New York City. Yissacharov, Yefet and dozens of other 'formers' are disliked by their ex-employers but generally laugh all the way to the bank.[12]

If at one time the kibbutznik in the shorts and simple hat of a happy worker in the fields was the symbol of the young Israel, emblazoned on all its early exports, the new symbols for Israel in the international community were the arms merchants and other 'formers'.

The leaking of secrets, the flood of information and the presence of hundreds of Israeli freelancers throughout all five continents were part of a general deterioration of standards and values in Israeli society. The low point came with the emergence of a traitor from the most secret depths of the Jewish state.

15

The Nuclear Traitor

The wiry and prematurely bald man was walking through London's Leicester Square, taking in the neon lights and bright signs of the many cinemas. It was Wednesday, September 24, 1986, and the next week he expected to shake the world.

Mordecai Vanunu had worked for nearly ten years as a technician in the top secret nuclear installation at Dimona, in the Negev desert. He knew that it was a bomb factory, that Israel had amassed a formidable arsenal of nuclear weapons. Vanunu had told one of Britain's newspapers and soon everyone would know. He wondered, looking at the crowds of people milling around the square, if their lives would be the same after hearing the frightening truth that the next Middle East war could lead to the end of the world.

Around the edges of the square, outside one of the discotheques, he noticed a tall, somewhat heavy-set and thick-lipped blonde. Mordecai looked at her and she glanced back. He had been lately lacking in female companionship, so he took an immediate interest and the first step.

Vanunu, who was 32 and unmarried, introduced himself as 'Mordy'. That was what his friends in Australia had called him, but at home in Israel, he said, he was Mordecai. She said she was Cindy, an American travelling alone in this age of the liberated woman. Talking and walking with her was by far the best pastime Vanunu had on offer that evening.

Vanunu thought that having responded favourably to his initial advance, she might be interested in sex. But the subject did not come up and as they parted that night, Vanunu gave her the telephone number of his hotel and they promised to see each other again soon.

Vanunu was born in Morocco in 1954, the second among seven children in a Jewish family who moved from Marrakesh to Israel in the early 1960s when the Mossad arranged clandestine emigration. The family settled in a slum neighbourhood of Beersheba, a place with a history dating back to the biblical days of Abraham, but now a dusty town in the middle of the desert. Vanunu's father Salumon struggled to make ends meet, selling religious and sacramental implements in the Beersheba market, where the mixed population of Jews and Bedouin Arabs mingled in commerce and conversation.

Vanunu served in the Israeli army, where he was a corporal and a mediocre member of the engineering corps. He then flunked out of a first-year physics course at Tel Aviv University. At age 21, he saw a newspaper advertisement for 'trainee technicians', and he applied to Kamag, the acronym for *Kirya le-Mechkar Gar'ini*, the Nuclear Research Centre in Dimona.

He was first interviewed by the centre's security officers, who worked closely with Shin Bet to screen applicants. They questioned him about drug or alcohol abuse, any crime he may have committed and about his political preferences. He went on the payroll in November 1976 and the Dimona centre sent him on accelerated courses in physics, chemistry, mathematics and English.

He passed an exam two months later, as did thirty-nine out of the forty-five other candidates, and in early February 1977 he took the official Volvo bus – which daily transported employees to their secret jobs – from Beersheba to the Dimona complex for the first time. In a classroom building within the high-security gates, Vanunu was required to sign a pledge not to reveal any secrets, under a law which specified a prison term of fifteen years for telling anyone – even his fellow employees – about his duties in Dimona.

There was another short course in nuclear physics and chemistry, including lessons on the plutonium and uranium with which the new recruits would be working. Vanunu and the other newcomers went through medical check-ups, received security passes and then were given ten weeks to become acquainted with the facility and its routine before starting work.

Vanunu quickly learned that he was now a special member of society, even if he would never be permitted to tell why. Like other Israeli men, Vanunu was called to the army for a month's reserve duty, but was immediately sent home when his unit was informed that he was now employed in an unspecified, but sensitive, defence project.

There was one more oral test to be passed at the Dimona compound, before a panel of three examiners, and finally he reported on August 7, 1977, for his full shift. He was a *menahel mishmeret*, or shift manager, between 11.30 pm and eight in the morning.[1]

Vanunu could have remained in the darkness, diligently toiling deep in the bowels of the Dimona complex, as do all the other anonymous workers. Sudden changes in his personality, however, put him on a different track. The first was when he tore himself away from his religious upbringing: the product of an Orthodox home, Vanunu became completely secular and cut all links with his family.

The second and most dramatic change occurred after the bloody Israeli invasion of Lebanon in 1982. Although he had once been like the other Moroccan immigrants – a nationalistic Zionist who believed in Menachem Begin and his Likud and in depriving Arabs of their rights where necessary – Vanunu had a political reawakening and his ideology turned radically in the other direction.

He became increasingly involved with radical circles on the fringes of Beersheba University. He enrolled in the philosophy department and befriended Arab students. Vanunu even applied for membership in the Israeli Communist Party, although he left the application form blank where it enquired about his employment.

He joined the vociferous campaign for the freedom of one of his teachers who had been jailed for refusing to serve in the army in occupied Arab lands. 'But even among us, the left-wingers on campus, he was exceptional,' recalled Dr Ze'ev Tzahor, political activist and history lecturer at Beersheba University. 'He radiated a deep sense of deprivation.'

Vanunu also turned out to be a notorious eccentric. College chums photographed him doing a musical striptease at a campus party. He became a nude model for art students. More seriously, he held picket signs along with Palestinian students in various protests. The university newspaper quoted Vanunu as saying: 'Stop oppressing the Arabs.'[2]

All these extracurricular activities should have caught the eye of Shin Bet agents, who track groups which they consider subversive. If the right and left hands of the security agency had known what each other were doing, Vanunu would have to have been judged a terrible candidate for clandestine defence-related work. For months, however, nothing happened. Vanunu kept riding the Volvo bus to Dimona and his work continued as normal.

By late 1985, security officers at Dimona learned that one of their employees – instructed to be silent, or at least unobtrusive – was making a public, anti-establishment spectacle of himself. Vanunu was warned to stop. When he continued on his unorthodox path, the nuclear authorities decided to fire him. To avoid public fuss or scandal, they did not officially brand him as a security risk. They paid Vanunu his severance pay and sacked him along with 180 other workers in a cost-cutting move in November 1985.

Within a month, Vanunu sold his old car and his small apartment and, like many other young Israelis, he set out on a long journey to the Far East. Unlike the others, who usually return after a few adventurous months in the exotic Orient, Vanunu found himself on a soul-searching excursion which led to the third change in his life.

He arrived in Sydney, Australia, in May 1986, and one Friday evening – ironically, the Jewish Sabbath – he drifted towards the lights and open doors of St George's Anglican Church. The Reverend John McKnight was there and recalls: 'Mordy came in, he looked around, talked to me and we became friends.'[3]

Two months later, Vanunu made the final break away from his boyhood and background: he converted to Christianity. It was a total divorce from the Jewish state.

Almost like a refusal to return the wedding ring, however, Vanunu held a tiny bit of his past in his pocket. He had never told anyone about this, but after becoming friends with an odd Colombian named Oscar Guerrero, Vanunu's secret was irretrievably out. Guerrero was a hyperactive freelance journalist who, due to unemployment, had put away his pen and notebook in favour of a painter's brush. Guerrero was painting the church fence when Vanunu met him. After several weeks of friendship, the Israeli revealed his secret.

He told Guerrero that he had been carrying two rolls of colour film since he had left Israel and was unsure of what to do with them. Guerrero could scarcely believe it when Vanunu said they were photographs he had covertly snapped inside the Dimona nuclear centre during his night shifts.

The Colombian, propelled into profit-seeking enthusiasm by his freelance instincts, did not bother to ask Vanunu how he had smuggled a camera into Dimona – or his films out of Israel – but instead marvelled at Vanunu as a chicken about to lay golden eggs.

Guerrero persuaded the Israeli that his story could be

sold – and for enough money to last a lifetime. The idea appealed to Vanunu, once he finished wrestling with his conscience, as he had reached the conclusion that Israel's secret nuclear project was immoral and should be revealed.

Guerrero appointed himself as Vanunu's 'literary agent' and together they contacted several international publications to offer a sensational scoop. But wherever they told their story, no one wanted to believe that Vanunu was a former employee of the most secret installation of the Jewish state. His tale was rejected by *Newsweek* magazine and even by local Australian newspapers, until the British *Sunday Times* decided to give him a try.

The free-spending newspaper, owned by the Australian-born press magnate Rupert Murdoch, sent investigative reporter Peter Hounam to Sydney to meet the Israeli and assess his fantastic tale. Vanunu and Guerrero suddenly found themselves lavishly treated in the city's finest restaurants, answering endless strings of questions until Hounam reached his verdict.

They especially impressed Hounam, who had a degree in physics, by showing him the photographs, which they had processed at an ordinary sixty-minute developing lab. The British journalist decided that it was worth bringing Vanunu to Britain for further inquiries. Hounam offered $75,000 for the exclusive rights to the story and the photos, including the eventual publication of a book.

But *The Sunday Times*, like any other business-minded publisher, wanted to cut out the middleman. It did not like either Guerrero's style or his credibility, so he was dropped.

On September 11, 1986, Mordy's friends brought him to Sydney airport and he promised them he would return within three weeks. Hounam and Vanunu landed in London the next day, not knowing that Guerrero – displaying an almost wild journalistic frenzy – followed them on a separate flight. None of them knew that two Mossad men were also following.

A few weeks earlier, the Mossad had received a message from its counterpart, the Australian Secret Intelligence

Organization. The ASIO sent a brief file about an Israeli who was engaged in a peculiar form of solicitation: trying to seduce the news media into buying a 'secret' story. The ASIO thought the Mossad might like to know. When it learned that Vanunu was heading to London, the Australian agency also told Britain's MI5.

Israeli intelligence officials now knew that they had a problem and would have to take swift action. Two Shin Bet agents visited Vanunu's brother Albert at his carpentry workshop and asked him whether he had heard from Mordecai. Without telling Albert why, one of the agents said: 'If you get a letter from your brother, bring it to us.'

The Sunday Times editors may not have been aware they were under surveillance, but they must have known they were holding a live bomb in their hands: an Israeli traitor with a story never told before.

Vanunu provided more than sixty photographs he had taken inside the grounds of the Dimona compound and more spectacularly, inside one of the buildings, which he named as Machon 2. *Machon* is a word for institute or facility which suggests a place of learning or a production centre.

Vanunu said he was one of only 150, out of a total of 2,700 Dimona employees, with security clearance for Machon 2, which he revealed to be an underground bomb factory – pure and simple. Beneath the surface of the desert, he disclosed, Israeli scientists and technicians extracted plutonium from uranium fuel rods after their use in the silver-domed nuclear reactor above. The plutonium, Vanunu said, was used to make bombs.

The world had long assumed that the reactor, occasionally photographed from a distance by foreign military attachés and journalists defying press censorship, was secretly used to produce a few, simple atomic bombs. Vanunu's photos, taken inside, offered close-up views of the famous dome and the first evidence suggesting Israel was manufacturing advanced, thermonuclear weapons, probably including neutron or hydrogen bombs – compact, but incredibly powerful.

Vanunu offered a detailed sketch of six hitherto unknown, below-ground levels of Machon 2. The building appeared above ground to be a two-storey, little used, unimportant warehouse. It was actually, he said, the key to Israel's development of nuclear weapons.

As a roving photographer, his camera recorded a tour of the corridors, laboratories, storage rooms and control panels. Above one set of dials, screens and meters was a neat Hebrew sign identifying one Yehida 95, or 'Unit 95'. Vanunu told the British reporters what many of the units did in the process of separating plutonium. The photos showed 'radioactivity!' warning signs in Hebrew and chambers where large rubber gloves built into the thick glass walls were used to handle the contents. Some also showed metal spheres, which Vanunu said were models of bombs.

Vanunu said the only outsiders who ever visited were senior military men, defence ministry officials, and Israel's prime ministers. One inspection point was known within Dimona as 'Golda's Balcony' after Israel's woman Prime Minister stood there and saw the 'production hall' below.

Everything which Vanunu had heard, while chatting with older colleagues who had worked at the nuclear facility for years, accorded with reports that France had built Dimona for the Israelis. The French had dug the pit which contained most of Machon 2 and they installed the bomb-making equipment.

The facts and figures he gave also indicated that the 26-megawatt reactor provided by the French in the late 1950s had been substantially upgraded by the Israelis – apparently to 150 megawatts. Vanunu's information supported the suspicions by foreign governments and their intelligence agencies, echoed in the world's media, that Israel had far more nuclear capacity than it admitted. The facility had been fed by the extra uranium obtained from Zalman Shapiro's Numec and from the ship-switching 'Plumbat' ruse in 1968.

The experts and physicists enlisted by *The Sunday Times* studied the pictures, spoke with Vanunu and considered the 'flow rates, measures, temperatures and other scientific data' he had memorized. Their conclusion was that Israel could easily have made at least 100 bombs during his decade in Machon 2.[4]

The newspaper team was convinced. Vanunu was genuine and his would be a great story. They had not reckoned, however, on the obstructive plans of Guerrero.

Cross at both Vanunu and *The Sunday Times* for abandoning him, the Colombian went to a rival newspaper, the *Sunday Mirror*, with his own, slightly garbled version of the nuclear revelations. The *Sunday Mirror* did not believe in Guerrero at all, but used him and a handful of Vanunu's photographs that he had kept for himself – buying his tale for a few thousand dollars – simply to publish a two-page barb poking fun at *The Sunday Times* for falling for Vanunu and this patent nonsense.[5]

Israel's nuclear potential was being used as a weapon in the war of the Fleet Street press barons, then raging between Murdoch and his arch rival, *Mirror* owner Robert Maxwell.

Vanunu was angry and afraid when he saw the *Sunday Mirror* and his picture alongside the front-page story. He was furious at *The Sunday Times* for hesitating with the real story and he now felt certain that Israeli agents were following him.

To defuse the tension and to protect him, the newspaper had been moving Vanunu from hotel to country house and back again, from the suburbs to the forests and into the centre of town every few days. Now, he was in the Mountbatten Hotel, in London's theatre district, under an assumed name. Only two newspaper staffers knew his location. The journalists tried to calm him, but they also told him that for the sake of good news standards they would need to get an official Israeli reaction before publishing the story the following week. It would, they told him, only make his account more credible.

On September 23, *The Sunday Times* sought a response from the Israeli embassy in London by giving it an outline of the Vanunu story. The embassy issued a denial and also tried to portray Vanunu as a minor technician who would not know anything anyway.

Deep inside, however, Ambassador Yehuda Avner was extremely concerned and so were his superiors in Jerusalem. They were on the verge of panic, realizing for the first time the breadth and scope of what the nuclear traitor had revealed.

Prime Minister Peres, shocked but unable to do much to control information once it leaked beyond Israel's borders, summoned a special meeting of a committee of newspaper editors within the country itself. He begged them to minimize – rather than emphasize – the story, once the British paper published its version. Abandoning pure news judgment for patriotism, as they often do, the editors agreed to cooperate.

The meeting was supposed to be confidential, but word of it reached London. Ironically, Peres's bid to minimize the story was the final push to give it maximum exposure. *The Sunday Times* assumed that his plea to the Israeli editors must mean that the story being prepared in London was truly important. If the Prime Minister was concerned, Vanunu must have revealed genuine secrets – notwithstanding the Israeli embassy's denials.

Peres, at the same time, consulted Rabin and Shamir in the Prime Ministers' club and decided to order the Mossad to arrest Vanunu – wherever he may be – so that he could be tried in Israel. It would be a lesson to the rest of the population that no one could get away with treason.

Peres was well aware, however, of Prime Minister Margaret Thatcher's sensitivity about British sovereignty, so the Mossad was also ordered not to violate British law. He understood what damage the Iron Lady's wrath could wreak on Israeli-British cooperation, which was one of Peres's pet diplomatic projects.

The mission was thus even more difficult than it would otherwise have been. To abduct a man, in a foreign land, was hard enough when he was alert to the danger, was under protection and was being moved among secret locations. The ban on illegality made the assignment almost impossible, as it tied the kidnappers' own hands.

The Mossad knew, however, that it could rely on two elements: the readiness of British intelligence men to co-operate in locating Vanunu – or, at least, to turn a blind eye; and the certainty of finding, in any man, the human frailties which can be exploited.

A team of Mossad men and women was sent to London to search for the nuclear traitor. The Mossad even stationed two men with a professional video camera to look out for Vanunu at the high-security entrance gate of Times Newspapers in Wapping, near the docks of East London. It was a stroke of good fortune that the angry British printers' union had a constant picket line outside Murdoch's publishing fortress. The security guards were already accustomed to seeing many television crews covering the labour protesters for one or another TV news programme. This particular video crew was itself videotaped, *The Sunday Times* camera seeing a six-foot-tall fellow who said he was covering for a student union, with an unshaven partner who said nothing.[6]

The Israelis spotted their man leaving Wapping in a taxi. Other Mossad teams picked up the trail, using cars and motorcycles, and had no trouble following Vanunu to his hotel. It was simple, then, for Israeli agents on foot to follow Vanunu wherever he went in the coming days. When he was walking in Leicester Square one evening, it was the perfect time to send 'Cindy' on stage to play her role.

For Vanunu, she seemed to be a gift from heaven. His *Sunday Times* babysitters had found him to be extremely nervous, perhaps not surprisingly, but this expressed itself in sexual hunger. The Israeli repeatedly and shamelessly propositioned the female members of the reporting team.[7]

Hoping now that his desires would be satisfied, he was anxious to see the American blonde again after their first meeting. She did call, the very next day. But the newspaper telephoned, too, to arrange another round of interrogation. When Vanunu complained that he had a date, a *Sunday Times* reporter drove him to the appointed rendezvous, the Tate Gallery on the north bank of the River Thames, so he could meet his girlfriend and cancel the date. The reporter noticed that the plump, bleached-blonde woman, in high heels, was reluctant to approach the car.

It was the only time that anyone other than Vanunu came face to face with 'Cindy'. The Israeli, reluctant to talk about her, told the newspaperman that she was an American make-up artist on a tour of Europe. Obsessed with sex, Vanunu also remarked plaintively that Cindy was refusing to go to bed with him.[8]

In the following days, they did have a few dates and exploiting his sexual appetite, his disgust with *The Sunday Times* delays and then the fright of the *Sunday Mirror* story on September 28, Cindy persuaded Vanunu to get away from it all. He ignored the advice his newspaper friends had given him time and again: not to leave the country, not to fly and not to check into any hotels which required him to show his passport.

Cindy was taking care of everything, however. She paid cash for two business-class tickets to Rome. Forgetting his fears of being followed by the Mossad, Vanunu accompanied her to London's Heathrow Airport and onto British Airways flight 504 on September 30. Before leaving, he telephoned *The Sunday Times*, said he was 'going to leave the city' and promised to return within three days. The newspaper never heard from him again.[9]

It was similar to the seduction of the Iraqi pilot Munir Redfa twenty years earlier: Israel's female agent was promising Vanunu that once they got to a safe house – this time, in Rome – everything would be all right. He could expect to get what he desired. It was a 'safe house', but only in the professional, espionage sense of a protected and anonymous shelter for the Mossad.

Vanunu simply vanished from the face of the earth for forty days and forty nights. Only on November 9 did Israel's

Cabinet Secretary Elyakim Rubinstein announce: 'Mordecai Vanunu is legally under arrest in Israel, in accordance with a court order following a hearing in which a lawyer of his choice was present.'[10]

Why, after weeks of silence, did the Prime Ministers' club decide to confirm that Vanunu had been captured? Firstly, his family had threatened to go to the Israeli supreme court to force the truth out of the government. Secondly, Israel was concerned that the growing speculation in the media – that Vanunu was kidnapped on British soil – would harm relations with London. British Members of Parliament were complaining, Scotland Yard was investigating and even *The Sunday Times* reported that Vanunu was abducted, packed into a crate as diplomatic baggage and flown to Israel.

The government chose to take the high road, declaring that Vanunu was under arrest on normal legal grounds. To cover the tracks of the covert operation in Europe, official sources in Jerusalem leaked various versions of the nuclear traitor's capture. All the distorted leaks shared one vital element, meant to protect Israel's relations with Britain: that no kidnap had taken place on British soil and that he had legally and willingly left the country.

To guard the venues and precise methods used, one leaked version had Vanunu stepping onto a yacht with a female Mossad agent in the South of France, only being arrested once the vessel reached international waters. Another said he had happily flown to Paris, where he was then drugged and carried onto an El Al flight from France to Israel.

The truth was left in doubt, although the uncertainty was somewhat removed by the criminal himself. Vanunu showed that, even under arrest and the duress of interrogation, he still had enough spirit and nerve to shatter Shin Bet security. Arriving at Jerusalem district for a pre-trial hearing, he flattened his palm against the window of the police van in which he was being closely guarded.

There, before the eyes and lenses of the world's press, the ink he had scrawled on his flesh told the truth. Written on his palm was:

I WAS HIJACKED
IN ROME ITL
30.9.86 AT 21.00 CAME
TO ROME ON B.A. FLIGHT 504

Vanunu, having limited space on his palm, could not hold his entire odyssey in his hand. In further court appearances, he arrived with his arms restrained, the van's windows painted dark and with a motorcyclist's helmet on his head so that the press could not hear any messages he might shout.[11] Even after Shin Bet took away his pens and pencils, Vanunu – in an added mystery – found other ways to tell family members how he had been captured.

His brother Meir went abroad and filled in what he claimed were the missing links in the Vanunu arrest: that as soon as British Airways flight 504 touched down at Fiumicino airport, Cindy pretended to hail a taxi which promptly drove the couple to an address she gave – her supposed love nest.

As soon as they entered an apartment there, Vanunu was pounced upon by two Israeli men, who held him down while Cindy injected him with a powerful anaesthetic. Meir Vanunu added that his brother was then chained, driven to an Italian port and transported to Israel by sea. After a week in the Mediterranean, he arrived on October 7, was tied to a stretcher when taken ashore at dawn and then thrown into a cell with no light and a bare mattress on the floor.

Only when interrogated by Shin Bet did Vanunu learn that *The Sunday Times* had finally published his story. He had been in chains, at sea, when the newspaper filled most of its front page with the headline 'Revealed: The Secrets of Israel's Nuclear Arsenal', followed by Vanunu's inside story of the work conducted at Dimona and a detailed blueprint of the nuclear facility, produced by one of the newspaper's mapmakers and based on Vanunu's description of the underground Machon 2.

What the defendant could not know, as he was about to face treason and espionage charges and his family were experiencing the harsh reaction of their neighbours, was that *The Sunday Times* – its staff, feeling somewhat guilty about its amateurish attempts to protect its news source – was attempting to repay its debt to Vanunu by pursuing the story.

The newspaper's investigative reporters discovered that the Israeli embassy in Rome had hired a van at the beginning of October and that the number of kilometres clocked up when it was returned precisely matched the distance to and from the port of La Spezia. An Israeli merchant vessel, the *Tappuz*, Hebrew for orange, had been there at the same time – but only after being diverted from another sea route. The implication was that the ship had brought the chained prisoner home.[12]

The British newspaper came up with some more circumstantial evidence, in its hunt for the unknown seductress who had snatched Vanunu. The journalists discovered that a 'C. Chanin' had sat next to 'M. Vanunu' at the front of the British airliner and that a certain Cheryl Chanin Ben-Tov was a woman from America who was married to a captain in Aman. Mrs Ben-Tov, based on a wedding photograph obtained by *The Sunday Times*, appeared to fit 'Cindy's' general description. Intriguingly, her sister-in-law in Florida was a cosmetician named Cynthia (Cindy) Chanin.[13]

It might appear – from the hire of the van, the ship diversion and the borrowed identity of a relative – that the Mossad had left a sloppy, even unprofessional trail. But Israel's intelligence chiefs did not really care. Vanunu was in custody and that was what mattered.

Grey, mundane Shin Bet, still licking its wounds from the Vanunu failure – permitting him to work at Dimona, allowing him to snap photographs, letting him keep the film for a year before taking it abroad and then watching helplessly as he told even more secrets while behind bars – was once again in the shadow of the glorious, globe-trotting Mossad, which basked in the glory of a successful mission.

Acting on short notice, the Mossad had captured the fugitive while obeying its instructions to remain on the right side of British law. Prime Minister Peres was able to telephone Prime Minister Thatcher to assure her that none of her country's statutes had been violated.

Neither leader, although happy with the smooth outcome of the Vanunu affair and exchanging pleasantries, knew that beneath the surface a bitter confrontation was brewing between their intelligence communities.

The unusual clash began in 1986 with the discovery of eight forged British passports in a telephone booth in West Germany. They had been left there by a careless Israeli intelligence courier, whose shoulder bag was found to contain the bogus documents, a genuine Israeli passport and other papers linking the bag to Israel's embassy in Bonn. Britain's Foreign Office strongly protested and elicited an apology from Israel – a tacit admission that the Mossad's forgers choose the United Kingdom as one of the many fake nationalities with which to equip Israeli spies.

A year later, relations between the Mossad and British security agencies were strongly rocked in the wake of a murder in broad daylight near London's Sloane Square, within sight of the punks and tourists rubbing shoulders in the trend-setting boutiques of the King's Road. This popular shopping area is not only a favourite with yuppies and Sloane Rangers, but also with visitors and exiles from the Arab world. Unfortunately, it was also the hunting ground for gunmen stalking a fellow Palestinian, Ali al-Adhami.

He had moved, with his wife and five children, from the lawlessness of Lebanon to seemingly safe London only two years earlier. Adhami was a cartoonist for a Kuwaiti newspaper in London, *al-Qabas*, and was known for his bitter caricatures of Yasser Arafat as a political schemer who had an Egyptian mistress and was enjoying the high life while his people starved in refugee camps. On July 22, 1987, at age 42, Adhami was gunned down outside his office.

Scotland Yard could not find the killer, even though the British and Arabic press guessed, from the start, that Arafat had ordered the assassination. The complete truth did not emerge until a trial, ten months later.

Ismail Sowan, a Palestinian who was 28 years old, was charged with the illegal possession of arms and explosives in his Hull flat. He had been in the country for four years, as a research assistant at the Humberside College of Higher Education. When the British police raided his home on an anonymous tip, they found an impressive arms cache including sixty-eight pounds of the devastating plastic explosive Semtex, made in Czechoslovakia and favoured by terrorists because it is not detectable by the security devices used at the world's airports.

Sowan told the police that he had no idea what was in the suitcases hidden in his bathroom and that he had been keeping them for his friend Abdel Rahim Mustapha. They had known each other for many years, in Beirut, Paris and lately, in Britain.

Mustapha was 37 and was running a petrol station in Leigh-on-Sea, on the eastern fringe of London's commuter belt. Beneath his cover as a legitimate businessman, however, he was a major in the PLO's Force 17, the élite unit set up for Arafat's protection by Ali Hassan Salameh who was blown up by a Beirut car bomb after a long Mossad manhunt in 1979. After Salameh's death, Force 17 expanded its functions: no longer merely defensive, it became a special assault force, often attacking from the sea – almost a PLO version of an Israeli *sayeret*.

Trained as Arafat's bodyguard, Mustapha was sent by the guerilla chairman to Britain to organize an underground cell. He already had some offensive, operational experience, having taken part in an attack on El Al passengers at Munich airport, on February 10, 1970, killing one Israeli and wounding others. He and his colleagues were freed by the West German authorities seven months later, as part of the ransom for a hijacked Greek airliner – showing how important Mustapha was to Arafat.[14]

Mustapha showed his gratitude to his beloved leader by supervising the liquidation of the critical cartoonist. He had been expelled, as an undesirable alien, by the British Government in April 1987, but had the dedication and daring to return under a false name in July for the Adhami shooting. When he had left in April, he had handed his terrorist arsenal – in the suitcases – to his trusted friend Sowan.

Arrested in August and pressed by British interrogators, who suggested he was involved in killing Adhami, Sowan first told them about Mustapha and then astonished them even more: he said he had been working, all along, for Israel.

Sowan said that for many years, he had been receiving a monthly salary of around $1,000 from Israeli intelligence. Born in East Jerusalem, then under Jordanian jurisdiction, he fell under Israeli control with the rest of the city in 1967. As in the case of other Palestinians who see no prospects in the occupied West Bank, Sowan went to Lebanon to study. In Beirut, he was recruited by the PLO.

Back in Nablus, on the West Bank for a family visit, he was picked up by Shin Bet. Rather than being charged with contact with a hostile guerilla organization, he was instead 'turned' to work for the Israelis in 1978. It was a typical pattern for the recruitment of Palestinian agents, whose families can enjoy some benefits in the occupied territories, while the agent is allowed to travel and study abroad, receiving money as the final binding element.

When Sowan moved to England, the Israelis even paid his rent. In return, he was sent on various intelligence missions to the Lebanon, where he befriended Mustapha, and to France. At one point, Israeli intelligence gave him a small electronic signalling device, which he kept in his pocket and pressed when he met a PLO contact. He was one of the Arab informers in the Middle East and Europe, who were run in a joint operation by the Mossad and Shin Bet in their hit-and-run war against Palestinian terrorists.

Sowan told the British police that he had tried to cut his links with Israeli intelligence, but it was not the sort of job you can quit. That was no wonder, because he was an important asset who had managed to penetrate one of the circles closest to Arafat himself. Sowan had accomplished a feat which was always near and dear to the heart of Israeli intelligence.

When the cartoonist Adhami was shot in London, Sowan happened to be in Israel – on vacation, seeing his family as well as his Israeli handlers. He had been so valuable that the Israelis could not resist sending him back to Britain, despite his warnings that the murder had made it too dangerous to remain in place. He even told his intelligence bosses about the suitcases which Mustapha had left in his Hull flat, but the Israelis merely told him to wait patiently and someone would come to relieve him of the burden.

It was ignorant, arrogant and unrealistic of the Mossad and Shin Bet handlers to press on with a mission which had most likely run its course. The Adhami killing changed everything, yet the Israelis acted as though Sowan could simply proceed as before. Worse still, they let him sit on the arms cache which only got him into deep trouble. Israeli intelligence had learned little from its recent run of mistakes.

Now in the hands of the British police, Sowan sang to save his skin. He named all his Israeli case officers, working undercover at the Israeli embassy in London. Sowan assumed that would help his case in British judicial eyes, but it did not. He was sentenced to eleven years in prison.[15]

His conviction was the trigger for firm British action against Israeli intelligence. On June 17, 1988, Her Majesty's Government carried out an unprecedented sweep against a friendly nation's spies – expelling Israeli embassy attaché Aryeh Regev and announcing that another diplomat, Yaakov Barad, could not re-enter Britain after his holiday at home. Soon afterwards, Israel withdrew another three operatives from its embassy in London – acting either on its own delayed initiative to smooth ruffled feathers, or on strong MI5 hints.

The British were furious. Perhaps they thought that Israel should have given Britain some warning that the Palestinian cartoonist was about to be murdered. Even if such expectations were too high, considering that the Israelis would have had to 'burn' their own agent inside Force 17, the

British hoped that the Mossad liaison in London would at least provide a full briefing after the killing of Adhami. Even failing that, the Israelis could certainly have given the arms cache to the authorities.

The Mossad and Shin Bet were hoping, instead, to have their cake and eat it, too. They were not especially concerned about the cartoonist, deceased in any event, and instead hoped against hope that Mustapha – or another big fish – would one day return for his very special suitcases. The Israelis wanted the best of all worlds, but everything turned sour.

Intelligence chiefs were extremely reluctant to examine the Sowan disaster and draw the necessary conclusions. They did not find any culprits and they did not dismiss anyone. It was typical of Admoni's easy-going and relaxed administration of the Mossad, at times focusing primarily on minimizing internal disputes. As with the failure to detect and deter Vanunu's treason, Israeli intelligence behaved as though it would be too painful to face its own deficiencies.

Israel lost its valuable inside agent, Sowan, near the top of the PLO leadership. It lost its complete infrastructure in London, when the angry British publicly blew the whistle. The Israelis nearly wiped out all their friendly ties with British intelligence, already frayed by the suspicions surrounding the Dikko kidnap affair and the capture of Vanunu.

Above all, the mishandled operation destroyed the last vestige of prestige which the Mossad had worked so hard to rescue, after the failures of the 1980s, by luring Vanunu into prison.

Vanunu was convicted of treason, espionage and disclosing state secrets on March 24, 1988. The three judges rejected his claim that he had acted out of ideological concerns. But, after he said, 'I am not a traitor and did not intend to damage the State of Israel,' the judges sentenced him to a relatively lenient eighteen years in jail.

The clouds of mystery were not lifted, however. Vanunu

himself, shown the photograph of Cheryl Chanin Ben-Tov, waved it off with: 'That's not the Cindy I knew.'[16]

Even more puzzling were the conclusions of Italy's famous counter-terrorism magistrate, Domenico Sica. After investigating whether the crime of kidnapping had been committed by Israelis in Rome, he issued the surprising conclusion in September 1988 that Vanunu had not been kidnapped at all.

The investigating judge said that the English written on the Israeli's palm was too good to believe, and the photographs of Dimona's bomb factory, which Sica borrowed from *The Sunday Times*, convinced him that they could only have been taken with official cooperation. The 'tourist's presentation' through the corridors and laboratories, with no people in sight, made little sense to Sica, who said that such dials and instruments would have had to be watched round the clock.

The Italian findings convinced some newspapers and magazines that Vanunu had been pretending to be a traitor and that Israel had arranged the entire charade – 'a well-organized disinformation operation', in Sica's words.[17] The Italian judiciary, rarely independent of political considerations, preferred to drop the entire incident. 'No kidnap' meant no need to investigate.

The intelligence communities of Israel and Italy have a long record of close cooperation, dating back to the 1950s. Was it just coincidence that the Mossad chose Rome as the place to capture Vanunu?

Sica's suppositions were taken seriously, however, by an international press which felt that Israeli intelligence must have been incredibly clever – not unforgivably stupid to allow Vanunu's treason. The media could not believe that the almighty Israeli secret services could be caught so off guard and assumed instead that Israel's spies had used Vanunu in a sophisticated plot to frighten the Arabs by revealing that Israel has a nuclear arsenal.

Only a highly conspiratorial mind could believe, however, that any organization – even the best intelligence agency in the world – could undertake such a long-term, complicated operation: to win the consent of the three top politicians in the Prime Ministers' club and coordinate the actions of all the secret service and military chiefs; to recruit a poor Moroccan with no physics training and then plot his extreme political changes; to equip him with photographs; to send him to the farthest conceivable foreign country and arrange his conversion to Christianity; to sell the story to the press; to set up a meeting of the Israeli Prime Minister with newspaper editors; to arrange Vanunu's disappearance and stage a trial in such a way as to fool his judges; to let his family suffer; and presumably, to make him rot in jail.

And what for? So that Israel could remind the world of its unassailable military superiority in the Middle East, without formally announcing the existence of the nuclear arsenal? The Arabs and the rest of the world have long taken it for granted that Israel has the bomb. Reminding them does no good; it spurs, instead, an unconventional arms race, with the Syrians and Libyans competing to develop chemical and even nuclear weapons.

The ironic outcome of the Vanunu affair was that Israel's most secret of secrets – its ultimate taboo topic, never discussed in any forum greater than ten people – was suddenly on the front pages around the world, in full detail, exposed to public discussion at a time not of the government's choosing. The story contains all the ingredients of the Israeli obsession with censorship and security.

16

A World Without Trust

The authors of this book were recently in Mossad head-quarters in Tel Aviv. Admittedly, their visit did not take in the part of the building which houses one of the world's most respected intelligence agencies. Let us say we were just next door.

We could give the address. We could describe the rather unremarkable premises. We could say, from experience, whether one gets around by escalator, by lift, or simply by climbing stairs. But we would be crossing the line into potential violations of Israeli law.

No one is entirely sure about the line, although journalists based in Israel usually know when they are speeding right through the grey area unto unlawful activities. The trick, both foreign correspondents and Israeli reporters have found, is to coast along the grey area without crossing to the other side.

In the case of the authors, we declare quite honestly that the one who lives outside Israel learned the addresses of

Mossad and Shin Bet headquarters, as well as the names of the current chiefs, from sources in Washington, DC. It is generally assumed that the intelligence services of the Soviet Union and of most Arab countries possess the same information – although we certainly did not tell them.

Most well informed Israelis – politicians, journalists and even others – know the secret names, too. It has become something of a game, at chic parties, to jump into conversations with 'The Shin Bet chief told me the other day . . .', or 'I met the head of the Mossad and he said . . .' and those who do not know the identities are simply not 'in' enough. They are 'out'.

One Israeli newspaperman, out to impress the élite among his audience and even to tell Shin Bet that he knows what it knows, played a game of cat-and-mouse with the name of the new agency chief in 1988 – appointed the same day Mordecai Vanunu was convicted. The inside joke was in the headline over an article purportedly about American TV detective Perry Mason: 'What will Perry follow?' At the risk of violating the ban on naming Shin Bet's director, the clue is somewhat bolder in Hebrew: '*Akhrei Ma Yaakov Perry?*'

What did the writer achieve? He gave enough hints, heavy as elephants, to anyone who might seek them, pointing to a name which is officially secret; and yet, he was travelling on the safe side of Israel's secrecy border, not giving the censor the ammunition to shoot him down. Perhaps the Shin Bet chief was lucky that the clever headline appeared in a small newspaper, but this did not prevent him telephoning the chief editor the next day to ask: 'Why did you do it to me?' The ostensibly anonymous intelligence chief called the editor directly because he knew he could trust her.

The flurry seemed entirely absurd when, in February 1989, the unnamed Shin Bet director celebrated his forty-fifth birthday amidst ridiculous publicity. It seems that he was separated from his wife, Israeli newspapers told the nation and the world, and his mistress – a well-known socialite – organized a huge surprise party in Jerusalem with the connivance of secretaries and others in Shin Bet.

Government ministers, parliamentarians of the Knesset, and even newspaper reporters were among the one-hundred and fifty guests. The press said later that Shin Bet operatives were drunk, as their famous but anonymous chief played 'Summertime' and other jazz favourites on his trumpet. His party, in the Israel Museum cafeteria, went on until three o'clock in the morning.

Prime Minister Shamir, the austere former Mossad agent, was livid when he heard of the exceedingly public celebration. Shamir knew that the newspaper accounts were a potential gold mine to hostile intelligence services seeking to compile a file on the Shin Bet chief. The Prime Minister called him onto the carpet and then permitted reports of the scolding to be leaked to the press.

The seemingly trivial event was a watershed in the four decades of the domestic security agency. Once a secret brotherhood, all its activities – from torture and perjury to late-night parties – were now fully exposed. It was said half-jokingly that confronted by a crowd of surprise-celebrants, previous Shin Bet chiefs would have reacted very differently: Isser Harel would have sent them all letter bombs, Yosef Harmelin would have been shocked into silence, Avraham Ahituv would have sacked them all and Avraham Shalom might have had them killed.

The fact that journalists were invited to the fête had its own implications. Any reporter so cosy with the clandestine authorities of his or her nation might some day be called upon to do a favour or two. Intelligence operatives do, on occasion, contact journalists directly – urging them not to pursue matters which they say would threaten Israel's security. The individual reporter must decide how to respond, but it is clear that in a small country it is far better to be on speaking terms with military and intelligence sources. If the personal pleas should fail, in any event, the officials do have enforcement power in the person of the censor.

Journalists and editors play by the rules and they even receive briefings from prime ministers, defence ministers and secret service directors. It is a unique system established in 1949, shortly after the War of Independence.

The first Prime Minister, David Ben-Gurion, could have kept using the old British Mandate's emergency regulations, restraining press and other freedoms, but he wanted to play the democrat while still enjoying the powers of the emergency laws. He found the newspaper editors to be perfect partners, willing to be censored voluntarily. They signed an agreement, with no legal force but great survival power.

Under the accord, the chief of staff and minister of defence appoint a military commander, who has an intelligence background, to the post of Chief Censor, with the rank of brigadier general. With the office, considered part of Aman, comes a staff of seventy military officers and civilian employees, working in two 'bases' in Tel Aviv and Jerusalem.

The agreement also says that the Israeli newspapers, radio and television, and foreign correspondents based in the country are honour-bound to submit their articles and news items to the censor, who enjoys the same authority as his scissor-wielding British predecessor. He and his staff can shut down newspapers and they have done so at least twice, in 1952 and in the Shin Bet scandal of 1984. These were Hebrew newspapers which presumably violated the accord, but it has happened far more frequently to the Arab press in Jerusalem and the occupied territories – even more so since the *intifada*, or uprising, began.

The censors have the legal right to listen in on a journalist's telephone, using outmoded equipment which is connected when news items are being phoned abroad, and they can read telex items as they are typed to the outside world.

The censor's powers extend well beyond military secrets and include the perfectly understandable identifications of army units, codes, names of intelligence officers, troop movements and specific topics such as nuclear weapons. The subjects which may also be censored include immigration to Israel, the construction of new roads, new Jewish settlements in the occupied territories, energy supplies and oil-storage facilities and both trade and political links with countries that do not have diplomatic relations with Israel; in other words, anything which could be interpreted as the defence of the state in its broadest, most exaggerated sense.

What do the Israeli editors receive in return? The censor usually acts sensibly, not overstepping his authority and usually – when not under heavy political influence – only sniffs around genuine military issues. But he sometimes is pressed to stick his nose into other matters, thus becoming a political censor. A working relationship has been forged, however, even with the foreign reporters based in Israel, who are covered by the same accord.

The 1949 agreement has been modified on three occasions, each time narrowing the list of topics subject to censorship. The list remains long, however, and includes sixty-nine subjects.[2]

A golden path has been found through this minefield and the participants in the game generally know where they stand. There is a tacit understanding that subjects such as road construction and economic relations do not have to be submitted in advance to the censor, unless they touch upon specific, sensitive topics such as the intelligence community.

If an Israeli or foreign correspondent wishes to name the secret service chiefs or their addresses in a dispatch, he is supposed to know that the copy goes first to the military censor. The secret facts will then duly be excised. So why write them down in the first place? The threat of censorship often becomes self-censorship.

By the same token, when reporters and editors feel they can 'get away' with a technical violation of censorship, they will take the risk. In 1981, for instance, an Israeli journalist working for an American newspaper revealed that the head of Shin Bet was then Avraham Ahituv. The newsman's main aim was to tell the world that the secret service chief had clashed with Prime Minister Menachem Begin over security policy regarding West Bank settlers and their alleged involvement in bombings against Palestinians. The chief censor recommended that the journalist be put on trial, but the attorney general decided not to press charges.[3]

The censor did even less in similar circumstances in 1986, when an American television network exposed Avraham Shalom as the head of Shin Bet, who was being investigated in connection with the killing of the two Palestinian bus hijackers.[4]

The Israeli system occasionally reaches the rock bottom of absurdity when it prevents local newspapers from publishing certain facts, even though the foreign press – beyond the reach of the censor – does publish the full story. The intelligence scandals of the 1980s all serve as excellent examples, when Israeli newspapers were permitted to quote, at length, stories which appeared in foreign publications. These were often based on Israeli sources whose lips were supposedly sealed by the censor.

Newspapers in America had already predicted, in the weeks before Nahum Admoni retired as Mossad chief in March 1989, that he would soon be replaced after nearly seven years as chief and twenty-eight years of Mossad service beforehand. At least in the short term, the fact that Admoni was replaced by his deputy – and the name of the new Mossad chief – remained secret.

The authors of this book know who he is but will not violate the censor's absolute ban as did some Israelis when they leaked Admoni's identity to Britain's *Sunday Times* within days of his appointment in September 1982. One or more 'formers' or privateers, who did not like Prime Minister Begin's selection, spelled the new chief's name on an open telephone line to London. It was pure luck that the journalist could not hear the letters clearly and gave the name as Nahum Adnoni.

Quoting and even reprinting entire pages from English, French or any other foreign-language publication was done on such a colossal scale that it was half-jokingly remarked that Israel's press would do a better job if it fired all its journalists and simply hired translators.

The censor and other Israeli authorities seem to feel that

the country's own newspapers are some sort of official mouthpiece. This view is based on the old Communist notion of trying to control every possible aspect of a centralized state. It is as though anything which appears in an Israeli publication will be seen as more authoritative and therefore more damaging – instead of the Israeli papers being seen as independent as any other newspaper in the West. The authorities are tacitly denying the right of the press to be free and independent and to be perceived as such.

Two principal reasons are given for maintaining the petty secrecy which goes hand in hand with Israeli censorship – itself a controversial institution in a democracy which proudly features a free press. One reason is mystical and the other is practical.

In a habit adopted from the British, who never publish the accurate names of the secret agencies known as MI5 and MI6 or the identities of the service chiefs, the Israelis preserve a similar mystique around their intelligence community. The intelligence community believes that the people of Israel sleep better at night knowing that they *are* protected and not because they know precisely *who* is protecting them and *how*.

It is, at all times, an ingrained habit in the world of espionage – based on both convenience and tradition – not to tell anything, when silence can be maintained instead. In the words of secret service veteran Rafi Eitan: 'The best thing an intelligence man can do is to keep out of the media.' When it came to saving his own skin, in the Lakam and Pollard affair, however, Eitan was giving interviews and background briefings left and right.

As for the practical reason, defence officials justifiably point out that many small terrorist groups – whether Palestinians, Marxists or anarchists – can actually be helped by details which may seem petty. If such terrorists, so the argument goes, were easily to obtain the names and addresses of intelligence agents and agencies, these would become potential targets for attack. Yes, the officials admit, the Russians, the Syrians and even the PLO know everything there is to know about the Mossad chief and his head-quarters, but there is no reason that every little troublemaker in the world should know.

The mystical argument – silence, for the sake of silence – meets with opposition, however. In the post-Watergate spirit of governmental openness which spread from the United States to other Western democracies, the blind faith that citizens had in their governments and defence establishments has worn thin. There are growing calls for greater public accountability on the part of politicians, civil servants, the military and even intelligence agencies.

Israel is different from the US in its form of government. All executive power lies with the cabinet formed by the prime minister, whose authority is based on the majority he or she commands in parliament. Checks and balances oper-ate quite differently from those in Washington.

Perhaps envious of the regular hearings held by commit-tees of the US Congress on subjects ranging from the defence budget to CIA assassination plots, vigorous demo-crats in the Israeli Knesset would dearly love to have the power to confirm or veto candidates for the directorships of the Mossad and Shin Bet.

They are not satisfied by the fact that there is a small, six-member subcommittee of the foreign affairs and defence panel, the Committee of the Services, which is supposed to oversee the secret agencies. Although the agency chiefs or their deputies do appear before these Knesset members, the committee's investigative instincts are usually washed away when it hears saucy details of covert operations. They are bought off, in a sense, with the excitement of hearing inside information. The committee has no real powers, aside from that of using its ears to listen. Some members have even complained that the intelligence agencies, which are sup-posed to brief them, instead bypass the committee and leak stories to foreign journalists.

What harm could there be in making the intelligence officials accountable to parliament? Supporters of the present arrangement respond by pointing out that members of the Knesset leak information day and night – almost as the second oldest profession in the land of the Bible – and that in a parliamentary system, it is the prime minister who is accountable for his entire ministry. He must bear the blame if the Mossad or Shin Bet commits an unacceptable act and if necessary, it is the prime minister who must resign.

In Israel, however, a noteworthy habit has developed among cabinet ministers: not to accept responsibility.

All that remains is a powerless civil servant – the State Comptroller, usually a wise, elderly and retired judge – who is charged with overseeing the intelligence agencies and, indeed, all government offices. They, in turn, all have one thing in common: they usually ignore his reports. These are encumbered by dense language and statistics, enveloping the harsh realities of wasted resources, stolen goods and corruption.

In looking into the activities of intelligence agencies, the comptroller has the definite handicap of having access to the expense accounts and budgets of the Mossad and Shin Bet, without knowledge of the covert operations which necessitated the expenditures. There is nothing he can meaningfully criticize and he has little choice but to accept the explanations offered by the secret service chiefs.

Even when the agencies need a few million dollars more than originally apportioned, they can approach the budget committee of the Knesset without explanations beyond, 'It is for a vital mission,' and the extra funds are always granted.

Israel is in an almost permanent state of war and has been since its creation in May 1948. Surrounded by hostile nations and a constant terrorism threat, the rules of defence and intelligence simply differ from those which apply in America or other Western countries. Many secrets do have to be better kept than they are in other nations because the slightest error or security lapse could easily cost lives in Israel. Censorship is understandable when it concerns battles while they are raging, counter-terrorism missions while the troops are still in motion, and details of operational methods including names of intelligence operatives and informers whose lives would be endangered. But these arguments hold up only when they are not pursued to an exaggerated degree.

It seems ludicrous that Israel confirms nothing about its intelligence agencies, while often having something of which to be proud. It even took the authors several days to get an accurate reply from the Prime Minister's office when asking for the precise and full name of the Mossad.

We wanted the exact name, used by the Mossad in its English-language correspondence. We know that the agency is not in the habit of writing official letters too often, but considering their liaison relationships with foreign espionage agencies the Mossad must have a name.

Officials responded to our enquiry with various names. At one point, we were advised to see the annual report of the State Comptroller. But it is in Hebrew and the names of the agencies can have varying translations.

Eventually, the Prime Minister's press spokesman returned with an answer and an explanation: 'It took me a hell of a long time to check it. I eventually talked to the head of the Mossad, who was very suspicious and could not understand why I was demanding to know. But I got it for you. Here is the name.'

And with the triumph of sharing exclusive information, he whispered: 'The Israeli Secret Intelligence Service.' The ISIS is a dour, British-style, pale reflection – for official foreigners only – of the legendary and proud name of the Mossad, or Institute for Intelligence and Special Assignments.

Asking who is the current director of the agency is somewhat easier, because the Prime Minister's spokesman will simply say: 'You know I cannot tell you that.'[5] This seems ridiculous when the heads of foreign secret services know the name, when many former Mossad and Shin Bet operatives believe there would be no harm in revealing the names of the chiefs and when the name of the head of the most important agency to the national defence – Aman – is publicly known. The only interested party kept firmly in the dark is the great Israeli public, the taxpayers who foot the bill. Some veterans have even proposed establishing a press office, at least for Shin Bet, which is little more than a police force with the added spice of secrecy.

Official responses vary when journalists ask whether the Mossad was responsible for an adventure or exploit somewhere in the world. Usually the reply is some form of 'no comment', but spokesmen in Jerusalem will often say: 'LaHaDaM,' a pronounceable Hebrew acronym for *Lo Hayu ha-Dvarim Mi-olam*, which means these things never happened.

Long experience has shown that these answers have absolutely no value. To put it bluntly, Israeli officials are often lying. It is difficult to believe anything in this world without trust. When it comes to matters of life and death and high politics, the officials defend vehemently their right to lie. Journalists similarly point out their obligation to keep asking.

Problems arise when officials abuse their power to sidestep the censor, often with the censor's consent, in order to leak a favourable interpretation of potentially embarrassing events. When Israeli leaders wished to give their own version of the Jonathan Pollard espionage affair, to pacify an angry and hurt American public, they privately unveiled the whole story – or one side of it – to a major US newspaper in November 1985. They even told the correspondent, through their assistants, that he would not have to submit his article to the censor; everything would pass.[6]

After Vanunu was spirited away from England, officials in October 1986 leaked various versions intended, above all, to emphasize that he was not kidnapped from under British jurisdiction. The Mossad's true operational details were still blurred, however. It was a case of revealing an inch, while covering up a yard. The censor, knowing his political masters' wishes, took no action despite these obvious violations of the regulations.

It took sheer gall, then, for the censor to punish foreign

correspondents who, in April 1988, received a leaked account of the killing of the PLO's Abu Jihad in Tunis. Officials such as Prime Minister Yitzhak Shamir, who claimed to colleagues that he simply heard about it on the radio, feigned ignorance. But others in authority, knowing that one of the purposes of the assassination was to intimidate the Palestinian enemy, chose their conduits: correspondents for an American TV network and a leading US newspaper. They duly published the story and were stunned when the Government Press Office then stripped them of their accreditations as foreign correspondents.

One arm of government often seems ignorant of what the others are doing. Journalists in the Israeli democracy have to cope with not knowing when and what they will be able to publish. The same is true in the field of personal memoirs. The haphazard nature of secrecy and censorship yields different rules for different cases and different people.

Secret service veterans have had to cope with the inequalities of the censor's judgment and have to guess when the climate is right for revelations. Several have written books which the censor refused to clear, but ex-*Memuneh* Isser Harel is a prolific author. This one-man book factory knew, without asking, how much he could reveal about intelligence operations such as the kidnapping of Eichmann.

Some veterans, to bypass the censoring authorities, turn their factual knowledge into extremely plausible fiction. Their urge to write produces novels. While they are obviously autobiographical at times, publishing no precise facts means no problem with the censor and no infringement of the lifelong pledge of secrecy signed by every intelligence operative.

Other Israelis, who have left the secret agencies or special military units, reveal secrets without publishing a word. They are to be found throughout the world, sharing their craft with foreigners who pay them for Israel's expertise in defence and security. The consultants obtained their knowledge while working for the Israeli Government.

Simply by doing – and teaching others how to do – they are revealing as many secrets as someone who produces the written word.

The censorship system targets only published and broadcast material, while the enemy – Arab and other intelligence services – closely follow both open and covert sources. True, a great deal of information in modern espionage comes from openly available material. But the secretly obtained information is also important and has to be targeted as well. The Israeli censor's work seems predicated on the thought that a person who loses a coin in a dark alley will only be searching where the streetlight shines.

Israel tries to stem the flow of news items in the media, while turning a blind eye to the flood of revelations coming from former operatives. If Israel is so concerned to stop the leak of classified information, why have a censor concerned only with publications? What about the activities of people holding secrets?

Perhaps it is a matter of convenience. It is far easier to keep track of the public media than it is to spy on what people are doing. Consider also that the people involved are former members of the defence and security 'family', precisely the same sort of 'old boys' still to be found in Jerusalem making the decisions. In fact, the Jerusalem team might expect in the future to be out there as consultants, too.

The worst damage has often been done by officials still serving in the government. Foreign Minister Moshe Dayan's statement in 1978, which confirmed the secret relationship with Ethiopia, did more harm than the mountain of ink and bits of newsprint deleted by the small army of worker ants employed by the military censor. And when a Jewish Agency official revealed the clandestine exodus of the Ethiopian Jews in 1985, he ruined more lives than any journalist in the history of Israel.

News reporters are usually less dangerous, yet they are decidedly more accountable. The men and women of the media can be punished, by a variety of sanctions, while politicians and other officials blithely survive their verbal misdemeanours.[7]

In judicial proceedings, too, the Israeli authorities jealously preserve their right to pick and choose the times at which they will demand absolute secrecy, or permit full disclosure. Espionage trials involving Israelis or foreigners who have spied against the State of Israel are almost always totally secret. Even the name of the accused is banned from publication. More than one 'Mr X' has stood trial in a Jerusalem or Tel Aviv courtroom.

Mordecai Kedar, Avri El-Ad, Ze'ev Avni and, more recently, Marcus Klingberg were tried in total secrecy and were even imprisoned as anonymous Xs. In the cases of Mordecai Vanunu and Shabtai Kalmanovitch, it was officially announced that they were accused of serious crimes, but there was absolutely no access to their trials.

It is a manipulative system, in which the authorities use their powers, not necessarily to protect secrets regarding national defence, but to keep embarrassing failures under wraps. That was the motive in the enforced disappearance of the prisoners, as it was in the totally unpublicized case of Peter Puhlman.

A German Jew born to parents who perished in the Holocaust, Puhlman was an engineer recruited by *Hauptverwaltung Aufklärung*, the HWA or East German Central Office of Information. His Communist intelligence masters planted him in West Germany, where he married a young Israeli woman and moved to Tel Aviv. In November 1971, Israel Aircraft Industries hired him to work on aerodynamics, where he displayed skill and professionalism until Shin Bet arrested him for espionage five months later.

As an East German spy, Puhlman had penetrated one of the most sensitive defence manufacturers in Israel. In strict secrecy, he was sentenced to fifteen years in prison. Nothing was published about his arrest, the charges, the trial, or his fate. In 1982, he was released and only a tiny item was printed by an Israeli news agency.[8]

How can a democracy, with a free press and full civil

rights, conduct itself in such silence and secrecy? The intelligence agencies, the military censor, the government and the judicial system walk a thin tightrope between protecting national security and preserving the primacy of law. The potential dangers are great: if people, both Israeli citizens and foreigners, can disappear – even the families, in rare cases, are not informed – there is the possibility that people in all walks of life could have their rights infringed.

There are signs that official bodies are demanding such powers and trying to whittle down civil rights. The Knesset passed the Secret Eavesdropping Law in 1979, and has modified it several times since, to set up the first orderly system of bugging by state agencies. Authorization was thus given, by statute for the first time, to the police, Shin Bet and Aman to plant microphones and intercept telephone calls as their needs might require.

The police are permitted to use such tools to catch offenders and solve crimes, but only with a warrant from a senior judge. Only one of the top commanders of the police is empowered to seek such a warrant.

The 'security authorities', as the two intelligence agencies are defined in the law, have a far easier time. They are required to secure the approval of the government minister in charge of them: the prime minister, in Shin Bet's case, or the defence minister in Aman's, would normally give written authority. But the law adds that if the secret agency needs to begin eavesdropping without delay, the agency chief himself can approve forty-eight hours of bugging without higher approval.

The Mossad asked for similar powers, but the legislative committee refused because the agency is not supposed to work domestically.

In the United States, even defence and espionage cases require judicial warrants for wiretapping. The CIA and the National Security Agency are permitted, but only with warrants, to mount surveillance within the US on foreign citizens who are not protected by the Constitution.

The Israeli intelligence community has few limitations in

such activities. Targets for eavesdropping can be either Israelis or foreigners and Aman can wiretap them all. The law specifically permits intelligence agencies to keep the transcripts of eavesdropping sessions, even if the tapes themselves are destroyed.

The army Chief of Staff, General Raful Eitan, ordered Aman, in the early 1980s, to record the telephone conversations of his generals when he feared there were leaks to the press. A military chief would have the authority to intercept the conversations of civilians on military telephones – even those of the prime minister or the defence minister who, in a democracy, are in charge of the army. As a vestige from needs of wartime security, the defence ministry also has a small unit with authority to intercept mail arriving from or going abroad.[9]

When the Knesset committee seemed reluctant to grant all the powers sought by the community, intelligence chiefs hurried to testify. As though they were offended, they said: 'What? Don't you trust us?' This happened to be in the midst of Shin Bet's cover-up of the bus hijacker killings and the committee members naturally felt they were dealing with a world without trust.

How can the public feel confident that generals and secret agents, who lie to their own superiors and government, will stick to a strict interpretation of the law on wiretaps?

The answer is that there can be no such confidence. There is a need for clearer regulations, without twilight areas on the fringes of legality. Depending on goodwill often leaves the door open to bad intentions.

Similarly, a democracy cannot rely on voluntary censorship, conducted on the basis of old accords from the days before computers, facsimile machines and satellite communications. In a democracy at war, censorship has its place, but only if it is coherent and consistent.

Finally, the accountability of the intelligence community to the public – as represented by parliament – must be increased. All the scandals of the 1980s showed that while individual missions can be accomplished with great success and aplomb, the agencies fail when they display misjudgments and dangerous abuses of power.

There need not be a contradiction between the openness of democratic society and its defence by covert means. Life in a free country need not be overshadowed by the sometimes dark security apparatus at its heart, so long as it is clear who is in charge: the public, through the government elected in the light of day.

The business of intelligence is too serious to be left to the intelligence agencies and a handful of politicians alone.

Into the Future

Israel entered the space age on September 19, 1988. A rocket blasted into the sky from a launch site near the Mediterranean coast, south of Tel Aviv, a short distance from the research nuclear reactor at Nahal Sorek.

A Jericho missile, based on an earlier French rocket and developed as a possible delivery vehicle for Israel's secret nuclear bomb, was carrying a satellite which the Israelis called *Ofek*, Horizon. The authorities said it was an experimental craft, orbiting the earth for about a month.

It was clear, however, that this was an important technological breakthrough for the Jewish state. After joining the exclusive nuclear club, Israel became the eighth nation in the select group possessing rockets capable of launching satellites.

By injecting *Ofek* into its intended orbit, an ellipse ranging from 620 miles to 155 miles from the earth, the Jericho proved its ability to hit a precise target – in this case, a trajectory high in the sky and beyond.

More significant was the future potential for spying from space. Israel planned a further series of satellites. These would have cameras and sophisticated communications and would remain on-station, passing over the Middle East every ninety minutes.

Once Israel sets up a permanent system of eyes in the sky, it will have more information than ever to prepare for war with its Arab neighbours. Previously, Israel has had to rely on reconnaissance flights and unmanned drones – or remotely piloted vehicles – which carried television cameras over and behind enemy lines.

As in other areas of technology, Israel – above all – wanted to eliminate any dependence on favours from foreigners: begging the United States to provide satellite photographs, or using agents such as Jonathan Pollard to steal them. Former Mossad chief Meir Amit said: 'If you are fed from the crumbs of others according to their whim, this is very inconvenient and very difficult. If you have your own independent capability, you climb one level higher.'[1]

Even as Israel reached its technological zenith, its intelligence community, ironically, was at a low ebb. Looking into the future, in many ways, is a welcome distraction from viewing the past. Israel could easily find itself looking back in anger.

The intelligence community cannot rid itself of the memory and reality of failures and setbacks which came in quick succession:

The Mossad's misjudgments in Lebanon; Shin Bet's killings and cover-up; using Pollard to spy on their best friends in America; intercepting a Libyan executive jet in the mistaken belief that Palestinian terrorists were aboard; the disarray of the covert Iran–America connection; losing control over freelancers and 'formers' around the world; allowing nuclear secrets to get out; being caught and expelled from London; operating an outdated and irrelevant censorship system; and misleading the government over the future of the occupied territories, just as a Palestinian uprising was beginning.

The entire litany of blemishes was symptomatic of the

diseases endemic in other countries' secret agencies: internal rivalries, lack of control by politicians, a desire to expand beyond reasonable limits, poor coordination among agencies, overlapping duties and duplicated efforts. Israel's intelligence community had suffered these in the early 1950s and early 1960s as childhood diseases, but had overcome them. In the 1980s, they were surfacing again.

The maladies could all be healed through better management, greater accountability, improved coordination and more selectiveness in recruiting agents and taking on missions.

It would take longer, however, to repair the serious damage to the image of the intelligence community. Deep cracks shattered the mystique of Israeli intelligence as precise, professional and even invincible.

Image is surprisingly important for seemingly faceless, secret agencies. The morale of Israeli operatives is closely linked to their perception among friends and enemies. In addition to the feelings of Israel's own operatives, there is also an impact on the readiness of other nations to cooperate with the intelligence community.

Riding high on a sea of triumphs makes it easier to recruit agents and informers. Who wants to work for a loser? Who would risk their life in the service of intelligence agencies which cannot protect their employees? Everybody wants to be on a winning team.

There is also the fact that nothing succeeds like success. In operations requiring pinpoint timing, precise training and more than a little good fortune, secret agents and operatives make their own luck. Not only do they feel more confident – although not foolishly over-confident, it is to be hoped – knowing that they are with a team of winners, but their enemies are, quite helpfully, intimidated: they fail to put up a good fight when convinced that they cannot beat the mighty Israelis.

It is easier for any soldier, whether in uniform or undercover, to fight in the knowledge that his nation is behind him. The intelligence community, when its mystique was intact, could depend on the goodwill and support of the Israeli people – as well as on the respect of people around the world.

There is keen fascination, in the media, books, and public discussion, with the shadowy world of espionage. People are enthralled by the daring and sophistication of secret operations, the intrigues, deceptions and even the sex appeal of spies. Israel was always high on the list in capturing the imagination of curious onlookers.

Foreigners and Israelis alike marvelled at the ability of the Jewish state's intelligence – usually ascribing all the credit to the Mossad – to capture Eichmann in Argentina and to rescue hostages at Entebbe. Experts abroad also considered Israel the definite leader in preventive intelligence and in the general fight against international terrorism.

The Mossad leaked some details of its feat in persuading the Iraqi pilot Munir Redfa to defect to Israel with his MiG-21. Tears flowed freely, when Israeli intelligence became Jewish intelligence to bring Ethiopian Jewry to the Promised Land and the same had been done for the Jews of Iraq, Morocco and other countries. Out of the publicity spotlight, Lakam helped build Israel's defences by obtaining scientific and industrial secrets abroad.

In its diplomatic role, the Mossad has opened doors and maintained relations with dozens of countries which prefer these connections not to be known. When digging beneath the surface, however, a question presents itself: What is the great value in having an intelligence agency doing something which the foreign ministry should do? There is no great value in maintaining clandestine relations with countries which find it more convenient not to have open, diplomatic ties with Israel. The Mossad simply gives the other nations an easy way out.

The foreign states do, on the other hand, insist on doing it the secret way. Fearing leaks to the press, they do not want to deal with Israel's foreign ministry. They have developed complete confidence in the Mossad's ability to be the great guardian of secrets.

Israel has also achieved startling success in penetrating the very heart of Arab officialdom: agents among the senior officials of Syria and Egypt, a secret dialogue with Jordan, an intelligence exchange with Morocco and spies within Yasser Arafat's PLO.

The foundations of both the achievements and the legends accompanying them are not well understood. Israel's intelligence community, just as those of other nations, is a mirror of the society which it serves and from which it draws its power and inspiration. Each country has an intelligence structure shaped in its own image. In parallel with the covert work itself, a certain folklore and mythology develop. They reflect the individual country's national temperament and the character of its culture.

The British, as in other areas of human activity, consider intelligence to be a game. The stress is on the contest, which is more a struggle of the human mind and less the application of muscle and brute force. British intelligence prefers to be depicted as elegant, brainy, sophisticated and brimming with schemes. It is based on human qualities: understanding and intellect. It may be characterized as British gentility, with an added air of romanticism and adventure.

The French play a sport in which governments say one thing, but intend something entirely different. Their secret services bridle at having to follow orders and even try to undermine the decisions of their political masters. For French spies, nothing is final; a deal is not a deal; there is always an official willing to look the other way.

The Americans have made intelligence into big business. Their stress is on quantity. American espionage is a massive conglomerate based, not on the virtuosity of the individual, but primarily on the efficiency and methodology of the entire system. The emphasis is on teamwork, supported by the best equipment and latest technology. In their actions, they can be exceedingly cruel, bombing civilians when deemed necessary, toppling regimes and even plotting to liquidate heads of state. The American agent always presents the justification that he is acting for the free world and democracy, not simply in the selfish interests of the US.

The Soviets, on the other hand, regard intelligence primarily as a tool for preserving their own regime and the survival of the Communist system. The individual within the organization is perceived as a small cog who is only a part of the collective. He is an obedient instrument of a rigid bureaucracy which is, by nature, hierarchical.

The influence of all four models can be found in the Israeli intelligence community. The experiences of Britain, France, the United States and the Soviet Union have, wittingly or unwittingly, left their mark on Israel's secret services since 1948.

The Israeli community is a synthesis of various traditions which were learned, adopted, inherited, copied or even purloined from other countries which have had longer histories as states and have more deeply ingrained intelligence customs.

Reuven Shiloah was, without doubt, one of the British-style gentlemen patricians overseeing the birth of Israeli intelligence. He loved secret schemes, diplomatic intrigues and broad strategic concepts. He romanticized the role of the spy, while also showing a great deal of inefficiency.

Isser Harel improved the efficiency, largely on Soviet-style lines. Russian characteristics coloured Israeli intelligence, perhaps subconsciously, as an inherent part of the spirit brought by the Jewish state's founding fathers from Russia and Eastern Europe. The Russian input included socialism, pioneering, centralization and placing the state above the individual. Harel was influenced by all these elements, although he added a lot of Harel to the Russian model.

Meir Amit also injected much of himself into an American-style management of intelligence. Great efforts were made to incorporate efficient use of both personnel and gadgets. The latest computers and technology were essential tools in Amit's self-shaped community.

Shimon Peres and Yitzhak Shamir, uncomfortably sharing the reins of government and of the intelligence community in the 1980s, both gained their early experience in French-style clandestine dealings. Peres practically commuted to Paris on Lakam and defence projects, and Shamir was there as a senior Mossad operative. They inherited the deceptive practices of the labyrinthine French secret services and introduced them in Israel. The now-traditional wink of the eye means that Israelis feel they will always get away with it – whatever it may be.[2]

Indeed, it is the Israeli character which dominates the history of the nation's intelligence community. Above all, regardless of rockets in orbit, electronic eavesdropping, or other space-age inventions added to its arsenal, Israel has always relied on *humint*. Its human intelligence resources – its people – have given it the decisive edge.

Whenever a chief of intelligence resigns or retires from the community, he invariably claims that things are not as they used to be. The 'formers' contend that everything that was wonderful is collapsing and that little excellence survives.

The truth, however, is that they are the ones who are succumbing to the difficulties of adjusting to life as a civilian. To reassure themselves that they were good back in their heyday, they go public – usually for the first time in their lives – to criticize the way things are run now.

Mossad veteran Dave Kimche claims the agency is in decline, saying the men and women working there now are not the same kind of operatives who were there when he joined in 1953. 'The main difference was in the great motivation of our people,' Kimche says. 'It was a matter of mission and readiness to work day and night with unlimited dedication.'[3]

The graveyards of the world, however, are filled with people who believed they were irreplaceable. The 'formers' who leave are constantly replaced by newcomers, who with proper control and inspiration can overcome the shattering scandals and failures. They can lead the Israeli intelligence community into the future, based on the same goals and requirements set forth in Ben-Gurion's time.

The existential needs of Israel have not changed, at their

roots, in over four decades. The state is still surrounded by hostile nations, which are increasingly willing to accept the reality of Israel's existence, but continue to plot and fight to weaken it. Even as Arafat and the PLO embark on a new, diplomatic path, Israel is faced with extremist Palestinian terrorists whom it must counter.

The demographic statistics looming over Israel will continue to demand Jewish immigration into Israel, so as not to be outnumbered by Arabs within Israeli territory, and this will require Jewish intelligence. In addition, Israel will need to research and develop its technological and industrial advantages, using inventiveness, as well as the kind of espionage which was Lakam's speciality, to keep ahead of the Arabs.

Israel has always been strong when it comes to facts and ideas. The intelligence community is extremely successful at obtaining them. It is also among the best in the world at executing specific missions, such as an assault against targets far from Israel's borders.

Israeli intelligence is not so good, however, at processing, analysing and evaluating the information it obtains. Problems of coordination persist in disseminating the data to the various 'customers' in official Israeli circles.

Intelligence analysts did not realize, in 1967, that a long-term occupation of the West Bank and Gaza Strip would be harmful to Israel. They did not foresee the peace initiative of Egypt's President Anwar Sadat ten years later. They did not correctly evaluate the situation in Lebanon when plotting the Israeli invasion of 1982. They did not predict war between Iran and Iraq in 1980, nor the end of the conflict in 1988. They did not detect that, in reaction to the Gulf War, Saudi Arabia would purchase Chinese medium-range missiles which could reach Israel.

It has become fashionable in Israel, in a sharp departure from the once automatic praise for the intelligence agencies, to blame them for events taking unexpected or unwelcome turns. The Middle East defies simple predictions, but in the new critical spirit Israelis express disappointment when their secret services cannot wave a magic wand and solve all outstanding problems.

Expectations are too high and the intelligence community cannot meet them all. The failures of foresight should not be exaggerated. Intelligence is simply an extension of the nation's policies. If the policies are faulty, even the best intelligence in the world cannot repair them.

It is doubtful that even if given all the proper warnings by Aman, Golda Meir and Moshe Dayan would have gone to war on Yom Kippur in 1973. They were still prisoners of 'the Concept' that the Arabs were incapable of beating Israel. The government leaders of 1982, or at least Menachem Begin and Ariel Sharon, were determined to sweep the PLO out of Lebanon and nothing the Mossad could say would have stopped them.

Prime Minister Shamir seemed to give little weight to an intelligence assessment delivered by Aman in March 1989, warning that Israel had few alternatives but to negotiate with the PLO. First, Shamir said publicly that there was no such report, and then he condemned whoever it was who leaked it from the cabinet. In another context, Shamir revealed his love of secrecy: 'Events are usually known to those who should know, and whoever does not know should continue not knowing.'[4]

A senior aide to the Prime Minister is said to have criticized Aman's assessment in a letter to agency chief General Amnon Shahak, adding that if published the report could be used by the United States to apply pressure on Israel to talk to the PLO.[5]

Even if politicians do pay close heed to the advice, analysis and wisdom of their intelligence chiefs, does it really help the decision-making process? Are the great energies and resources put into secret services absolutely necessary for Israel?

Israeli intelligence failed to predict the surprise attack by Egypt and Syria in 1973. As in the 1941 surprises of Adolf Hitler's invasion of Russia and the Japanese attack on Pearl Harbor, the individual facts which could have formed a composite picture of aggression on the horizon were available. They were simply not put together into a coherent and convincing whole and the warning signs were ignored by the leaders of the target countries.

These were intelligence failures of a strategic nature – blindness to major questions of war and peace. Intelligence can definitely be useful on a tactical level. Modern history has shown that intelligence communities usually do not have much say in formulating policies, but they do have a role in pursuing limited and specific goals set by their political masters.

In preparing for and fighting a war, advance information on the disposition of enemy troops and firepower is clearly a key element in achieving victory – so long as the information is analysed and disseminated correctly. Similarly, preventive intelligence can save lives by providing advance word of an expected terrorist attack. Secret agents are also the ideal choice for executing well-defined, precise assignments.

By dwelling excessively on grand design and inflated ambitions, Israeli intelligence has betrayed its own true nature. The outer bounds of what can be accomplished should be recognized. Israel should not expect its intelligence community to be more than it can be: an excellent example of what a small nation – with meagre resources – can do by using intelligence to the utmost. The community's history has exposed both the inescapable limitations and the maximal achievements of intelligence.

Reference Notes

Chapter 1: *The Death of the Informers*
1. *Jerusalem Post*, February 26, 1988; *Los Angeles Times*, February 27, 1988; *Washington Post*, March 1, 1988.
2. *New York Times*, February 17, 1988.
3. *Washington Post*, April 17, 1988.
4. *Sunday Times*, April 24, 1988.
5. Ibid.
6. Yossi Melman, *The Master Terrorist: The True Story Behind Abu Nidal* (London: Sidgwick and Jackson, 1987), pp. 142–3, 170–4.
7. Reuter news agency, November 5 and 7, 1988.
8. Retired General Ariel Sharon, in charge of that operation, revealed the details in a *New York Times* interview, reprinted in *Ma'ariv*, November 10, 1988.

Chapter 2: *First Steps*
1. Hagai Eshed, *One-Man 'Mossad': Reuven Shiloah, Father of Israeli Intelligence* (Tel Aviv: Edanim Publishers, Yediot Aharonot edition, 1988), p. 120.
2. Ibid., p. 31.
3. Abba Eban, interviewed by the authors, August 27, 1988.

4. Eshed, *One-Man*, p. 42; also Tom Segev, *1949: The First Israelis* (Jerusalem: Domino Press, 1984), p. 34.
5. Eshed, *One-Man*, pp. 84–8.
6. Ibid., pp. 97–102.
7. Ibid., pp. 14–16.
8. Eyewitness Herzl Ehrlich, interviewed by the authors, September 19, 1988; also Stewart Steven, *The Spymasters of Israel* (New York: Ballantine Books, 1980), p. 23; and Zeev Schiff and Eitan Haber, *Israel, Army and Defence: A Dictionary* (Tel Aviv: Zmora, Bitan, Modan, 1976), pp. 222–3.
9. Eshed, *One-Man*, p. 120; also Michael Bar-Zohar, *Isser Harel and Israel's Security Services* (Jerusalem: Weidenfeld and Nicolson, 1970), pp. 32–5.
10. Bar-Zohar, *Isser Harel*, p. 40.
11. *Yediot Aharonot*, April 7, 1988.
12. Schiff and Haber, *Israel, Army and Defence*, p. 189.
13. Eshed, *One-Man*, p. 127; Bar-Zohar, *Isser Harel*, pp. 62–4; Steven, *The Spymasters of Israel*, pp. 33–9.
14. Eshed, *One-Man*, pp. 127–9.
15. Isser Harel, *Security and Democracy* (Jerusalem: Edanim/Yediot Ahanorot, 1989), pp. 170–5.
16. Steven, *The Spymasters of Israel*, p. 39.
17. Yaakov Frank, interviewed by the authors, September 20, 1988; also *Ma'ariv*, January 30, 1984.
18. Frank interview.
19. Frank interview; also Shlomo Hillel, *East Wind: On a Secret Mission to the Arab Lands* (Jerusalem: Edanim/Yediot Aharonot and Ministry of Defence, 1985).
20. Hillel, *Mission*, pp. 236–45.
21. Interview with Avraham Dar in *Yediot Aharonot*, January 1, 1988.
22. Avri El-Ad, *Decline of Honor* (Chicago: Regency Books, 1976), pp. 60–2; see also Aviezer Golan, *Operation Susannah* (New York: Harper and Row, 1978).
23. Interview with Jean Bennett and her daughter Michele, in *Ha'aretz*, January 1, 1988; also *Davar*, November 26, 1987.

24. Avraham Dar in *Yediot Aharonot*, January 1, 1988.
25. *Ha'aretz*, January 1, 1988.
26. *Ha'aretz* and *Davar*.
27. Eshed, *One-Man*, p. 136, and authors' interview with Ben-Natan
28. El-Ad, *Decline of Honor*, pp. 181–193.
29. Segev, *1949: The First Israelis*, pp. 119–120.
30. Eshed, *One-Man*, p. 137.

Chapter 3: *Strategic Alliances*

1. Eshed, *One-Man*, pp. 164–5.
2. David C. Martin, *Wilderness of Mirrors* (New York: Harper and Row, 1980), p. 11.
3. Martin, *Wilderness of Mirrors*, p. 20.
4. Stephen Green, *Taking Sides: America's Secret Relations with a Militant Israel* (New York: William Morrow and Company, 1984), p. 19, quoting a memorandum to Secretary of Defense James Forrestal.
5. Martin, *Wilderness of Mirrors*, p. 21; and Eshed, *One-Man*, p. 163; Harel, *Security and Democracy*, pp. 381–2.
6. Steven, *The Spymasters of Israel*, p. 32.
7. Eshed, *One-Man*, p. 164. There are various versions, but nearly all credit Israeli intelligence with obtaining the secret speech.
8. *The Guardian*, May 13, 1987.
9. William Colby and Peter Forbath, *Honorable Men: My Life in the CIA* (New York: Simon and Schuster, 1978), p. 365; quoted in John Ranelagh, *The Agency: The Rise and Decline of the CIA* (London: Weidenfeld and Nicolson, 1986), pp. 560–3.
10. Peter Wright, *Spycatcher: The Candid Autobiography of a Senior Intelligence Officer* (New York: Viking Penguin, 1987), pp. 346–7.
11. Martin, *Wilderness of Mirrors*, p. 57; Eshed, *One-Man*, p. 160; and *Washington Post*, December 5, 1987.
12. *Ha'aretz*, May 13, 1988; also *Ma'ariv*, May 25, 1988, based on an interview published a few days earlier in London's *Sunday Times*, in which Harold (Kim) Philby admitted

his past for the first time. See also Chapman Pincher, *Their Trade is Treachery* (London: Sidgwick and Jackson, 1981), p. 14.

13. Pincher, *Their Trade is Treachery*, p. 186; and Richard Deacon, *'C': A Biography of Sir Maurice Oldfield, Head of MI6* (London: Futura Books, 1985), pp. 29, 69, 80, 230, 250–5. .

14. Deacon, *'C': A Biography of Sir Maurice Oldfield*, p. 250.

15. Chapman Pincher, *Traitors: Labyrinths of Treason* (London: Sidgwick and Jackson, 1987), p. 93.

16. Pincher, *Traitors: Labyrinths of Treason*, p. 98; and *Ha'aretz*, December 1, 1982.

17. Yossi Melman and Dan Raviv, *Behind the Uprising: Israelis, Jordanians, and Palestinians* (Westport, Connecticut: Greenwood Press, 1989).

18. Jonathan Bloch and Patrick Fitzgerald, *British Intelligence and Covert Action* (London: Junction Books, 1983), pp. 128–9.

19. Aryeh (Lova) Eliav, *Rings of Testimony* (Tel Aviv: Am Oved, 1984), pp. 156–64.

20. Samuel Segev, *The Iranian Triangle: The Secret Relations between Israel and Iran* (Tel Aviv: Maariv Books, 1981), p. 88.

21. Yossi Melman, *The CIA Report on the Intelligence Services of Israel* (Tel Aviv: Erez, 1982), p. 57, quoting a classified report by the CIA dated 1976 and published in 1979 by the Islamic militants who seized the US Embassy in Teheran; Eshed, *One-Man*, pp. 262–4; Bloch and Fitzgerald, *British Intelligence and Covert Action*, p. 113; Deacon, *'C': A Biography of Sir Maurice Oldfield*, p. 113 and Shmuel Segev, *The Iranian Triangle: The Untold Story of Israel's Role in the Iran–Contra Affair* (New York: Free Press, 1988), p. 32.

22. Israel Defence Ministry memorandum on Weizman–Tufanian meeting in Tel Aviv, dated July 18, 1977, marked 'Top Secret', but published by the Islamic militants who seized the US Embassy in Teheran in 1979.

23. US State Department memorandum from Washington

to Teheran, dated November 25, 1970, published in 1983 by the militants in Teheran.

24. Bloch and Fitzgerald, *British Intelligence and Covert Action*, pp. 159–60.

Chapter 4: *Lakam and the Nuclear Bomb*

1. Article by Mordecai Bar-On, aide-de-camp to Chief of Staff Moshe Dayan, in *Yediot Aharonot*, October 24, 1986; also Ben-Natan, interviewed by the authors, December 12, 1988.
2. *Ma'ariv*, October 24, 1986.
3. Michael Bar-Zohar, *Bridge over the Mediterranean: Israeli–French Relations, 1947–1963* (Tel Aviv: Am Hasefer, 1965), referring to its title.
4. *Ma'ariv*, December 5, 1986.
5. *Davar*, December 29, 1986.
6. Green, *Taking Sides*, pp. 149–50.
7. Matti Golan, *Peres* (Tel Aviv: Schocken Books, 1982), p. 54.
8. Ibid., pp. 71–4.
9. Peter Pringle and James Spiegelman, *The Nuclear Barons: the Inside Story of How they Created our Nuclear Nightmare* (London: Michael Joseph, 1982), pp. 295–6.
10. *Yediot Aharonot*, May 29, 1987.
11. Pringle and Spiegelman, *The Nuclear Barons*, p. 296.
12. *Yediot Aharonot*, September 9, 1986.
13. The complete story appeared in *Newsweek* and was quoted in *Ha'aretz*, January 5, 1978.
14. *Ha'aretz*, January 5, 1978.
15. *Washington Post*, December 5, 1987.
16. *Los Angeles Times*, June 16, 1986; and *Washington Post*, June 5, 1986.
17. Pringle and Spiegelman, *The Nuclear Barons*, p. 297. The complete story was published in Elaine Davenport, Paul Eddy and Peter Gillman, *The Plumbat Affair* (London: Andre Deutsch, 1978). Also, see *Ha'aretz*, June 26, 1978.
18. *Ha'aretz*, January 5, 1978.
19. *Ha'aretz*, April 17 and May 22, 1987.

20 Israel Defence Ministry memorandum on Weizman–Tufanian meeting in Tel Aviv, dated July 18, 1977, marked 'Top Secret', but published by the Islamic militants who seized the US Embassy in Teheran in 1979.

21. *Ma'ariv*, September 20, 1988; also Amos Perlmutter, Michael Handel, and Uri Bar-Joseph, *Two Minutes over Baghdad* (London: Vallentine Mitchell and Company, 1982), p. 46.

22. Steven, *The Spymasters of Israel*, pp. 210–20; and Dennis Eisenberg, Uri Dan, and Eli Landau, *The Mossad: Inside Stories* (New York: New American Library, 1978), pp. 177–98 and 212–27.

23. *Washington Post*, October 30, 1986; *Ha'aretz, Davar*, and *Al Hamishmar*, November 2, 1986.

24. Melman, *CIA Report*, p. 52.

Chapter 5: *Harel's Crusades*

1. *Al Hamishmar*, weekend magazine, September 5, 1975, and Harel, *Security and Democracy*, pp. 226–47.

2. Segev, *1949: The First Israelis*, pp. 292, 294.

3. Ibid., p. 264.

4. Bar-Zohar, *Isser Harel*, p. 264.

5. Ibid., p. 99.

6. Ibid., pp. 135–8.

7. Ibid., pp. 1–32.

8. Ibid., pp. 106–8, 148.

9. Ibid., pp. 106–8, 148; Harel, *Security and Democracy*, pp. 199–216.

10. Israel Beer, *Israel's Security: Yesterday, Today, Tomorrow* (Tel Aviv: Amikam, 1966); and Isser Harel, *Soviet Espionage: Communism in Israel* (Tel Aviv: Edanim, Yediot Aharonot, 1987), pp. 93–169.

11. *Yediot Aharonot*, October 24, 1986.

12. Harel, *Soviet Espionage*, pp. 131–6.

13. Ibid., p. 20.

14. Ibid., p. 21.

15. El-Ad, *Decline*, pp. 282–4; and Moshe Zak, *Israel and the*

Soviet Union: A Forty-Year Dialogue (Tel Aviv: Ma'ariv Book Guild, 1988), pp. 301–2.

16. Harel, *Soviet Espionage*, pp. 169–75; and *Ma'ariv*, November 14, 1986.
17. Melman, *CIA Report*, pp. 61–3.
18. Ibid., p. 67; and Green, *Taking Sides*, p. 19.
19. *Ha'ir*, September 26, 1986.
20. According to former operative Eliyahu Ben-Elissar, interviewed on Israel Defence Forces Radio, 1986.
21. El-Ad, *Decline*, p. 31.
22. Ibid., pp. 267–8.
23. *Hadashot*, November 14, 1986.
24. Ibid.; Harel, *Security and Democracy*, pp. 270–3; and *Jerusalem Post Magazine*, January 20, 1989.
25. *Monitin* [Israeli magazine], May 1987.
26. Yigal Mossensohn, interviewed by the authors, December 6, 1988.
27. Peter Mann and Uri Dan, *Eichmann in My Hands* (Tel Aviv: Massada Publishers, 1987), p. 164.
28. *Monitin*, August 1986, p. 37.
29. One of the journalists concerned, Samuel Segev, interviewed by the authors, October 21, 1988; and Bar-Zohar, *Isser Harel*, p. 240.

Chapter 6: *Amit Cleans the Mossad Stable*
1. Eitan Haber, *Today War Will Break Out: Reminiscenses of Brigadier General Israel Lior, Aide-de-Camp to Prime Minister Levi Eshkol and Golda Meir* (Tel Aviv: Edanim/ Yediot Aharonot, 1988), p. 62.
2. Ibid., p. 62.
3. Steven, *The Spymasters of Israel*, pp. 158, 180, 186–7; Yair Kotler, *Joe Returns to the Limelight* (Tel Aviv: Modan, 1988), p. 40.
4. Kotler, *Joe Returns to the Limelight*, p. 61; also Haber, *Today War Will Break Out*, p. 62; and *Yediot Aharonot*, October 16, 1987.
5. Kotler, *Joe Returns to the Limelight*, pp. 66–8; and Harel, in *Yediot Aharonot*, October 16, 1987.

6. Kotler, *Joe Returns to the Limelight*, p. 61; and Steven, *The Spymasters of Israel*, pp. 186–7.
7. A long-time Mossad operative, who wished to remain anonymous, interviewed by the authors, 1988.
8. Yitzhak Shamir, in an interview with the authors, September 10, 1987.
9. Kotler, *Joe Returns to the Limelight*, p. 45.
10. Steven, *The Spymasters of Israel*, pp. 188–93; also Melman, *CIA Report*.
11. *Hadashot*, July 23, 1987.
12. *Ha'ir*, September 2, 1988.
13. *Yediot Aharonot*, May 3, 1987.
14. *Ha'ir*, September 2, 1988.
15. Ibid.
16. Melman, *CIA Report*, pp. 41–56; and Walter Laqueur, *A World of Secrets: The Use and Limits of Intelligence* (New York: Basic Books, 1985), p. 220.
17. Steven, *The Spymasters of Israel*, pp. 188–93.
18. Bar-Zohar, *Isser Harel*, pp. 184–9.
19. Eisenberg, *Mossad*, pp. 51–65.
20. Ibid., pp. 60–1.
21. Ibid., p. 61; also Steven, *The Spymasters of Israel*, pp. 214–20.
22. Steven, *The Spymasters of Israel*, p. 171; also Wolfgang Lotz, *The Champagne Spy* (New York: St Martin's Press, 1972).
23. This claim appears in E. H. Cookridge, *Gehlen: Spy of the Century* (New York: Random House, 1971), as quoted in Steven, *The Spymasters of Israel*, p. 171.
24. Samuel Segev, *Alone in Damascus: The Life and Death of Eli Cohen* (Jerusalem: Keter, 1986), p. 60.
25. Ibid., p. 23.
26. Ibid., p. 14.
27. Ibid.; and *Ha'aretz*, July 14 and 21, 1972, and March 8, 1974.
28. Joshua Tadmor, *The Silent Warriors* (New York: Macmillan, 1970), pp. 93–5.
29. Ibid., pp. 119–23.

30. Laqueur, *A World of Secrets*, p. 22; Melman, *CIA Report*, pp. 46 and 56; and Bloch and Fitzgerald, *British Intelligence and Covert Action*, pp. 162–3.
31. Melman, *CIA Report*, p. 58.
32. *Yediot Aharonot*, January 2, 9, and 16, 1987; and *Ma'ariv*, October 24, 1986.
33. Melman, *CIA Report*; also *Ma'ariv* and *Observer*, March 15, 1988.
34. Steven, *The Spymasters of Israel*, pp. 240–52; also *Monitin* quoting *Time*, December 29, 1975.
35. *Monitin*, June 1987.
36. *Yediot Aharonot*, October 16 and 19, 1987.
37. Ibid.
38. Amos Kenan, *Your Land, Your Country* (Jerusalem: Edanim, Yediot Aharonot, 1981), pp. 62–79.

Chapter 7: *Shin Bet Has its Day*

1. Ehud Yaari, *Fatah* (Tel Aviv: Levin-Epstein Books, 1970), pp. 101–2.
2. Ibid., pp. 90–1.
3. Haber, *Today War Will Break Out*, pp. 130–1.
4. *Ma'ariv*, December 4, 1987; and *Hadashot*, June 19, 1987.
5. Ibid., and *Ma'ariv*, April 7, 1988.
6. Haber, *Will War Break Out Today*, pp. 130–1.
7. Shlomo Gazit, *The Stick and the Carrot: the Israeli Administration in Judea and Samaria* (Tel Aviv: Zmora Bitan, 1985), p. 107.
8. Ibid., pp. 133, 223, 284.
9. Melman, *CIA Report*, p. 93, quoting a CIA report on the Israeli intelligence community, dated 1976 and published by the Iranian militants who seized the US Embassy in Teheran in 1979.
10. Ibid.
11. Ibid.
12. Yaari, *Fatah*, pp. 91–103.
13. *Yediot Aharonot* devoted an investigative issue in April 1988 to Israel's occupation of the territories; see also David Grossman, *The Yellow Wind* (Jerusalem: Keter,

1987, Hebrew edition); see also *Koteret Rashit*, 'The Swiss Scenery', April 29, 1987.

14. *Hadashot*, November 6, 1987.
15. *Hadashot*, June 19, 1987.
16. Yossi Melman and Dan Raviv, 'Expelling Palestinians', in *Washington Post*, 'Outlook' section, February 7, 1988.
17. Haber, *Today War Will Break Out*, p. 324, and *Ma'ariv*, February 2, 1989.
18. *Ma'ariv*, November 10, 1988; Associated Press, 'Former Mossad Chief Named as Suspect in 1973 Crash', February 1, 1989; and authors' interview with Zvi Zamir, January 30, 1989.
19. Haber, *Today War Will Break Out*, pp. 343–4; and Haber and Schiff, *Israel's Army and Defence*, p. 74.
20. *International Herald Tribune* and *Washington Post*, April 22, 1988; see also *Hadashot*, December 2, 1988.
21. *Ma'ariv*, September 23, 1987 and February 5, 1988.
22. Haber, *Today War Will Break Out*, pp. 328–30.
23. Steven, *The Spymasters of Israel*, pp. 304–5; and Haber and Schiff, *Israel's Army and Defence*, p. 195.
24. *Hadashot*, November 6, 1987.
25. Steven, *The Spymasters of Israel*, pp. 309–10.
26. Yoel Marcus was the first journalist to expose the activities of 'Committee X', in *Ha'aretz*, June 10, 1986.
27. Operational details can be found in David B. Tinnin with Dag Christensen, *The Hit Team* (London: Futura Books, 1977).
28. *Monitin*, February 1988.
29. Steve Posner, *Israel Undercover: Secret Warfare and Hidden Diplomacy in the Middle East* (Syracuse, New York: Syracuse University Press, 1987), pp. 20–78.
30. Michael Bar-Zohar and Eitan Haber, *The Quest for the Red Prince* (London: Weidenfeld and Nicolson, 1983), pp. 215–21; and David Ignatius in *Wall Street Journal*, February 10, 1983.

Chapter 8: *The Surprises of War and Peace*
1. *Ha'ir*, October 2, 1987; also Haber and Schiff, *Israel's Army and Defence: A Dictionary*, p. 219.

2. *Ha'ir*, October 10, 1986.
3. James Bamford, *The Puzzle Palace* (Boston: Houghton Mifflin, 1987).
4. Melman, *CIA Report*, pp. 69–75.
5. Richard Nixon, *RN: The Memoirs of Richard Nixon, Volume 2* (New York: Warner Books, 1978), p. 475.
6. Sadat, quoted in Marvin Kalb and Bernard Kalb, *Kissinger* (New York: Dell Publishing, 1975), p. 514.
7. Haber, *Today War Will Break Out*, p. 20; also Yoel Ben-Porat in *Al Hamishmar*, September 20, 1988. Ben-Porat was in charge of an Aman research unit which investigated 'the Yom Kippur surprise' and traded accusations with Zvi Zamir in *Monitin* magazine, September and December 1988; Zamir threatened to sue Ben-Porat and the magazine.
8. Dayan told Israeli newspaper editors on October 8, 1973; also Perlmutter, *Two Minutes over Baghdad*, pp. 43–9.
9. *Koteret Rashit*, November 16, 1988.
10. Perlmutter, *Two Minutes over Baghdad*, pp. 43–51.
11. *Davar*, weekly supplement, December 7, 1987.
12. Classified CIA report on Israel's intelligence community, published by the Islamic militants who seized the US Embassy in Teheran in 1979.
13. Melman, *CIA Report*, pp. 101–4.
14. Melman and Raviv, *Behind the Uprising: Israelis, Jordanians, and Palestinians* (Westport, Connecticut: Greenwood Press, 1989).
15. Bob Woodward, *Veil: The Secret Wars of the CIA 1981–1987* (New York: Simon and Schuster, 1987), p. 381; earlier revealed by his *Washington Post* colleague Don Oberdorfer.
16. Woodward, *Veil: The Secret Wars of the CIA*, p. 308; and Steven, *The Spymasters of Israel*, p. 240.
17. Haber and Schiff, *Israel's Army and Defence: A Dictionary*, p. 203.
18. Melman, *CIA Report*, p. 57.
19. Davenport, Eddy and Gilman, *The Plumbat Affair*, pp. 178–9.

20. William Stevenson, *90 Minutes at Entebbe* (New York: Bantam Books, 1976), pp. 76–88; Bloch and Fitzgerald, *British Intelligence and Covert Action*, pp. 128–9, 159–60; *Ha'aretz*, April 3, 1981; and *Davar*, May 28 and 29, 1978.

21. Kol Israel radio report, June 8, 1983.

22. Ali told the tale to Israeli official Dan Pattir, who later told *Ma'ariv*, November 22, 1987.

23. Moshe Dayan, *Breakthrough: A Personal Account of the Egypt–Israel Peace Negotiations* (New York: Alfred A. Knopf, 1981), pp. 43–4, 52.

24. Major General Shlomo Gazit, in *Ma'ariv*, January 7, 1983.

25. Ze'ev Schiff, *A History of the Israeli Army* (New York: Macmillan Publishing, 1985), p. 204.

26. Ehud Yaari, in *Monitin*, September 1986.

Chapter 9: *For the Good of the Jews*

1. Tudor Parfitt, *Operation Moses* (New York: Stein & Day, 1985), serialized by *Yediot Aharonot*, October 25, 1985.

2. Ibid.; also Yehiel Kadishai, interviewed by the authors, October 31, 1988.

3. Segev, *1949: The First Israelis*, pp. 119–20.

4. *Ha'ir*, October 23, 1987; also Harel, *Soviet Espionage*, p. 65 and *Davar*, November 26, 1984.

5. Eliav, *Rings of Testimony*, p. 165.

6. Ibid.

7. Amos Ettinger, *Blind Jump: The Story of Yeshayahu (Shaike) Dan* (Tel Aviv: Zmora Bitan, 1986), p. 35.

8. Harel, *Soviet Espionage*, p. 66; Ettinger, *Blind Jump*, p. 352.

9. Ettinger, *Blind Jump*, p. 356; and Eliav, *Rings of Testimony*, pp. 166–70.

10. Zak, *Israel and the Soviet Union*, pp. 301–2; and Harel, *Soviet Espionage*, p. 22.

11. Ettinger, *Blind Jump*, p. 356.

12. *Ha'aretz*, January 11, 1988; and Ilya Dzhirkvelov, *Secret Servant: My Life with the KGB and the Soviet Elite* (London: Collins, 1987), pp. 244–9.

13. *Ma'ariv*, November 4, 1988.
14. Ibid.; and *Ha'aretz*, January 11, 1988.
15. *Al Hamishmar*, May 15, 1988; *Yediot Aharonot*, February 26 and May 15, 1988; and *Davar*, December 6, 1988, quoting Jack Anderson's column.
16. *Ha'ir*, October 23, 1987.
17. *Ha'aretz*, May 4, 1981.
18. *Ha'ir*, October 23, 1987.
19. Eliav, *Rings of Testimony*, pp. 166–70.
20. *Ha'aretz*, May 29, 1987; *Yediot Aharonot*, January 22, 1988; and Reuter news agency, December 28, 1988.
21. Ettinger, *Blind Jump*, p. 13.
22. Ibid., p. 386; and Harel, *Soviet Espionage*, pp. 24–5.
23. *Ma'ariv*, October 19, 1987; and Ettinger, *Blind Jump*, p. 386.
24. *Ha'aretz*, November 18, 1988.
25. Kadishai, interviewed by the authors.
26. *Koteret Rashit*, October 30, 1985; *Yediot Aharonot*, October 25 and November 2, 1985, serializing Parfitt, *Operation Moses*.
27. *Koteret Rashit*, October 30, 1985; and *Ma'ariv*, November 3, 1988.

Chapter 10: *The Age of Adventurism*

1. *Ma'ariv*, May 13, 1988, report by Shin Bet operative Noam Federman.
2. Haber and Schiff, *Israel's Army and Defence: A Dictionary*, pp. 521–3.
3. *The Guardian*, May 6, 1984.
4. Shlomo Nakdimon, *Tammuz in Flames* (Jerusalem: Edanim/Yediot Aharonot, 1986), pp. 38–47; also Perlmutter, *Two Minutes over Bagdhad*, pp. 58–60.
5. Nakdimon, *Tammuz in Flames*, p. 88; and Perlmutter, *Two Minutes over Bagdhad*, pp. 69–70.
6. Perlmutter, *Two Minutes over Baghdad*, pp. 69–70; and *Yediot Aharonot*, October 16, 1987.
7. Nakdimon, *Tammuz in Flames*, pp. 83, 100.

8. Avraham Tamir, interviewed by the authors, November 28, 1988.
9. Nakdimon, *Tammuz in Flames*, pp. 294–5; *Ha'aretz*, June 18, 1981; and *Ma'ariv*, June 22, 1981.
10. Speech by Ariel Sharon on November 7, 1981, at the Jaffe Centre for Strategic Studies at the University of Tel Aviv.
11. *Davar*, April 22, 1984.
12. The events were related to the authors by separate sources who took part in the secret contacts but insisted on anonymity.
13. *Ha'aretz*, August 14, 1983, October 10, 1983, January 25, 1983; based on reports in the 'Foreign Report' of *The Economist*.
14. Woodward, *Veil: The Secret Wars of the CIA*, pp. 204–12.
15. Shimon Shiffer, *Snow Ball: The Story Behind the Lebanon War* (Jerusalem: Edanim/Yediot Aharonot, 1984).

Chapter 11: *Killings and Cover-Ups*
1. *Hadashot*, September 23, 1987.
2. Alex Libak, interviewed by the authors, November 13, 1988.
3. *Koteret Rashit*, May 28, 1986.
4. Ibid.
5. Ibid.
6. Karp Commission Report, published by Government of Israel, December 30, 1987.
7. *Washington Post*, April 12, 1987.
8. *Hadashot*, September 23, 1987.
9. *Yediot Aharonot*, May 29, 1987.
10. *Yediot Aharonot*, June 2, 1987.
11. *Yediot Aharonot*, May 29, 1987.
12. *Hadashot*, November 4, 1988.
13. *Yediot Aharonot*, November 11, 1987.
14. *Koteret Rashit*, December 2, 1987.
15. Landau Commission Report, published by Government of Israel, December 1, 1987.

Reference Notes

Chapter 12: *A Spy in America*

1. *Washington Post*, November 24, 1985.
2. *New York Times*, November 27, 1985; and *Washington Post*, November 30, 1985.
3. *US News and World Report*, June 1, 1987.
4. Eitan told his life story to *Washington Post*, May 31, 1987.
5. *US News and World Report*, June 1, 1987.
6. Wolf Blitzer, *Territory of Lies* (New York: Harper and Row, 1989), pp. 129–30.
7. The Stanford professor was quoted in *Washington Post*, November 23, 1985. Agee's account was in *US News and World Report*, June 1, 1987.
8. *Washington Post*, June 7, 1986 and Blitzer, *Territory of Lies*, pp. 142–4.
9. *Los Angeles Times*, November 27, 1985.
10. Classified CIA study on Israeli intelligence community, dated 1976, published by Islamic militants who seized US Embassy in Teheran in 1979.
11. *New York Times*, March 5, 1987.
12. *Time*, March 16, 1987.
13. *Washington Post* and *New York Times*, December 21, 1985.
14. *Hadashot*, March 15, 1987.
15. *Los Angeles Times*, March 7, 1987.
16. *Christian Science Monitor* and *Los Angeles Times*, March 4, 1987.
17. *Los Angeles Times*, March 7, 1987.
18. A former Director of Central Intelligence, who preferred not to be named, interviewed by the authors, April 14, 1988.

Chapter 13: *The Chaos of Irangate*

1. Stephen Green, *Living by the Sword: America and Israel in the Middle East, 1968–1987* (London: Faber and Faber, 1988), p. 218.
2. Haber and Schiff, *Israel's Army and Defence: A Dictionary*, p. 502.
3. BBC Television, 'Panorama', February 1, 1982.

4. Kimche, interviewed in *Yediot Aharonot*, January 2, 1987.
5. The authors have read Ghorbanifar's secret study written for the Mossad.
6. *Davar*, December 12, 1986.
7. *New York Times*, December 3, 1988; *Washington Post*, December 2 and 3, 1988.
8. The sequence of events of Irangate were related to the authors by separate sources, who took part in the events and even shared some relevant documents, but insisted on anonymity.

Chapter 14: *Business at All Costs*
1. *Christian Science Monitor*, December 27, 1982.
2. *The Military Balance 1981/82* (London: International Institute of Strategic Studies, 1982).
3. Yossi Melman and Dan Raviv, 'Israel's Other Arms Deal', *Washington Post*, 'Outlook' section, November 30, 1986.
4. Aaron Klieman, *Israel's Global Reach: Arms Sales as Diplomacy* (McLean, Virginia: Pergamon-Brassey's, 1985), pp. 2–7; also, *Hadashot*, February 10, 1989.
5. *Los Angeles Times*, August 4, 1988.
6. *Christian Science Monitor*, April 24, 1986.
7. *Ha'ir*, June 5, 1987; *Ma'ariv*, January 22, 1988.
8. *Yediot Aharonot*, May 20, 1988.
9. Jonathan Marshall, Peter Dale Scott, and Jane Hunter, *The Iran–Contra Connection* (Boston: South End Press, 1987), pp. 115–120.
10. Dan Raviv, in the *Glasgow Herald*, July 12, 1984; and the *Sunday Telegraph*, July 8, 1984.
11. *Ma'ariv*, April 25, 1988.
12. *Yediot Aharonot*, August 5, 1988 and March 3, 1989.

Chapter 15: *The Nuclear Traitor*
1. Vanunu told his tale to *The Sunday Times*, October 5, 1986.
2. *Hadashot* and *Yediot Aharonot*, November 3, 1986.

3. Reverend McKnight, interviewed by the authors, December 16, 1986.
4. *Sunday Times*, October 5, 1986.
5. *Sunday Mirror*, September 29, 1986.
6. *Sunday Times*, November 16, 1986.
7. Ibid., and authors' interviews with members of *Sunday Times* reporting team.
8. Ibid.
9. *Sunday Times*, November 16, 1986.
10. *Jerusalem Post*, November 9, 1986.
11. *Jerusalem Post*, August 9, 1987.
12. *Yediot Aharonot*, March 28, 1988.
13. *Sunday Times*, February 21, 1988.
14. Haber and Schiff, *Israel's Army and Defence: A Dictionary*, p. 416; *Daily Telegraph*, June 16, 1988.
15. *Daily Star*, August 18, 1987; *Sunday Telegraph*, May 8 and July 24, 1988; *Daily Telegraph* and *The Independent*, June 16, 1988; *Daily Mail*, June 17, 1988; and *The Guardian*, June 18, 1988.
16. *Ma'ariv*, February 23, 1988.
17. *The Economist*, September 24, 1988.

Chapter 16: *A World Without Trust*

1. Amir Oren in *Davar*, April 1, 1988.
2. *Ma'ariv*, March 4, 1988; also *Yediot Aharonot* and *Ma'ariv*, February 24, 1989.
3. The journalist was David Halevy, writing in the *Washington Star*.
4. The network was ABC News and the censor had no proof that its correspondent in Israel was behind the disclosure.
5. Avi Pazner, Prime Minister Shamir's spokesman, interviewed by the authors, September 22, 1988.
6. The Israeli version of the Pollard affair appeared in the *New York Times*, November 29, 1985; the major participants in the leak were interviewed by the authors.
7. In 1988, Glenn Frankel of the *Washington Post* and Martin Fletcher of NBC News temporarily lost their Israeli

government-granted press credentials for reporting that
Israel killed Abu Jihad in Tunisia. Similar action was
taken, later that year, against Paul Taylor and Steve
Weizman of the Reuter news agency, for reporting
rumours of Israeli death squads in the West Bank; in
1980, against one of the authors, Dan Raviv of CBS
News, for reporting on Israel–South Africa nuclear development; and, in 1970, against CBS newsman Tony
Hatch, when Israeli officials were especially angry that
he reported on a commando raid into Egypt while it
was still in progress.

8. *Ha'aretz*, September 1, 1982.
9. *Davar*, April 13, 1987.

Chapter 17: *Into the Future*

1. *Washington Post*, September 20, 1988; and *Time*, August
   29, 1988.
2. *Koteret Rashit*, June 11, 1986.
3. *Yediot Aharonot*, January 2, 9, and 16, 1987.
4. Reuters, 'Shamir Accused of Lying on PLO Report',
   March 22, 1989.
5. *Davar*, February 9, 1989, citing New York's *Village Voice*.

Bibliography

Books in English

Adams, James. *Secret Armies: The Full Story of SAS, Delta Force and Spetsnaz*. London: Hutchinson, 1987.

Bahbah, Bishara. *Israel and Latin America: The Military Connection*. New York: St Martin's Press, 1986.

Bar-Zohar, Michael and Eitan Haber. *The Quest for the Red Prince*. London: Weidenfeld and Nicolson, 1983.

Barnaby, Frank. *The Invisible Bomb: The Nuclear Arms Race in the Middle East*. London: I. B. Tauris, 1989.

Beit-Hallahmi, Benjamin. *The Israeli Connection: Who Israel Arms and Why*. New York: Pantheon, 1987.

Blitzer, Wolf. *Territory of Lies*. New York: Harper and Row, 1989.

Bloch, Jonathan, and Patrick Fitzgerald. *British Intelligence and Covert Action*. London: Junction, 1983.

Breecher, Michael. *Decisions in Israel's Foreign Policy*. London: Oxford University Press, 1974.

——. *The Foreign Policy System of Israel*. London: Oxford University Press, 1972.

Cookridge, E. H. *Gehlen: Spy of the Century*. New York: Random House, 1971.

Davenport, Elaine, Paul Eddy and Peter Gillman. *The Plumbat Affair*. London: Andre Deutsch, 1978.

Dayan, Moshe. *Breakthrough: A Personal Account of the Egypt-Israel Peace Negotiations*. New York: Alfred A. Knopf, 1981.

Deacon, Richard (Donald McCormick). *'C': A Biography of Sir Maurice Oldfield, Head of MI6*. London: Futura, 1985.

——. *The Israeli Secret Service*. London: Sphere, 1979.

——. *Spyclopaedia*. London: Macdonald, 1988.

Deacon, Richard, with Nigel West. *Spy!* London: Grafton, 1988.

Dzhirkvelov, Ilya. *Secret Servant: My Life with the KGB and the Soviet Elite*. London: Collins, 1987.

Eisenberg, Dennis, Eli Landau and Menahem Portugali. *Operation Uranium Ship*. Tel Aviv: Steimatzky's, 1978.

Eisenberg, Dennis, Uri Dan and Eli Landau. *The Mossad, Israel's Secret Intelligence Service: Inside Stories*. New York: New American Library, 1978.

El-Ad, Avri. *Decline of Honor*. Chicago: Regency, 1976.

Elkins, Michael. *Forged in Fury*. London: Corgi, 1982.

Gabriel, Richard A. *Operation Peace for Galilee: The Israeli-PLO War in Lebanon*. New York: Hill and Wang, 1984.

Golan, Aviezer, and Danny Pinkas. *Shula, Code Name the Pearl*. New York: Delacorte Press, 1980.

Green, Stephen. *Living by the Sword: America and Israel in the Middle East, 1968–1987*. London: Faber and Faber, 1988.

——. *Taking Sides: America's Secret Relations with a Militant Israel*. New York: William Morrow and Company, 1984.

Haber, Eitan, Ze'ev Schiff and Ehud Yaari. *The Year of the Dove*. New York: Bantam, 1979.

Hart, Alan. *Arafat: Terrorist or Peacemaker?* London: Sidgwick and Jackson, 1984.

Henderson, Bernard R. *Pollard: The Spy's Story*. New York: Alpha, 1988.

International Institute of Strategic Studies (IISS). *The Military Balance 1981/82*. London: IISS, 1982.

Jonas, George. *Vengeance: The True Story of a Counter-terrorist Mission*. London: Collins, 1984.

Kalb, Marvin and Bernard Kalb. *Kissinger*. New York: Dell, 1975.

Kessler, Ronald. *Khashoggi: The Rise and Fall of the World's Richest Man*. London: Corgi, 1987.

Kissinger, Henry. *Years of Upheaval*. Boston: Little, Brown and Company, 1982.

Klieman, Aaron S. *Israel's Global Reach: Arms Sales as Diplomacy*. McLean, Virginia: Pergamon Brassey/International Defence, 1985.

Knightley, Philip. *The Second Oldest Profession: The Spy as Bureaucrat, Patriot, Fantasist and Whore*. London: Pan Books, 1987.

Laqueur, Walter. *A World of Secrets: The Use and Limits of Intelligence*. New York: Basic Books, 1985.

LeCarré, John (David J. M. Cornwell). *The Little Drummer Girl*. London: Hodder and Stoughton, 1983.

Lotz, Wolfgang. *The Champagne Spy*. New York: St Martin's Press, 1972.

Marshall, Jonathan, Peter Dale Scott and Jane Hunter. *The Iran-Contra Connection: Secret Teams and Covert Operations in the Reagan Era*. Boston: South End Press, 1987.

Martin, David C. *Wilderness of Mirrors*. New York: Harper and Row, 1980.

Martin, David C., and John Walcott. *Best Laid Plans: The Inside Story of America's War Against Terrorism*. New York: Harper and Row, 1988.

Melman, Yossi. *The Master Terrorist: The True Story Behind Abu Nidal*. London: Sidgwick and Jackson, 1987.

Melman, Yossi, and Dan Raviv. *Behind the Uprising: Israelis, Jordanians and Palestinians*. Westport, Connecticut: Greenwood, 1989.

Ninio, Marcelle. *Operation Susannah*. New York: Harper and Row, 1978.

Nixon, Richard M. *RN: The Memoirs of Richard Nixon*. New York: Warner Books, 1978.

Parfitt, Tudor. *Operation Moses: The Untold Story of the Secret Exodus of the Falasha Jews from Ethiopia*. New York: Stein and Day, 1985.

Perlmutter, Amos, Michael Handel and Uri Bar-Joseph. *Two Minutes over Baghdad*. London: Vallentine Mitchell, 1982.

Pincher, Chapman. *Traitors: Labyrinths of Treason*. London: Sidgwick and Jackson, 1987.

Posner, Steve. *Israel Undercover: Secret Warfare and Hidden Diplomacy in the Middle East*. Syracuse, New York: Syracuse University Press, 1987.

President's Special Review Board. *The Tower Commission Report*. New York: Bantam and Times Books, 1987.

Pringle, Peter, and James Spiegelman. *The Nuclear Barons: The Inside Story of How They Created our Nuclear Nightmare*. London: Michael Joseph, 1982.

Randal, Jonathan. *The Tragedy of Lebanon*. London: Chatto and Windus, 1984.

Ranelagh, John. *The Agency: The Rise and Decline of the CIA*. London: Weidenfeld and Nicolson, 1986.

Sachar, Howard M. *A History of Israel*. New York: Alfred A. Knopf, 1985.

Schiff, Ze'ev. *A History of the Israeli Army: 1874 to the Present*. New York: Macmillan, 1985.

Segev, Samuel. *The Iranian Triangle: The Untold Story of Israel's Role in the Iran-Contra Affair*. New York: Free Press, 1988.

Sterling, Claire. *The Terror Network*. New York: Berkley, 1982.

Steven, Stewart. *The Spymasters of Israel*. New York: Ballantine Books, 1980.

Stevenson, William. *90 Minutes at Entebbe*. New York: Bantam, 1976.

Tadmor, Joshua. *The Silent Warriors*. New York: Macmillan, 1970.

Tinnin, David B., with Dag Christensen. *Hit Team*. London: Futura, 1976.

Toronska, Teresa. *Oni*. London: Collier, 1986.

Turner, Stansfield. *Secrecy and Democracy: The CIA in Transition*. London: Sidgwick and Jackson, 1986.

Woodward, Bob. *Veil: The Secret Wars of the CIA, 1981–1987.* New York: Simon and Schuster, 1987.

Wright, Peter. *Spycatcher: The Candid Autobiography of a Senior Intelligence Officer.* New York: Viking-Penguin, 1987.

Books in Hebrew

Bar-Zohar, Michael. *Bridge over the Mediterranean: Israeli-French Relations, 1947–1963.* Tel Aviv: Am Hasefer, 1965.

———. *Isser Harel and Israel's Security Services.* Jerusalem: Weidenfeld and Nicolson, 1970.

Beer, Israel. *Israel's Security: Yesterday, Today, Tomorrow.* Tel Aviv: Amikam, 1966.

Eliav, Arie-Lova. *Rings of Faith.* Tel Aviv: Am-Oved, 1983.

Eshed, Hagai. *One-Man Mossad: Reuven Shiloah, Father of Israeli Intelligence.* Jerusalem: Edanim/Yediot Aharonot, 1988.

Ettinger, Amos. *Blind Jump: The Story of Yeshayahu (Shaike) Dan.* Tel Aviv: Zmora Bitan, 1986.

Freundlich, Yehoshua, ed. *Documents on the Foreign Policy of Israel, Volume 5: 1950.* Jerusalem: State of Israel Archives, 1988.

Gazit, Shlomo. *The Stick and the Carrot: The Israeli Administration in Judea and Samaria.* Tel Aviv: Zmora Bitan, 1985.

Goren, Dina. *Secrecy, Security and the Freedom of the Press.* Jerusalem: Magnes/Hebrew University Press, 1976.

Golan, Matti. *Peres.* Tel Aviv: Schocken, 1982.

Grossman, David. *The Yellow Wind.* Jerusalem: Keter, 1987.

Haber, Eitan. *Today War Will Break Out: The Reminiscences of Brigadier General Israel Lior, Aide-de-Camp to Prime Ministers Levi Eshkol and Golda Meir.* Jerusalem: Edanim/Yediot Aharonot, 1988.

Harel, Isser. *Security and Democracy.* Jerusalem: Edanim/Yediot Aharonot, 1989.

———. *Soviet Espionage: Communism in Israel.* Jerusalem: Edanim/Yediot Aharonot, 1987.

Hillel, Shlomo. *Operation Babylon*. Jerusalem: Edanim/Yediot Aharonot, 1985.

Kenan, Amos. *Your Land, Your Country*. Jerusalem: Edanim/Yediot Aharonot, 1981.

Kotler, Yair. *Joe Returns to the Limelight*. Tel Aviv: Modan, 1988.

Mann, Peter, and Uri Dan. *Eichmann in My Hands*. Tel Aviv: Massada, 1987.

Melman, Yossi. *The CIA Report on the Israeli Intelligence Community*. Tel Aviv: Erez/Zmora Bitan Modan, 1982.

——. *A Profile of a Terrorist Organisation*. Tel Aviv: Hadar, 1984.

Nakdimon, Shlomo. *Tammuz in Flames*. Jerusalem: Edanim/Yediot Aharonot, 1986.

Schiff, Ze'ev, and Eitan Haber, eds. *Israel, Army and Defence: A Dictionary*. Tel Aviv: Zmora, Bitan, Modan, 1976.

Segev, Samuel. *Alone in Damascus: The Life and Death of Eli Cohen*. Tel Aviv: Keter, 1986.

——. *The Iranian Triangle: The Secret Relations Between Israel-Iran-USA*. Tel Aviv: Ma'ariv, 1981.

——. *The Iranian Triangle*. Jerusalem: Domino Press, 1988.

Segev, Tom. *1949: The First Israelis*. Jerusalem: Domino Press, 1984.

Shiffer, Shimon. *Snow Ball: The Story Behind the Lebanon War*. Jerusalem: Edanim/Yediot Aharonot, 1984.

Yaari, Ehud. *Fatah*. Tel Aviv: A. Levin Epstein, 1970.

Zak, Moshe. *Israel and the Soviet Union: A Forty-Year Dialogue*. Tel Aviv: Ma'ariv Book Guild, 1988.

Zvi, Ofer, and Avi Kober. *Intelligence and National Security*. Tel Aviv: Maarachot/Ministry of Defence, 1987.

Index

Abadan, 91

Abbas, Abul, 362

ABC News, 39, 306

Abdullah, King of Trans-Jordan, 87, 222

Abu Hassan (Mohammed Hassan Buheis), 24

Abu Jihad (Khalil el-Wazir), 25, 26–33, 35, 414

Abu Kassem, 312–13, 314

Abu Nidal (Sabri el-Banna), 34, 285

Abu Sherif, Bassam, 21–2, 25, 200

Abu Tayeb, 256, 259, 261, 279

Abutbul, Felix, 377–8

Achille Lauro, 362

Adam, Major General Yekutiel (Kuti), 276, 289

al-Adhami, Ali, 396, 397–8, 399–400

Admoni, Nahum, 20, 21–3, 26, 30, 289–90, 331–2, 358, 400, 408

Adwan, Kamal, 208

Africa, 91–4, 172–4, 224–6, 233, 280, 282–3

Agaf ha-Modiin see Aman

Agee, Commander Jerry, 334

Agranat, Shimon, 220

Agranat Commission, 220

Ahituv, Avraham, 188–90, 193, 205, 227, 263–5, 267, 276, 318, 405, 407

Aldouby, Zwy, 140–1

Alexandria, 66–7, 246

Algeria, 97, 99, 103, 175, 183, 184, 195

Ali, General Kamal Hassan, 228–9

Aliyah B, 44, 52, 54, 58, 61, 73, 78, 79, 116, 234

Allon, General Yigal, 178, 266

Almog, Mordecai, 148

Aman (Military Intelligence), 9, 117; formation of, 43; and the *intifada*, 19; assassination of Abu Jihad, 28–9; and the 'revolt of the spies', 56; operations in Egypt, 64–70, 71–2; functions, 137, 216–17; Amit as head of, 146–7; rivalry with Mossad, 147–8; and the occupied territories, 188; Yom Kippur War, 213–15, 217–21, 428; and peace negotiations with Egypt, 229–30; destruction of Iraqi nuclear reactor, 268–70; contacts in Lebanon, 285–7; and the invasion of Lebanon, 288–9, 292; television censorship, 306; bugging activities, 417–18

Amar, Field Marshal Hakim, 178

Amin, Idi, 172, 224, 373

Amit, Major General Meir, 226, 421; head of Aman, 146–7; as head of Mossad, 145–6, 148–81; Six-Day War, 171, 181; and the assassination of Ben-Barka, 175–6; rivalry with Isser Harel, 177–9; and the occupied territories, 187; leaves Mossad, 201–2; Jewish emigration from Morocco, 249; character, 425

Amnesty International, 316

Amster, Jules (Yehuda), 50–1

Andropov, Yuri, 240–1

Angleton, James Jesus, 77–82, 87, 97, 107, 226

al-Ansari, Rifaat, 85–6

Anti-Terrorism Alert Center (USA), 324–5, 328–9, 333–4

Antwerp, 107

Anya-nya, 93

Aphrodite, 246

Arab League, 175, 256

Arab Legion, 42, 49, 222

Arabs *see* Palestinians *and individual Arab countries*

Arafat, Yasser, 25, 29–30, 396; and

Index

Index

Chad, 282–4; invasion of Lebanon, 284–5, 287–93, 428; leadership struggle in Likud, 295; Pollard spy case, 342
Sharon, Lily, 278
Shayetet 13, 30
Shcharansky, Anatoli, 245
Sherut Yediot see Shai
Shi'ite Moslems, 18, 290, 346
Shiloah, Reuven, 54, 116, 117, 148; background, 44–9, 425; and the Kurds, 46–7, 88; *Va'adat*, 52; revolt of the spies, 55–6; creation of Mossad, 56–7; operations in Iraq, 57–8; operations in Egypt, 71; resignation from Mossad, 73–4; secret contacts with CIA, 75–9; meetings with King Abdullah, 87, 222; meetings with Turks, 89
Shin Bet, 9, 35, 43, 54, 79, 117, 361; and the *intifada*, 12–20, 36, 38–40; brutality, 14, 193–4; interrogates El-Ad, 72; infiltration of political parties, 117–19, 121–2; functions, 130–1; and the assassination of Ben-Barka, 177; and the occupied territories, 184–94; recruits, 192; anti-terrorist activities, 195–203; and Soviet spies, 242–3; and Jewish terrorism, 264–8, 296; invasion of Lebanon, 290–1, 311; and the hijacked bus, 295–311; disciplinary court, 302; scandals, 311–21; and arms sales, 367, 369; Vanunu affair, 387, 394, 395; and the murder of Adhami, 399–400; secrecy, 404–5, 407–8, 410–11, 413; bugging activities, 417–18
Shkolnick, Norman, 370
Shomron, General Dan, 19, 28
Shomron, David, 132
Shoshan, Danny, 315–16
Shubak, 259
Shultz, George, 12
Sibat, 367–8, 370, 372
Sica, Domenico, 401
Sidi Boussaid, 30–1
Siman-Tov, Lieutenant Binyamin, 218

Sinai Peninsula, 11, 25, 96, 180, 181, 183, 218, 219, 229
Sion, Colonel Dov, 110
Sirota, Garcia, 250
Sitta, Kurt, 128–30
Six Day War (1967), 109, 171, 178–81, 183, 215, 216
Smyth, Richard, 111–12
Snir, Danny, 313
Société Général de Minaro, 107
Sofaer, Abraham, 339
Sokolow, Victor, 123
Sol Phryne, 20–5
Solomon, Flora, 83
Somalia, 233, 254, 379
South Africa, 108, 241, 366, 370
South Lebanese Army (SLA), 286–7
Soviet Union: Cold War, 54; support for Israel, 76; Jewish emigrants, 78–9; Khrushchev's speech to Twentieth Congress, 80; recruits Canadian spy, 84–5; influence in Egypt, 86–7; and the Suez crisis, 98; Pines' alleged spy network in, 115–16; spies in Israel, 122–8, 240–3; Mossad acquires MiG plane, 162–3; detects Israeli spies in Egypt and Syria, 169; Jews in, 234–6, 239–40, 244–5; Israeli agents in, 236–9; attitude to intelligence operations, 425
Sowan, Ismail, 397, 398–400
Spain, 140–1, 172, 248–9
Special Air Services (SAS), 198
La Spezia, 395
Stalin, Josef, 121, 235
Stansted airport, 377
State Comptroller, 411, 412
State Department (USA), 332
Stern Gang, 118, 132, 151
Sudan, 88, 91–3, 172, 255–62, 279–82
Suedani, Colonel Ahmad, 167, 168, 184
Suez Canal, 217, 218, 219
Suez crisis (1956), 95–8
Sukarno, President, 237
Sunday Mirror, 389, 392
Sunday Times, 386, 387–95, 401, 408
Sunni Moslems, 18

THE IMPERFECT SPIES

Surdin, Maurice, 98
Switzerland, 56, 109–10, 172, 196, 243
Syria: attempts to blow up Israeli
  airliner, 34–5; and the *intifada*, 17;
  Israeli War of Independence, 42;
  war plans, 53; Druze, 88; Israeli spies
  in, 163, 165–9; spies in Israel, 170;
  Six-Day War, 178, 181; Yom Kippur
  War, 212, 213–15, 219, 223, 428–9;
  and the Israeli invasion of
  Lebanon, 284–5; chemical
  weapons, 333

Tacuara, 250
Tajar, Yehudah, 63
Tamari, Brigadier General Dov,
  241–2
Tamimi, Mohammed Bassem Sultan
  (Hamdi), 22–4
Tamir, Major General Avraham, 275,
  279, 282–4, 288
Tammuz project, 268–71
Tangier, 248
Tappuz, 395
Tawil, Muhammad, 263
Techno-Kfitz, 57
Teheran, 59
Tel Aviv, 37, 58, 152
Tel Nof airbase, 341–2
Teller, Edward, 113
Thatcher, Margaret, 363, 390, 396
Thomas, Jack, 157–9
Time magazine, 291
Tohami, Hassan, 228–9, 231
Toledano, Shmuel (Amnon), 140,
  148–9, 185, 247, 250
Torrijos, General Omar, 374
TOW missiles, 355, 359
Tower, John, 113, 364
Trachtenberg-Dan, Yeshayahu
  (Shaike), 47, 251–3
Trans-Aseatic, 91
Trans Europe Airlines, 260
Trans-Jordan, 42, 49, 87; *see also*
  Jordan
trials, secret, 9, 416
Trident, 89
Tripoli, 34, 197
Truman, Harry S., 75

Tubianski, Captain Meir, 49–50, 51,
  55
Tufanian, Hassan, 90–1
Tunis, 27, 30, 333
Tunisia, 27–33, 250, 333
Turkey, 62, 89, 108, 172
Turkish National Security Service
  (TNSS), 89
Tzahor, Dr Zeev, 384

Uganda, 172, 224–6, 373
Umm Jihad, 32
Umma Party (Sudan), 91–2
Unit 131, 56, 64–8, 72, 135, 150, 166
United Nations, 5, 37, 180, 225
United Nations High Commission
  for Refugees, 256
United States of America: and the
  intifada, 12–13, 39; intelligence
  service, 48, 424–5; Cold War, 54;
  influence on organization of
  Israeli intelligence, 56–7; links
  between Mossad and CIA, 75–82;
  and the Suez crisis, 97–8; and the
  Israeli nuclear project, 103, 106–7,
  111–13; Shin Bet surveillance, 131;
  Mossad acquires MiG plane, 162;
  and the Six-Day War, 181; and the
  Yom Kippur War, 217, 219; and
  the Ethiopian Jews, 257–9, 261;
  Pollard spy case, 9, 322–43;
  Irangate, 344–65; and Israeli arms
  sales, 370–2; attitude to
  intelligence operations, 424–5
United States Information Centre
  (Egypt), 67
uranium, 106–8
US Army, 131
US Atomic Energy Commission, 106
US Congress, 410
US Customs Service, 112
US Justice Department, 113
US Navy, 323, 324–5, 328–38

Va'adat Rashei ha-Sherutim, 19–20,
  21, 52, 54, 117, 187–8, 214–15, 276,
  367
Vanunu, Albert, 387
Vanunu, Meir, 394

[468]

Index